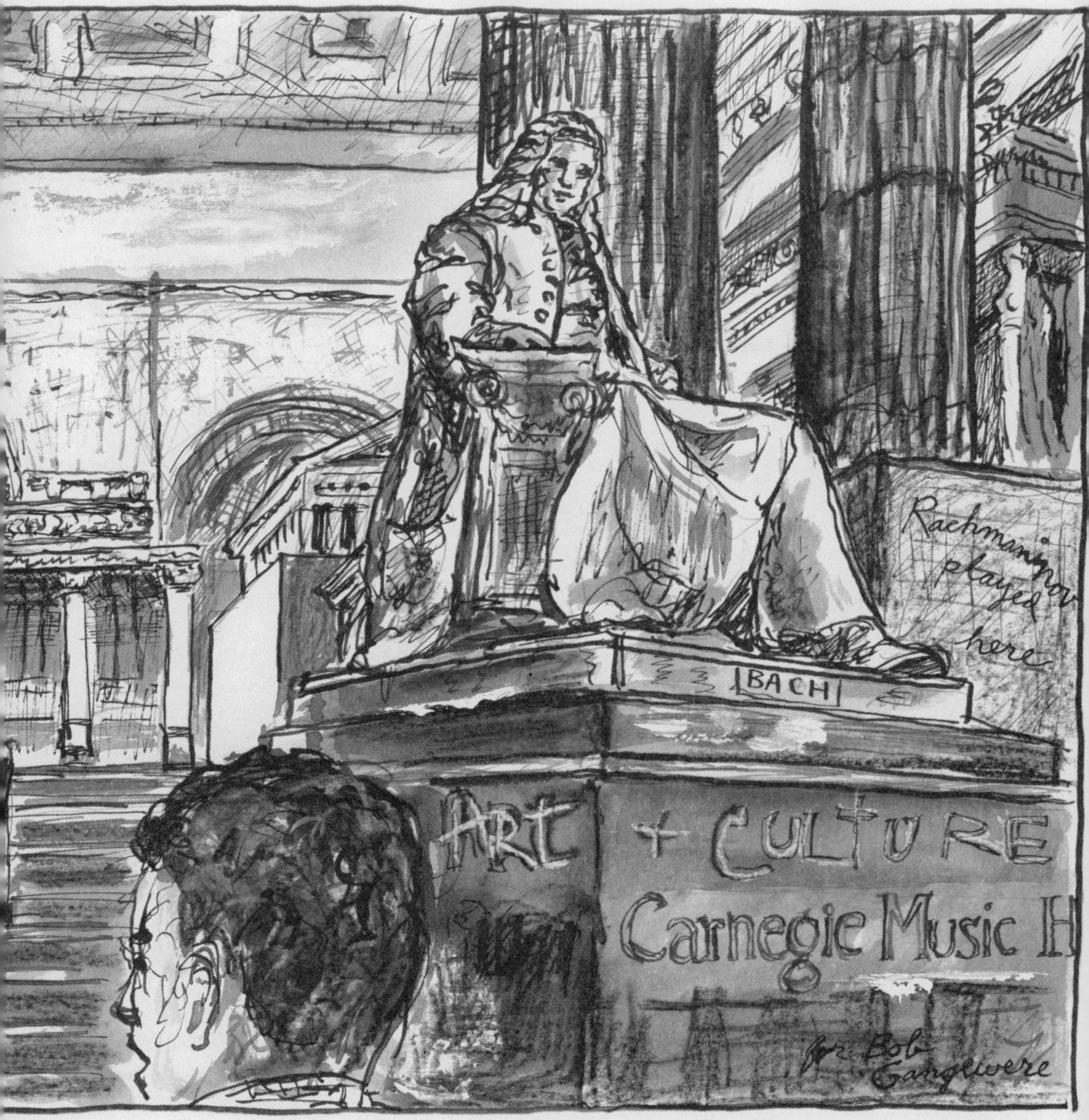

Rachmaninov played here
BACH
ART + CULTURE
Carnegie Music H
for Bob
Gangewere

PALACE

OF CULTURE

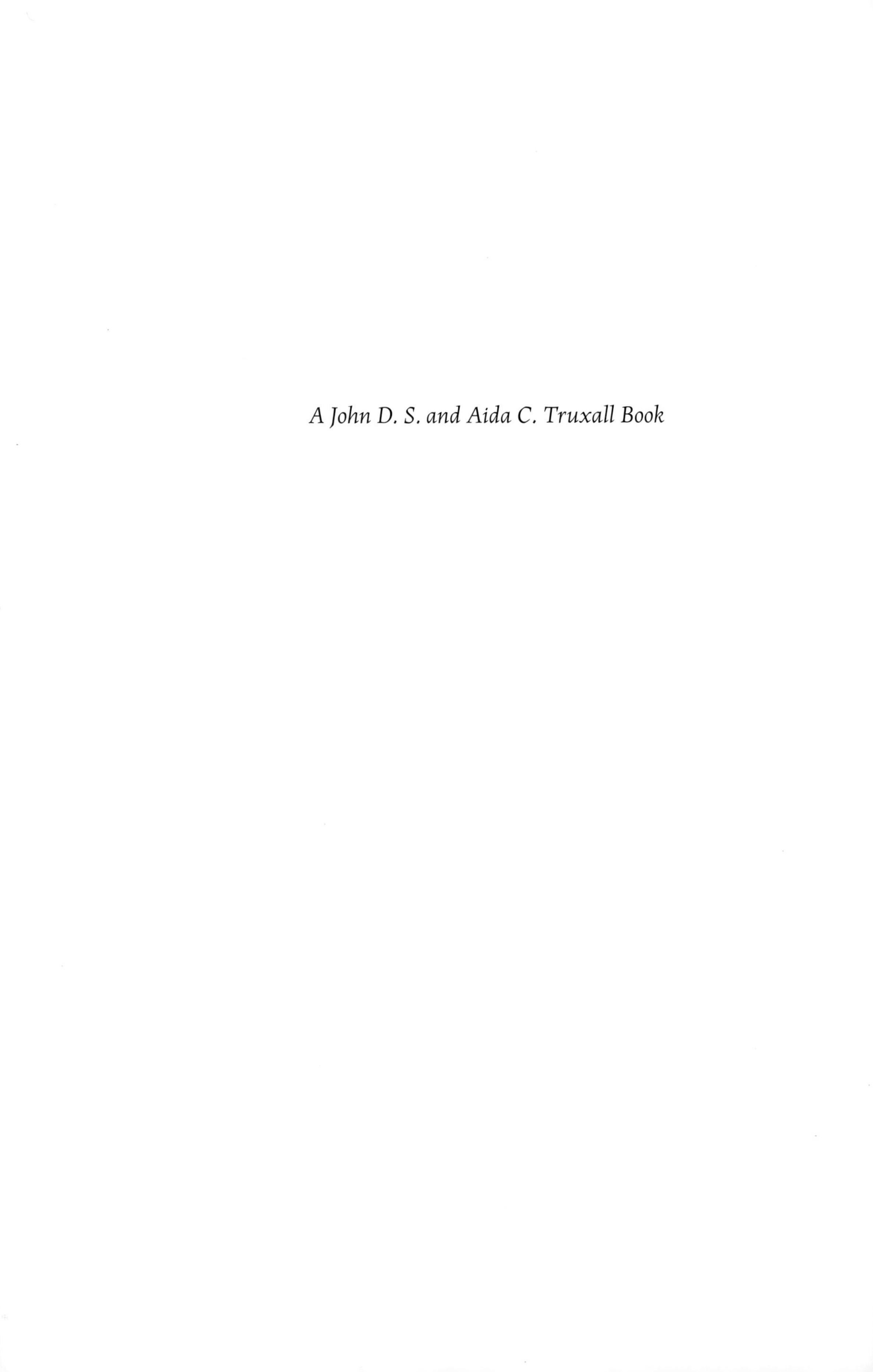

A John D. S. and Aida C. Truxall Book

PALACE
OF CULTURE

Andrew Carnegie's Museums and
Library in Pittsburgh

ROBERT J. GANGEWERE

University of Pittsburgh Press

Published by the University of Pittsburgh Press, Pittsburgh, Pa., 15260
Copyright © 2011, University of Pittsburgh Press
All rights reserved
Manufactured in the United States of America
Printed on acid-free paper
10   9   8   7   6   5   4   3   2   1

Text design and typesetting by Kachergis Book Design

LIBRARY OF CONGRESS CATALOGING-IN-PUBLICATION DATA

Gangewere, Robert J. (Robert Jay), 1936–

Palace of culture : Andrew Carnegie's museums and library in Pittsburgh /

Robert J. Gangewere.

p. cm.

Includes bibliographical references and index.

ISBN-13: 978-0-8229-4397-6 (cloth : alk. paper)

ISBN-10: 0-8229-4397-2

1. Carnegie Institute—History.   2. Carnegie Library of Pittsburgh—History.

3. Pittsburgh (Pa.)—Intellectual life—20th century.

4. Pittsburgh (Pa.)—History—20th century.   5. Carnegie, Andrew, 1835–1919.

I. Title.   II. Title: Andrew Carnegie's museums and library in Pittsburgh.

AS36.P79G36 2011

069.09748'86—dc23   2011020990

For my wife, and first reader, Linda

CONTENTS

PREFACE

The story of Andrew Carnegie's Palace of Culture has many themes, from changes in American museums and libraries in the twentieth century, to changes in art, technology, and science, and to Pittsburgh's own remarkable rebirth from a dirty mill town into one of the nation's most livable cities. Generations of people, in Pittsburgh and the United States, and internationally, have been influenced by Carnegie's remarkable Institute and Library. This is a rare story about the myriad ways that one cultural institution shaped the life of a city and a region, a story whose roots lie in a singular experiment in bringing middle- and high-class culture to the masses in a city notably isolated in western Pennsylvania, without the richness in the arts and sciences that the great East Coast cities were developing. Pittsburgh was for many years a microcosm of America, tucked away in the mountains of western Pennsylvania, and in that regard a kind of laboratory Petri dish, where one might see over the course of a century "the higher things of the spirit," as Carnegie phrased it, develop and grow on their own.

As I wrote *Palace of Culture,* I realized that I had to think more broadly and deeply about the museums of Carnegie Institute and Library that I knew so well. As the editor of *Carnegie Magazine* for over thirty years, I could have simply recast much of what I knew. I was steeped in the culture of Carnegie Institute and Library, knew the familiar institutional stories, and at first thought my primary challenge would be organizing information. But this presumption was faulty for several reasons.

It was a mistake to think that Carnegie Library, founded in 1895, and Carnegie Institute, founded three months later in 1896, were only about 110 years old. Collectively, all the institutions whose stories I was starting to tell had about five times that amount of history: Carnegie Library was 110, Carnegie Museum of Natural History was 110, Carnegie Museum of Art was 110, and Carnegie Music Hall (perhaps no longer an equal partner, but with its own powerful history and presence) was 110. Each institution, then, had more than a century's worth of accomplishments and memories.

In addition, Carnegie Science Center, built in 1991, in fact stood on the shoulders of the Buhl Science Center; it was not 15 years old, but about 70, starting with the Buhl's founding in 1939. The Andy Warhol Museum, which opened in 1993, was the only recent institution, at about 14 years old. In effect, I was dealing with more than 500 years' worth of institutional and communal memories. A linear cultural history of five centuries would have had to begin in the 1500s, the time of Shakespeare.

In addition, the official literature that museums produce—marketing brochures, catalogs, tributes to benefactors, and wall copy explaining exhibits—ignores all the nuances and complexities that mark institutional growth. There are few conflicts and no failures, and the debates that once animated public opinion are absent, whether they were about religion versus scientific truth, exhibiting plaster casts instead of real objects, depicting benign Native Americans rather than savage Indians, or collecting comforting traditional art versus disturbing abstract art. Andrew Carnegie, in an 1894 telegram, once advised Institute president William Nimick Frew, "I hope nothing in gallery or hall will ever give offense to the simplest man or woman."[1] Yet the stories of museums are complex, and museums have long stood poised at the intersection of many issues, including censorship, changing management strategies, adopting new technologies, obtaining large sums from private and public sources, and competing against entertainment choices in the modern consumer-driven marketplace.

Most connoisseurs and historians of museum life—and I have read my share—have reason to be humble as they tell their stories. Picking which stories to tell is arbitrary by nature, and a complete, definitive history is impossible. Walter Muir Whitehill, author of the two-volume centennial *History of the Museum of Fine Arts, Boston* (1970), who "had known the institution fairly intimately nearly half of its life" and been a trustee for years, said of his own book, "It is, however, in no sense an official history. The form, style and character are my own, as are the opinions expressed and the conclusions reached. Many of the works of art reproduced are ones for which I have a particular affection: they include both very old and recent friends."[2] If this author, writing two volumes about an institution with which he had a lifelong love affair, could not produce a definitive history, what hope is there for other museum chroniclers? Similar disclaimers are made by all serious lovers of museums. This is implicit in the personalized approach to the Metropolitan Museum of Art taken by Calvin Trillin, in his delightful *Merchants and Masterpieces* (1989); in the feisty confessional of retired Met director Thomas Hoving, *Making the Mummies Dance: Inside the Metropolitan Museum of Art* (1994); and in *The Whitney Women and the Museum They Made: A Family Memoir*, by Flora Miller Biddle (2001).

Museum histories are a difficult genre, and not many museums relish the challenge of crafting one. The usual trigger for a history is an anniversary, and the usual result is a self-congratulatory narrative. But this is a matter of degree and depends upon who pays for the publication. Great museums, like elephants, ignore the gnats of personal criticism because they belong visibly to the world of ideas and controversy. But smaller museums, so dependent on local goodwill and support, are very sensitive to criticism and sedulously hide their problems, while they proclaim their successes. Their close cousins, academic institutions like universities, are sometimes different in this respect. In Pittsburgh, Carnegie Mellon University has published four volumes detailing its decades of evolution, each by a different distinguished professor, while Robert C. Alberts wrote a great history entitled *Pitt: The Story of the University of Pittsburgh, 1787–1987,* for that university's bicentennial. Competition among ideas is at the basis of academic life, and university historians usually recognize this.

Yet another reason why comprehensive museum histories are rare is that often some of the stories behind museums have already been published piecemeal, in exhibit catalogs, subject histories, and memoirs. Andrew Carnegie wrote at length about his motives in his *Autobiography,* in the chapter "Colonel Anderson and Books," and also in his "Gospel of Wealth," explaining why rich people should support libraries; to the extent that we accept his reasoning, then, the origins of Carnegie Library of Pittsburgh were decided long ago. A handful of books also exists about the phenomenon of building Carnegie libraries across America. But up to this time, the only specific accounts regarding the history of Carnegie Library of Pittsburgh in the twentieth century are the unpublished manuscript written by former director Ralph Munn in 1970 and the chronology of events published online by Barry Chad of the Pennsylvania Department of the library. Interest in the details of a library's evolution seems to be for a niche audience, if a large one, even for a library as iconic as Carnegie Library of Pittsburgh.

Carnegie Museum of Art has long published catalogs of its paintings, prints, and collection highlights by curators and experts, but one must have a library of these publications and then fit them together like the pieces of a puzzle if one wants to understand the whole picture. Too, some of these books are very expensive. Diana Strazdes's excellent *American Paintings and Sculpture to 1945 in the Carnegie Museum of Art* (1992) is large, beautiful, graceful, and scholarly, but it deals with only one area of the collection and is an expensive volume that not many readers will need to own. Other books, like Kenneth Neal's *A Wise Extravagance: The Founding of the Carnegie International 1895–1901* (1996) and *International Encounters* (1991), edited by Vicki Clark, give detailed but selective histories of Carnegie Museum of Art.

So it is with Carnegie Museum of Natural History, which has Tom Rea's *Bone Wars: The Excavation and Celebrity of Andrew Carnegie's Dinosaur* (2001), among other dinosaur books, detailing essentials about the museum's history. But there is so much more to this museum—anthropology, entomology, botany, geology, birds, mammals, and more—that the institution's full scope has scarcely been explained. As for the other institutional "parts" of Carnegie—Carnegie Music Hall, Carnegie Science Center, the Andy Warhol Museum—each has stories, but these are seldom told in the context of the embracing "corporation" (as Institute president Ellsworth Brown liked to call it), previously known as "Carnegie Institute," "The Carnegie," and by 1996 as "Carnegie Museums of Pittsburgh." Further, Carnegie Library of Pittsburgh was dropped from the central administration in the 1990s and from the standpoint of Carnegie Institute is a separate, unrelated organization, even though it shares with the art and natural history museums the same magnificent building in Oakland.

Only two attempts have ever been made to summarize the legacy of these varied institutions devoted to art, natural history, science, music, and literature. One is Ellen Wilson's brief *The Carnegie,* a seventy-two-page pictorial overview published in 1992, under president Robert Wilburn, drawing on the author's experience as assistant editor of *Carnegie Magazine.* But this was destined to fall out of favor when the Brown administration eliminated the moniker "The Carnegie," which had replaced the long-held title "Carnegie Institute," by marketing yet another new corporate idea: "Carnegie Museums of Pittsburgh." The second compilation is Agnes Dodds Kinard's *Celebrating the First 100 Years of the Carnegie in Pittsburgh, 1895–1995,* which evolved through several editions. A lawyer and a long-time volunteer, Kinard published privately, at her own expense, three versions of her celebration of Carnegie, the first in 1982, the last in 1995, the Institute's centennial year. A veritable scrapbook of information gathered from old *Carnegie Magazine* articles and newspaper stories, including lists of works of art and donors, names of trustees, and statistical data, Kinard's collection reminds the public how much material about these organization exists—and that no real synthesis has ever been attempted.

To make a subject like Carnegie Institute and Library popular, one has to tell stories. For some years, in many interviews, I asked each interview subject, toward the end of our conversation, if there were some story he or she wanted to see in this book, some theme or point of view that needed to be expressed. It seemed a novel question to many, but they responded in interesting ways, bringing up ideas they felt strongly about.

My friend the writer Abby Mendelson offered an immediate and deceptively transparent answer to the question of what would make a good book on this subject. There were, he said, three things the book would need: it should be well-written; it should tell a story with a beginning, middle, and end; and it should tell the reader something that he or she did not know before. As an experienced English teacher, I knew well the ground rules of writing, and yet, as I drowned in five centuries' worth of information, I saw that this advice could help me. The delights of the intellectual chase are infinite: one can research forever and never finish a book. There is a character in George Eliot's *Middlemarch* named Reverend Edward Causabon, who devotes his life to pursuing an endless "Key to All Mythologies." A sad, dry stick of a scholar, he never uncovers all the connections he wishes to make or publishes his key. His problem is like that of the frustrated pope who shouted at Michelangelo, who had labored for years lying flat on his back, painting the gods and heroes of the Bible on the ceiling of the Sistine Chapel: "But when will you make an end?"

It was necessary, then, to make an end to this complex, infinitely interesting subject, and to organize it simply. I gave each institution its own chapter, and I also wrote chapters focusing on several larger themes, such as the influence of Andrew Carnegie and the makeup of the central administration that guided the Institute and Library through the challenges of the twentieth century. This approach was more reader-friendly than one long chronology would have been. In an institutional chapter, for example, one can simply follow the story of the Museum of Art, without searching out pieces of its narrative in chapters on the Great Depression, the World Wars, or the rise of the digital age. It followed from this approach that I had to be arbitrary about which anecdotes and moments of decision to convey. Each organization has more stories to tell than could ever actually be included, and a large and splendid cast of characters ranging from presidents and curators to board members, volunteers, and patrons. One could never do justice to them all.

Still, there are specific themes that shaped the life of each institution—dinosaurs for natural history, the Carnegie International for the Museum of Art, and the library's financial struggle to survive on meager tax support. Further, broad American cultural rhythms have also affected every institution, such as the changing museum profession, the rise of cultural competition in other venues, the advent of computers and databases, and the way the Internet is changing how organizations communicate. Powerful trends in marketing and branding forced museums to capture their market share of the entertainment dollar. Locally, the Pittsburgh Renaissance, after World War II, raised the bar for what the region expected of its museums. Later, the creation of the Allegheny Regional Asset District (ARAD), a county-wide tax-based funding source, assisted cultural organizations, including Carnegie Institute and Library.

But whoever the leaders at the Carnegie were, and whatever national and local themes shaped the museums and library, all were subject to an important common denominator: they were part of an original educational experiment in the arts and sciences developed by Andrew Carnegie, whose reasons were personal and local to Pittsburgh, but whose ambitions were national and international. "My cathedral is in Pittsburgh," he told the bishop of the Cathedral of St. John the Divine in New York, as he turned down his request to fund a pipe organ in that church. For the last twenty years of his life, he boasted about his Pittsburgh experiment to American presidents, the king of England, the chancellor of Germany, and the other world leaders he met. He loved to see Pittsburgh on the international stage. Pittsburgh never got over the influence of this Star-Spangled Scot, and through his benefactions the city became a culturally richer place than it had been before, a place where everyone might gain a worldly education. Because of Carnegie, the ugly proletarian city of 1895 now had a glorious palace on a hill in Oakland, devoted to art, science, music, and literature. The idea of working "at the museum" as a staff member, volunteer, trustee, or patron, or just visiting it, had a resonance in Pittsburgh that could not be matched in any other American city. The Carnegie was a powerfully symbolic place, and that reputation never went away, even as the institution changed its name several times and expanded into a larger corporation by absorbing the Buhl Science Center and sponsoring the Andy Warhol Museum.

The story of Carnegie Museums and Library is an American story that deserves to be told and better known. It reveals how one visionary experiment in educating the nineteenth-century masses played out in the twentieth century and into the twenty-first. There is no other story like it in America, unless one looks to the Smithsonian in Washington, D.C., and that is another story altogether.

My final manuscript, encompassing all the people, anecdotes, facts, and themes that I felt were important to this subject, was nearly twice as long as this published book could accommodate. I hope that through some easily used archive or other resource, I will be able to make available more information, to help those who want a closer, more detailed look at Andrew Carnegie's fascinating Pittsburgh legacy.

ACKNOWLEDGMENTS

This is not an official history produced by Carnegie Museums of Pittsburgh. Its form and character are my own, as are its opinions and conclusions. I wish to thank Cynthia Miller and the University of Pittsburgh Press for undertaking this project, with its large ambitions, and for seeking funds for its publication.

Since my retirement, many people at the Carnegie Museums and Carnegie Library have been generously cooperative, from presidents, board members, directors, and curators, to staff and volunteers. Working at the Carnegie is something of an honor in Pittsburgh, and former employees often become volunteers, seemingly institutional family members for life. An informal Carnegie veterans group even meets occasionally to talk about their shared experiences. In my over three decades of interaction with employees at all levels of the Carnegie Museums and Library, I can scarcely acknowledge all those who have helped me.

But I did have immediate advisors in my writing and editing, especially my wife, Linda Gangewere, who has faithfully read everything I wrote, and Carnegie Institute and Library readers who obliged me by reviewing the subjects in which they had expertise. These include, among others, Bernadette Callery, Barry Chad, Vicky Clark, Mary Dawson, Deborah Harding, Mike Kainaroi, Sarah Nichols, Louise Lippincott, Brad Livezey, Pat McShea, Cynthia Morton, Tim Pearce, Mary Ann Perkins, John Rawlins, James Richardson III, Steve Rogers, Tey Stitler, Dave Watters, Don Wentworth, James Wilkinson, Suzanne Wilkinson, and Marc Wilson. The Buhl historian Glenn Walsh also helped me, as did the coin and stamp specialist Wayne Homgren. Carnegie volunteer Robert Flood assisted me in conducting interviews and making transcripts. The Pennsylvania Department and the Music and Art departments of Carnegie Library of Pittsburgh were invaluable in my research. I am indebted as well to Carol Sickman-Garner for her scrupulous copy editing of the manuscript.

Gil Pietrzak of the Pennsylvania Department and Kathryn Logan of the Music and Art departments of Carnegie Library of Pittsburgh were invaluable in my research, as was the staff of Carnegie Museum of Art, and the Library of Carnegie Museum of Natural History. So too in my search for images were Rick Armstrong, Jeff Boyd, Greg Burchard, Stan Franzos, Susan Geyer, Frank Heny, Nancy Lewis, Robert Raschak, and Madelyn Roehrig.

The notes to most chapters mention the interviews that I taped while writing articles for *Carnegie Magazine* and researching this book. I have donated all the taped interviews that I still possessed to Greg Priori of the William Oliver Special Collections Department of the Carnegie Library of Pittsburgh to help future historians. I am indebted to these interviewees, some of whom provided me with hours of candid conversation. They are listed in the appendix to the book.

PALACE

OF CULTURE

THE CARNEGIE YEARS

*"Pittsburghers Knew I Was One
of Themselves"*

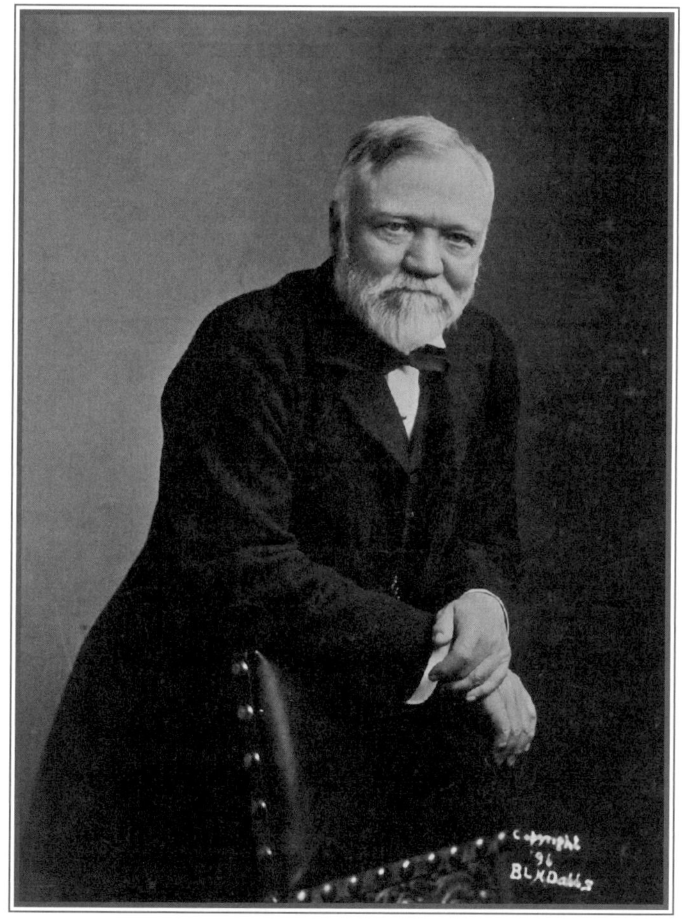

*Andrew Carnegie in 1896, the year he dedicated his
Institute in Pittsburgh.*

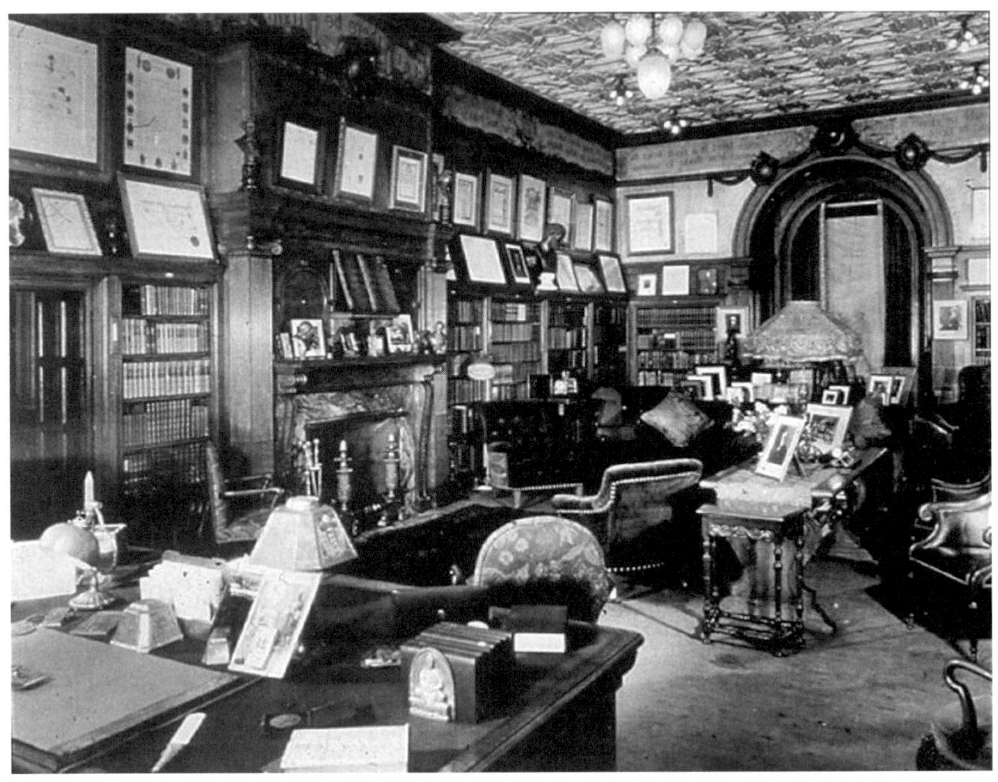

The library of Carnegie's mansion on Fifth Avenue and 91st Street, New York, now the Cooper Hewitt National Museum of Design of the Smithsonian.

ANDREW CARNEGIE, one of the richest men in America, was short of cash when he turned down a request to donate a church organ to the Cathedral of St. John the Divine in New York in 1897. He explained to Bishop Henry Codman Cotter of the New York Diocese, "I am pledged to spend millions and more in and around Pittsburgh, your starting place as it was mine. This is my cathedral work. Some day I should so like to have you go there with me and see the latent desires for the higher things the Institute has called forth—music, literature, painting and the museum. . . . Not less than five million dollars shall I spend on this work, as rapidly as I receive it. Just now I am a little behind on cash. Must concentrate on my Pittsburgh work."[1]

Carnegie's priorities were clear: Pittsburgh was the zenith of his first experiment in large-scale philanthropy, and his efforts there symbolized the scale of his benefactions in a way that none of his other gifts could. He had dedicated the Carnegie Library in 1895, then the Carnegie Institute in 1896, and by 1897 he was considering expanding the entire facility, which he would do with a colossal addition that opened in 1907. While nearly all Carnegie's other large gifts could be housed anywhere, this one had to be in Pittsburgh, an expression of that particular city and of Carnegie's devotion to it. In Pittsburgh he was enshrined in a three-story mural as the Black Knight of Labor, rising heavenward amid clouds of smoke from his mills, while angelic creatures present to him the spiritual rewards of manual labor—the gifts of music, art, literature, and science. In 1913 he was again represented, this time in a bronze sculpture, seated like Lincoln in a classical chair, wearing his business suit and gazing over the crowds entering Carnegie Music Hall. His 1895 dedication speech for the Carnegie Library summed up his intent: "Pittsburghers knew I was one of themselves, for here it was that fortune came to me, and it is as a Pittsburgher I have labored for Pittsburgh. This Institute is built by a Pittsburgher with Pittsburgh money for Pittsburgh."[2]

Andrew Carnegie was a man of contradictions, and his need to triumph in business at all costs was balanced and contradicted by his need to give his money back to the working class from which he had sprung. Already by his thirties he was well aware of this internal conflict, confessing his limits and hopes in December 1868, at age thirty-three, in a private, penciled note of year-end resolutions. Carnegie, who had recently settled in at the

St. Nicholas Hotel in New York to promote his business interests in the nation's financial center, wrote:

Thirty three and an income of 50,000$ per annum.

By this time two years I can arrange all my business as to secure at least 50,000$ per annum—Beyond this never earn—make no effort to increase fortune but spend surplus each year for benevolent purposes. Cast aside business forever, except for others.

Settle in Oxford & get a thorough education making the acquaintance of literary men. This will take three years active work—pay special attention to speaking in public. Settle then in London & purchase a controlling interest in some newspaper or live review & give the general management of it attention, taking part in public matters, especially those connected with education & improvement of the poorer classes—

Man must have an idol—the amassing of wealth is one of the worst species of idolatry—no idol more debasing than the worship of money—Whatever I engage in I must push inordinately, therefore should I be careful to choose that life which will be the most elevating in character—To continue much longer overwhelmed by business cares and with most of my thoughts wholly upon the way to make money in the shortest time must degrade me beyond hope of permanent recovery.

I will resign business at thirty five, but during the ensuing two years I wish to spend the afternoons in receiving instruction, and in reading systematically.[3]

Carnegie did not "resign business" until 1901, when he was sixty-six, but he was engaged in self-improvement throughout his life, taking trips around the world, owning a newspaper chain, writing newspaper and magazine articles that he eventually collected in books. Gradually he ascended to national and international acclaim as a rich American outspoken on the meaning of American democracy and then as a philanthropist obsessed with devising methods to give away his fortune. In 1889, just before his library and institute began to take shape, he published the first version of his famous "Gospel of Wealth," arguing that every rich person had an obligation to return his wealth to the masses. His personal plan was to help working-class Americans improve their lot through self-education at libraries, where they could acquire the anglophile culture revered by the Victorian age.

Carnegie's autobiography, published posthumously in 1920, remains an inspirational American story and one of the best things he ever wrote, and like Benjamin Franklin's autobiography, it has influenced generations of readers. Carnegie shaped his rags-to-riches tale to support a philosophy that he had promoted for decades in oratory and articles, employing the same vignettes and themes when he dedicated his libraries or delivered the keynote address at universities, technical schools, institutes, libraries, and economic conferences. To understand Carnegie's work in Pittsburgh, we have to understand how he saw his life as a rise from poverty to power, culminating in friendships with philosophers, statesmen, presidents, and kings.

BEGINNINGS AND EARLY SUCCESS

Behind Andrew Carnegie's aggressive drive to improve himself and promote change for those around him lay his Scottish ancestry. Carnegie never lost his working-class family's outspoken contempt for the British class tradition of inherited family wealth. In the rigid class structure of nineteenth-century Scotland and England, the inherited wealth of the upper class doomed poor weavers and cobblers like his two grandfathers and forced his father, the political activist William Carnegie, into a life of perpetual poverty. The new steam-powered looms in Dunfermline had made his handloom weaving obsolete, and the day came when William, a master weaver at age forty-four, had to tell his son, "Andra, I can get nae mair work."[4]

The need to leave Dunfermline and move to America, where they had to live with his mother's sister, was a deep shame to twelve-year-old Andrew. After arriving with his family in Allegheny City, across the river from Pittsburgh (now the North Side), Andrew penned long, precocious letters home to his cousin "Dod" in Scotland, justifying new American economic opportunities and praising American democracy. Witnessing how technological innovations changed manufacturing and dislocated the lives of the British working class, he articulated early the classic American immigrant's argument for choosing the New World over the Old.

In spite of his son's optimism, William Carnegie—perhaps more of a dreamer than a suitable worker in industrialized Pittsburgh—struggled unsuccessfully to make a living wage as a handloom weaver in America, and his family remained poor. The obligation to support the family fell to William's wife, Margaret Morrison Carnegie, who repaired shoes in Allegheny City (cobbling was her family's trade) to keep her two sons in decent clothing. She held the family together, and Andrew, to the end of his life, regarded her as a heroine for her labors. William Carnegie died a few years later, and Andrew, at age twenty, became the male head of the family.

His rise to success had already begun. At fourteen, he began working as a telegraph messenger boy, delivering messages to important Pittsburgh businessmen. Quick-witted, he had an excellent memory—so good that he was one of the first telegraph operators in the country to translate the dots and dashes of the new Morse code immediately into words, without writing down notes or referring to the cumbersome printed-out tapes used by translators. He took every opportunity to improve himself. When he gained entry to the theater to deliver messages to businessmen, for example, he stayed to enjoy the language of the theater, especially Shakespeare's plays. A small boy, and only five-foot-three even as an adult, Carnegie was a born communicator who learned early to use words rather than physical force to get what he wanted.

A turning point in Andrew's life—one that supported his belief in the power of language—came at age seventeen, when he found himself forced to pay a fee to borrow the formerly free library books of a retired business-man, Colonel James Anderson. Anderson had opened his library of four hundred volumes to working boys and then acted as librarian, lending each boy one book per week. When he retired as the librarian, he donated his little library to Allegheny City, whose librarian wanted to establish a new fee-based lending policy that discriminated between poor children with no income and poor children who had jobs. Since Andrew worked as a messenger boy, no longer as an unpaid apprentice, he now had to pay a fee, but since he dutifully turned his small wage over to his mother, he had no money of his own. He saw the new policy as unfair and wrote a letter of protest to the newspaper, arguing that it discriminated against young wage earners. His letter got the library policy reversed, and this became his first victory against the establishment. He never forgot this early success, made possible by his ability to articulate his beliefs, and he used the example of Colonel Anderson's library for the rest of his life to support his establish-ment of free public libraries.

Thanks to his hard work and ambition, Carnegie was soon singled out and asked to be the private telegrapher for Thomas Scott, the superin-tendent of the Western Division of the Pennsylvania Railroad. Carnegie promptly distinguished himself as a master dispatcher and with Scott's tutelage began to understand the financial side of railroading, eventually investing small sums of his own money (which Scott lent to him at the beginning). Railroads were expanding aggressively in the 1850s, and the discovery of oil in Pennsylvania in 1859 increased the tempo of industrial-ization even further. When the Civil War broke out in 1861, Thomas Scott was drawn away to work in Washington, D.C., and Carnegie, at age twenty-seven, became the supervisor of the Western Division. His responsibilities included transporting troops and war materials from Pittsburgh to the Union Army. Like other businessmen at the time, Carnegie paid someone to be his substitute as a soldier, but he was injured while working on the tele-graph lines, as he tried to pin down a wire that snapped upward and struck him in the head. He suffered from sunstroke, and his health deteriorated, so he was granted three months off from his job to recover and decided to return to Scotland to visit his birthplace, Dunfermline. This triumphant

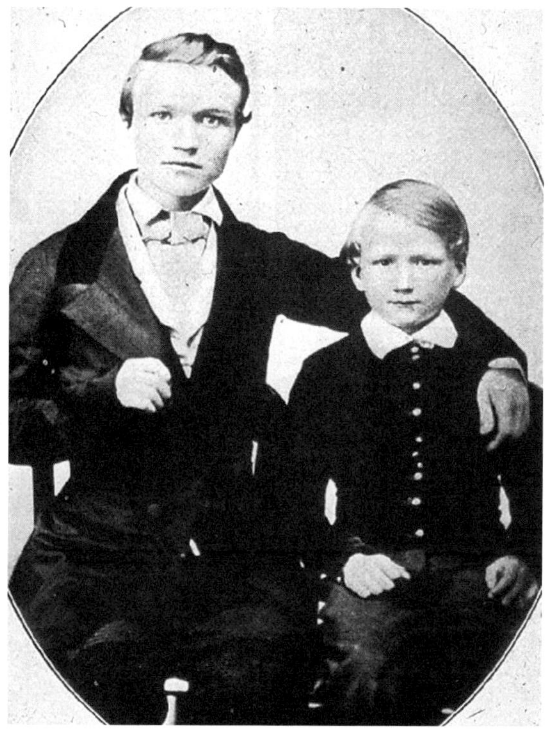

*Andrew Carnegie, age sixteen, with his brother
Thomas Morrison Carnegie, age ten, as professionally
photographed in Allegheny City
in 1851.*

return for a once poor boy whose impoverished family had left in disgrace in 1848 set a pattern Carnegie would continue to follow throughout his life, of leaving business in the hotter months for extended vacations that allowed him to see the world.

Carnegie decided to leave the Pennsylvania Railroad in 1865, instead beginning to use the insider information he had gained from railroad executives and industrial entrepreneurs to pursue success as a salesman and investor in stocks and bonds, including stocks in Western Union. Relatively rich by age thirty, he still worked with railroads but now focused on the products railroads transported—iron, coal, coke, and eventually steel. Repeating the pattern that had led to his own success, he always found bright partners and hired "young geniuses" as managers.

Despite his business success, Carnegie's scant four years of formal schooling in Scotland had left him feeling keenly his insufficient polish and lack of a university education. As his wealth brought him into increasing

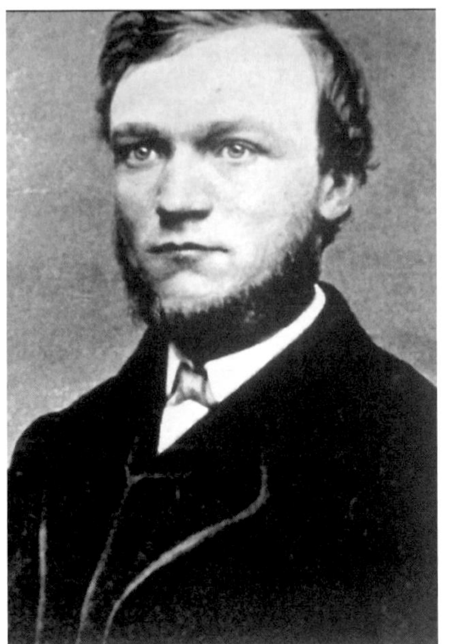

Carnegie in the late 1860s, about the time he moved to New York City and resolved to give up "business cares."

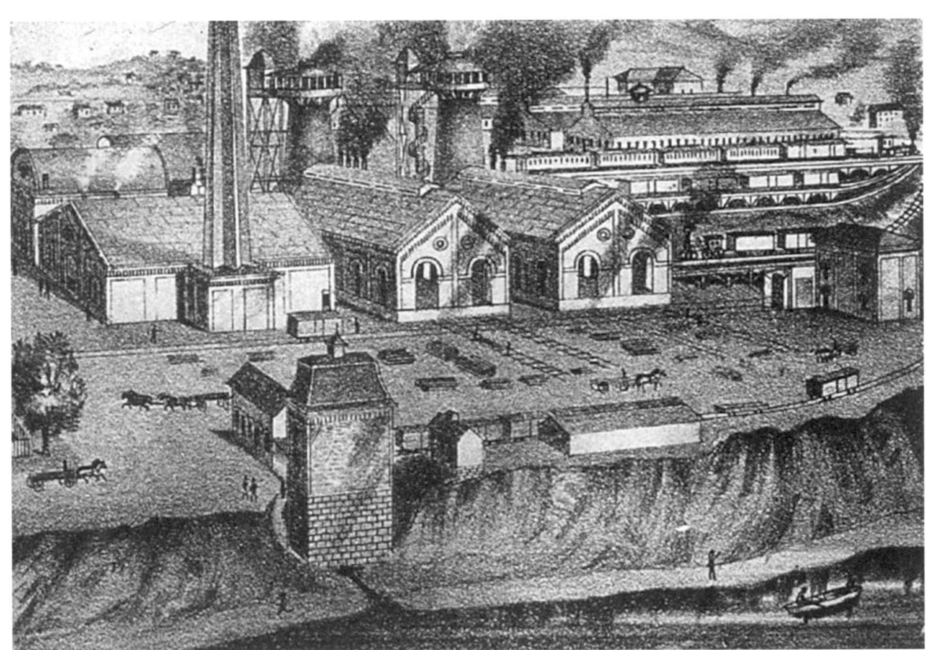

The Carnegie brothers' first steel mill, named Lucy Furnace after Tom Carnegie's wife, was located in the Lawrenceville neighborhood of Pittsburgh and went into production in 1872.

contact with sophisticated people, he worked to erase from his behavior the raw manners and untutored speech of a Scottish immigrant. He first tasted cultured conversation in the gatherings held at Judge Thomas Wilkins's home in the outskirts of Pittsburgh's East End. He liked debating important issues with cultivated people, and as he continued to rise in power, his new friends were regularly surprised to see that he was consistently driven more by ideas than by money.

After his 1867 move to New York, his love of conversation and debate carried on at Madame Anna Botta's literary salon. The wife of a professor of Italian literature, Madame Botta presided over elevated conversations with many of New York's fashionable writers, intellectuals, and statesmen—the sophisticates of the era.[5] After marrying in 1887, Carnegie himself used his homes in New York and Scotland as salons for invited guests, regularly inviting interesting people, rich and poor alike, to visit him, often at his own expense. At Skibo Castle, the irrepressible Carnegie had a piper lead the parade of guests to the dinner table every evening. At breakfast they were accompanied to the table by the dramatic music of composers such as Richard Wagner, played on the castle's pipe organ. His wife eventually persuaded Andrew to build a smaller house on the castle grounds, where they could actually be alone with each other and their daughter, but Carnegie never lost his enthusiasm for company. He was a founding member of the New York Author's Club, a literary salon where he regularly traded opinions with famous writers and philosophers, such as Mark Twain. In an era of vast and ruthless wealth, many of Carnegie's business associates, such as Henry Frick, Andrew Mellon, and J. P. Morgan, built exquisite art collections through the advice of sophisticated experts. However, none could articulate their personal feeling for art with the enthusiasm and style of the gregarious and articulate Carnegie, who easily extemporized on literature, art, and science.

OUTREACH

Carnegie's book *Triumphant Democracy* (1886) opened in dramatic journalistic style: "The old nations of the earth creep on at a snail's pace; the Republic thunders past with the rush of an express. The United States, the growth of a single century, has already reached the foremost rank among nations, and is destined to outdistance all others in the race. In population, in wealth, in annual savings, and in public credit; in freedom from debt, in agriculture, and in manufactures, America already leads the civilized world."[6] The American Republic, Carnegie declared simplistically, had faced two great threats: human slavery, overcome twenty years earlier by the Emancipation Proclamation, and now, in the late nineteenth century, "the millions of foreigners who came from all lands to the hospitable shores of the nation, many of them ignorant of the English language, and all unaccustomed to the exercise of political duties." It was this crisis in civilized culture that his free libraries and Carnegie Institute were supposed to alleviate. The Institute, Carnegie held, would be a center of refinement in the heart of an industrial wasteland—a home for scientists, artists, and intellectuals, as well as the common man, where all could gather, learn, and exchange views, in keeping with the founder's belief in promoting democracy through civilized discussion and debate.

The year 1886, beyond marking the publication of *Triumphant Democracy,* was a watershed for Carnegie in other respects, for his strong-willed mother and his younger brother and business partner Tom both died, and he himself nearly died of pneumonia in the mountains at Cresson, Pennsylvania. The next year he married Louise Whitefield, twenty-one years younger, who had long waited for him while he remained under the spell of his mother, whom he had held in saintly respect. He began a renewed life, returned to health at age fifty-one, with a devoted wife to help him, and he began in earnest to put his ideals into practice.

These ideals were challenged, however, in 1892, three years before his library opened in Pittsburgh, when the Homestead strike put him at the center of a national controversy. At the Homestead Mill, which his partner Henry Clay Frick managed, the workers had struck in protest over a plan to reduce wages. Carnegie, vacationing in Scotland, let Frick do the dirty work of breaking the strike by hiring the notorious Pinkerton guards. Violence broke out, men were killed, and the Pennsylvania National Guard occupied Homestead to restore order. Soon afterward, Frick himself was shot and stabbed by an anarchist in his downtown office, although he recovered. Homestead was a disaster on a national scale, altering the relationship between the steel unions and management for decades.

The relationship between Frick and Carnegie also started to disintegrate as a result of the strike. Frick nevertheless remained on the board of Carnegie Institute until 1899, when he resigned from the Carnegie Steel Company. Carnegie then began proceedings against Frick under the "Iron Clad Agreement," which guaranteed that partners could purchase each other's shares at their original purchase price rather than their much greater appreciated value. In the famous personal confrontation that ended their relationship, Frick threw Carnegie out of his office in downtown Pittsburgh and called him a liar. The case went to court, and the two never spoke again.

During the controversy surrounding Homestead and its aftermath, Carnegie's critics labeled him a sanctimonious hypocrite. To defuse their accusations, he reprinted his famous "Gospel of Wealth," arguing that

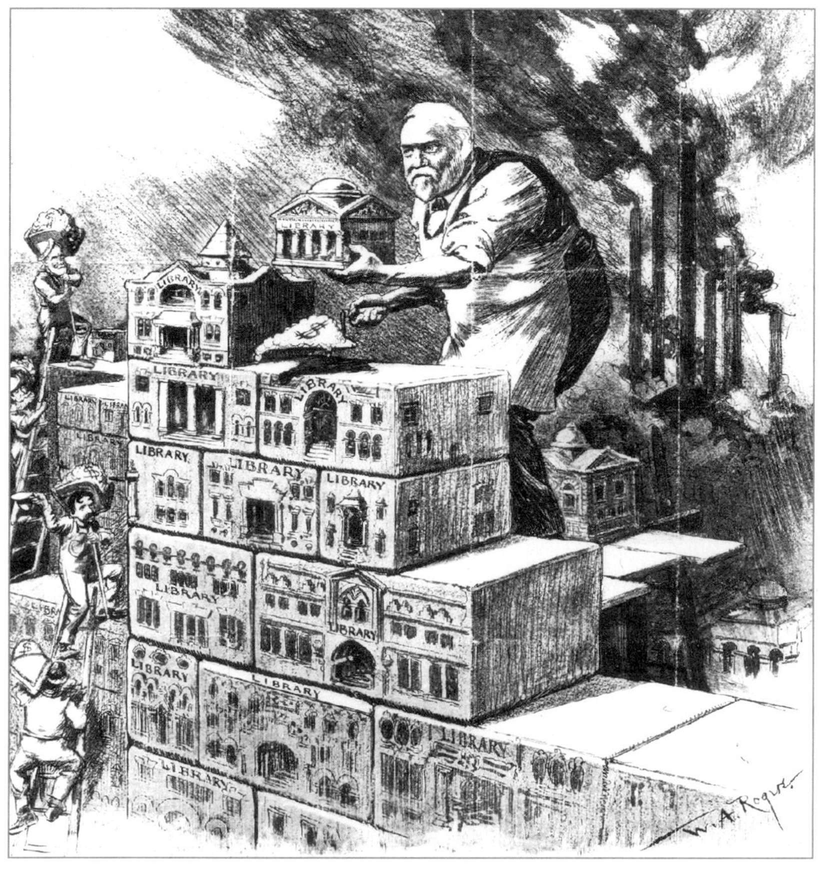

Cartoonist W. A. Rogers pictured Carnegie using workers to establish his own
"temple of fame."

enlightened benefactors had a duty to uplift the masses. His cynical, or
perhaps realistic, belief was that most people would inevitably spend slight
wage increases on pleasures, rather than on high-minded self-improvement.
He held, paternalistically, that he could spend this money more wisely for
the masses than they could for themselves. After 1900, his gifts of free
libraries multiplied, and a national debate developed about the morality of
accepting Carnegie's "tainted money." Carnegie's enemies held that his free
libraries were mere sops to American workers and the public, an attempt to
win back their favor after breaking the steelworkers' union and enforcing
low wages. The era's cartoonists and satirists showcased the controversy, the
Chicago-born journalist Finley Peter Dunne using his fictitious Irishman
Mr. Dooley to caricature Carnegie's views: "The way to abolish poverty an'
bust crime," he mused, "is to put up a brown-stone buildin' in ivry town in
the country with me name over it."[7]

Carnegie's enemies accused him for the rest of his life, overlooking the fact that Carnegie had resolved to give away his fortune long before the Homestead controversy arose. His moral philosophy is usually traced to several of the foremost thinkers of the Victorian Age, particularly Thomas Carlyle, Matthew Arnold, and Herbert Spencer. Carlyle, a fellow Scot, espoused the role of heroic leaders in transforming society, and Carnegie believed in such great men all his life, identifying and associating with them whenever he could. Arnold, the British poet and essayist, advanced a theory of high culture that provided the "best that was thought and said" as the touchstones of education, confirming Carnegie's belief that exposure to literature, music, art, and science led to a higher plane, where "sweetness and light" reigned. Spencer, a proponent of Social Darwinism, verified Carnegie's conviction that human society was evolving to ever higher and more refined forms. Both Arnold and Spencer became Carnegie's friends and were his guests on tours of America. Both too, not surprisingly, found the depth of American civilization thin compared to Europe, but they submitted to their host's enthusiastic patriotism with good grace.

Many agreed with him out of politeness, and few bothered in their memoirs to describe their candid feelings. One who did was his friend Samuel Clemens (Mark Twain), who joked with him often in letters he addressed to "Saint Andrew" from "Saint Mark," and always hoped Carnegie would help him out financially, although Carnegie never did. A few years before the end of his life, Clemens wrote in his memoirs, in 1907, "If I were to describe him in a phrase I should call him the Human Being Unconcealed." He added, "He never has any but one theme, himself. . . . He is his one darling subject, the only subject he . . . seems stupendously interested in." Carnegie, Clemens pointed out, kept strict account of the great men who had paid him compliments and always implied that they sought him out, rather than he them: "He is an astonishing man in his genuine modesty as regards the large things he has done, and in his juvenile delight in trivialities that feed his vanity." Of the famous incident in which Carnegie had entertained the king of England (who asked him about *Diplodocus carnegii*) at Skibo Castle four years earlier, Clemens noted, "Mr. Carnegie cannot leave the King's visit alone; he has told me about it at least four times, in detail. When he applied that torture the second, third, and fourth times, he certainly knew it was the second, third and fourth time, for he has an excellent memory. . . . He has likable qualities, and I like him, but I don't believe I can stand the King of England visit again." To Clemens, Carnegie was "always a subject of intense interest. . . . I like him; I am ashamed of him; and it is a delight to me to be where he is if he has new material on which to work his vanities where they will show him off as with a limelight."[8]

Carnegie believed wholeheartedly in benevolent capitalism and individualism. Putting aside those who benefited from inherited wealth and special privileges, he argued that everyone could reach for opportunities in the new republic, but that only those who applied all their energy and intelligence in the workplace and in the world of ideas could succeed. He saw poverty, which he had personally experienced, as useful in developing inner strength ("Adversity makes men, prosperity monsters"), and he believed that the way to avoid suffering among the masses was to alleviate it with legislation and charity, both private and public. He estimated that those capable of lifting themselves out of poverty and ignorance amounted to about one-tenth of the total population—the "swimming one tenth" he called them, people with the energy and determination to get ahead in life. He believed that the social reformers of his day focused so exclusively on the hopelessly poor—the wretched one-tenth at the bottom of society—that they ignored the relatively slight assistance needed to lift up the hardworking and hopeful one-tenth, who also typified the working class.

Today Carnegie's enthusiasms seem clichéd and Victorian, and he certainly glossed over darker aspects of America's past, such as the long consequences of slavery. Contemporary critics declared him addicted to "sweetness and light" in his portrayal of triumphant democracy. Nevertheless, his principles were clear, based on personal experience, and he was true to them for his entire life.

PHILANTHROPY

Agencies in the Forward March of Humanity
Henry S. Pritchett

Andrew Carnegie never stopped denigrating "the debasing worship of money," and after he retired in 1901, he never even visited the bank in Newark where he had deposited some $350 million in stocks and bonds. "Watch the pennies," one of his mottoes declared, "and the pounds will take care of themselves." He insisted, "The man of wealth who dies rich dies disgraced." After he sold Carnegie Steel and his other interests in 1901 in the creation of U.S. Steel, the world's largest corporation, J. P. Morgan called him the richest man in the world. Ready to make philanthropy his first order of business, Carnegie now began to give away millions.

Believing in the uplifting power of music, he gave away some seven thousand church organs and built grand music halls in New York and Pittsburgh. He gave to two-year trade and technical schools, rather than four-year colleges, and founded Carnegie Technical School in 1900, putting it under the governance of Carnegie Institute trustees. He considered founding a university in the Washington, D.C., area but considered the great schools that already had their roots in the area, such as Baltimore's Johns Hopkins, and instead threw his support to the predominantly African American Howard University.

Taking a national view of science, he decided in 1902 to fund a research institution for $10 million to help the country's universities by conducting primary research under the control of great scientists—Carnegie Institution of Washington, D.C. Among its many projects was the scientific mission of the ship *Carnegie,* built without iron so its compass would register true north, a ship that sailed around the globe correcting inadequate navigational charts to make the world safer for oceanic shipping and travel. Under Carnegie Institution of Washington was Mount Wilson Observatory, in Southern California, devoted to astronomical research. But his gifts promoting "pure science" began in Pittsburgh with his funding of Carnegie Museum and its paleontological research out west.

In Scotland he endowed the four venerable but poor major universities with one large gift: the Carnegie Trust for the Universities of Scotland. This $10 million donation assured the financial stability of the centuries-old seats of learning at St. Andrews, Glasgow, Edinburgh, and Aberdeen. He gave another $10 million to the Carnegie Endowment for International Peace, and in 1905 he donated $13 million to create the Carnegie Foundation for the Advancement of Teaching, which, in 1917, produced the Teachers Insurance and Annuity Association of America (TIAA), still the backbone of retirement funds for teachers and other nonprofit employees. He created the Carnegie Hero Fund Commission in 1904 (its U.S. headquarters in Pittsburgh) with $5 million, to reward ordinary citizens who risked their own lives to save the lives of others.

By 1905, his single-handed efforts to give away his money wisely were frustrating him, and he was tired of being constantly pilloried by the media. Conservatives criticized him as a socialist for his support of two-year schools and black colleges, while liberals accused him of trying to prostitute colleges and scientific research by making institutions indebted to him. In 1906, he complained to a friend: "The final dispensation of one's wealth preparing for the final exit is a heavy task—all sad. . . . You have no idea of the strain I have been under."[9] While giving a speech at the jubilee celebration of an institute in Scotland, he departed from his text to say, "Millionaires who laugh are rare, very rare, indeed." He had given away $180 million and had just as much still left to give. The capitalist return of 5 percent per year on his fortune was accumulating wealth more quickly than he could wisely administer giving it away.

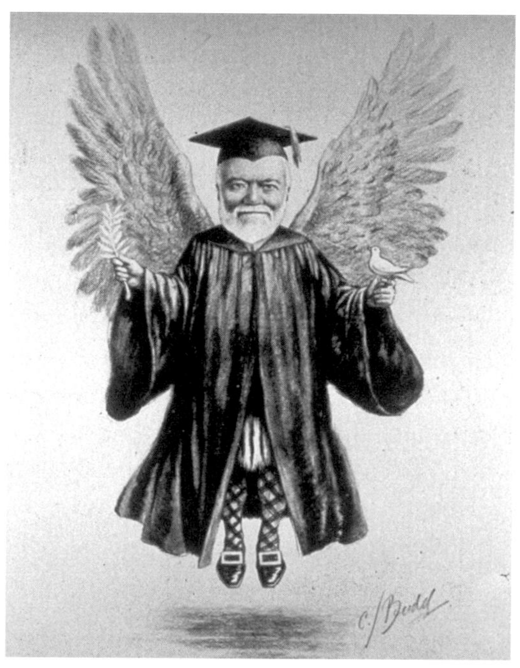

*Andrew Carnegie, who funded the Carnegie Endowment
for International Peace, is depicted by Charles Budd as the
angel of the international peace movement.*

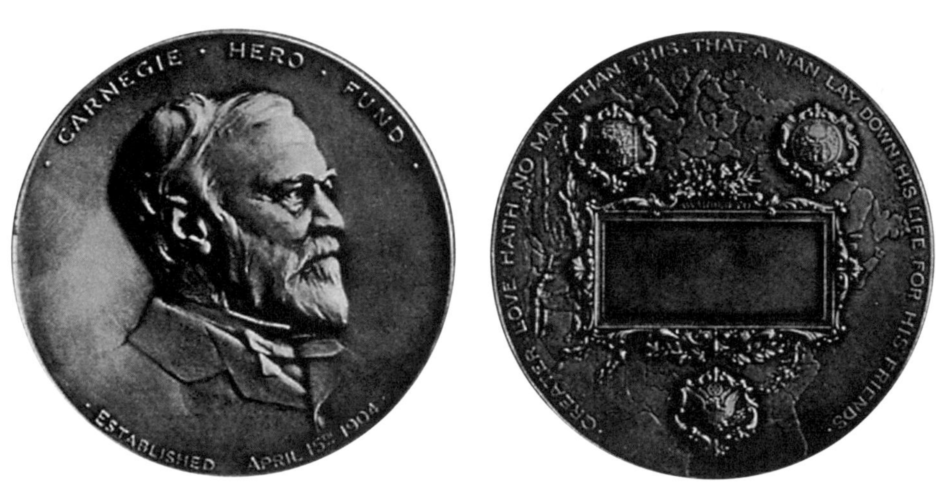

*The Carnegie Hero Fund Commission awards this medal to ordinary people who
risked (and often lost) their lives to help others.*

At one point, he lamented that he was doomed to die in disgrace, having failed to dispense his wealth, and his friend Elihu Root, the secretary of state, cheered him by saying, "You have had the best run for your money I have ever known." Root suggested that he give up this mission as a personal goal and create a trust that would leave the task in others' hands. Thus, in November 1911, Carnegie created Carnegie Corporation of New York, transferring to it in a series of grants his remaining fortune of $125 million, noting (using his simplified English spelling system—one of his various enthusiasms that did not catch on) that the money would be used "to promote the advancement and diffusion of knowledge among the people of the United States by aiding technical schools, institutions of higher lerning, libraries, scientific reserch, hero funds, useful publications, and by such other agencies and means as shall from time to time be found appropriate therefor."[10] He became the president of Carnegie Corporation, and the heads of his various other institutions all served as board members—including, over time, both William Nimick Frew and Samuel Harden Church, the presidents of Carnegie Institute and Library in Pittsburgh. The Carnegie Corporation dominated American philanthropy until the death of Henry Ford in 1947, which led to the expansion of the Ford Foundation for charitable giving.[11]

The scale of Carnegie's philanthropy was unprecedented, and in 1915, to honor the anniversary of the Carnegie Institute of Technology and Carnegie's eightieth birthday, Henry S. Pritchett, the president of the Carnegie Foundation for the Advancement of Teaching and the former president of Massachusetts Institute of Technology, came to Carnegie Tech and spoke to Carnegie's legacy:

The chief causes which Mr. Carnegie has sought to stimulate are these: the promotion of good reading through public libraries, the cause for scientific research through a research-institution, higher education through the Carnegie Foundation, human idealism through the Hero Fund, international Peace through the Peace Endowment, discriminating philanthropy through the Carnegie Corporation; last, and in some ways most interesting of all, service to his home city through the Carnegie Institute of Pittsburgh, of which this great school is a part. These are great causes—good reading, research, education, idealism, world-peace, wise philanthropy, and fittest of all, a ministry to the old home and its aspirations.

Referring to the war that had broken out in Europe, Pritchett argued grandly that while "these are days in which humanity is crucified," the "constructive institutions which Mr. Carnegie has conceived and put in motion . . . are to have immortal lives. Decade after decade, century after century, they will make their contributions to the progress of their age and of their generation. They are immortal agencies in the forward march of humanity. To have conceived and to have set in motion such immortal forces for human upbuilding is to become oneself a partaker of immortality."[12] Pritchett was being grandiose, but his attempt to grasp the whole impact of Carnegie's philanthropy was unique. At this point the presidents of Carnegie Institute also sat on the board of the Carnegie Corporation of New York and on the boards of other Carnegie institutions, and the leadership in Pittsburgh maintained for decades the common bonds of idealism, internationalism, and pacifism, all legacies of Andrew Carnegie. The broader view was gradually lost sight of after Carnegie's death, as each institution moved in its own direction, and their common bonds grew weaker.

THE PITTSBURGH GIFT

It was a combination, as I believe, not before attempted,
of library, art gallery, museum, and hall of music.

Andrew Carnegie, 1907

Carnegie first offered Pittsburgh a free public library on November 25, 1881, the same year he dedicated his first library in the city of his birth, Dunfermline, Scotland. He wrote a letter to the mayor of Pittsburgh, Robert W. Lyon, offering to donate $250,000 for a free library, providing the city would appropriate $15,000 annually for its maintenance. But under Pennsylvania law, despite the city's willingness to accept the gift, Pittsburgh had no authority to tax its citizens for the maintenance of a library, and the offer could not be accepted without a change in state law.

In 1886 it was determined that the state could pass legislation enabling Pittsburgh to accept the gift, and a city ordinance was passed accepting Carnegie's offer and empowering the mayor and the presidents of the Select and Common councils to serve ex officio on a board of trustees to be named by the donor. Finally, in 1887, the enabling act was passed by the Pennsylvania legislature, and Carnegie was informed that his gift had been accepted.

One of Carnegie's close advisors, William J. Holland, the chancellor of the University of Pittsburgh (then the Western University of Pennsylvania) and later the director of Carnegie Museum in Pittsburgh, advised Carnegie to create more than a simple library. Carnegie thus wrote another letter to the Pittsburgh mayor on February 6, 1890, now offering $1 million, pointing out that since the city was growing rapidly in size, he wanted to provide a more extensive building that would include rooms for reference and circulating libraries, galleries displaying works of art, assembly rooms for scientific societies, and branch libraries in the city's various neighborhoods. He suggested four branches—in Birmingham (the South Side), Temperenceville (the West End), East Liberty, and Lawrenceville—and perhaps a fifth in an older part of the city. "All of these," he noted, "should be thoroughly fireproof, monumental in character and creditable to the city."[13]

Not everyone agreed that the city deserved such a generous second offer, especially after refusing the first. Carnegie's friend the dyspeptic philosopher Herbert Spencer, after reading in the newspapers the accusation that Carnegie wanted only to build a monument to himself, declared the city unworthy of Carnegie's generosity. Spencer's belief in social evolution inclined him to punish human or civic ingratitude, perhaps as a penalty for a society's failure to evolve. But Carnegie replied that since he sincerely wished to promote the good of Pittsburgh, not his own, he was not at all wounded by the first refusal. Indeed, he rejoiced that Pittsburgh had changed its mind. Throughout his life, once Carnegie decided to support an enterprise, he seldom changed his mind, often adding more funds to ensure its success and thus illustrating yet another of his favorite mottoes: After a decision has been made, put all your eggs in one basket and watch that basket.

Over the next thirty years, Andrew Carnegie and the Carnegie Corporation of New York provided over twenty-five hundred libraries in the English-speaking world, requiring every community or organization that received a library to pay for its maintenance and management. In the long run, this approach revolutionized the landscape of public library administration, politicizing the process. Local officials now had to vote each year to authorize funding for their public library.

Among Carnegie's close associates appointed to the Pittsburgh Library Board were James B. Scott (president), Henry Clay Frick (treasurer), and William Nimick Frew (secretary). Scott was also named chair of the all-important Building Committee, which decided early on that a useful interior was more desirable than a beautiful exterior, a decision that doubtless reflected Carnegie's own frugal views. For the Pittsburgh library, the Building Committee selected the plan of Boston architects Longfellow, Alden and Harlow, a decision that was approved by the board. In February 1894 Scott died in the midst of construction, and Frew took over his position. He reported on the management of the facility at its 1895 dedication:

The several departments of the main Library building are under the supervision of a corps of gentlemen, each selected because of his peculiar fitness for his position.... Each ... is held responsible to the Board of Trustees for the proper management of his own department, and has the sole right to employ and discharge his assistants.

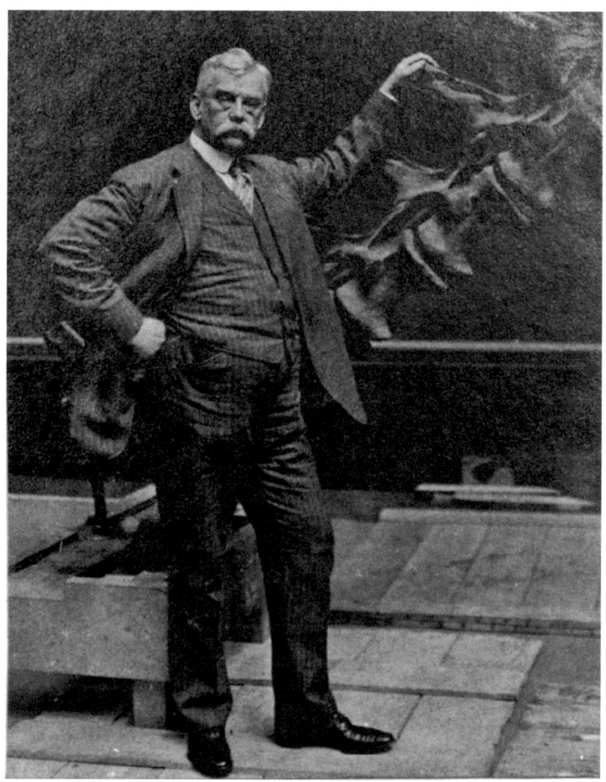

William Holland, Presbyterian minister, chancellor of the University
of Western Pennsylvania, director of Carnegie Museum, and
Carnegie's close advisor on the Institute,
with a cast of Diplodocus carnegii.

Arrangements have been made with the Academy of Science and Art to occupy and control the meeting and lecture rooms in the Science wing, with the
understanding that numerous lecture courses shall be free to the public. Similar
contracts have been made with the Art Society and the Mozart Club. The School
of Design for Women has been given commodious quarters in the basement, and
the Art Student's League has found a home on the third floor on the conditions
that the skilled instructors be secured from the best schools, and that male and
female classes be formed which shall be open to any desiring to study art.[14]

This was truly a multipurpose educational facility with few parallels elsewhere. Carnegie Hall in New York City (built in 1892, originally called the
"Music Hall") was also used for lectures, music, and classes, and there
were multipurpose educational buildings in Liverpool and Manchester,
England, that featured art galleries and museum displays. Carnegie had

studied the gifts of other American benefactors, and he reeled off examples in his 1895 dedication:

The surplus money gathered in one great sum and spent for the Cooper Institute of New York, the Pratt Library of Baltimore, for the Pratt Institute of Brooklyn, the Drexel Institute of Philadelphia, or by my friend and partner, and your distinguished fellow-citizen, Mr. Phipps, for the conservatories . . . , or by Mrs. Schenley for our park . . . or spent by Seth Low for the Columbia College Library, is put to better and nobler ends than if it had been distributed from week to week in driblets among the masses of the people.

He also brought up Colonel Anderson's free library, which had so influenced his youth, and his family history of giving books to libraries:

Our newspapers have recently quoted from a speech in which I referred to the fact that Colonel Anderson—honored be his memory—opened his four hundred books to the young in Allegheny City, and attended every Saturday to exchange them; and that to him I was indebted, as was Mr. Phipps . . . , for admission to the sources of knowledge and that I then resolved that if ever surplus wealth came to me—and nothing then seemed more unlikely, since my revenue was one dollar and twenty cents a week as a bobbin boy in a factory; still I had my dreams—it should be devoted to such work as Colonel Anderson's. The opening to-night of this library, free to the people, is one more realization of the boyish dream. But I also come by heredity to my preference for free libraries. The newspaper of my native town recently published a history of the free library in Dunfermline, and it is there recorded that the first books gathered together and opened to the public were the small collections of three weavers. Imagine the feelings with which I read that one of these three was my honored father. He founded the first library in Dunfermline, his native town, and his son was privileged to found the last. . . . Another privilege is his—to build a library for the people, here in the community in which he has been so greatly blessed with material success. I have never heard of a lineage for which I would exchange that of the library-founding weaver. Many congratulations have been offered upon my having given for this purpose, which I have declined to receive, always saying, however, that I was open to receive the heartiest congratulations upon the City of Pittsburgh having resolved to devote part of its revenues to the maintenance of a library for its people.

Turning from the library to the art gallery and the museum, he explained his rationale for adding them to the facility:

We now come to another branch, the Art Gallery and Museum, which the City is not to maintain. These are to be regarded as wise extravagances, for which public revenues should not be given, not as necessaries. These are such gifts as a citizen may fitly bestow upon a community and endow, so that it will cost the City nothing.

The Art Gallery and also the Museum you will to-night have an opportunity to see. Already many casts of the world's masterpieces of sculpture are within its walls. Ultimately, there will be gathered from all parts of the world casts of those objects which take highest rank. The Museum will thus be the means of bringing to the knowledge of the masses of the people who cannot travel many of the most interesting and instructive objects to be seen in the world; so that, while they pursue their tasks at home, they may yet enjoy some of the pleasures and benefits of travel abroad. If they cannot go to the objects which allure people abroad, we shall do our best to bring the rarest of those objects to them at home. Another use we have in view is that the objects, rare, valuable and historical, belonging to this region will here find their final home. We think we see that there will be gathered in this Museum many of the treasures of Western Pennsylvania, so that after generations may be able to examine many things in the far-distant past, which our present will then be, which otherwise would have been destroyed.

As for the Music Hall, he pointed out:

It is unnecessary to say one word in explanation of, or apology for, its existence. It has already spoken for itself, and is fully vindicated in your opinion. You know from the public press what has already been arranged, and what the masses of the people are to obtain here, without money and without price. That this Hall can be and will be so managed as to prove a most potent means for refined entertainments and instruction of the people and the development of the musical taste of Pittsburgh, I entertain not the slightest doubt, and Goethe's saying should be recalled, that "Straight roads lead from music to everything good." . . . Let us trust that here, also, the great organist whom the committee has been so fortunate as to secure . . . , and the manager of the Hall will ever bear in mind that there has not been in view the entertainment of the cultured musical few, but that it is intended as an instrument for spreading among the masses of the people the appreciation and the love of music which musical people already possess.

After thanking many on the board, and city officials, and Mrs. Mary Schenley (in her heart a true Pittsburgher), and identifying the first gifts to the art gallery and museum, he stressed the importance of his wife, Louise Carnegie, who had counseled him throughout his philanthropy (and indeed continued his efforts in the decades after his death, in concert with the Carnegie Corporation of New York). "We," he said, now made this gift to Pittsburgh using "our surplus wealth":

I have dropped into the plural, for there is one always with me to prompt, encourage, suggest, discuss, and criticise; whose heart is as keenly in this work as my own, preferring it to any other as the best possible use of surplus wealth, and without whose wise and zealous co-operation I often feel little useful work could be done. . . .

Mrs. Carnegie and myself, who have given this subject much thought, and have had it upon our minds for years, survey to-night what has been done; the use to which we have put our surplus wealth, the community to which we have devoted it, and say to ourselves, if we had the decision to make again we should resolve to do precisely as we have done. . . . We feel that we have made the best use of surplus wealth according to our judgment and conscience; beyond that is not for us; it is for the citizens of Pittsburgh to decree whether the tree planted in your midst shall wither or grow and bear such fruits as shall best serve the county where my parents and myself first found in this land a home, and to which we owe so much. . . .

There is nothing in what we have done here that can possibly work evil; all must work good, and that continually. If a man would learn of the treasures of art, he must come here and study; if he would gain knowledge, he must come to the library and read; if he would know of the great masterpieces of the world in sculpture or architecture, or of nature's secrets in the minerals which he refines, or of natural history, he must spend his time in the museum; if he is ever to enjoy the elevating solace and delights of music, he must frequent this hall and give himself over to its sway. There is nothing here that can tend to pauperize, for there is neither trace nor taint of charity; nothing which will help any man who does not help himself; nothing is given here for nothing. But there are ladders provided upon which the aspiring may climb to the enjoyment of the beautiful and the delights of harmony, whence comes sensibility and refinement; to the sources of knowledge, from which spring wisdom; and to wider and grander views of human life, from whence comes the elevation of man. . . .

We now hand over the gift; take it from one who loves Pittsburgh deeply and would serve her well.[15]

After Carnegie had handed his library over to the city, he officially added the Institute as a separate organization within the original building, by a deed of trust dated March 2, 1896. He was actively engaged in its success for another decade, making financial gifts to encourage the health of the art gallery and famously purchasing the fossil of the dinosaur *Diplodocus carnegii* for the museum.

Then, on November 15, 1900, he wrote to Pittsburgh's mayor, William Diehl, that he had read with great interest that the Central Board of Education had asked the City of Pittsburgh for one hundred thousand dollars to begin a technical school. He now hoped, he told Mayor Diehl, that he could bring to fruition a plan he had long nursed, of giving a technical in-

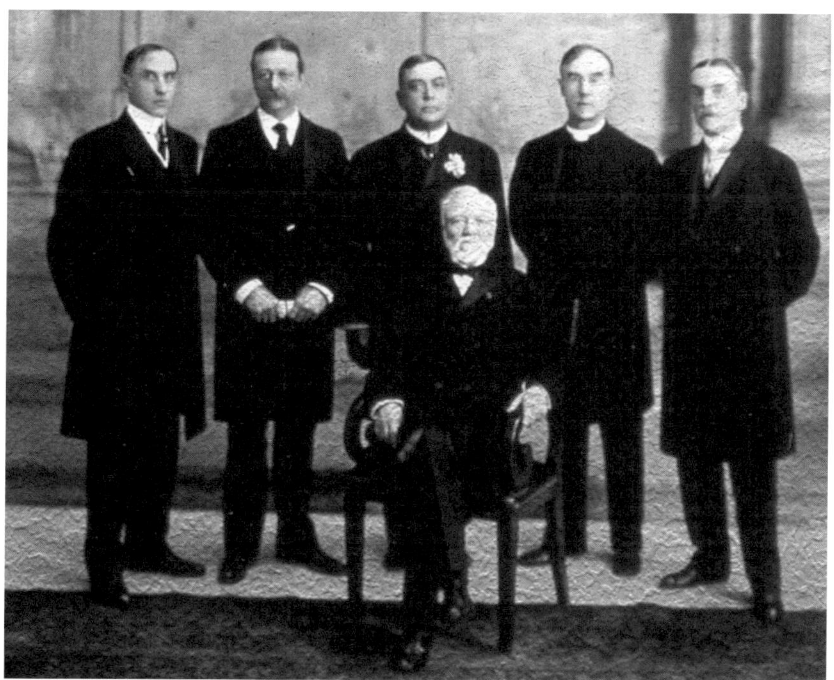

On Founder's Day, April 11, 1911, Carnegie poses with administrators and distinguished guests in the Hall of Architecture. At the photo's far right is the Institute's first president, William Nimick Frew; at far left is Secretary Samuel Harden Church, who succeeded Frew as president in 1914.

stitute to the city, to be under the governance of the Board of the Carnegie Institute: "The rare ability with which the trustees of Carnegie Institute have managed it, and the results which have so surprised and gratified me, naturally lead me to beg those gentlemen to take charge of the technical institute and its endowment."[16]

He proposed a plan for the school similar to that for the library: the city would furnish a suitable site, and he would endow it with $1 million in bonds, yielding revenue of $50,000 per year. This offer was soon accepted, and the Carnegie Technical School flourished during Carnegie's lifetime, soon bursting at the seams, a major component of Carnegie's Pittsburgh empire of education. The two-year Carnegie Technical School, with its focus on vocational skills and applied arts and crafts, including home economics at the Margaret Morrison Carnegie College for Women (named after the founder's beloved mother), evolved in 1912, against Carnegie's original advice, into a four-year college, the Carnegie Institute of Technology. In 1967, merging with Mellon Institute, Carnegie Tech obtained the national stature it had long craved and became Carnegie Mellon University.

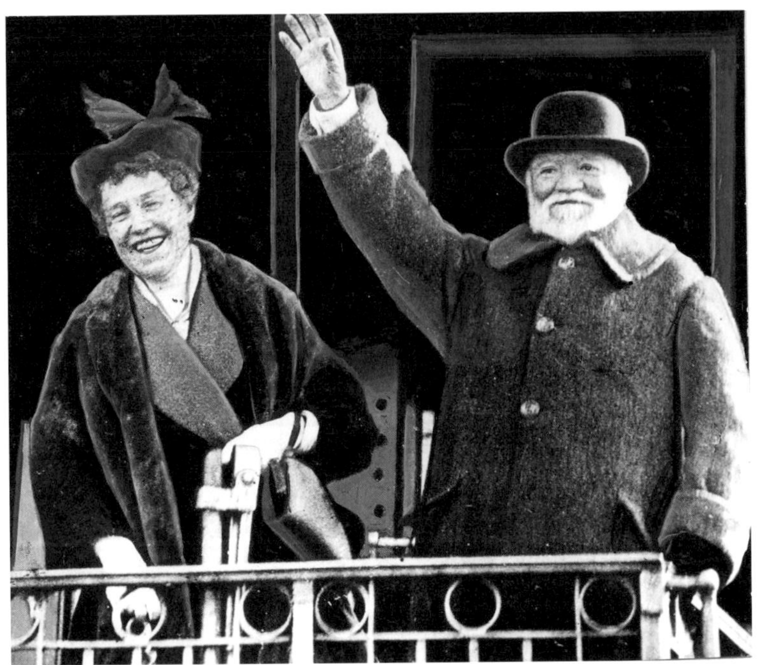

Carnegie and his wife, Louise, wave their final goodbye to Pittsburgh in 1914 as they leave by train from the East Liberty Station.

Carnegie made additional special gifts for accessions by the library, the Fine Arts Department, and the museum, as well as gifts "For Revenue" and "Endowments" to all departments. Still, however munificent these gifts were by the standards of that day, they could not by themselves sustain the library and the Institute in the decades ahead. When Andrew Carnegie died in 1919, his public gifts and bequest to his Institute and library totaled $11,729,471, and the Carnegie Institute of Technology had received an additional $7,274, 371. Carnegie Corporation of New York continued to support the Pittsburgh organizations, and Louise Carnegie remained active on its board, as did the president of Carnegie Institute, Samuel Harden Church. By 1940 the estimated total expenditures had reached $13,115,053, including support for thirty-nine international exhibitions of paintings.[17]

Andrew Carnegie's experience in business and his willingness to adapt to change led him to trust the judgment of those who managed his institutions. During his lifetime, he never laid down restrictions on the ways his institutions could develop in the future. He could no more know the future of these institutions, he declared, than he could guess whether his own afterlife would be spent in heaven or elsewhere.

BUILDING A
PALACE OF CULTURE

*"I Felt That Aladdin and His Lamp
Had Been at Work"*

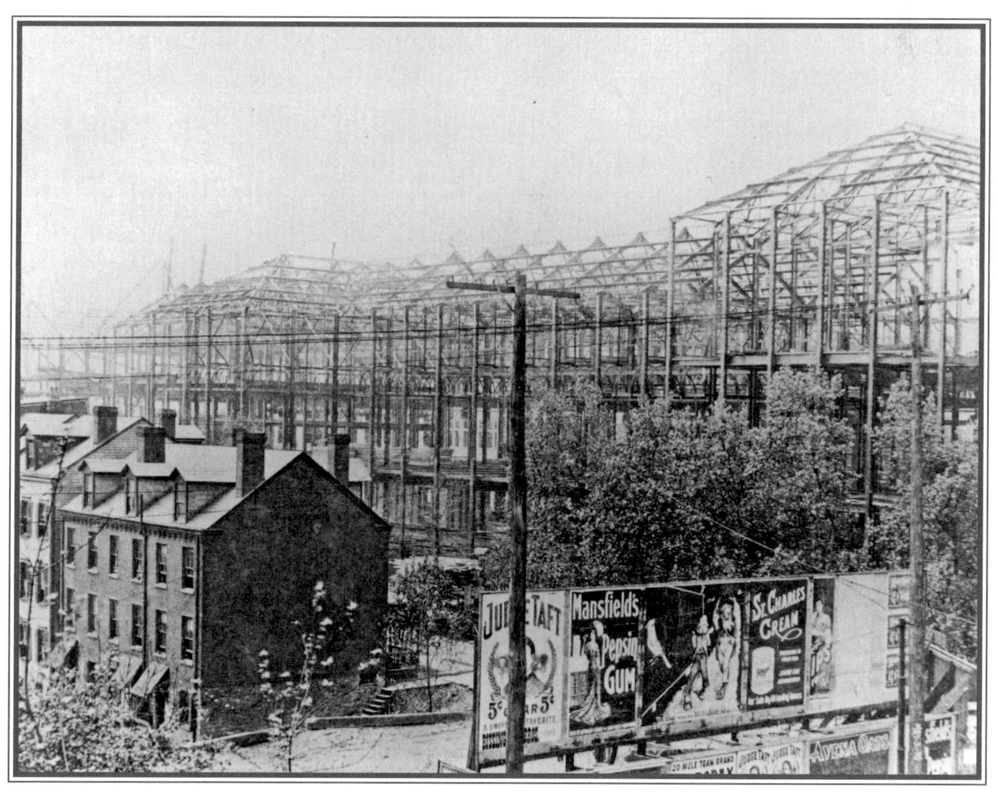

The 1895 library was such a success that Carnegie wanted an expansion, and used
Carnegie structural steel for his massive new Institute. Under construction by 1904,
it opened in 1907.

THE VISION

WHEN ANDREW CARNEGIE dedicated the completed Institute in 1907, he said first, "I have been in a dream from the moment I entered this Institute yesterday. I have been in a dream all morning and am not yet awake. . . . I really cannot understand at all. I think it is a defect in my nature. I confess to you, as I have had to confess to several, that I am totally unable to realize that I have had any part in creating this Institute."[1]

Playing the role of the bemused dreamer on the Music Hall stage, he skillfully glossed over the fact that he had in fact spent years planning Carnegie Institute and Library as the full embodiment of his philosophy in practice. In 1890 he had stood at the top of Herron Hill looking down at the panorama of Oakland, ready to choose the site for his library. With him were the mayor of Pittsburgh and George Scott, the head of the Library Building Committee, among others. Carnegie joked that like Moses he was leading people to the top of a mountain: the East End of Pittsburgh, now starting to develop, was the logical direction in which the city might grow, three miles distant from the smoky downtown, confined by industry and hills along the rivers. In addition, Oakland was accessible by streetcar, was above the industrial river corridors, and had cleaner air. Here, Carnegie believed, people would gravitate in the future.[2]

Today Herron Hill is a congested puzzle of academic buildings on the Upper Campus of the University of Pittsburgh, and Carnegie Institute and Library is surrounded by the University of Pittsburgh and Carnegie Mellon University. But in 1890 the land stretching away from the Carnegie site was sparsely populated with Victorian houses, and the name of the undeveloped Mount Airy Tract, with its steep ravines, was just being changed to Schenley Park.[3] The gully in front of the future library site was known as St. Pierre's Ravine, and Bellefield Bridge would be built across it in 1897 to allow visitors to reach its entrance by carriage. Behind the library to the south was Junction Hollow, cradling the tracks of the Baltimore and Ohio Railroad. Schenley Bridge would be built in 1897 to cross this valley, allowing visitors to reach the park and Phipps Conservatory (erected in 1893). Carnegie thus pictured his library on a hill bounded by steep ravines, at the entrance to a public park that was not yet developed.

Schenley Park was essential to Carnegie's vision. Public parks were high on his 1889 Gospel of Wealth list of what benefactors could give to the masses, and when Mary Schenley donated the land for this park in 1889, Carnegie, who knew Mrs. Schenley, acted quickly: the library site was selected in 1890, and the city passed an ordinance in 1891 authorizing the new Board of Trustees of Carnegie Library to build on this "free" public land.

Mary Schenley's story was famous in Pittsburgh. In 1842, at the tender age of fifteen, when she was still little Mary O'Hara Croghan, attending a fashionable boarding school in Staten Island, New York, she had eloped with the dashing British officer Captain Edward Schenley, forty-three years old, twice divorced, and often described as a fortune hunter. Mary, indeed, was positioned to inherit a vast estate: her despairing father was William Croghan, the husband of Elizabeth O'Hara Croghan, who had died the year after Mary was born, in 1828, as heir to the riches accumulated by her own father, General William O'Hara, after the Revolutionary War, when the new U.S. government awarded back pay to veterans in the form of Ohio country real estate, rather than cash. General O'Hara bought large swaths of this land from veterans for ready cash.

After young Mary Croghan's marriage, her father persuaded the Pennsylvania state legislature to terminate her inheritance and make him the guardian of her estate. He gave Mary and her husband part of her inheritance when she turned twenty-one, after he visited them in England and found them living in reduced circumstances. He bought them a house and even brought them to Pittsburgh to visit the family estate, hoping they would remain, but that was not to be: they returned to London, where they raised nine children. After her husband died in 1878, Mary took possession of the rest of her inheritance and leased or sold off portions of her Pittsburgh estate, including much of what is modern Oakland. She had lived in London for nearly fifty years when, in 1889, she donated three hundred acres in the steeply wooded Mount Airy Tract to the city of Pittsburgh for a public park, with an option to buy one hundred more acres for $125,000. The city council promptly bought the additional acres. One condition of Mary Schenley's gift was that the park be named after her and never sold.[4]

Carnegie, standing on Herron Hill, saw this convergence of Pittsburgh history and modern park development as an excellent opportunity. His library was dedicated in 1895—an event to which he invited Mary Schenley, asking her to take a carriage ride with him through the park named after her, although her health did not permit it—and in 1898, as a trustee of the University of Western Pennsylvania, he traveled to London again with the university chancellor William Holland to see Mrs. Schenley, They now wanted her to provide land allowing the school's campus to be relocated to Oakland, on property that was then called Schenley Farms. But in the British tradition, Schenley preferred having long-term leaseholders

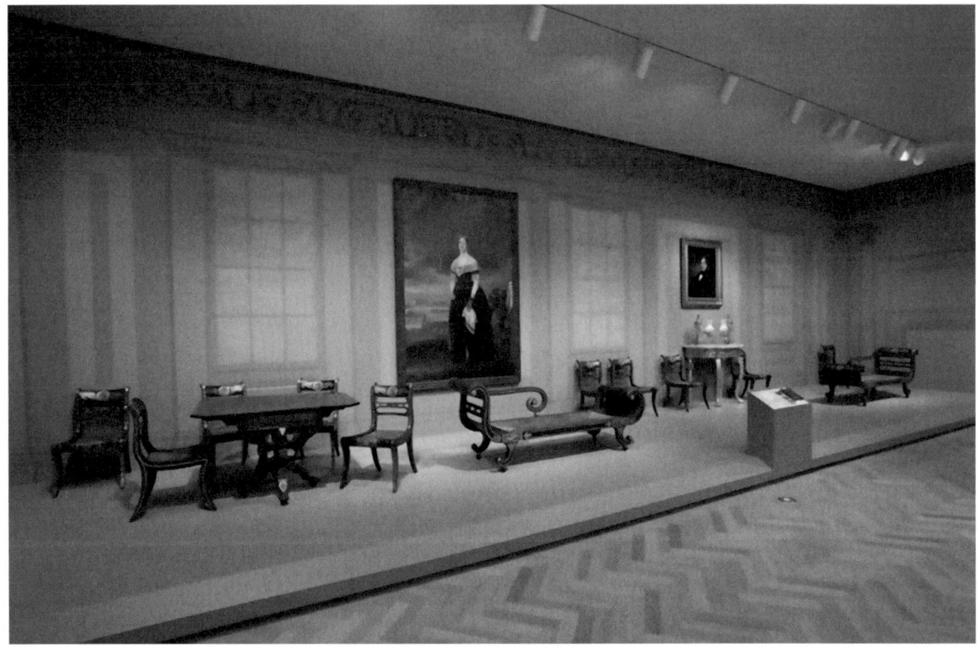

Thomas Lewis, Portrait of Mrs. Mary Schenley, *1842. Acquired in 1931 by Carnegie Museum of Art, it was installed in the renewed Ailsa Mellon Bruce Decorative Arts Gallery in 2009, along with furniture from Picnic House, the Schenley family's Pittsburgh home.*

to selling property outright, and she did not agree to this latest proposal. She died in 1903, and in 1905, in the biggest real estate deal in Pittsburgh history, the executors of her estate sold 103 acres of Schenley Farms to the developer Franklin Nicola for about $3 million.[5] This acquisition, along with the thirty-two acres that the city had provided for Carnegie's new technical school in 1903, meant that the development of modern Oakland was under way.[6]

THE LARGEST DESIGN COMPETITION IN AMERICA

Carnegie's vision triggered the largest architectural design competition held in America up to that time: ninety-seven architectural firms competed, and the winning firm was Longfellow, Alden and Harlow, only five years old but well-known in Pittsburgh. The firm's architects, Alexander W. Longfellow, Frank E. Alden, and Alfred B. Harlow, had been partners of the late Henry Hobson Richardson when he designed Pittsburgh's greatest building, Allegheny Courthouse and Jail, in 1884–88. From their office in downtown

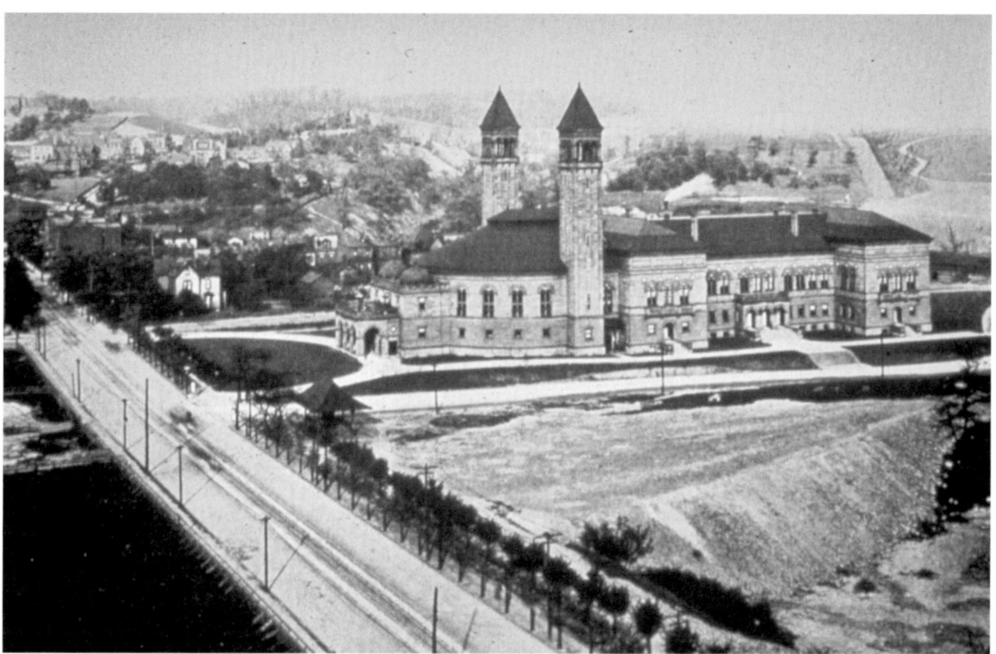

The building looked this way in 1895, with separate entrances for Carnegie Music Hall (including a circular drive for carriages), the art gallery, the library, and the museum.

Pittsburgh, they had already designed the Duquesne Club (1889) and would create Pittsburgh's first skyscraper, the Carnegie Steel Building, in 1895.

Their winning drawing featured the four elements Carnegie's vision required—a theater, a library, an art gallery, and a museum—as well as a cupola (never built) on the red-tiled roof above the library entrance. The structure would essentially be two buildings joined: the Music Hall to the north, a curved driveway from Forbes Avenue leading to its entrance and two renaissance towers flanking the theater, and the library building to the south, with rooms in its wings for the art gallery and the museum. Three separate entrances faced the westward ravine, for the library, the art gallery, and the museum. The entrance to the library, in the center, led inside to marble steps that took people upstairs to the middle of a spacious reading room on the second floor.

In the library's north wing, on the second floor, were three galleries for the Department of Fine Arts (later the library's Music and Art departments), reached via two sets of stairs that took visitors up to the side of the central gallery. The galleries' northern wall was the back wall of the Music Hall stage, an economical solution, but one that did not allow the

Music Hall sufficient space for props or scenery. Instead the pipes of the hall's large organ were crowded into the rear of the stage, and two dressing rooms were provided at stage right and left. Ultimately, the Music Hall stage proved too small for large modern symphony orchestras and ineffective as a theater for plays, serving best as a space for smaller orchestras and intimate musical performances, recitals, or lectures. The south wing of the library originally housed the Department of the Museum, with a lecture room and meeting rooms on the first floor and three halls for exhibits on the second floor. Today these are library rooms, with the Children's Room on the first floor. The museum's exhibit halls quickly proved inadequate for the growing collection, and the eighty-five-foot fossil dinosaur that Carnegie purchased required a very large hall, a reason for the great expansion that took place in 1907.

In 1895 the interior of the building was considered sensational. The walls of the library and the art galleries had been painted by the Boston interior designer Elmer Garnsey, who had worked on the Boston Public Library and the U.S. Capitol. The elaborate interior of the Music Hall, with its coffered ceiling and horseshoe design, was largely the work of Longfellow, who was enamored of the architecture he had studied at the Ecole des Beaux Arts. He used as his models elegant Parisian examples, such as the Theatre Lyrique and the Theatre Imperial, by Gabriel Davioud. The Music Hall's curved entrance, with its side towers, resembled Davioud's immense Trocadero Palace (1878). For the exterior of the buildings, Carnegie wanted brick and terra-cotta: brick had been used at his library in Braddock, and later at his libraries in Homestead and Duquesne, as well as at New York's Carnegie Hall, and terra-cotta was easy to keep clean in the soot-laden Pittsburgh atmosphere. His architects, however, wanted the monumental character of cut sandstone. It was more expensive, but he obliged them, adding one hundred thousand dollars to the seven hundred thousand the board had appropriated for the main structure. The foundation of the building was laid in the fall of 1892, and work on the superstructure began in July 1893, continuing without interruption until the building's completion in 1895.

Carnegie expressed opinions about many details of the building, but he usually gave way to his experts when they insisted. One example of this was the choice of the authors, artists, musicians, and scientists whose names would be carved on the entablature of the building. The Victorians often carved the names of famous individuals on the exterior of buildings, and both the 1895 and the 1907 buildings followed this practice. These names on the building's exterior were a symbolic reflection of what was going on in the interior: the names of authors were carved over the library entrance, the names of composers on the sides of the Music Hall, and the names of

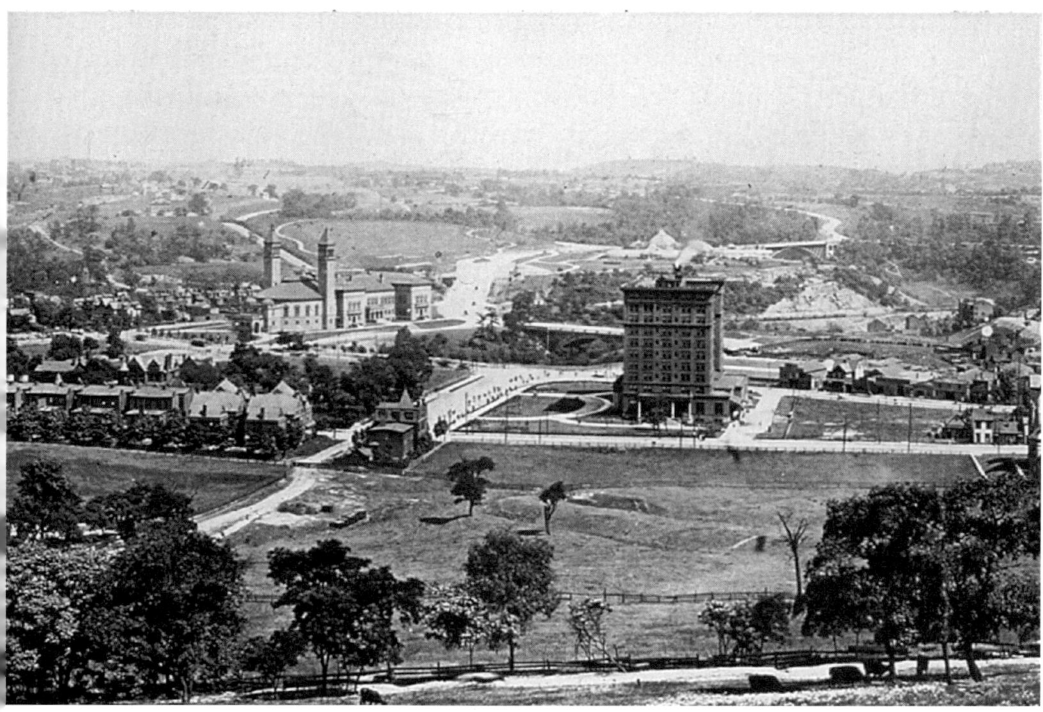

Pittsburgh's Oakland neighborhood, circa 1904, featured the Schenley Hotel and Carnegie's new library. Phipps Conservatory is in the distance, in the newly developing Schenley Park.

artists and scientists on the appropriate wings as well. This is why today the names of scientists appear over the south wing of the library, where the Children's Room is now located. In addition, from the courtyard of the modern Scaife Gallery, the names of scientists are visible above the waterfall, since that part of the building houses the scientific collections and the Hall of Dinosaurs.

To choose the names of great men (there are no women) for the walls of his buildings, Carnegie had a committee of experts who voted on the final list. When he saw their list, however, he became upset and wrote Institute president William Nimick Frew in protest, asking him to delay the final decision: "I cannot approve the list of names. . . . Some of the names have no business to be on the list. Imagine Dickens in and Burns out."[7] He wanted the name of plowboy-poet Robert Burns, his compatriot and favorite Scottish poet, on the front of the library, where the names of such literary gods as Homer, Virgil, Shakespeare, and Milton were to be placed, but he did not overrule the experts' decision to omit Burns, who was not usually placed in that rarified company. Rather, Carnegie quietly arranged with eight wealthy Pittsburghers of Scottish descent to erect their own monument to Robert Burns outside of Phipps Conservatory. (Henry Phipps was one of Carnegie's childhood friends from Scotland.) To carve the monument, they chose another Scottish American, John Massey Rhind, who had recently created the sculptures at Carnegie Institute. One of Carnegie's last acts in Pittsburgh was to dedicate the Burns sculpture on his final visit in 1914.[8]

Another decision he faced in 1895 was whether or not to produce copies of classical statuary in the nude, like the Greek originals, or to cover their genitals with modest Victorian drapery. In 1895 he telegrammed Frew his verdict: "I strongly recommend nude to be draped since question has been raised. Remember my words in speech. We should begin gently to lead the people upward. I hope nothing in gallery or hall will ever give offense to the simplest man or woman. Draping is used everywhere in Britain except in London. If we are to work genuine good we must bend and keep in touch with the masses. Am very clear on this question."[9]

The opening of Carnegie Institute and Library in Pittsburgh was such a success that within two years Carnegie wanted to capitalize on it. Pittsburgh was the best symbol of what he and the Gospel of Wealth could do for the masses, and he had the money to triple its size. By 1898, the Board of Trustees had received estimates from Alden and Harlow (their associate Longfellow had returned to his Boston practice) for the expansion Carnegie desired, and in 1899 they were forwarded to Carnegie. The first estimate called for $1.75 million, to which he agreed. Then the plan to erect a Music Hall foyer the size and scale of the Paris Opera brought the total cost to $3.6 million.[10] Carnegie agreed again. Over the next eight years, the firm of Alden and Harlow was devoted to this expansion, which had captured the attention of the international press as an illustration of what America's richest multimillionaire was doing for democracy.

Throughout this project, the appointed directors of each department shaped the Institute's intellectual mission and its operational details. One result of their varied opinions was the development of spectacular interior spaces, at the expense of an organic exterior. The architectural historian Margaret Henderson Floyd argues that the aesthetic challenge faced in the 1907 expansion was entirely different from the original 1895 building, "where the forms of interior spaces could be read from the exterior. . . . The Carnegie Institute Extension produced a ponderous entity that in the end resembled the Library of Congress more than any other contemporary building and sought to rival its richness as well."[11] The internal result was a disjointed series of giant spaces. Floyd concludes: "Thus the Carnegie must be experienced as a series of breathtaking surprises, each more astonishing than the last, in which the unsuspecting explorer is carried between

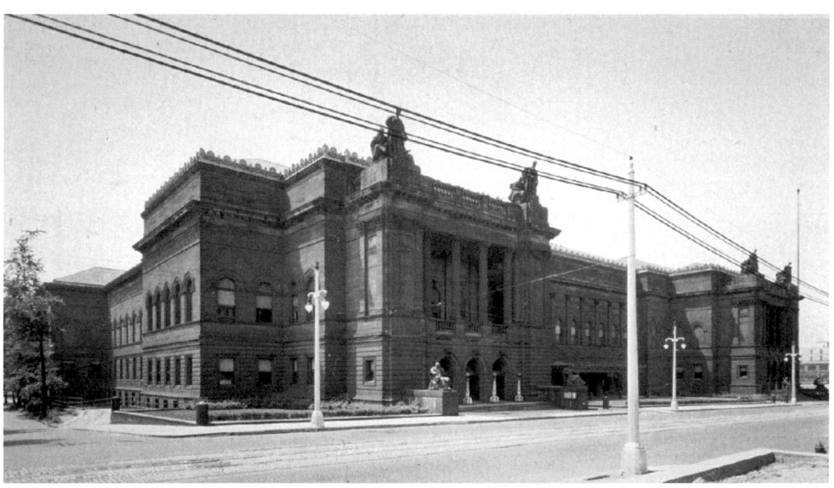

*The 1907 expansion of the Institute on Forbes Avenue reached east to Mawhinney Street,
a street later eliminated by the addition of the Scaife Gallery in 1974.*

unrelated worlds as in a time capsule. Such an aesthetic system reflects
the contradictions and inconsistencies of the antimodern culture of the
century's end." The Institute's disjunctive interior featured major spaces
that were tied together "by almost secretive intermediate connectors that
prevent their coordination into an organic whole."[12] While Floyd sees this as
evidence of the intellectual fragmentation characteristic of the start of the
twentieth century, it can also be seen as the physical birth of the four powers
that came to rule the politics of the Carnegie Institute and Library—the
departments of music, art, literature, and science, whose administrative
alliance might have been uneasy, but promised great rewards for the public.

In 1907, these four powers and the mission of the Institute as a whole
were symbolized outside the building by the allegorical sculptures of John
Massey Rhind and inside by the large mural painted by John White Alexander (*The Crowning of Labor,* never completed). John Massey Rhind (1858–
1936) was a prolific Scottish-born sculptor whose success in New York and
elsewhere had brought him to the attention of Carnegie and the architects
Alden and Harlow. At the Institute, he created the famous ensemble of
heroic figures at the Forbes Avenue entrance (1907), the Muses above, the
seated figure of Carnegie inside (1911), and finally the figure of the poet
Robert Burns by Phipps Conservatory (1914). Rhind's forte was sculpture
associated with architecture, especially grand figures with symbolic details.
The ensemble of iconic figures he sculpted at the Forbes Avenue entrance
is often referred to as the "noble quartet": Shakespeare (literature), Bach
(music), Michelangelo (art), and Galileo (science), all seated in classic Greek

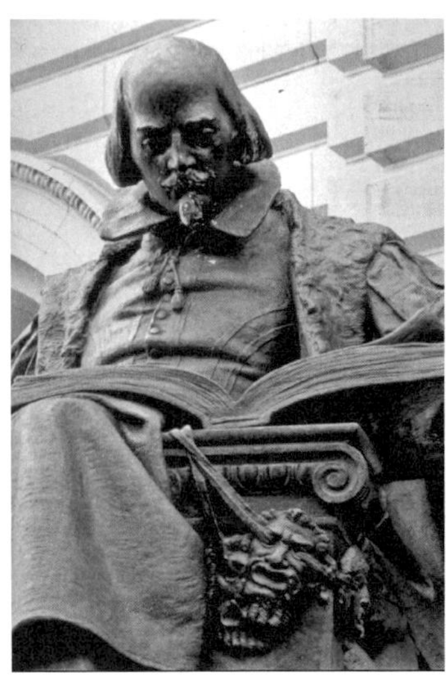

1

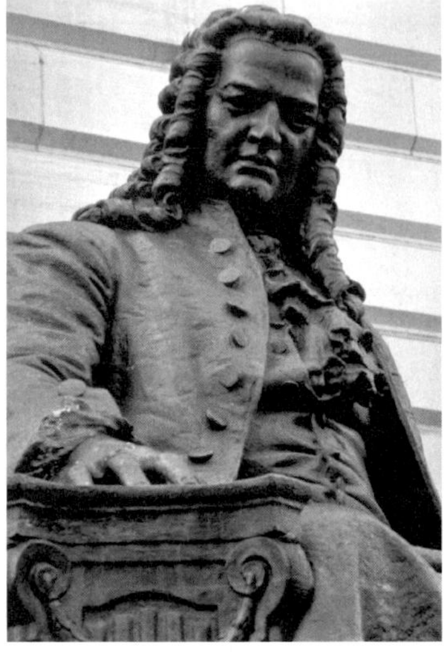

2

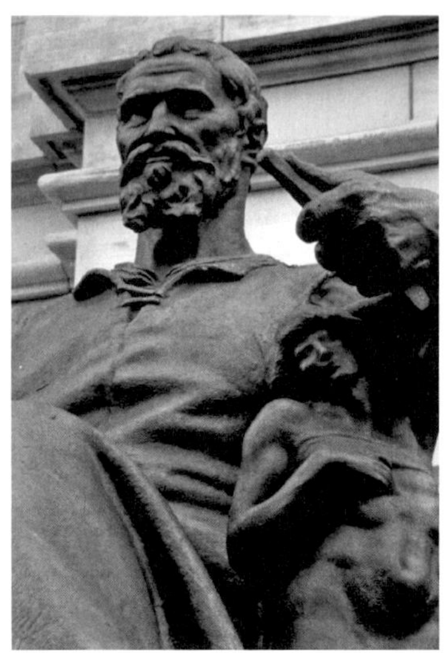

3

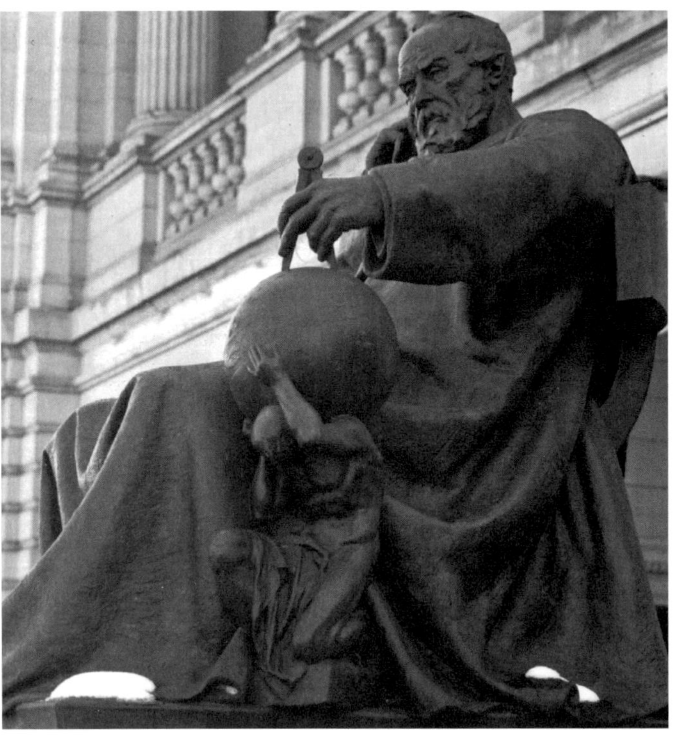

4

1. *John Massey Rhind sculpted four figures for the 1907 expansion to represent the "noble quartet" of the arts. Literature is represented by Shakespeare; the masks of comedy and tragedy appear on the pedestal beneath his book.*

2. *Bach, symbol of music, has his hand on a keyboard—you have to be standing beside him to see his fingers on the keys.*

3. *Michelangelo, symbol of art, with his chisel and his sculpture of the Dying Slave, which captures the moment when life gives way to death.*

4. *Galileo, symbol of science, with his calipers and Atlas holding up an armillary sphere—a model of objects in the universe.*

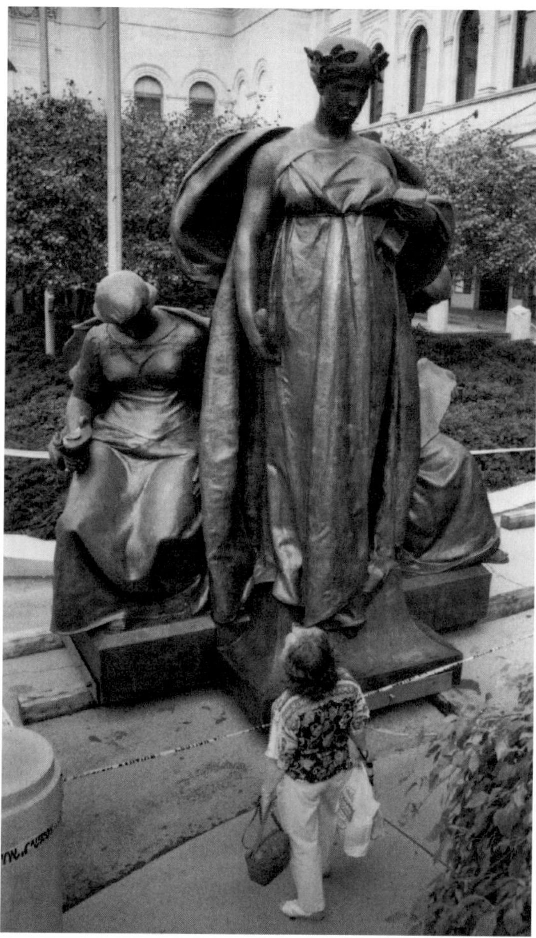

*In 1992, Rhind's four groups of allegorical figures on the
top of the building, representing literature, music, art, and
science, were lowered for restoration. For the first time,
the objects held by the three figures in each group could be
examined by viewers on street level.*

chairs, with the emblems of their crafts about them. Rhind's iconography
is predictably Victorian. The seated figures in the "noble quartet" are male,
while the Muses—the female allegorical spirits looking down from the
parapets—are female, symbolizing the same inspirational achievements in
literature, music, art, and science. The men in this iconography are earth-
bound, corporeal workers, while the unspecified Muses represent the higher
and finer life of the spirit, each holding symbols of the four disciplines: the
lamp of learning, a quill pen, and paper for literature; a palette, a flower, and

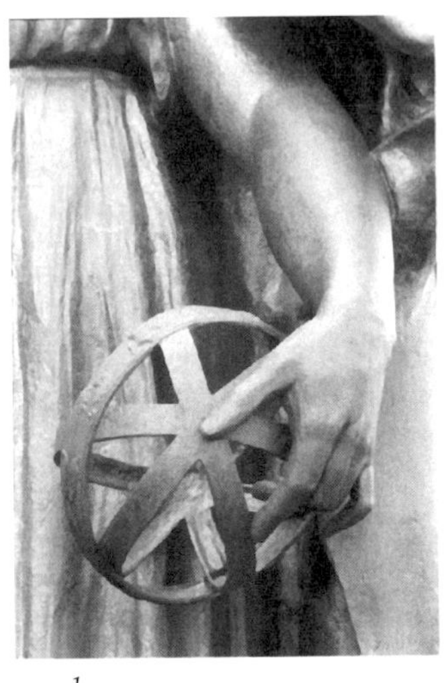

1

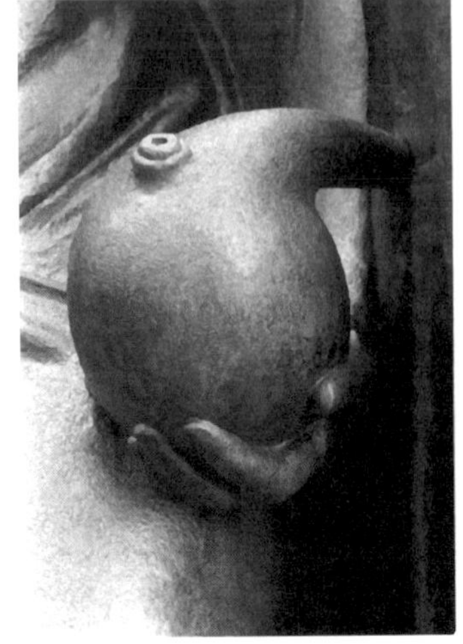

2

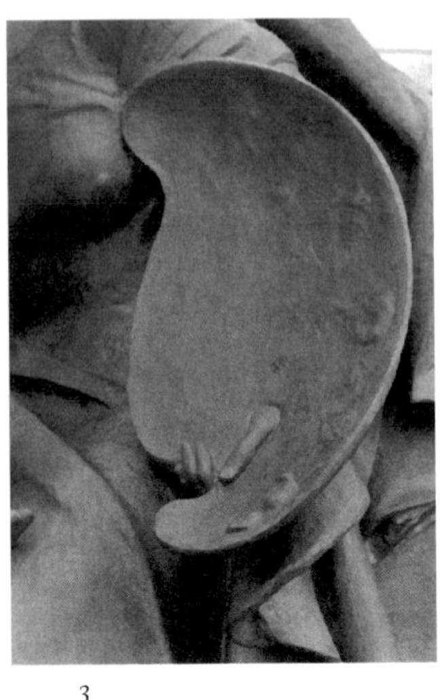

3

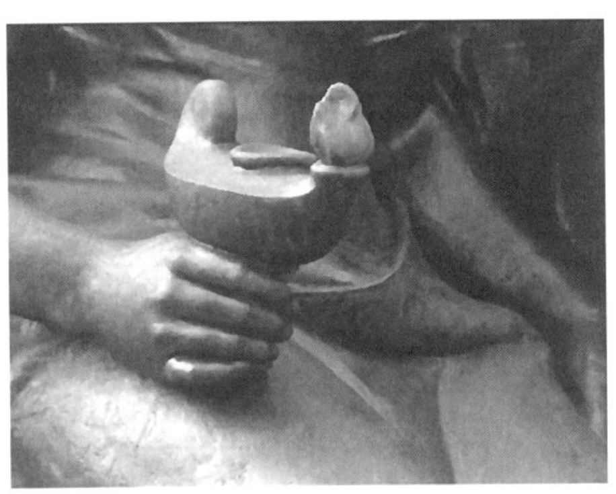

4

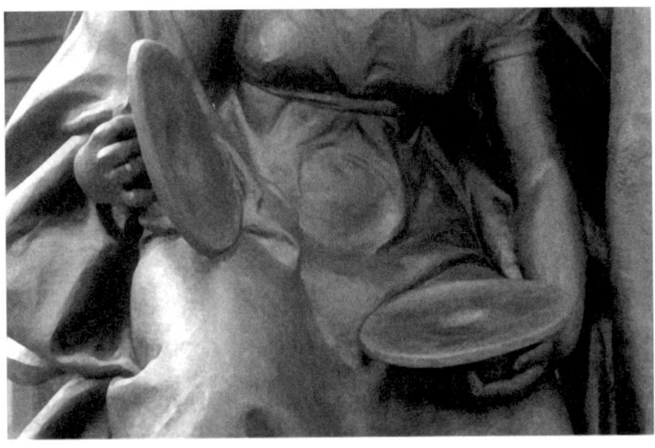

5

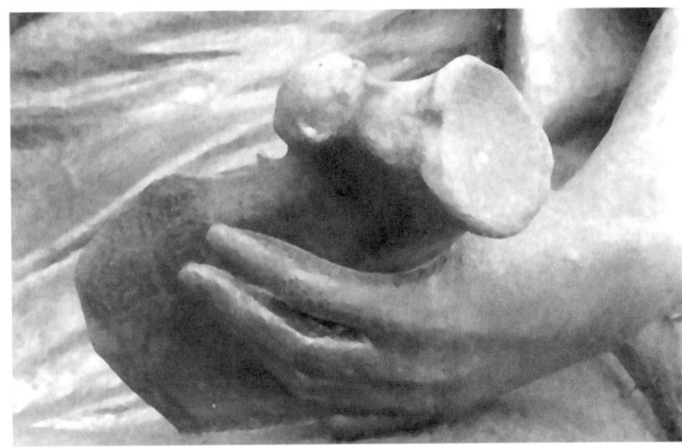

6

1. *A muse of science holds an armillary sphere.*

2. *A muse of science holds a chemist's flask.*

3. *Looking down from atop the Institute, a muse of art holds a painter's palette.*

4. *A muse of literature holds the lamp of learning.*

5. *A muse of music holds cymbals.*

6. *A muse of science holds a fossil bone to honor museum science.*

an architect's compass for art; cymbals, a pan pipe, and a lyre for music; and the armillary sphere, a chemist's flask, and a fossil bone for science. Rhind's twelve-foot-high Muses, nearly a hundred feet in the air, lean out slightly over Forbes Avenue to avoid appearing to fall backward when viewed from the ground. Rhind's symbolism on the exterior, echoed in the John White Alexander mural inside, led Cynthia Field, an architectural historian at the Smithsonian Institution, to say that the Institute had the most fully realized sculptural and architectural program of any museum of its era.[13]

SPECTACULAR SPACES

The 1895 library had provided a large reading room, while the Music Hall featured a fine performance space. The 1907 extension added the foyer of the Music Hall, the Hall of Architecture, the Hall of Sculpture, Staircase Hall, and the Hall of Dinosaurs. As the historian Floyd notes, the space inside the Institute is marked by a series of "breathtaking surprises," and the richly marbled Music Hall foyer is perhaps the most astonishing of these. Sixty feet wide and 135 feet long, with a 45-foot-high ceiling of sculptured plaster and gold leaf, the foyer was the largest marble project in the world. Harlow, its primary designer, used French and Italian artists to cut the rich marble detailing of the foyer's floors and walls and to mold the gilded plaster of its coved ceiling. The marble itself is European—the floor made of "richly patterned red Castelpoggia, white Italian, and Vert Antique" and the walls, in the vestibule and the corridor leading to the grand staircase, paneled in "light Montarenti Sienna marble."[14] The eighty-five plasterers employed to sculpt the foyer's ornamental plasterwork, including model makers, modelers, and casters—mostly Italians—set up a studio inside the building. Suspended from the ceiling, four gilded chandeliers show-cased hundreds of electric lightbulbs, only then starting to appear in public buildings, while a colonnade of twenty-four green marble columns, 28 feet high, supports an ornate balcony that circles the room. At the far end of the foyer is the seated bronze statue of Andrew Carnegie, holding court for those who visit the Institute but in fact wedged between two columns and often overlooked. The architectural historian James Van Trump notes the significance of the foyer's splendor: "In its lavish use of luxurious materials and the heavy elegance of its detailing, the Foyer is a true and representative monument of the Edwardian era—that period between 1900 and 1914—the high summer and heyday of the capitalist world."[15] Still, while the foyer's sumptuous display of marble and golden surfaces would befit a king, the message here is in fact the reverse: this is a people's palace, and the founder himself is present as a businessman.

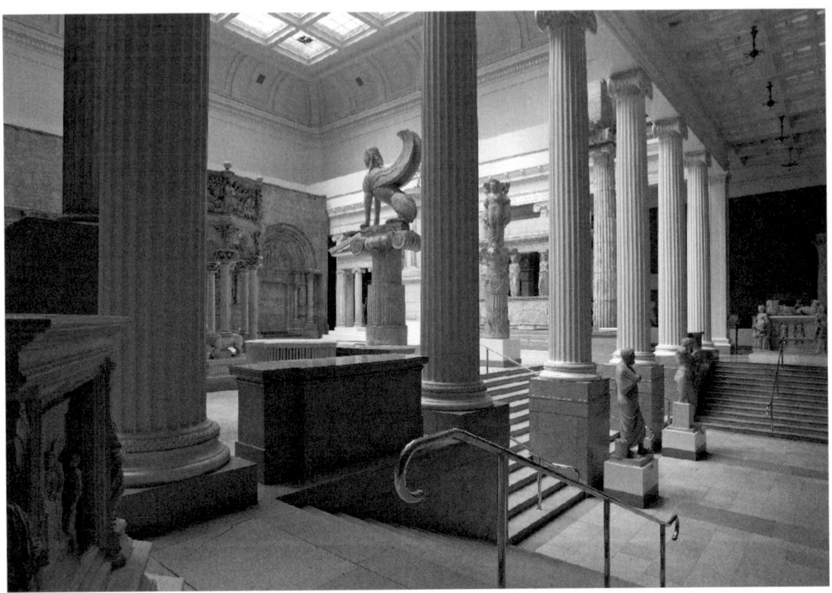

The Hall of Architecture has a glass roof; glass panels in the balcony floor admit even more light.

The Hall of Architecture was modeled after the great Tomb of Halicarnassus, built in 353 B.C. for the Asian king Mausolus. In ancient times, this was one of the Seven Wonders of the World, but it had long ago fallen into ruin, so its 1856 excavation by Sir Charles Newton had captured the world's imagination. Alden and Harlow now adapted the tomb's intriguing form for the Institute, conceiving a vast space in which to display ancient architecture and sculpture.[16] The resulting room is a giant cube 125 feet wide and 126 feet long and more than 76 feet high. Alden and Harlow transferred the tomb's colonnade from outside to the hall's inside, so that the twenty-eight Ionic columns surrounding the hall could carry a balcony. Above all is a great coved skylight that allows cool light down into the space, which is home to casts of the world's great sculpture and architectural fragments.

To James Van Trump, the Hall of Architecture, with its giant cast of St. Gilles du Garde as centerpiece, is "like some fabulous and forsaken city in a medieval tapestry[;] it hovers hauntingly under Mausolas dome, inhabited by silent, fantastic beasts and broken Roman columns, by frozen saints and fairy-tale foliage. However engaging as stage scenery, this plaster replica cannot, in the end be considered a valid historical document; it is an illusion, a mask, behind which we may discern dimly the real face of the past. But even if it is a mask of the past, it does strike the note of grace in the harsh industrial climate of Pittsburgh; it emphasizes an achieved state of artistic grandeur, albeit at one remove."[17]

The top-lit Hall of Sculpture, like the foyer, is two stories high, with rows of white marble pillars holding up the balcony and the roof, and with an important frieze at the top. Neoclassical and elegant, it is Greek in effect and reflects the interior look of the Parthenon, built of pentelic marble from the same quarry that was used to construct the original Temple of Athena in Athens. Its plaster frieze (funded by Carnegie in 1898) circles the room at the top, at the approximate height of the original Parthenon frieze, although the Institute's frieze is inside instead of on the exterior. The bas-reliefs of this fragmented scene are details from the ancient Greek

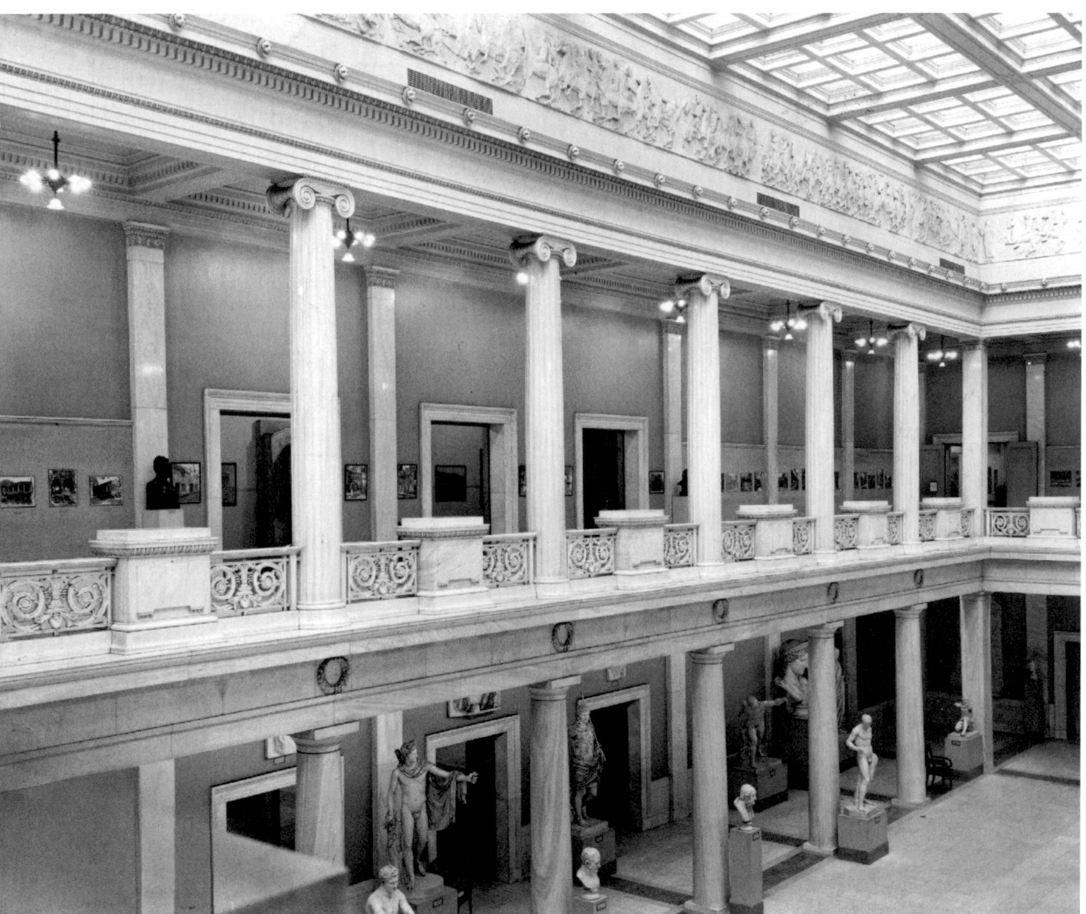

The Hall of Sculpture, made of pentelic marble from the same quarry used by ancient Greek architects to construct the buildings on the Acropolis in Athens.

religious festival of the Panathenaia, in which processions and games were held in Athens, replicas of originals that Lord Elgin took to England in 1806 to be preserved in the British Museum. In 1907, the Hall of Sculpture displayed its classical sculptures on the ground floor, but now some figures rest on pedestals on the balcony, while others have been placed in the Hall of Architecture. The glass floors of the balcony, like those of the balcony in the Hall of Architecture, allowed light into this cavernous room before electric lights became common.

Staircase Hall is the "stair of honor" for John White Alexander's three-story mural *The Crowning of Labor.* Van Trump's lush prose captures the effect:

Here the wide burnished expanses of Eschallion and Hauteville marble rising through three stories, the opulently pattered floor, and the swirling tenuosities of the murals set eminently the tone of the building, proclaim its subdued palatial richness, though the pride of the ascending flights is not royal, but municipal. The idea of *escaliers d'honneur* such as this is essentially baroque, and the prototype of our stairway is undoubtedly that of the Paris Opera, but the sinuous feminine pomp of Paris has been metamorphosed into a quiet, angular masculinity. Pittsburgh is an intensely masculine city and so is much of its architecture, and nowhere is that virility shown more straitly than in this stair hall.[18]

The hall grows more elaborate as it rises, moving from Doric to Corinthian orders on the capitals of the columns, and shifting from marble and iron balustrades up to the second level, with a curving iron rail reaching to the third level. Although incomplete, Alexander's three-story mural symbolizes the rise of the laboring masses to the spiritual heights of music, art, literature, and science and shows Carnegie as the Black Knight of Labor who made this possible. Once again the earthbound male workers labor below in the mills (first-floor murals); female spirits rise amid the smoke from the mills, bearing the artistic and intellectual gifts of labor (second-floor murals); and at the top level a procession of noble workers—men, women, children—marches confidently toward an apotheosis: music, art, science, literature (third-floor mural). Unfortunately, the artist died before painting the climactic last murals that depict the goal.

Dinosaur Hall was utilitarian, a powerful magnet for the public, and a prime reason behind the Institute's expansion. *Diplodocus carnegii,* displayed there, made the Pittsburgh site equal to the greatest scientific museums of the world. Surrounded by a balcony with iron railings, the two-story hall was illuminated by large windows opening to the east (now sealed) that now face the Sculpture Court. Before 1907, the only place in Pittsburgh to clean and prepare the bones of this eighty-five-foot-long fossil skeleton, and eventually to erect it, was Exposition Hall (1889) at the Pittsburgh

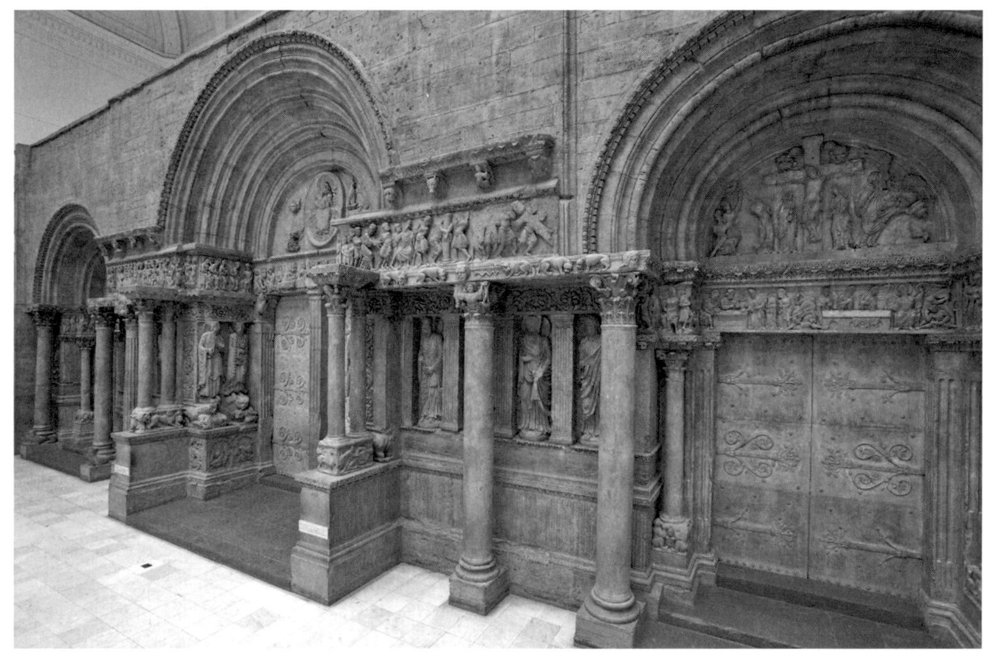

To bring the medieval facade of the Abbey Church of St.-Gilles-du-Gard to his Hall of Architecture, Carnegie gave the mayor of the town in southern France a considerable sum to make a plaster replica. The result was the largest architectural cast ever made.

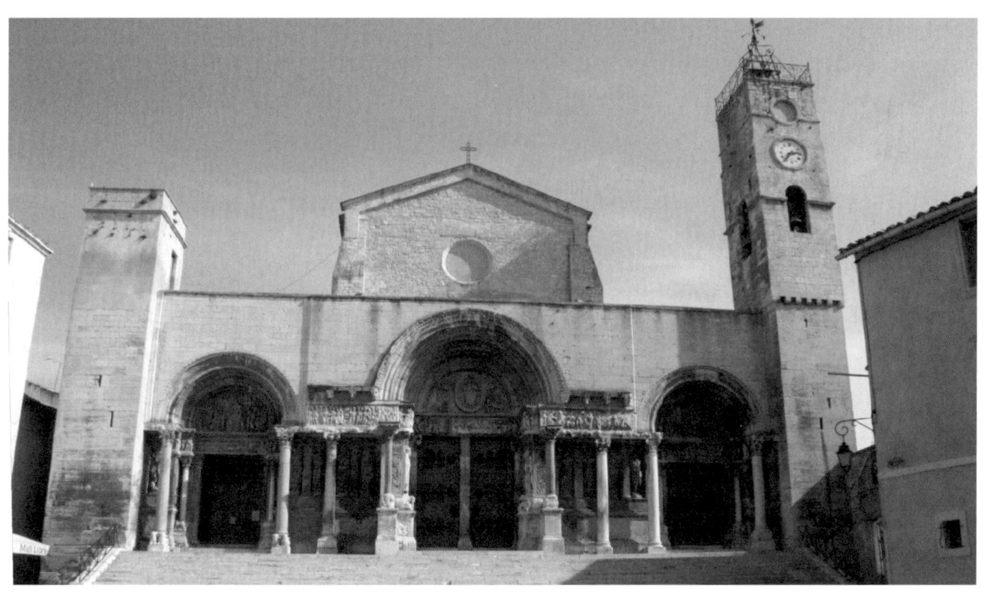

The ruins of the Benedictine Abbey Church, from which Carnegie's cast was made, still stand in St.-Gilles-du-Gard, France.

Point, and *Diplodocus* was first assembled there before being installed at Carnegie Institute.

The 1907 expansion created numerous other spaces within the Institute. Natural History halls took shape on three floors in the rear of the building, including the second-floor space that today holds the Hall of North American Mammals and African Mammals. A meeting room was devoted to the Boone and Crockett Club, one of the scientific societies that the Institute then encouraged and the home of big-game hunters and wildlife specimen collectors. The expansive art galleries on the Institute's Forbes Avenue side received the northern light favored by artists. In the second-floor galleries (now displaying decorative arts), high arched windows faced Forbes Avenue, while the third floor's top-lit galleries (eventually the anthropology halls for the Natural History Museum) were flooded with light. On the first floor, the Founder's Room, an elegant ceremonial space where Institute leaders and Carnegie formally posed for pictures, has today been faithfully restored, and the President's Office holds the painting of Andrew Carnegie that his wife, Louise, considered his best likeness. Local tradition has it that the roll-top desk and Victorian sofa in the President's Office belonged to Carnegie, but there is no documentation supporting that claim. Perhaps they came from the Carnegie Steel Building downtown, demolished in the 1950s.

THE BEAUX-ARTS EFFECT

The World's Columbian Exposition, held in Chicago in 1893, showcased the beaux-arts style propounded at Paris's Ecole des Beaux Arts, and architects across the nation, including Pittsburgh's Longfellow, Alden and Harlow, began to adopt many beaux-arts techniques. The beaux-arts style emphasized noble spaces, such as grand entrances and plazas; order and symmetry in boulevards and streets; and architectural imitations of historic building styles. It stressed precision in details such as balustrades, cornices, bas-relief panels, and sculpture and used garlands or cartouches for graceful effects. After the exposition closed, "City Beautiful" fever affected the United States for decades, producing grand vistas and avenues; eye-catching monuments; uniform cornice heights; and the harmonious, if somewhat theatrical, look of new large buildings. The exposition's closing, which coincided with the initial construction of Carnegie Institute and Library, found Pittsburgh on the verge of a building boom. Thus, Pittsburgh's Fifth Avenue and the adjacent streets in Oakland are one of the best U.S. examples of the beaux-arts principles that were sweeping the nation, thanks to the civic power and accumulated wealth of the city's leading citizens.

At the time, Oakland already enjoyed a grand pleasure ground in

Schenley Park: a racetrack (Schenley Oval), a golf course, a lake for rowing, bridle paths and walking trails, a flower conservatory, a merry-go-round, a parade ground (Flagstaff Hill), and picturesque roads skirting romantic ravines. Now, as Oakland became the cultural center of the city, the exclusive "clubhouses of Oakland" (as architectural historian Franklin Toker called them) proliferated: the Pittsburgh Athletic Club, the University Club, the Masonic Temple, Syria Mosque, the Jewish Community Center, the Twentieth Century Club. So too did public buildings such as the grandiose Allegheny County Soldiers and Sailors Memorial and the Italianate villa of the Pittsburgh Board of Education. The people who used the new clubhouses of Oakland and bought paintings from Carnegie Internationals to hang in them were the same people who attended the concerts at the Music Hall and enjoyed the museum's galleries. Their children went to Oakland universities, which for decades depended on the Carnegie Library for academic resources.

Spurred by the impetus of the City Beautiful movement, and the energy of developers like Franklin Nicola, the monuments and expensive residences that made Oakland distinctive took shape over a few scant decades. The universities planned new campuses featuring ennobling designs. The grassy swards of the Carnegie Institute of Technology fronted buildings such as the Fine Arts Building, the Margaret Morrison School, and Baker and Porter halls—leading visually to Machinery Hall at the end of a long court of honor. The University of Pittsburgh planned an acropolis of academic buildings on Herron Hill, designed by Henry Horbostle, although only a few were completed. Heinz Chapel and Rodef Shalom Synagogue were added to the mix, as were large hospitals and schools such as Central Catholic. The Schenley Hotel was built in 1898 to accommodate visitors to Carnegie Institute and Library, and Carnegie himself stayed there when visiting the city. Toward the end of the beaux-arts building boom, from 1931 to 1937, in the depths of the Depression, a classic temple for applied science, Mellon Institute, was built. Even more astonishing was the Cathedral of Learning, also begun during the Depression, which Chancellor John Bowman envisioned as a centerpiece for Pittsburgh itself. Architecture is often described as frozen music, and Bowman compared this impractical, thirty-six-story skyscraper to the crescendos of Richard Wagner's *Ride of the Valkyries.* The Cathedral of Learning changed the metabolism of Oakland, centered the university, and towered over the three-story Institute.

Yet another of Oakland's landmark structures is the Bellefield Boiler Plant, described by the novelist Michael Chabon as "the Cloud Factory."[19] Chabon's student narrator in *The Mysteries of Pittsburgh,* like countless others, enjoys watching the power plant, its high smokestack emitting the stuff of dreams—"great clouds, perfectly white and clean, white as new base-

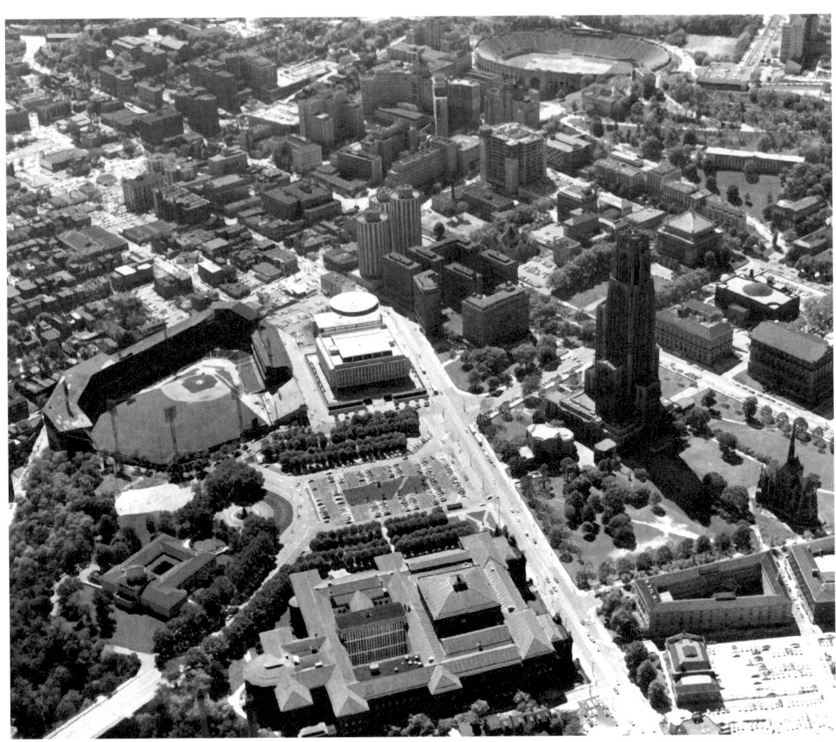

A bird's-eye view of Oakland just before Forbes Field was torn down in 1971. The Institute is in the foreground (without the Sarah Scaife Gallery of 1974); the monumental buildings on Forbes and Fifth Avenues show the beaux-arts influence.

balls"—as the plant generates steam for Oakland. The architect Phillip Johnson once contrasted the plant's smokestack to the elegant chimney atop Carnegie Mellon's Machinery Hall, across the ravine: the Machinery Hall chimney, designed by the campus architect Henry Hornbostel, struck Johnson as "the most beautiful smokestack in the world," the gray concrete smokestack of the Bellefield Boiler Plant as the ugliest.[20]

Still, the plant is integral to the Institute, designed by Alden and Harlow in 1904 at the time of the expansion to provide the steam heat the Institute required. Set logically in Junction Hollow, in the ravine below the Institute, the plant provided coal from the Baltimore and Ohio railroad line, a spur running directly into the plant and a small locomotive moving coal cars back and forth.[21] Alden and Harlow used brick, not stone, for its construction, a five-hundred-foot tunnel, twelve feet wide and seven and a half feet high, invisible to the public, connecting it to the Institute above.

From 1895 until 1904, a small boiler was used inside the building, but the expanded Institute required more steam and power. It was clearly safer

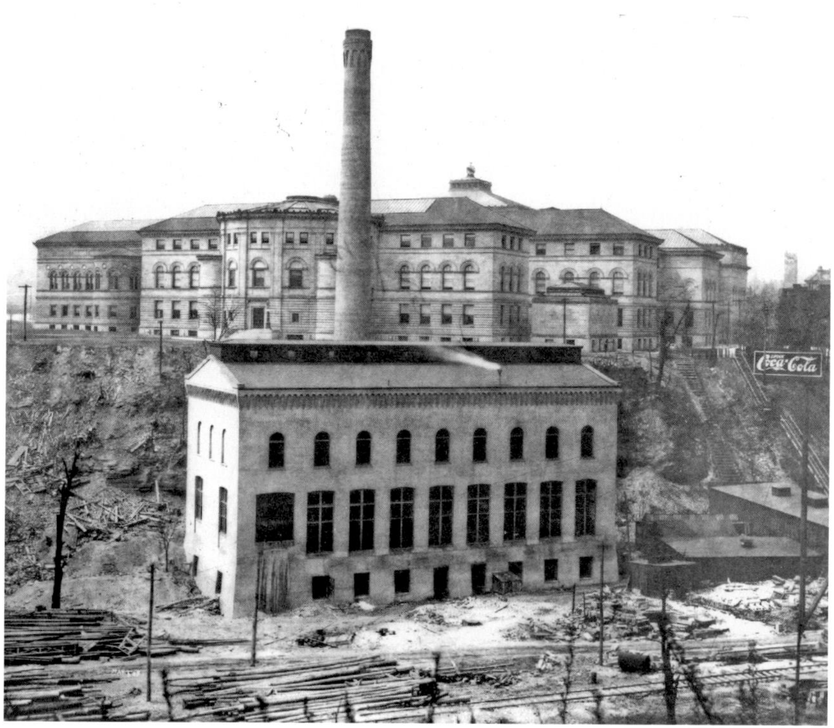

The Bellefield Boiler Plant was designed by Alden and Harlow in 1904 as an integral part of Carnegie Institute and Library.

to place the furnaces and boilers outside of a building that housed books, fine art, and rare artifacts, and the removed location kept dirt, smoke, and noise at a distance. In the Institute's basement, Alden and Harlow designed an elegant engine room with four steam-powered generators. This engine room celebrated the achievements of Pittsburgh's practical genius, and its marble floor, white terra-cotta walls, and instrument panels of marble and brass were proud features of the 1907 Institute. In 1943, the Bellefield Boiler Plant was enlarged to serve other buildings in Oakland.[22] Today it has worked safely and economically for more than a century, one of the last examples of nineteenth-century technology displayed in the urban heart of postindustrial Pittsburgh.

Carnegie, calling his expanded Institute the work of a genie who had rubbed a lamp, was countered by his wife, Louise: "Yes," she said, "and we did not even have to rub the lamp." By the end of the twentieth century, Oakland was the third busiest urban center in Pennsylvania, after Philadelphia and downtown Pittsburgh.

CARNEGIE INSTITUTE FLOORPLANS, 1895–PRESENT

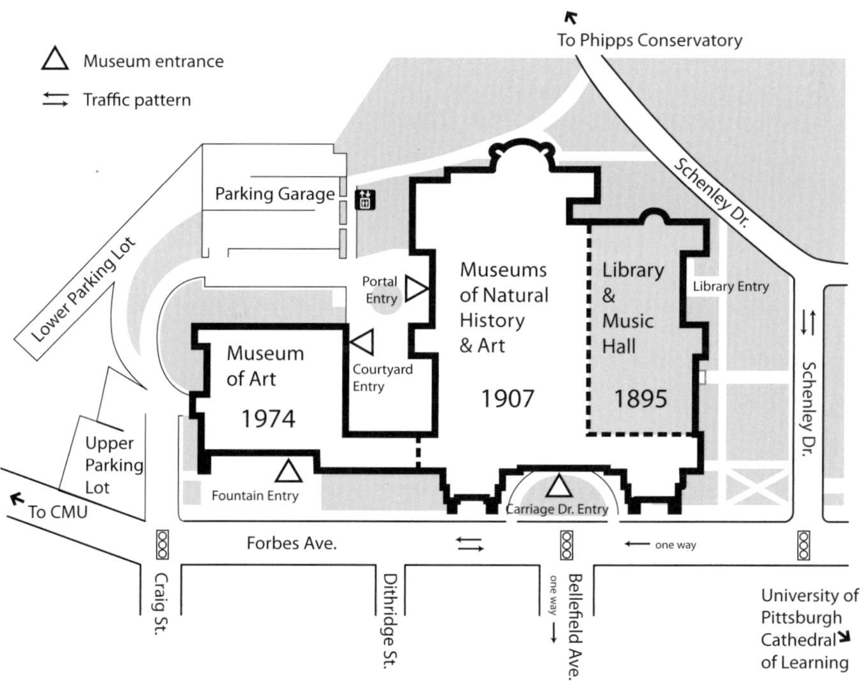

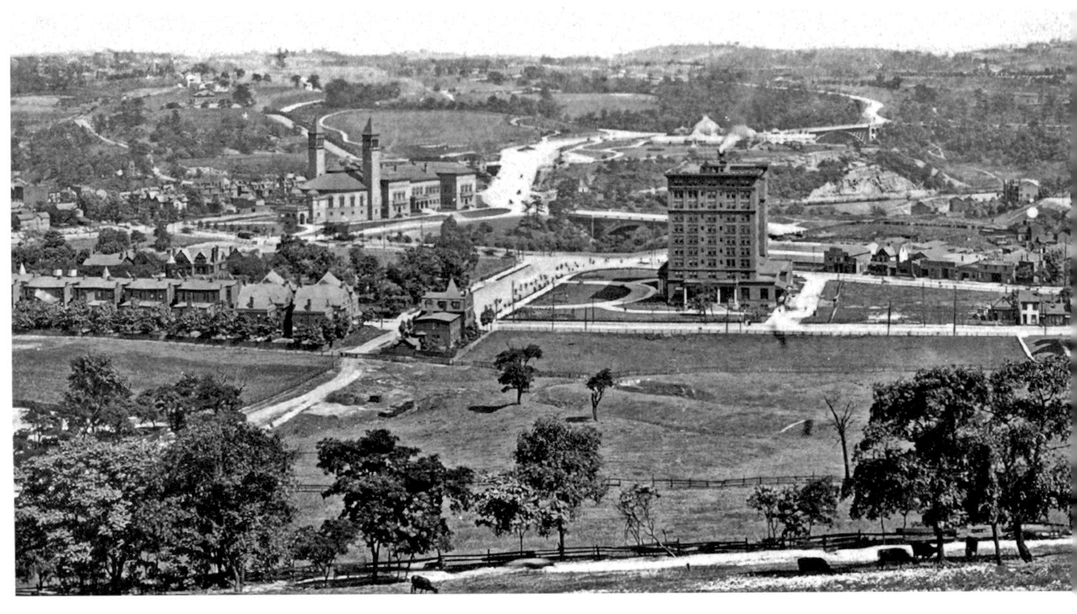

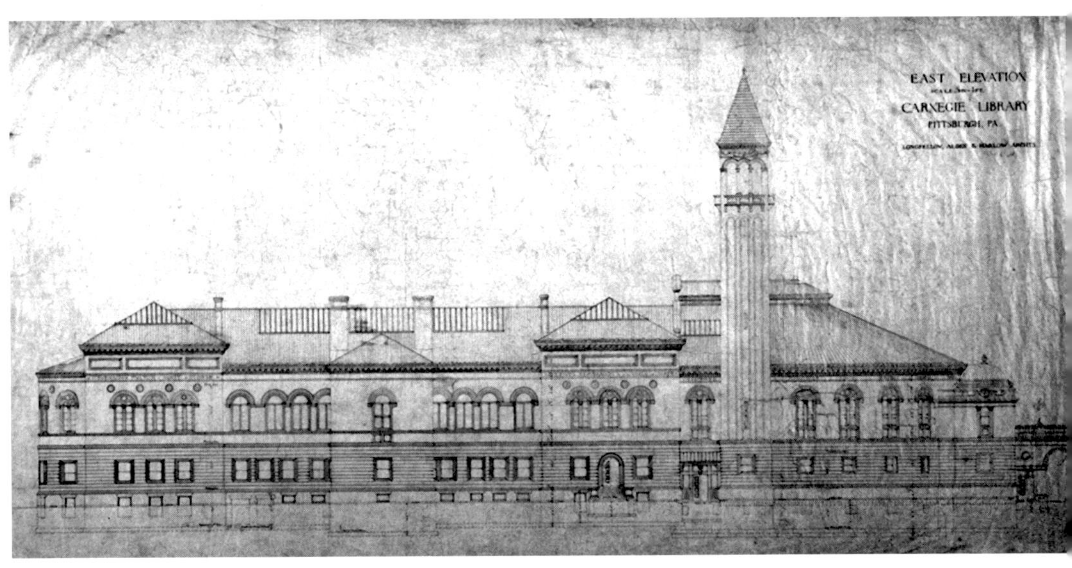

EAST ELEVATION
SCALE
CARNEGIE LIBRARY
PITTSBURGH, PA
LONGFELLOW, ALDEN & HARLOW ARCHITECTS

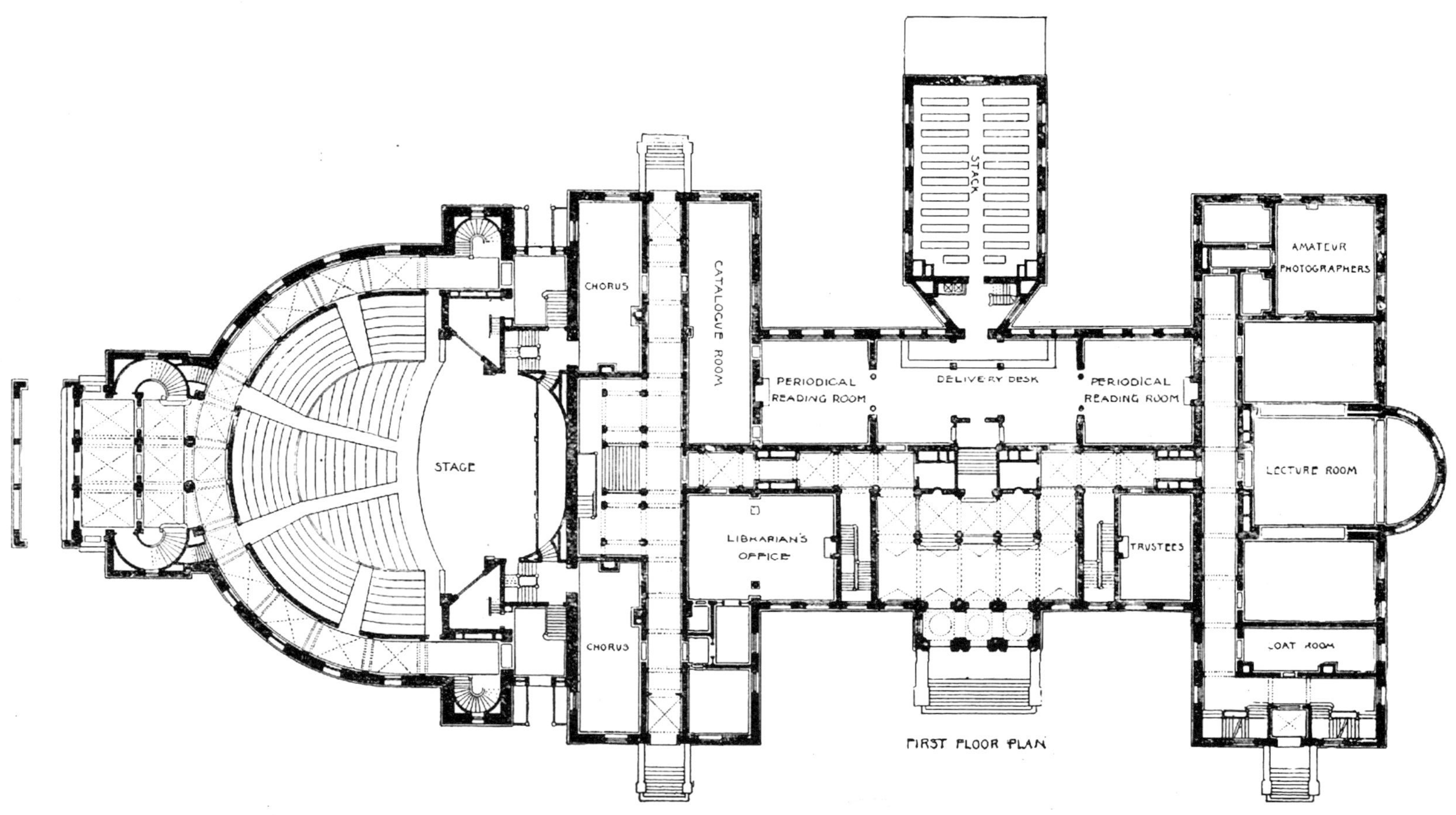

STACK
CHORUS
CATALOGUE ROOM
AMATEUR PHOTOGRAPHERS
PERIODICAL READING ROOM
DELIVERY DESK
PERIODICAL READING ROOM
STAGE
LECTURE ROOM
LIBRARIAN'S OFFICE
TRUSTEES
CHORUS
COAT ROOM
FIRST FLOOR PLAN

1895: SECOND FLOOR

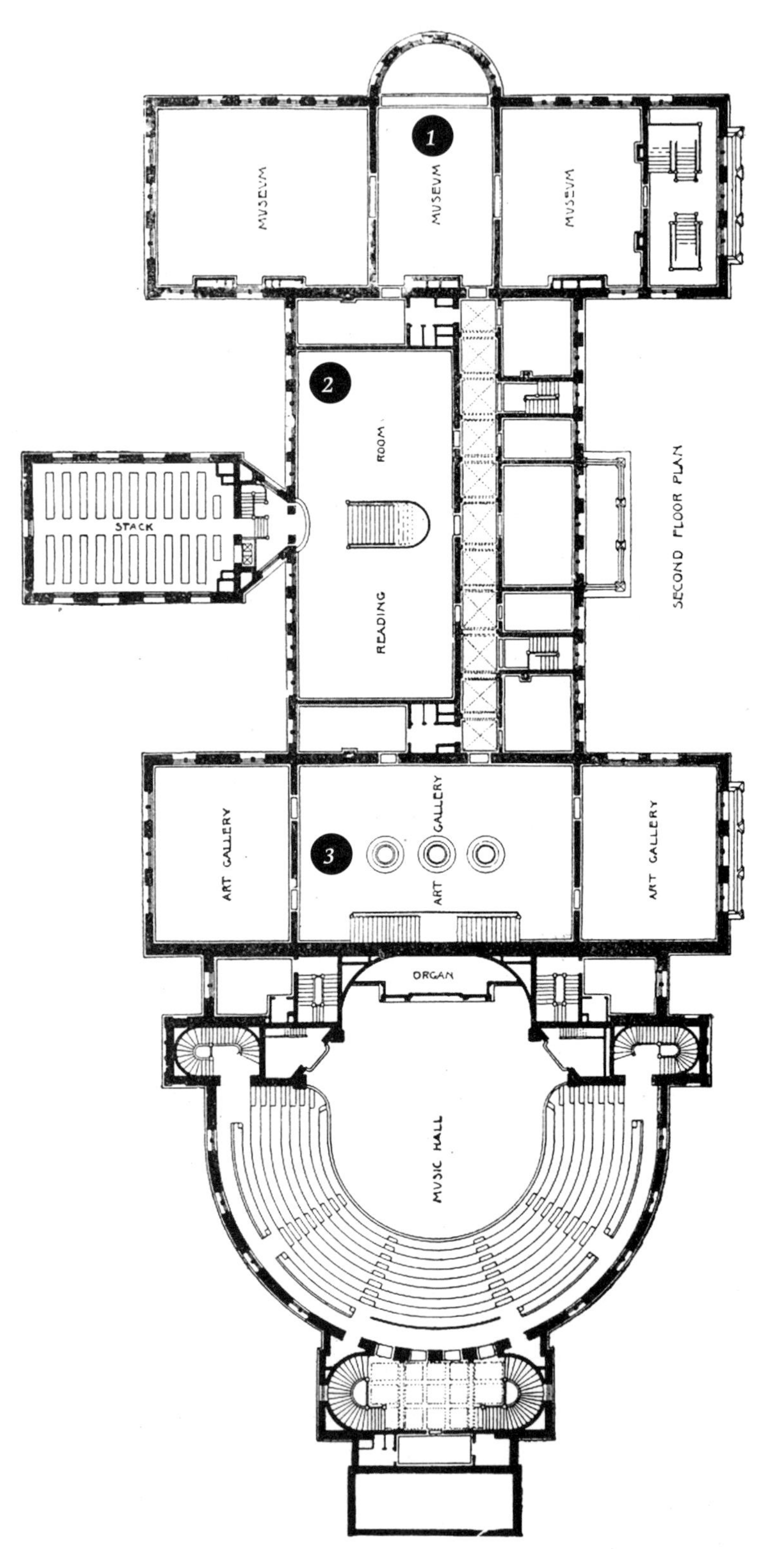

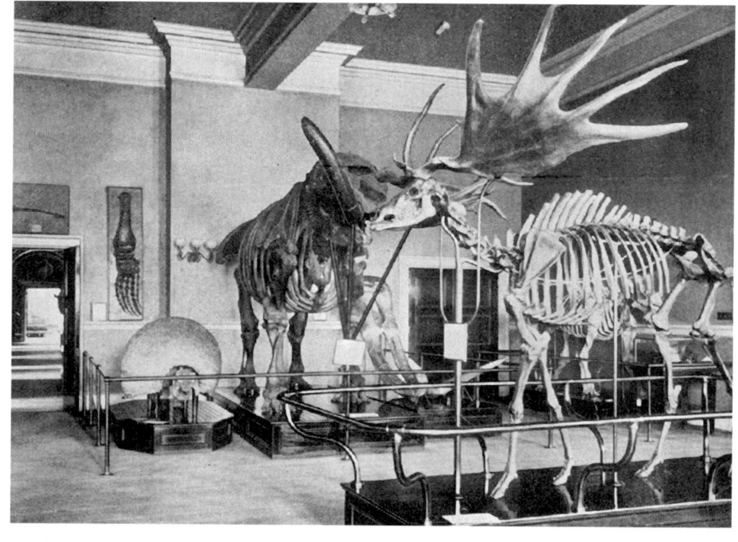

1. Mastodon and Irish elk skeletons in the first museum display

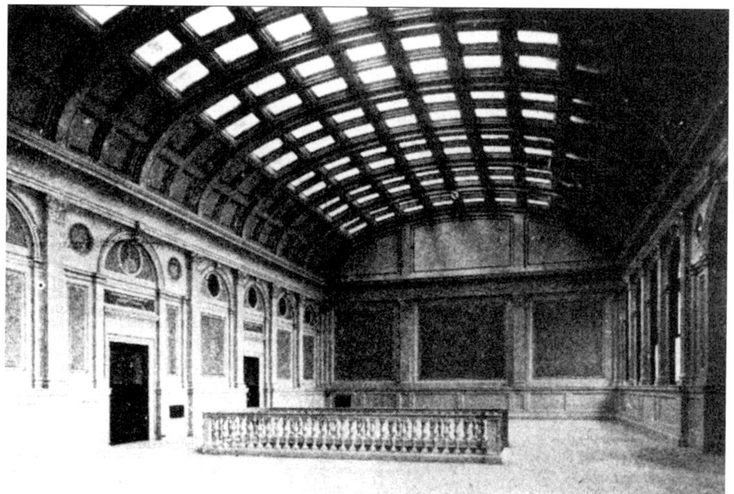

2. The second floor library reading room with the central staircase leading up from the first floor

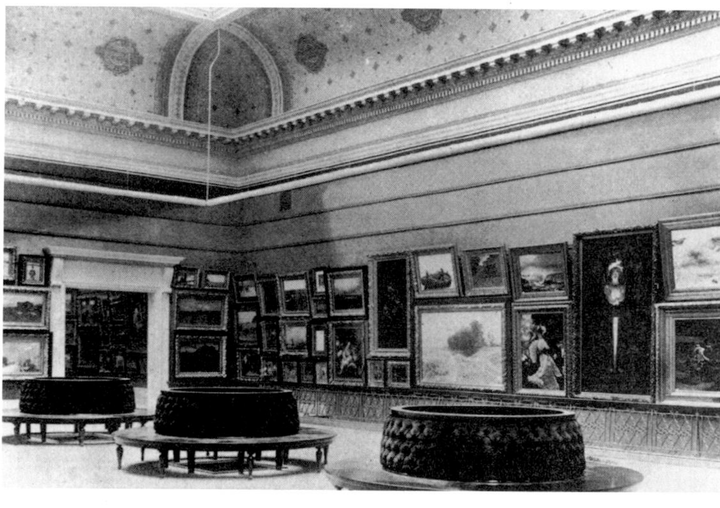

3. The central gallery of the Department of Fine Arts

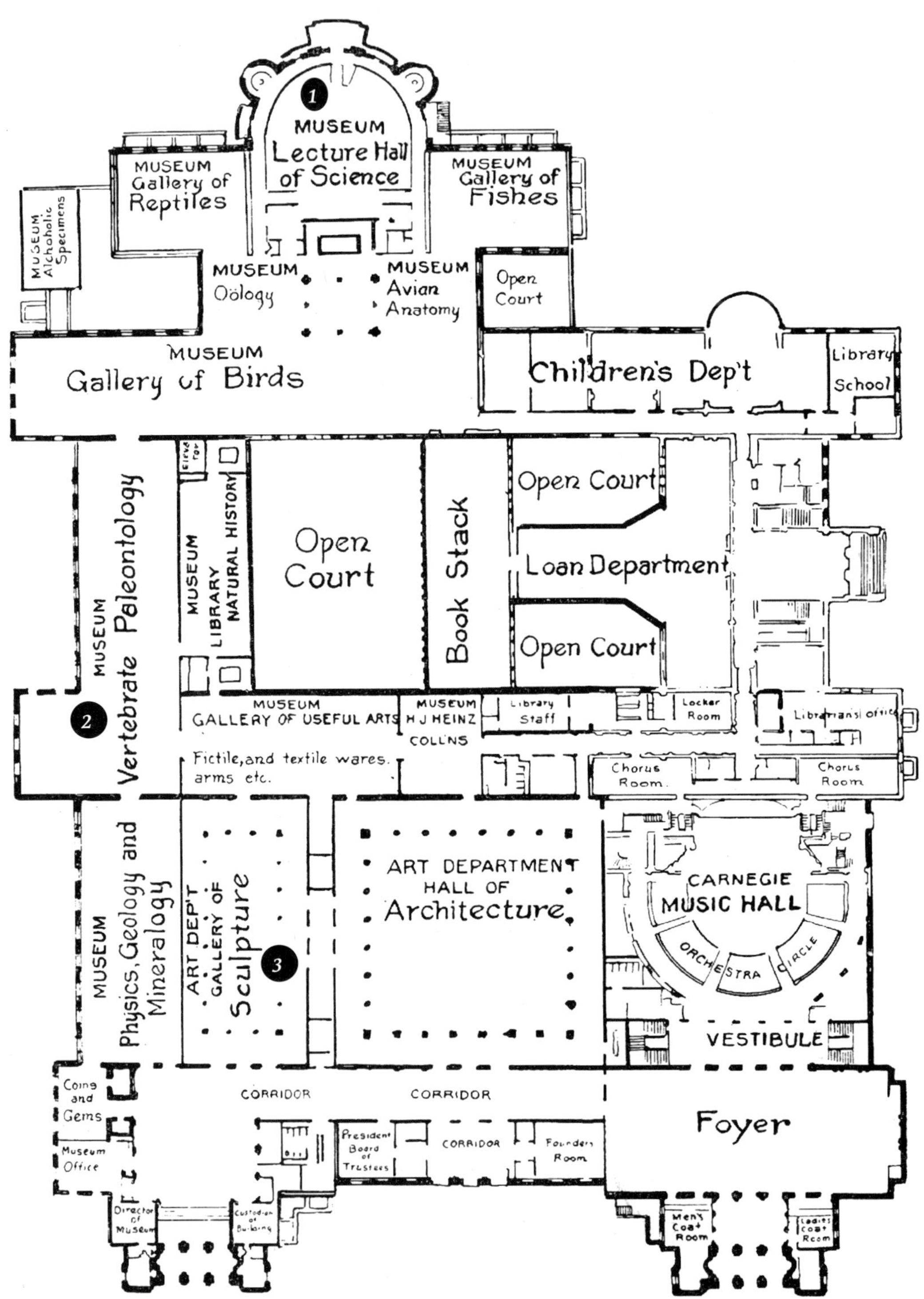
1
MUSEUM
Lecture Hall
of Science
MUSEUM
Gallery of
Reptiles
MUSEUM
Gallery of
Fishes
MUSEUM
Alchoholic
Specimens
MUSEUM
Oölogy
MUSEUM
Avian
Anatomy
Open
Court
MUSEUM
Gallery of Birds
Children's Dep't
Library
School
MUSEUM
Vertebrate Paleontology
Fire
Pro
MUSEUM
LIBRARY
NATURAL HISTORY
Open
Court
Book Stack
Open Court
Loan Department
Open Court
2
MUSEUM
GALLERY OF USEFUL ARTS
MUSEUM
H J HEINZ
COLL'NS
Library
Staff
Locker
Room
Librarians office
Fictile, and textile wares.
arms etc.
Chorus
Room.
Chorus
Room
MUSEUM
Physics, Geology and Mineralogy
ART DEP'T
GALLERY OF
Sculpture
ART DEPARTMENT
HALL OF
Architecture
CARNEGIE
MUSIC HALL
ORCHESTRA
CIRCLE
3
VESTIBULE
Coins
and
Gems
CORRIDOR
CORRIDOR
Foyer
Museum
Office
President
Board
of
Trustees
CORRIDOR
Founders
Room
Director
of
Museum
Custodian
of
Building
Men's
Coat
Room
Ladies
Coat
Room

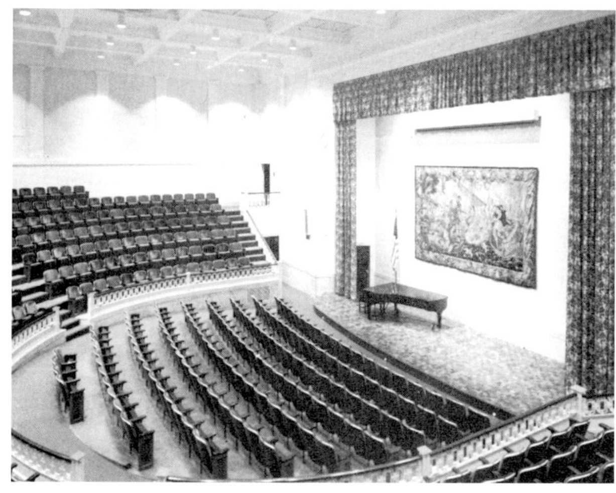

1. Lecture hall

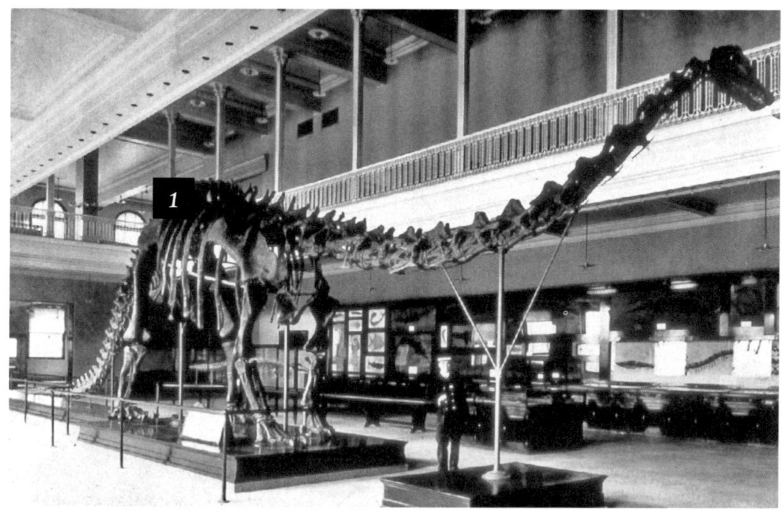

2. The early display of Diplodocus carnegii

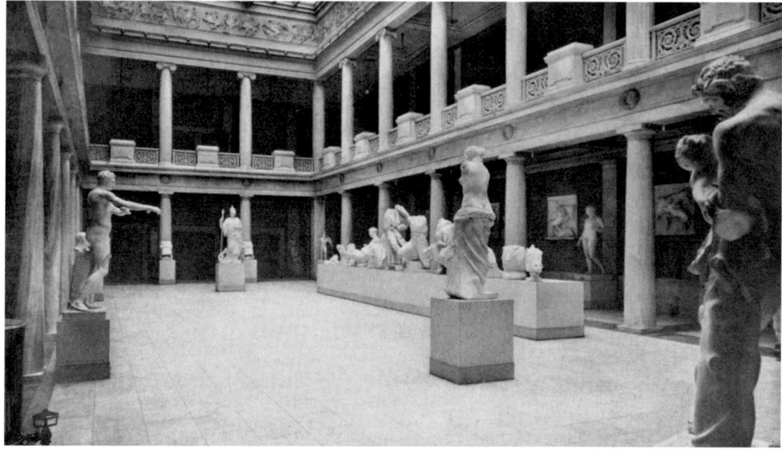

3. The Hall of Sculpture before the casts of statues were moved onto the second-floor pedestals and into the Hall of Architecture

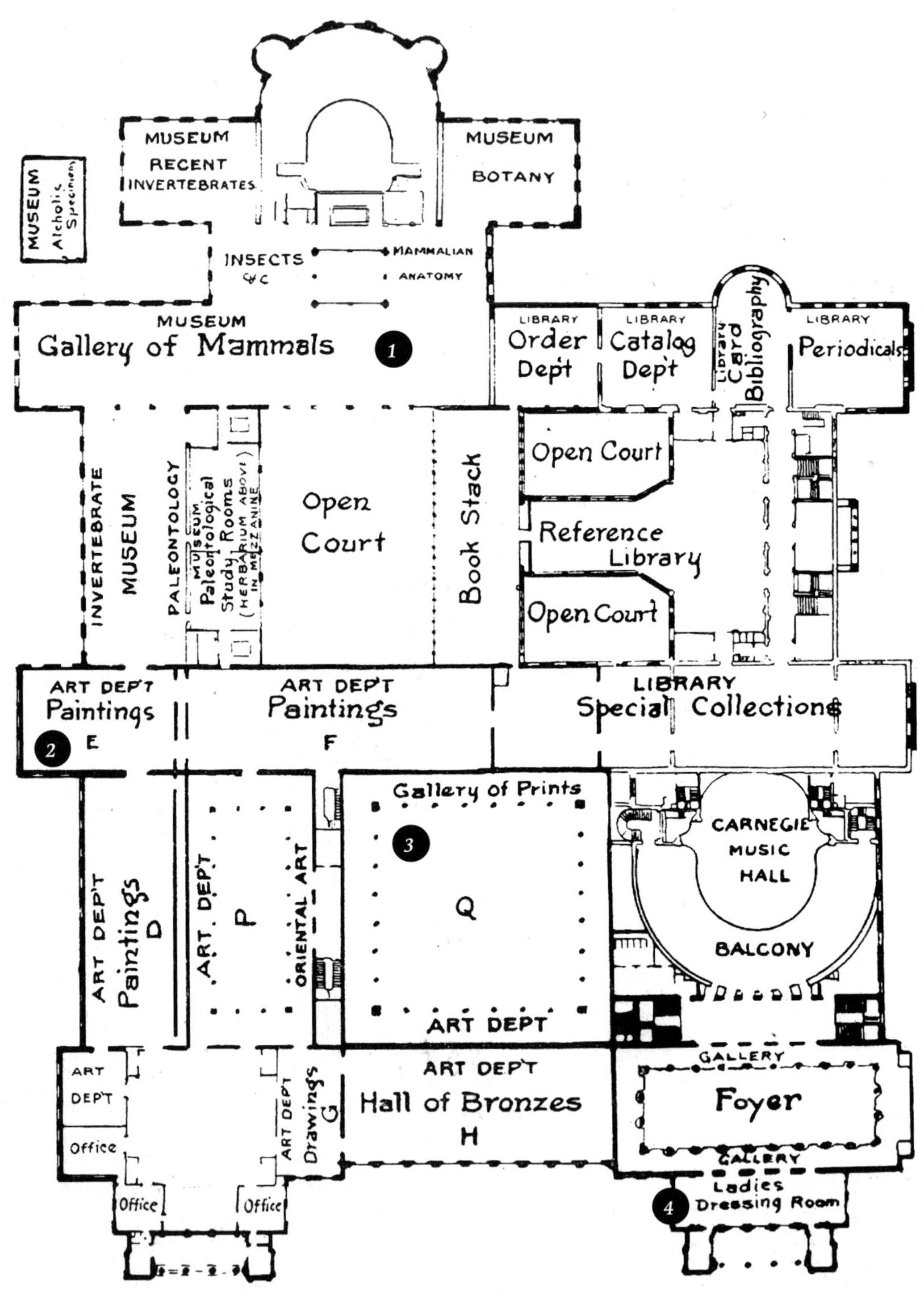
MUSEUM Alcholic Specimen
MUSEUM RECENT INVERTEBRATES
MUSEUM BOTANY
INSECTS &c
MAMMALIAN ANATOMY
MUSEUM
Gallery of Mammals
1
LIBRARY Order Dept
LIBRARY Catalog Dept
Library Card Bibliography
LIBRARY Periodicals
INVERTEBRATE MUSEUM
PALEONTOLOGY
MUSEUM Paleontological Study Rooms (HERBARIUM ABOVE IN MEZZANINE)
Open Court
Book Stack
Open Court
Reference Library
Open Court
ART DEP'T Paintings E
2
ART DEP'T Paintings F
LIBRARY Special Collections
Gallery of Prints
3
CARNEGIE MUSIC HALL
ART DEPT Paintings D
ART. DEP'T P
ORIENTAL ART
Q
BALCONY
ART DEPT
ART
DEP'T
Office
ART DEPT Drawings G
ART DEP'T
Hall of Bronzes H
GALLERY Foyer
Office
Office
GALLERY Ladies Dressing Room
4

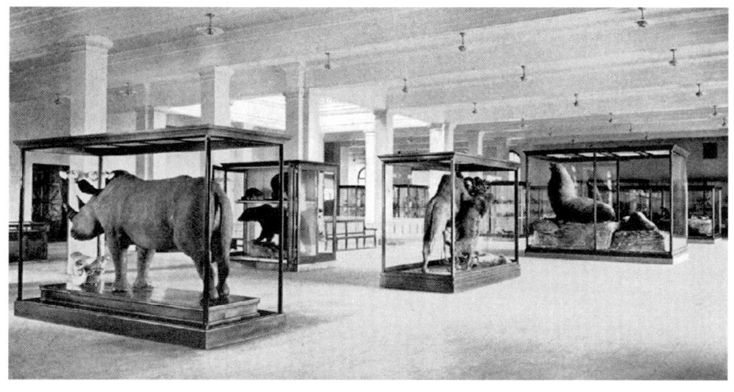

1. Gallery of Mammals

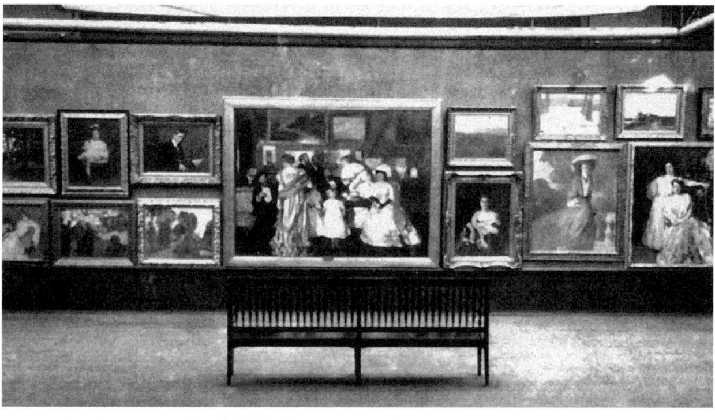

2. Painting gallery

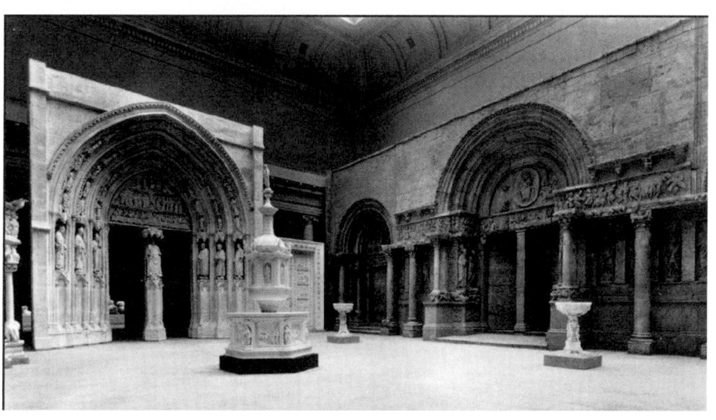

3. Hall of Architecture

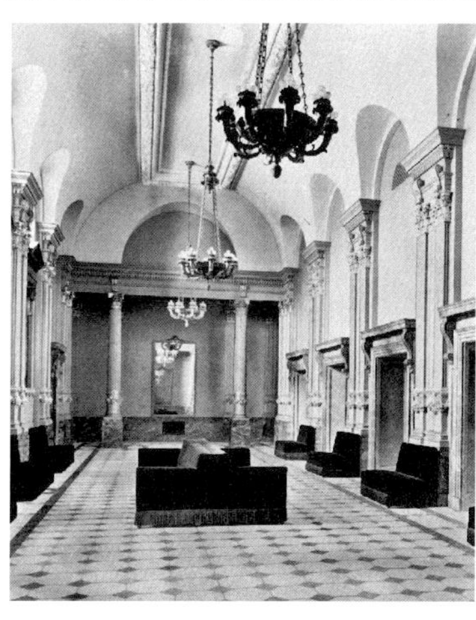

4. The Ladies Room
(The Green Room)

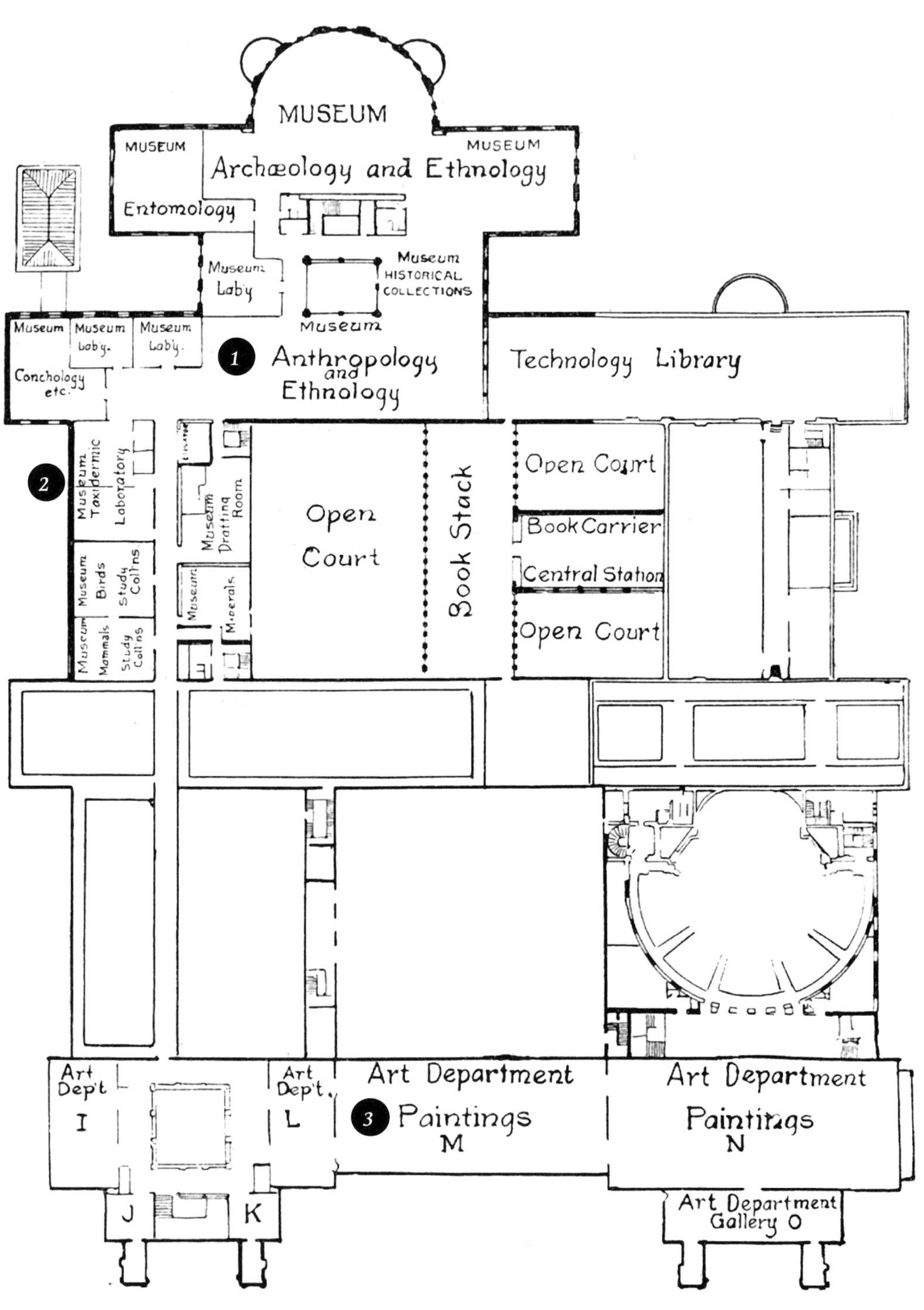
MUSEUM
MUSEUM
Archæology and Ethnology
MUSEUM
Entomology
Museum Lab'y
Museum HISTORICAL COLLECTIONS
Museum
Museum
Museum Lab'y.
Museum Lab'y.
Conchology etc.
Anthropology and Ethnology
Technology Library
Museum Taxidermic
Laboratory
Open Court
Museum
Drafting Room
Museum
Minerals
Book Stack
Open Court
Book Carrier
Central Station
Open Court
Museum Birds
Study Coll'ns.
Museum Mammals
Study Coll'ns
Art Dep't I
Art Dep't L
Art Department Paintings M
Art Department Paintings N
J
K
Art Department Gallery O

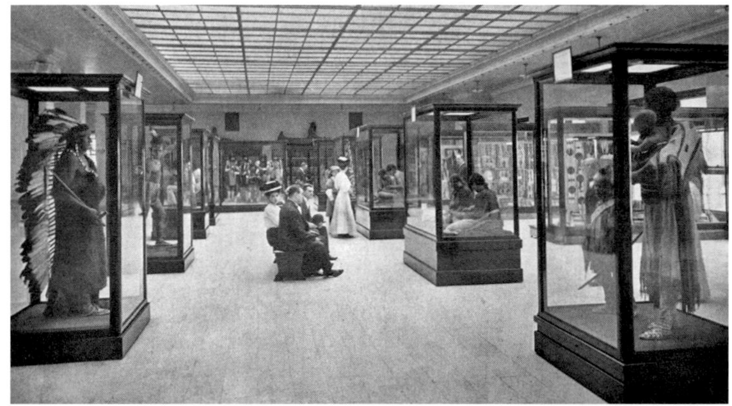

1. Indian models
in the Hall of
Anthropology

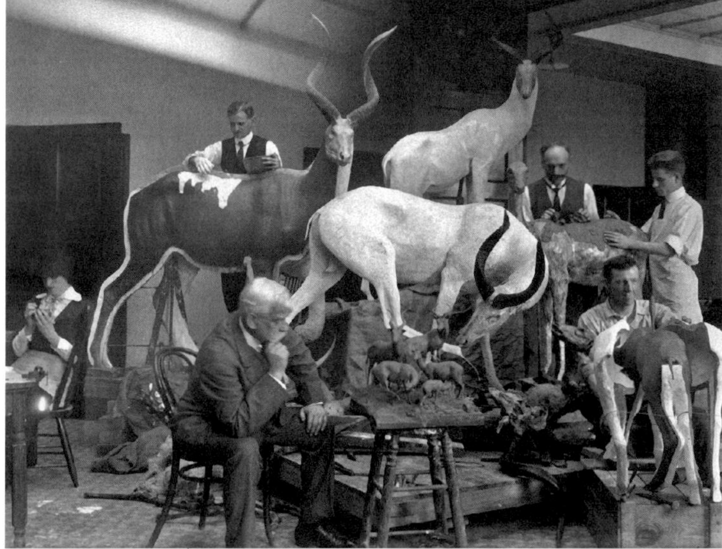

2. Preparing
the African
mammals exhibit
in the taxidermy
laboratory

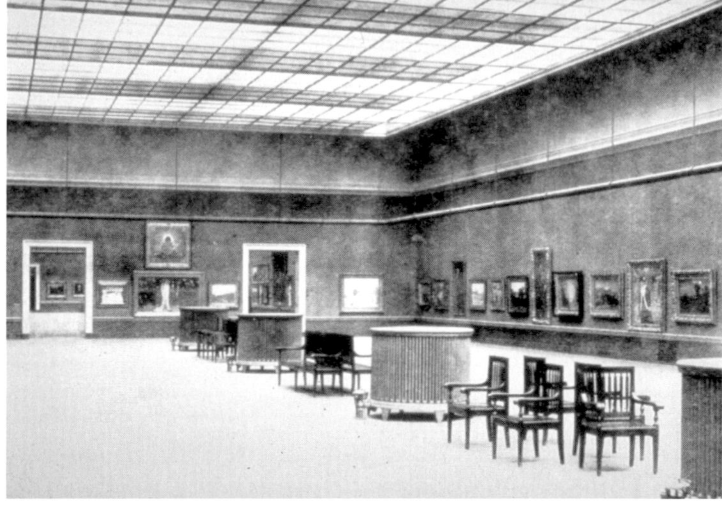

3. Painting
gallery with
skylights

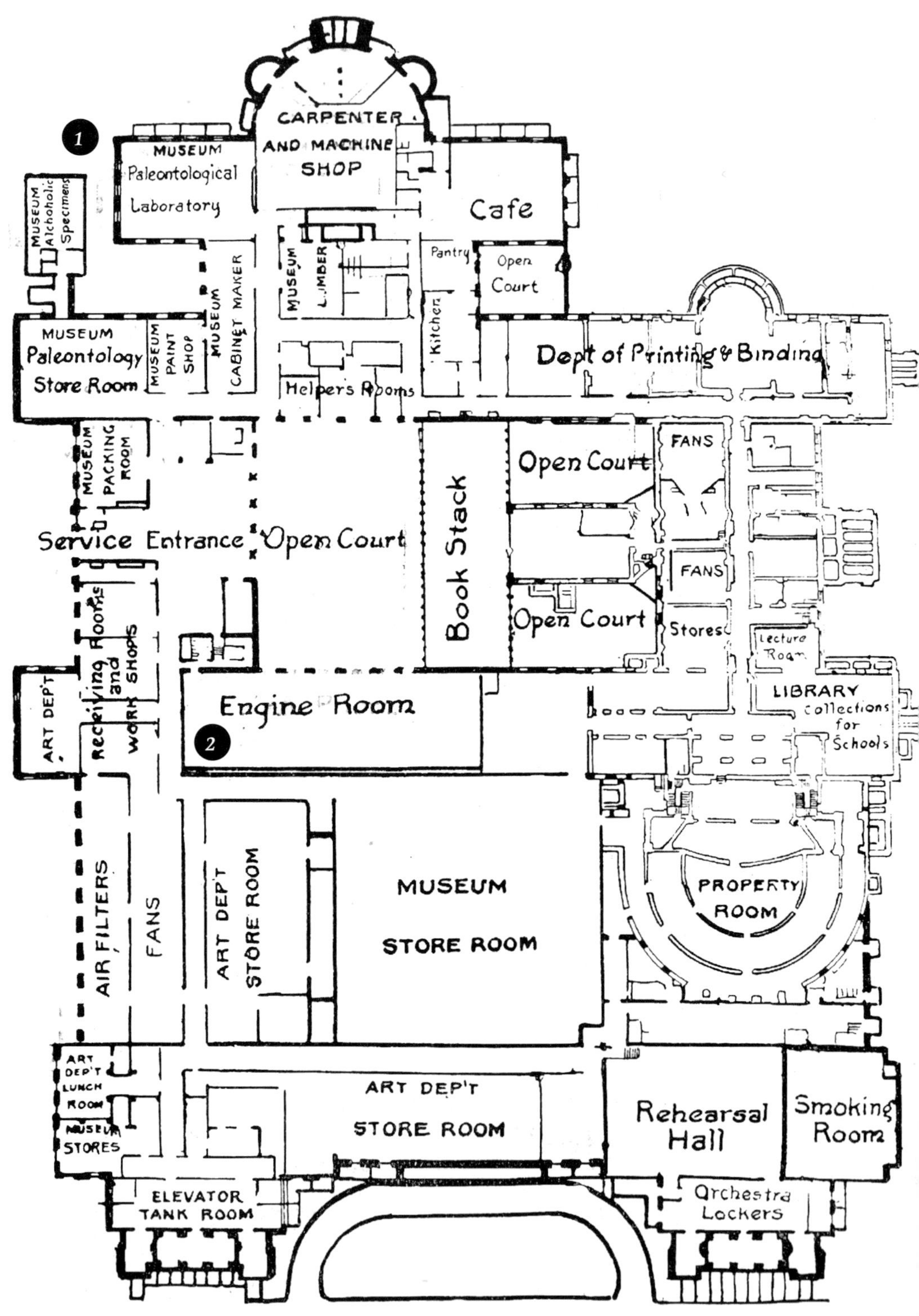
MUSEUM Alcoholic Specimens
MUSEUM Paleontological Laboratory
CARPENTER AND MACHINE SHOP
Cafe
MUSEUM LUMBER
Pantry
Open Court
MUSEUM Paleontology Store Room
MUSEUM PAINT SHOP
MUSEUM CABINET MAKER
Kitchen
Dept of Printing & Binding
Helpers Rooms
MUSEUM PACKING ROOM
Service Entrance
Open Court
Book Stack
Open Court
FANS
FANS
Open Court
Stores
Lecture Room
Receiving Rooms and Work Shops
ART DEPT
Engine Room
LIBRARY Collections for Schools
AIR FILTERS
FANS
ART DEP'T STORE ROOM
MUSEUM STORE ROOM
PROPERTY ROOM
ART DEP'T LUNCH ROOM
MUSEUM STORES
ART DEP'T STORE ROOM
Rehearsal Hall
Smoking Room
ELEVATOR TANK ROOM
Orchestra Lockers

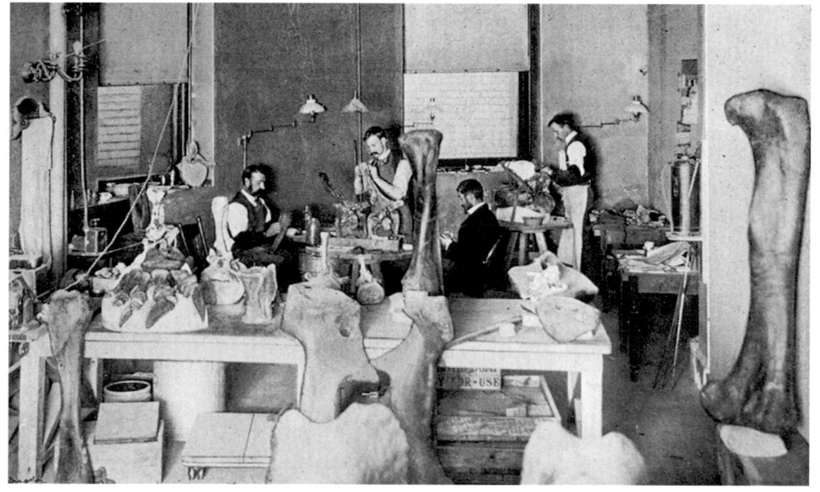

1. Preparing the
   dinosaur bones
   in the first
   paleontology
   laboratory

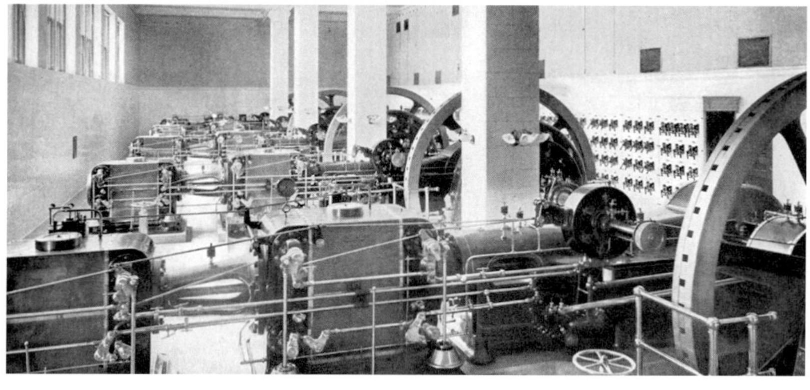

2. The engine room
   was a showplace in
   industrial-minded
   Pittsburgh

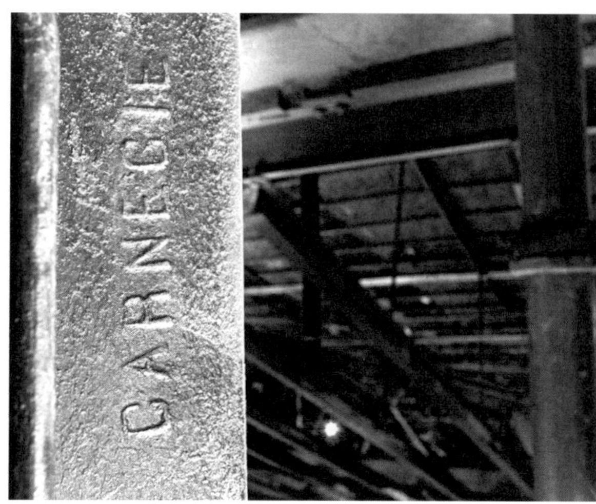

Carnegie structural steel filled the 1907
expansion from top to bottom.

THE PRESENT: FIRST FLOOR

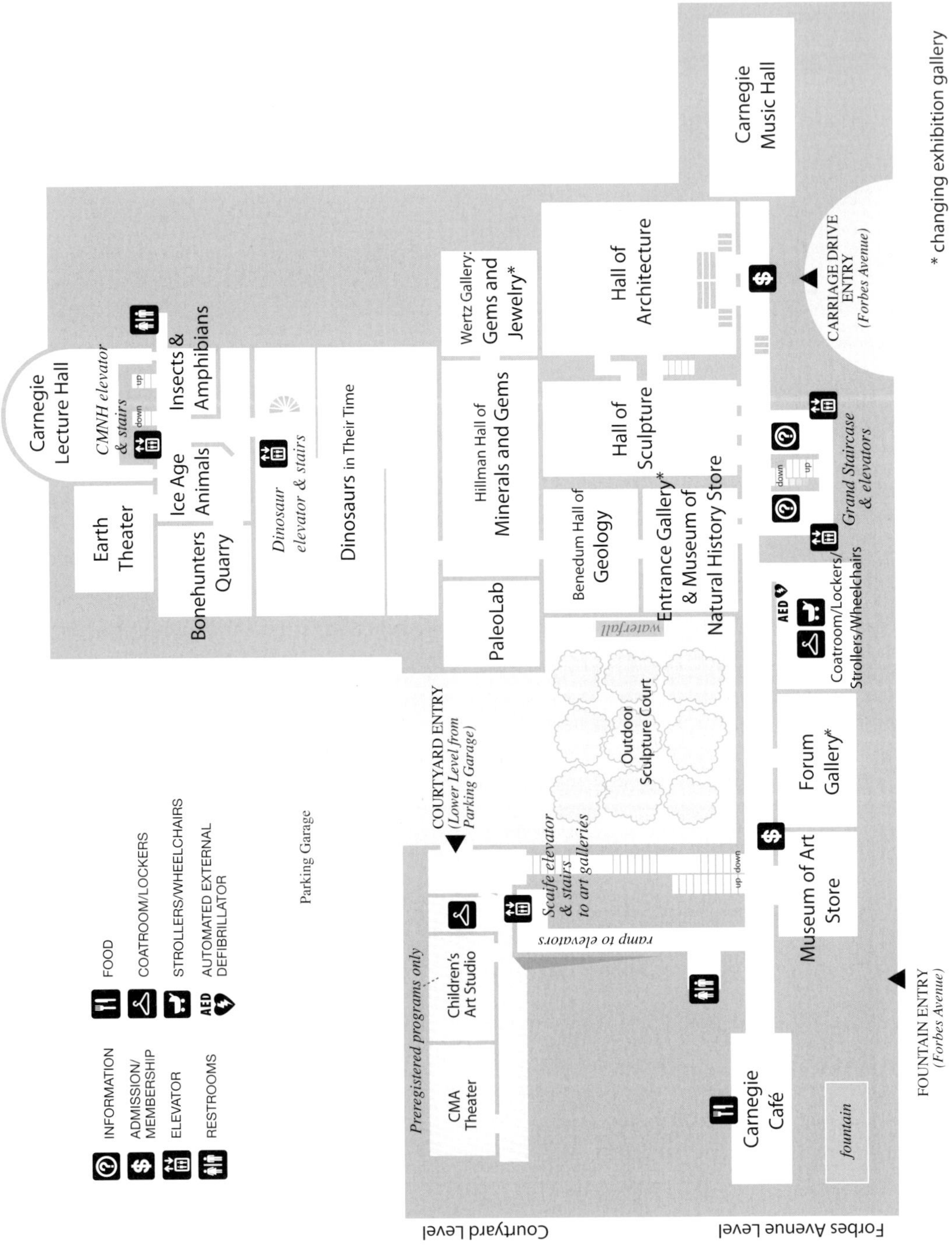

Carnegie Music Hall

Carnegie Lecture Hall

CMNH elevator & stairs

Earth Theater

Ice Age Animals

Insects & Amphibians

Bonehunters Quarry

Dinosaur elevator & stairs

Dinosaurs in Their Time

Hall of Architecture

Wertz Gallery: Gems and Jewelry*

Hillman Hall of Minerals and Gems

Hall of Sculpture

PaleoLab

Benedum Hall of Geology

Entrance Gallery* & Museum of Natural History Store

waterfall

Outdoor Sculpture Court

Grand Staircase & elevators

Coatroom/Lockers/ Strollers/Wheelchairs

AED

CARRIAGE DRIVE ENTRY *(Forbes Avenue)*

Forum Gallery*

Museum of Art Store

Scaife elevator & stairs to art galleries

ramp to elevators

COURTYARD ENTRY *(Lower Level from Parking Garage)*

Parking Garage

Children's Art Studio

CMA Theater

Preregistered programs only

Carnegie Café

FOUNTAIN ENTRY *(Forbes Avenue)*

fountain

Courtyard Level

Forbes Avenue Level

* changing exhibition gallery

INFORMATION

ADMISSION/ MEMBERSHIP

ELEVATOR

RESTROOMS

FOOD

COATROOM/LOCKERS

STROLLERS/WHEELCHAIRS

AED AUTOMATED EXTERNAL DEFIBRILLATOR

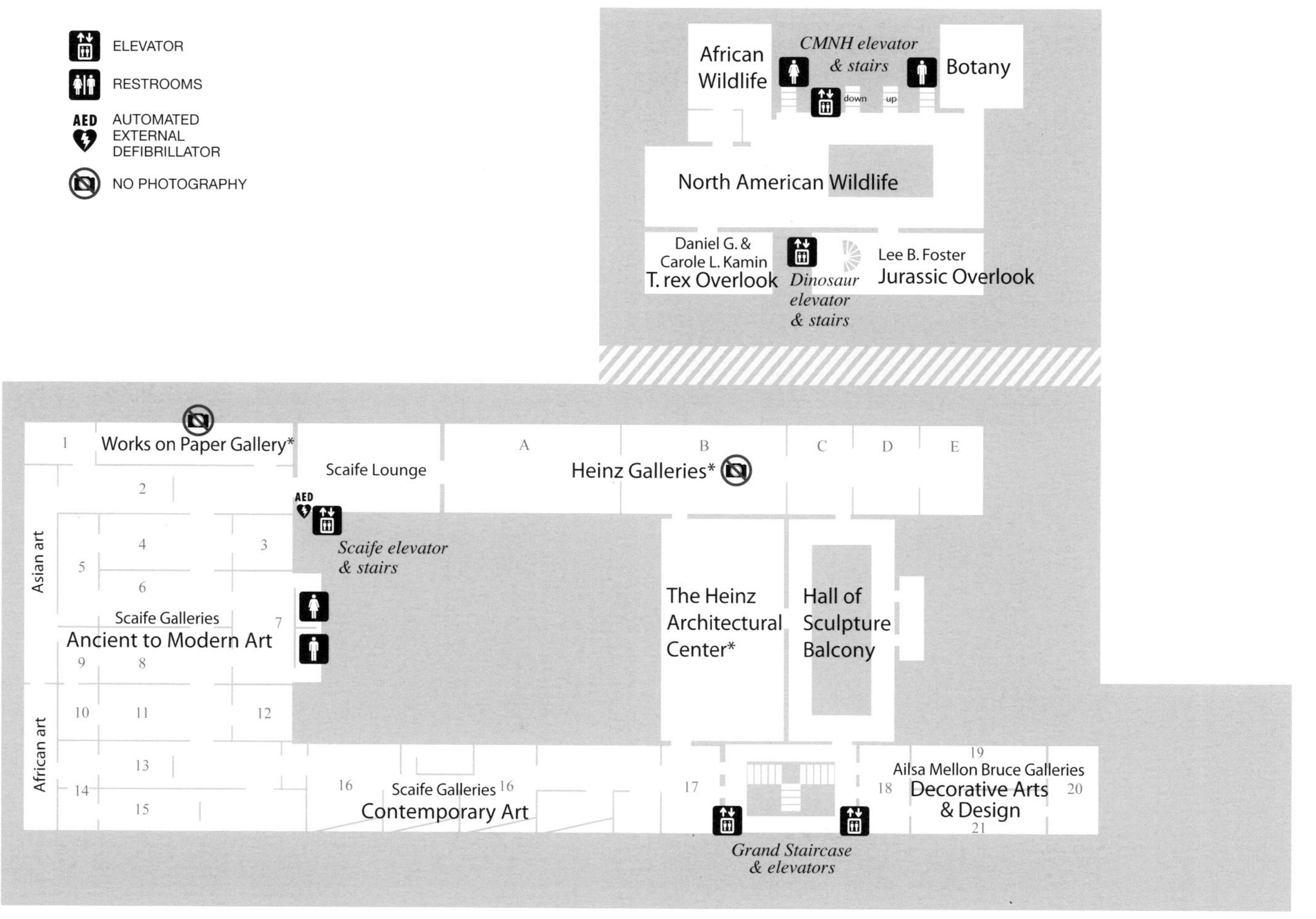

ELEVATOR
RESTROOMS
AED AUTOMATED EXTERNAL DEFIBRILLATOR
NO PHOTOGRAPHY
African Wildlife
CMNH elevator & stairs
Botany
down
up
North American Wildlife
Daniel G. & Carole L. Kamin
T. rex Overlook
Dinosaur elevator & stairs
Lee B. Foster
Jurassic Overlook
Works on Paper Gallery*
Scaife Lounge
Heinz Galleries*
A
B
C
D
E
AED
Scaife elevator & stairs
Asian art
Scaife Galleries
Ancient to Modern Art
The Heinz Architectural Center*
Hall of Sculpture Balcony
African art
Scaife Galleries
Contemporary Art
Ailsa Mellon Bruce Galleries
Decorative Arts & Design
Grand Staircase & elevators
1
2
3
4
5
6
7
8
9
10
11
12
13
14
15
16
16
17
18
19
20
21
* changing exhibition gallery

THE PRESENT: THIRD FLOOR

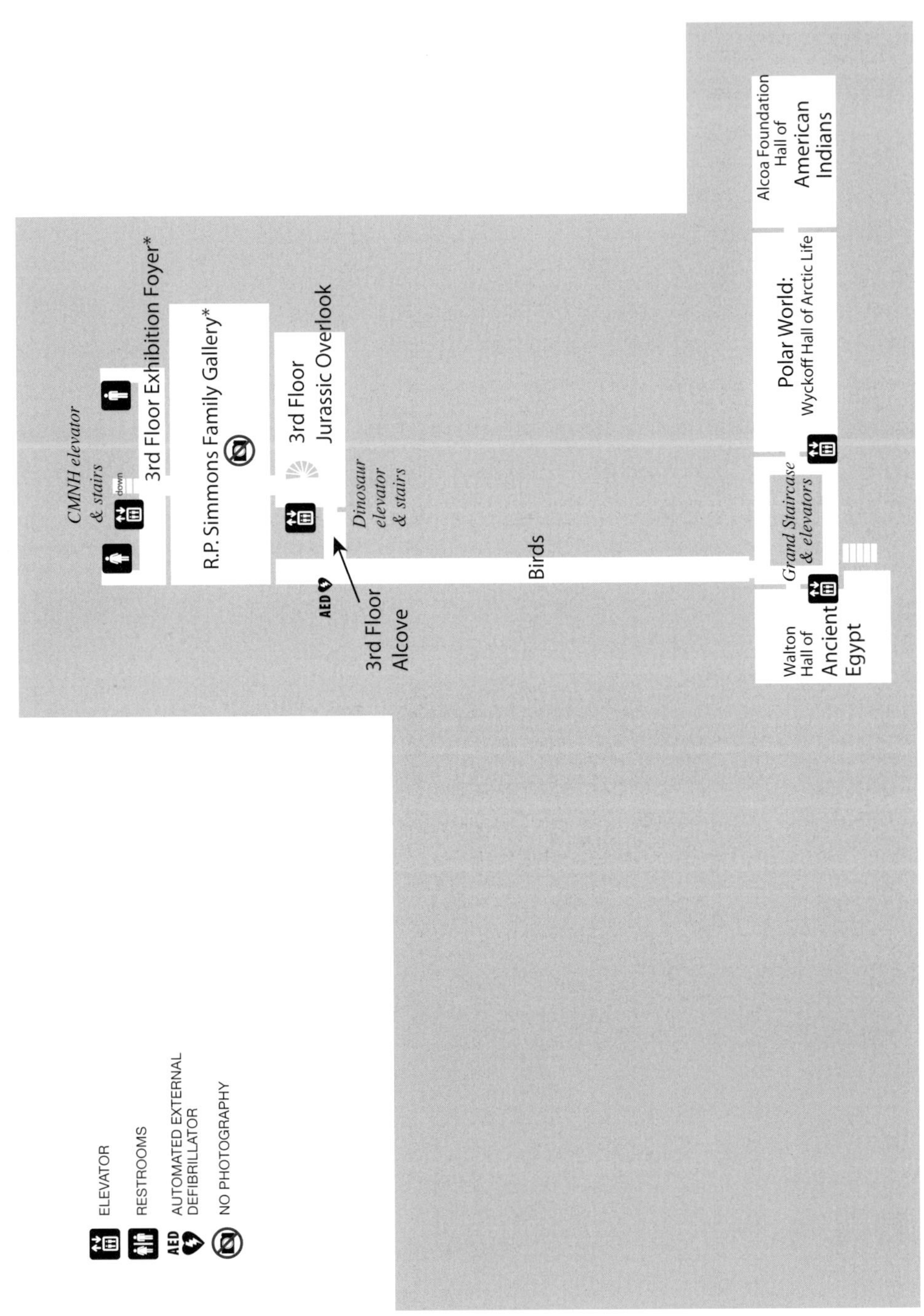

3

THE HIGH COMMAND—A CENTURY OF GOVERNANCE

"Men Capable of His Own Zeal"

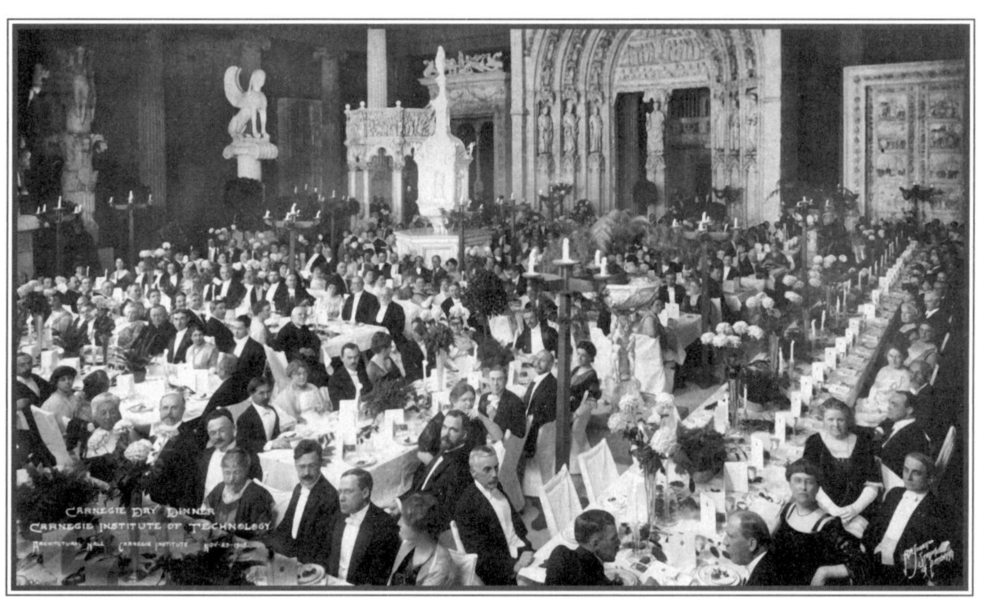

At the Carnegie Day Dinner of 1915, faculty and staff of Carnegie Institute of Technology filled the Hall of Architecture to hear Henry S. Pritchett, from the Carnegie Endowment for the Advancement of Teaching, speak about all the institutions created by Andrew Carnegie.

It has been his just pride and pleasure to find men capable of his own zeal, and to gather their time and attention without reward except the reward of conscience and public duty.

John, Viscount Morley, *Recollections*

JOHN MORLEY, one of Andrew Carnegie's "old shoes," as Carnegie termed his intimate friends, knew the founder for decades. A distinguished British statesman, Morley considered Carnegie an idealist "who lives and works with his ideals, and drudges over them every day of his life." He described how Carnegie chose his partners and successors and motivated them to share his aspirations: "Much too shrewd to suppose one man competent by himself to perfect and administer all the many schemes to which his name belongs, it is impossible not to admire the pains he has taken in inducing the right men to co-operate as trustees and in firing them with sympathy."[1] The aging Carnegie knew he must trust his legacy to men who would make their own decisions. Perhaps musing upon how his own accomplishments had been both praised to heaven and damned to hell, he confided to the mayor of Pittsburgh in 1900, "I would no more legislate for the next fifty years ahead than I would prepare my wardrobe for the next world when I did not know what the climate would be."[2]

The first three presidents of Carnegie Institute and Library—James B. Scott, William Nimick Frew, and Samuel Harden Church—were Carnegie's personal friends and continued his work just as he would have liked until 1943, when Church died. Frew's son then took up the charge of leadership, continuing as president until 1948. Following the second William Frew's death, James M. Bovard, another Pittsburgh executive and lawyer intimately tied to Mellon family interests, managed the Institute until 1967, when James Mellon Walton, yet another member of the Pittsburgh business elite and part of the extended Mellon family, took over as president, remaining in the position until 1984.

Thus, for eight decades, the Institute's high command—its presidents, who also served as chairs of the boards that controlled the library and for decades the Carnegie Institute of Technology—directly extended the reach of the founder's aspirations for his empire of culture. There are two ways to look at this extension of Carnegie's leadership. One is in Carnegie's own

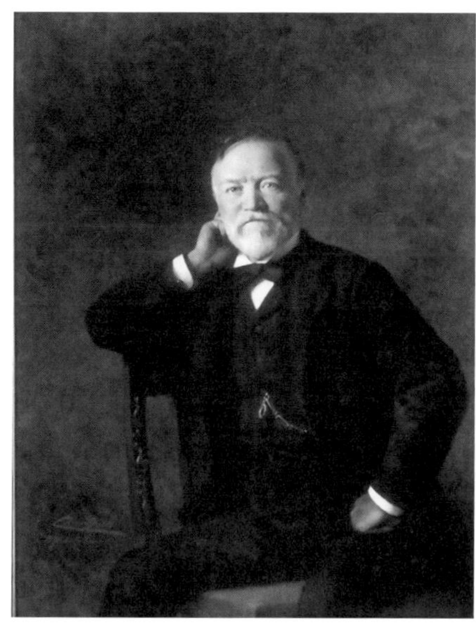

The portrait of Andrew Carnegie by Theobald Chartran, given to Carnegie by Henry Clay Frick, has been hanging in the President's Office for over a century.

terms: Carnegie viewed administration as a chosen form of self-abnegation by the great men who perform public service. He advised men of wealth to submit themselves before "the noble shrine in service to the race." "Members of this inner and higher circle," he wrote, "seek to do the right thing, and not be popular, saying with Confucius, 'It concerneth me not that I have high office; what concerns me is to make myself worthy of office.'"[3] By the late nineteenth century, Pittsburgh's ruling class was well established, a powerful group of primarily Scotch-Irish Presbyterian business executives. These were the men who led Pittsburgh's evolution into an industrial powerhouse of iron and steel manufacturing; banking; the production of oil, gas, and electricity; and food manufacturing. As this aging class of wealthy men began to divest themselves in their last years of their collected art and artifacts, many deposited their personal treasures in the Carnegie Institute.

Some believe the Calvinist spiritual heritage of Carnegie and the Institute's other benefactors is epitomized by the high-minded moral code of the Presbyterian Church, which emphasizes commitment to moral uplift, hard work, and charitable good deeds pursued without self-advertising. Others, however, view the situation differently. At the start of the Great Depression in 1930, as Pittsburgh's social future seemed bleaker than ever, an acerbic critic named R. L. Duffus examined Pittsburgh's Scotch-Irish ruling class for *Harper's Magazine.* Asking whether its members were "civilized," Duffus concluded that they were not:

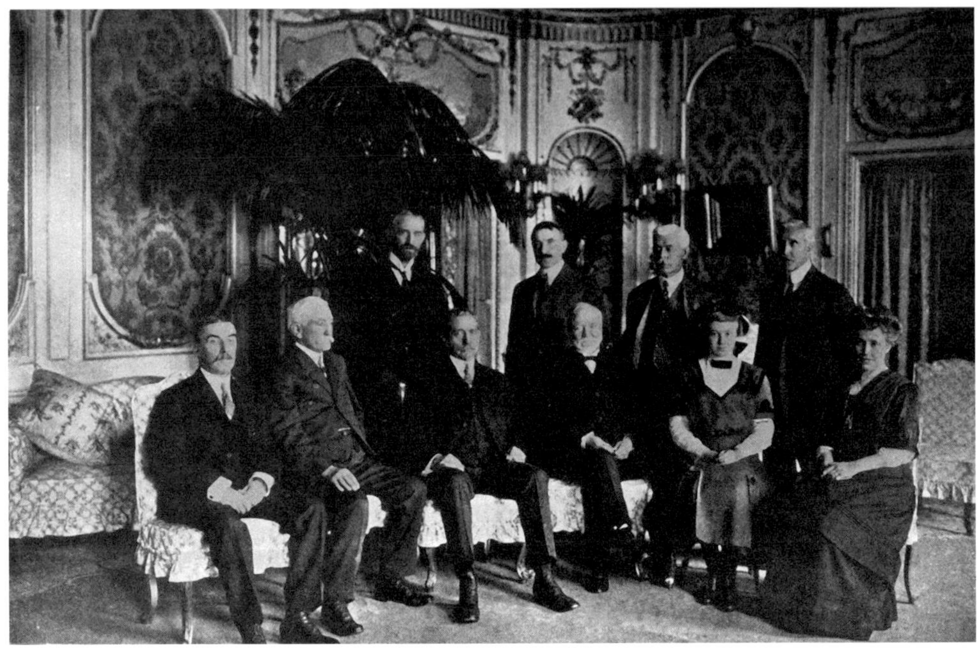

This 1911 photo was taken on the occasion of the founding of the Carnegie Corporation, which then continued Andrew Carnegie's philanthropy. Seated next to Carnegie are his daughter Margaret and his wife Louise. Carnegie Institute president William Nimick Frew is seated at the photo's far left; Henry S. Pritchett, head of the Carnegie Endowment for the Advancement of Teaching, is standing at the photo's far left.

The Scotch-Irish, including the notable Mellon Family, had the first pickings of the enormous wealth in and around Pittsburgh. They made a thorough job of it, not only without a sense of sin but with a sincere conviction that they were thereby serving the God of their fathers. They went to church regularly, ruled their families with rods of iron, and counted their pennies. To this day church membership is essential to participation in the higher social life of Pittsburgh. "What you want to do to promote yourself in Pittsburgh," said an old timer to an ambitious new arrival, "is to buy yourself a hundred thousand dollar house and join the proper church." . . . The situation could not have been summed up more neatly.[4]

In Pittsburgh power was exercised by an elite that governed politely, without self-assertion, and offered the example of "one of the gentlest, shyest and most mild-spoken of men," Andrew Mellon, who served as the secretary of the treasury under three presidents from 1921 to 1932 and was a long-time member of the board of Carnegie Institute. On one occasion

Mellon offered his rare opinion to the board about buying a work of art for the Institute: "Usually he said nothing. One day he mildly proposed that a painting by a certain Pittsburgh artist be acquired for the museum. A temperamental fellow trustee, with a lack of reverence almost unique in Pittsburgh, lit into the suggestion. He said that Pittsburghers couldn't paint—expressing a rather common belief among the elite. . . . Mr. Mellon blushed. 'My cousin,' he said mildly, 'knows something about these things and he says he's a very good artist.' Then he subsided and said no more."[5] A lifelong art collector, Mellon would soon spend a fortune to create the National Galley of Art in Washington, D.C., furnishing it with great art from his own collection and with paintings he bought for $7 million from the Hermitage in Soviet Russia. Financially, it was a good deal, for the cash-poor Soviet government now wanted to sell the art treasures of the old Russian nobility that had been overthrown in the Russian revolution. One estimate of the total cost of the National Gallery building, endowment, paintings, and sculptures Mellon gave to the American people during the depths of the Great Depression puts the total at $50 million, the largest gift ever made to a government by an individual.[6] The director of the National Gallery, John Walker, later described Mellon: "He was inarticulate on the subject of art. . . . But from the way he looked at his paintings, from the sheer intensity of his scrutiny, I knew he had a deep feeling for what he collected, a relationship to his pictures which I have rarely found in many collectors I have known."[7] Mellon knew that attaching his family name to the "National Gallery" in the nation's capital would deter other benefactors and wisely refused to do so.

This soft-spoken style of governance by an anglophilic ruling class characterized governance at the Institute. For whatever reason, the sharp, competitive instincts of Pittsburgh's business executives were sheathed in benevolence when it came to running the business of the Institute. When, for example, Carnegie Museum of Natural History came in over budget at one year's end, board chair Richard King Mellon turned to his secretary for a check to make up the difference. There was never a doubt that Pittsburgh's leading families, such as the Heinz family or the Hillmans, felt a civic responsibility to support the Institute in the generous manner established by Andrew Carnegie himself.

Such long-lasting, genuine philanthropy by a small group of wealthy, circumspect Pittsburghers, however, arguably kept the Board of Trustees from ever becoming visibly critical of Institute management. One problem that would not arise for nearly a century was the need to offer high salaries to top Institute leadership, since the chief administrators were either sufficiently wealthy not to demand high salaries or were motivated by the honor of playing such a role in public service. Even by the year 2000, when the Institute showed signs of financial trouble and sharp questions were being raised about its administrative direction, there was no visible public debate, because such issues were traditionally kept out of the public eye. For generations, the presidents of Carnegie Institute succeeded through executive skill, a strong idea of the institutional mission, and a personal work ethic in overseeing a perpetually underfunded empire made of disparate parts that did not always function together smoothly, including Carnegie Library of Pittsburgh; Carnegie Institute, with its art and natural history museums and Music Hall; and the aggressively growing Carnegie Institute of Technology.

WILLIAM NIMICK FREW, 1896–1914

When the Board of Trustees was organized on May 31, 1890, the first person appointed president and chair of the board was James B. Scott. The treasurer was Henry Clay Frick, and the secretary was William Nimick Frew. Until his death in February 1894, Scott labored at the head of the all-important Building Committee, running the complex competition among architects who submitted proposals for the Institute; overseeing the selection of Longfellow, Alden and Harlow; and seeing the foundation laid in 1892 and the superstructure begun in 1893. When he died suddenly in 1894, his place was quickly filled by Frew, who told the Music Hall audience at the 1895 dedication, "Mr. Scott contributed unsparingly of his time and skill in making this building what it is, and almost unaided succeeded in removing many serious obstacles to the success of the enterprise."[8]

Although Frew was not the first president appointed, he was the first to run the institution after the building opened, and his eighteen-year tenure included dedicating Carnegie Library, organizing the Institute, building eight branch libraries and the Carnegie Technical School, and guiding the monumental physical expansion of 1904–7. During construction, almost every day for three years, he spent part of each morning in the building and regularly called at the architect's office to study the plans. Frew, who "never sought office and ever shrank from applause," was also on the board of the Pennsylvania Female College, the Homeopathic Hospital, and other organizations.[9]

Frew, a member of an old Pittsburgh Scotch-Irish family, had a private school education and had graduated from the Western University of Pennsylvania. When oil was discovered in Pennsylvania, he was one of the first in the wildcatter's oil fields. With his partner, he built the first Pennsylvania refinery, Brilliant Oil Works, which laid the foundation of his

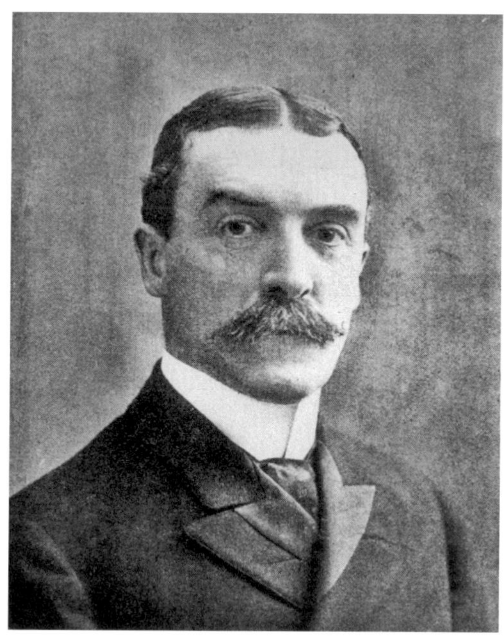

William Nimick Frew served as president the Institute and Library through the first decades, from 1894 to 1914.

fortune. During the Civil War, he achieved the rank of major and was later described as "gifted and lovable," with a "broad grasp of affairs" and "an exceptional knowledge of men." To his business associates, he was "genial, kindly and humorous, and his uniform justice and consideration towards his subordinates were beyond praise."[10] Such traits must have endeared him to Carnegie, who also asked him to serve ex officio on the boards of other Carnegie organizations, such as the Carnegie Hero Fund, Carnegie Institution of Washington, D.C., and Carnegie Corporation of New York.

A spare, elegant man with a full Victorian mustache, Frew shunned personal ostentation and took a modest role in early Founder's Day celebrations. Frew simply opened the ceremonies with a brief welcome and later read aloud the lists of winners in the annual art exhibitions. It was perhaps this ability to avoid the spotlight that allowed him to successfully manage his demanding directors and their pressing needs, including John Beatty, the industrious director of the Art Gallery, with his expensive international art agenda; William Holland, the opinionated director of the museum; Samuel Harden Church, Frew's secretary, who was often political and outspoken; Edwin Anderson, a visionary young librarian; and a number of cantankerous music directors.

Indeed, Frew made it clear that he valued such disparate personalities and the contributions they made to this monumental effort. At the 1895 dedication of the Institute, for example, Frew drew his audience's attention to an important issue:

To-morrow [we] will begin to answer the question whether the money, that has been provided with no grudging hand, has been wisely expended or wasted. Many circumstances augur in favor of a brilliant future for this great enterprise. One of these is the liberal and intelligent way in which it is being treated by the legislative and executive heads of our City Government, who have gone hand in hand with the Board of Trustees in bringing about a successful completion of this first part of the undertaking.... Another is the great and universal interest manifested by the people of this City, very many of whom have already contributed rare and valuable books, manuscripts, and works of scientific and artistic worth.

From his perspective, the enterprise so far had been a great team effort, dependent not only on government officials but on the architects, the mural painter, the contractor, and all the tradesmen who had "striven earnestly to erect a building that will do them honor."[11]

Frew's belief in the common effort the Institute signified gave him a sense of mission akin to Carnegie's, and three years after the building opened, he declared that "Carnegie Institute since its inception has taken no backward step, that its lines are extended farther today than ever before in its history, and that in all human probability it is destined to go forward until its mission is finally and fully accomplished.... It means the opening of a door into a higher life; it means recognition by a universe of arts and letters that our city has but little known before; it means an introduction to the circle of knowledge and refinement, not only of this country, but of the world, for assuredly the pebble dropped here creates a wave that dies only on the beaches of the farthest civilization."[12] By 1914 his health was failing; he resigned and died the following year.

SAMUEL HARDEN CHURCH, 1914–43

Samuel Harden Church served as the formidable president of Carnegie Institute and Library for twenty-nine years, from April 28, 1914, to October 11, 1943, having been part of the institution since the beginning. In some ways, Church's life paralleled Andrew Carnegie's. Born in a log cabin, he attended Pittsburgh's public schools until age eleven, when he became a cash boy at Joseph Horne's Company for $1.50 a week. He then worked as a telegraph messenger boy, before going to work for Pennsylvania Railroad at age seventeen in 1875. In 1890, he took a special assignment to edit the corporate history of the railroad, producing a fifteen-volume work after eight years. Like Carnegie a constant writer, he published books, newspaper columns, and plays.

Like Frew, Church oversaw many Institute milestones. During his administration, in 1926, Carnegie Institute was incorporated under the laws of the Commonwealth of Pennsylvania, legally defined as an organization controlled by a self-perpetuating board of thirty-six trustees.[13] In 1927, Church invented *Carnegie Magazine* as the Institute's vehicle of opinion and record, announcing, "We must have a magazine." He served as its editor until his death, publishing his political opinions about world affairs in a column called "Through the Editor's Window." Another Church column, "Garden of Gold," focused on fund-raising, asking readers to plant metaphorical financial seeds in the "garden" of Carnegie Institute, Carnegie Library, or the nearby Carnegie Institute of Technology, even holding a write-in competition to name his metaphorical Gardener. The name "Jason . . . he who sought the Golden Fleece," was selected, and his wife was the faithful Penelope, who was given to utterances such as, "Why dear Jason, this ought to be one of your most prosperous days." Usually, those days were. Jason labored in the metaphoric garden, attired in his Golden Fleece. On certain days his eyes filled with tears of gratitude as generous friends such as George H. Clapp showed up, hailed him with cheery greetings, and made gifts, wrapped in tissue paper, of funds to use for the museums' endowment. Fund-raising, in fact, drove Church constantly: the monetary flush of Andrew Carnegie's support was gone, and the burden of public support for the Institute now rested squarely on his shoulders. In 1928, he dourly observed, "The Institute is so short of fixed income that its Fine Arts and Museum departments, while walking forward, are walking with leaden feet."[14]

In spite of his frustrations, Church prided himself on *Carnegie Magazine,* and he celebrated its first anniversary with pride: "The little magazine has made its way into every corner of the habitable earth, and it is welcomed upon the tables of statesmen, diplomats, and literary men pretty much all through the world, while here at home in Pittsburgh it has become the subject of table talk in many of our cultured families."[15] The magazine, he believed, would not be limited to Pittsburgh, but instead follow the versatile life of Carnegie Institute itself, addressing the world at large. To that end, he published reviews of books and plays by local scholars (especially Carnegie Tech professors), celebrated the birthdays of great figures such as Andrew Mellon, and reprinted the speeches made by distinguished speakers at Founder-Patron's Day.

Church's interests also stretched beyond the Institute. A collector of books about Oliver Cromwell, the "Great Protector," he wrote a biography of the Puritan revolutionary and modeled his own dramatic adherence to

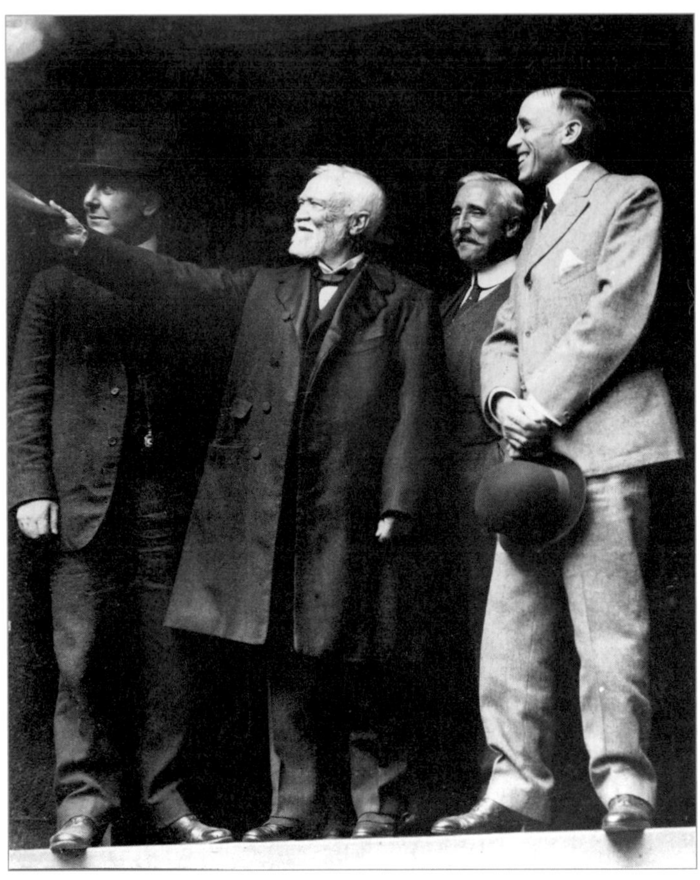

Carnegie stands next to the second Institute president, Samuel Harden Church, his host and confidant when he visited Pittsburgh in 1914. They are on the steps of the Duquesne Club, the membership club favored by Pittsburgh's leaders in business, industry, politics, and culture.

principle on Cromwell's example. Like Carnegie an outspoken advocate of world peace, Church campaigned for the cause on both the national scene and the world stage. When ninety-three German intellectuals declared that Germany was guiltless in provoking World War I, he wrote a famous article refuting that claim, entitled "The American Verdict on the War." Published internationally, it earned him a decoration from Belgium's king and queen: "Commander of the Crown of Belgium." In 1933, when major German cities were burning books written by and about Jews, he staged a retaliatory event at Carnegie Music Hall in which one hundred Jewish students from the University of Pittsburgh, wearing caps and academic gowns, paraded solemnly across the stage to deposit copies of the same

     THE HIGH COMMAND

books being burned in Germany into the care of Ralph Munn, director of Carnegie Library. In 1940, he famously offered, on behalf of Pittsburgh's leaders, a reward of one million dollars in 1940 to anyone who would deliver Adolph Hitler, "alive, unwounded and unhurt," into Allied custody. His one-month offer brought no results, but it did catapult him into the national news. In 1941, Church returned the French Legion of Honor he had been awarded in 1923 to the Vichy government, rejecting its collaboration with the Nazi occupation and declaring that "honor is dead in a country which abjectly bows to Hitler's wishes."[16] The idealistic Church was a figure to be reckoned with—by leaders within the Institute, from the strong-willed museum director William J. Holland to his sophisticated successor, the Russian Andrey Avinoff, and beyond its sphere, in government, business, and the arts and sciences.

Still vigorous at age eighty-five, Church was writing a letter inviting the Brazilian ambassador to the United States to give the Institute's Founder-Patron's Day speech when he was fatally stricken in his office. His obituary in the magazine he had founded quoted Shakespeare: "He was a man, take him all for all / We shall not look upon his like again."[17]

WILLIAM FREW, 1943–48

When Church died, William Frew, sixty-two years old and vice president of the Board of Trustees, became president. A lawyer by training and the son of the board's first president, Frew had worked as an assistant district attorney and as an army air corps captain in World War I and was now a partner in a private brokerage firm.

Frew's tenure began with the country pressed by World War II, and he faced the immediate challenge of raising $1.7 million by 1946, in order for the Carnegie Institute of Technology to meet the terms of a grant of $8 million the Carnegie Corporation of New York had promised years earlier. Frew met his deadline on June 30, 1946, with gifts ranging from one dollar to $333,000. Having secured the grant to Carnegie Tech, he then faced the stark reality that the Institute itself was failing financially because of rising costs and shrinking revenues from the original endowment. To save money, he reduced the hours the building was open, confessing, "We have pared the staff to an irreducible minimum."[18]

Considering the institutions that fell under his leadership, he saw that the library with its branches was supported by the city and that Carnegie Tech had a separate endowment and received income from tuition fees. The Institute, however, had relied solely on Andrew Carnegie's original endowment for forty years. Now, while the size of the endowment itself was

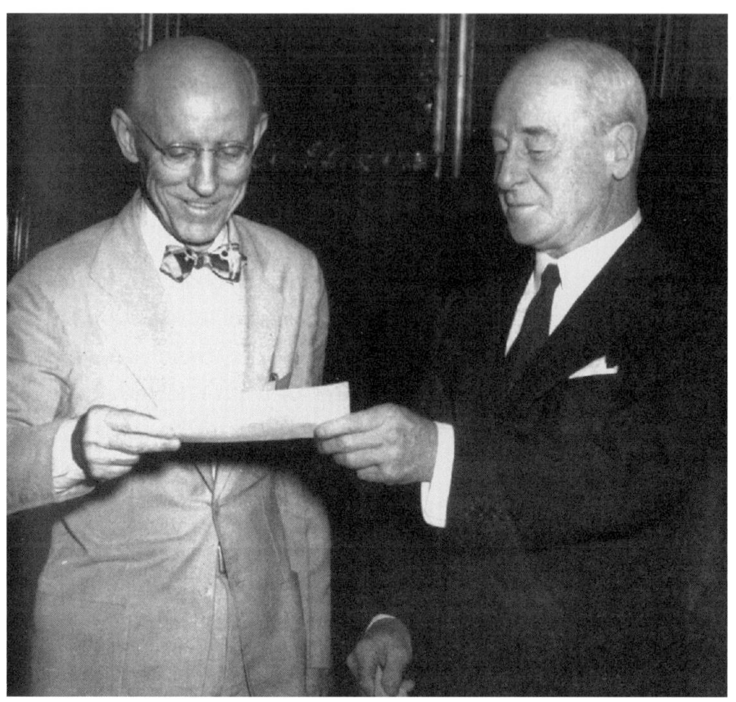

*William Frew (right), president of the Institute from 1943 to 1948,
hands over a large check to the president of Carnegie Institute of Technology,
Robert Dougherty, in 1946.*

the same, there was a serious decrease in return on the investments. Frew saw the situation—the original bonds were about to mature and would have to be invested at a lower rate of return—as "the same situation which confronts all endowed institutions today—hospitals, colleges, art galleries and museums of natural history alike." He did not want to raise revenue by charging admission, for he felt that the Institute must abide by the mandate "Free to the People," carved in stone above its doors. He thus proposed a voluntary membership program, the Fine Arts and Museum Society of Carnegie Institute, allowing the Institute's supporters to buy memberships both for themselves and for those who could not afford to do so. The price of "Sustaining" memberships was lower than comparable memberships elsewhere, prices ranging from five to fifteen to twenty-five dollars, and students could join for just two dollars. Members would enjoy notices of events and exhibitions, a subscription to *Carnegie Magazine,* and invitations to special programs and activities.[19]

Frew believed it was time for the Institute to extend its public outreach: "A new conception of the art and natural history museum has been gradu-

          THE HIGH COMMAND

ally evolving. No longer can we consider such institutions as static repositories of masterpieces or specimens. More and more they are becoming recognized as stimulating educational and social centers, active agents in group living, where concerts, lectures, classes, cultural programs of every sort, are to be enjoyed." Like Carnegie and Church, Frew wanted the Institute to be "no ivory tower, but a treasure house of art and natural history where a warm and hospitable welcome awaited the men and women and children for whose benefit it was created."[20] The trustee Augustus K. Oliver noted that Frew "experienced far more inward pleasure in watching the throngs of school children who visited the Institute every Saturday morning than he did from the raising of funds."[21] He had been president for only four and a half years when he died suddenly from a heart attack in 1948.

JAMES M. BOVARD, 1948–67

Following Frew's death, James M. Bovard, a lawyer associated with Mellon family interests, served as president for nearly twenty years, from February 20, 1948, to December 31, 1967. Like Frew, he had been an officer in the army air corps, had gone to Yale as an undergraduate, and had received a law degree from the University of Pittsburgh. The announcement of his appointment noted that he planned no drastic changes: "His guiding principle will continue to be close adherence to the Andrew Carnegie–charted course of service to the public."[22]

Bovard's twenty-year tenure was a stable period, and he enjoyed strong support from both the staff and the community. In 1955, the Institute building saw its first substantial rehabilitation, at a cost of more than $3.25 million: the leaking roof was covered with aluminum, and some decorative details, such the 1907 copper cheneaus along the roofline, were removed. The Women's Committee of the Museum of Art was organized in 1957, initiating a long period of continuous service to the Institute, its members raising funds not only for the museum but for general improvements to the building itself and for innovative programs such as the Three Rivers Arts Festival.[23] In 1959, the boards of Carnegie Institute and Carnegie Tech were finally separated, Bovard having advanced a development program that brought in some $61 million, including $30 million to Carnegie Tech. He also oversaw extended library services, including bookmobiles and shared resources in Allegheny County.

One of Bovard's most important legacies was the Institute's continuing emphasis on public outreach. He encouraged the development of a single Division of Education in 1948, the new department combining all education classes and services for both the art and the natural history museums.

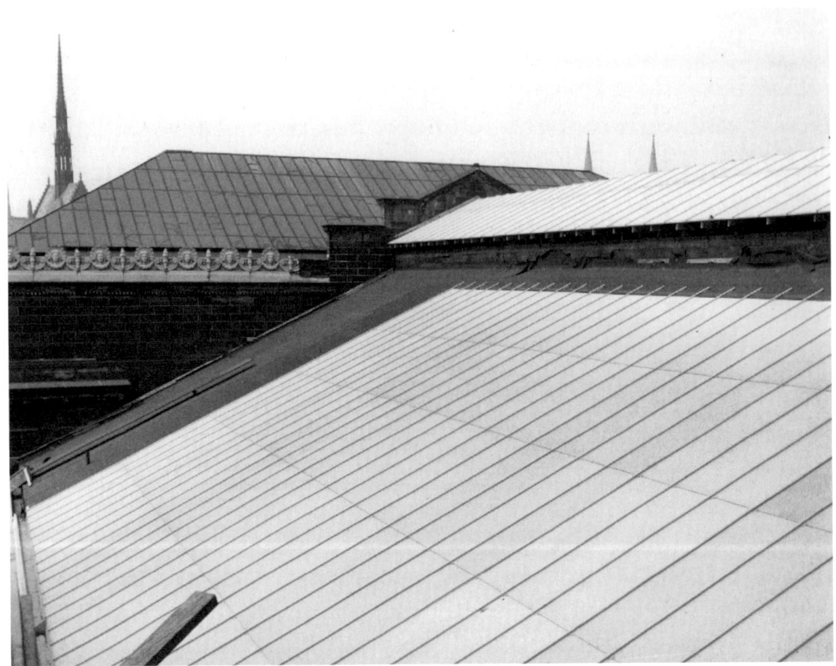

In the 1950s, Institute president James Bovard had to replace the original glass roof and decorative chenaus. Glass brought in light, but uncontrolled light also deteriorated the collections. The leaky glass roof was replaced by an aluminum one.

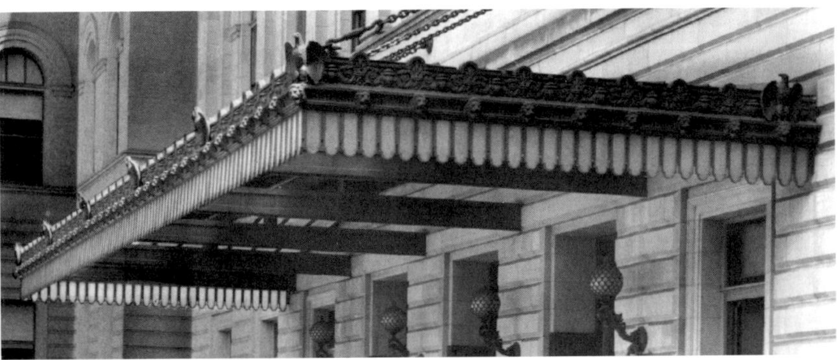

The new aluminum roof reacted with the decorative copper to produce a corrosive acid, so the copper heads as well as the original copper and glass canopy at the Carriage Drive entrance had to be removed.

He nurtured the Carnegie Institute Society (originally Frew's Fine Arts and Museum Society), its membership growing from eighteen hundred in 1948 to more than twelve thousand by Bovard's retirement. The society's members organized a notable film and lecture series supervised by Arthur S. Twomey, the well-traveled naturalist who headed the Division of Education. The weekly travel films and the addresses by world-traveled lecturers, greeted on stage by the tuxedoed Twomey, became a popular Pittsburgh entertainment, regularly packing the Music Hall and necessitating three additional screenings at other sites in the suburbs. Pittsburgh now had one of the most coveted series for lecturers on the national travel film circuit, and the program lasted for decades.

The Natural History Museum also continued to grow, and Bovard's tenure saw the construction of many exhibits that later became popular with museum-goers, such as Paleozoic Hall and the mammal and botanical dioramas. The Richard King Mellon Foundation started the Natural History Museum's International Program under Bovard, bringing students and scientists from around the world to study in Pittsburgh and strengthening the Institute's international reputation. Outside the Institute's formal boundaries, the Powdermill Nature Reserve near Ligonier was established in 1956, initially a 1,160-acre "outdoor laboratory for the scientists of the Museum" that provided "a recreational opportunity for the staff . . . and . . . an educational program for children of the area."[24] Some cynical western Pennsylvanians felt this generous gift was R. K. Mellon's way of insulating from public encroachment the beautiful forests and fields of the nearby Rolling Rock Club, whose exclusive game preserves, fox hunts, and horse shows were enjoyed by many of the Institute's board members, including Bovard.

James Bovard decided to retire in 1967, soon after the 1965 death of Sarah Scaife, a Mellon heiress who had been an avid art collector during her lifetime. Her family, including her son Richard Mellon Scaife, was interested in erecting a Memorial Pavilion for use by the Museum of Art in her honor and purchased land adjacent to the Institute. Bovard may have felt that the coming building campaign should be conducted by someone bringing fresh energy to the task, his two predecessors having died in office while managing just such stressful Institute affairs.

JAMES MELLON WALTON, 1968–84

This fresh energy was provided by thirty-eight-year-old James Mellon Walton, the grandson of Richard Beatty Mellon. His family connections to Carnegie Institute and Library were strong—his father, John Walton, had

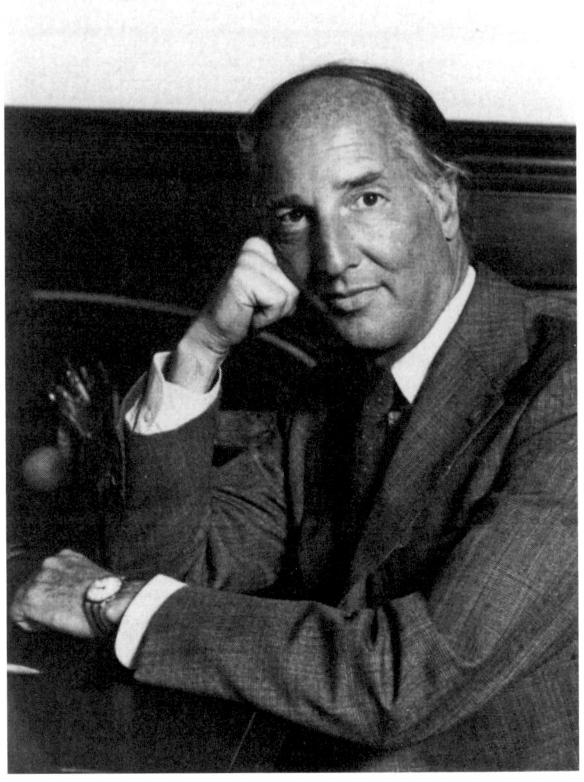

James Mellon Walton, Institute president from 1968 to 1984,
oversaw the addition of the Sarah Scaife Gallery.

served as a trustee for many years, as had his grandfather William Larimer
Mellon. His cousin Richard Mellon Scaife was deep in consideration of a
memorial project for his mother. Like his predecessors, Walton had also
gone to private school, earned an undergraduate degree from Yale University,
and served as an officer in the U.S. Army. He had earned a graduate
degree in business administration from Harvard and then embarked on
a career with the Gulf Oil Corporation, a company deeply connected to
Mellon Bank. He resigned as Gulf's director of sales in Rome to return
to Pittsburgh and accept the position as president of Carnegie Institute.

Jim Walton—president for sixteen years, from January 1, 1968, to July
8, 1984—oversaw the Institute's growth into the modern era: the Scaife Gallery
was added during his tenure, and the professional world of museums
began to change dramatically. Pittsburgh too underwent drastic changes,
and Walton was tasked with navigating the city's changing economic scene,

modernizing the nonprofit organization by making its business side more efficient as Pittsburgh lost its industrial base. In the face of such complexity, Walton created a new position in 1972: director of financial and general services, hiring Edwin C. Brueggman to fill it. A comprehensive computer system was installed in 1980 through a grant from the Richard King Mellon Foundation, to track the collections in both museums, general finances, development, and public relations.[25] The Estate Planning Program for donors was instituted under Walton's tenure, as was the Development Department, first with hired consultants, then with permanent staff. Walton's term saw the president become increasingly involved in library affairs, lessening the independence the library's director had enjoyed to that point. Anthony Martin, who served as director during the presidencies of Walton and his successor, Robert Wilburn, believed this new degree of involvement diminished his effectiveness as the sole recognized spokesperson for the library. Presidential involvement in library affairs marked the beginning of a schism between the Institute and the library that would evolve over the next thirty years into a territorial battle over shared services, common financing, and the use of space within Institute walls.[26]

Walton also introduced admission fees in 1974, with the opening of the Scaife Gallery; free entrances to the building were closed, and the public was directed to the admissions desks. More lucrative events were now booked in the Music Hall, the Lecture Hall, the new Museum of Art Theater, and other spaces in an effort to compete with other Pittsburgh venues. Having laid a firm groundwork for a more business-oriented approach, Jim Walton stepped down as president in 1984 but continued to serve as a member of the Board of Trustees.

ROBERT C. WILBURN, 1984–92

Robert C. Wilburn, appointed president on July 9, 1984, was the first president from outside the line of Pittsburghers attached by tradition to Carnegie or Mellon family influence. An economist by training, he had a sterling resume at Chase Manhattan Bank and had served as the secretary of budget and administration under Pennsylvania governor Dick Thornburgh and as the president of Indiana University of Pennsylvania. Wilburn, from a middle-class family, had grown up in a small western Pennsylvania town. His friendly style masked his genius for policy analysis, and he was widely admired at Carnegie Institute and Library by both staff and trustees. His experience in state government had taught him how to accomplish large goals: his forte was rekindling a sense of mission, increasing attendance, and achieving greater fiscal responsibility and donor participation. One

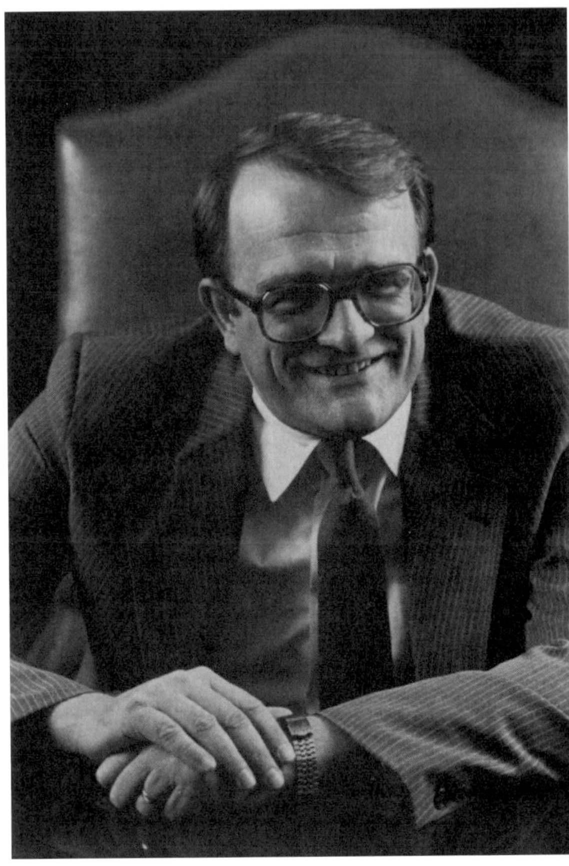

*Robert C. Wilburn, president from 1984 to 1992, brought
Carnegie Science Center and the Andy Warhol Museum
into the corporation.*

of his earliest initiatives was to solicit nominations from people active in
the Institute and library for Pittsburghers who would serve on the "Committee of One Hundred," tasked with advising on such issues as increasing
education programs, attendance, and membership; utilizing the Music
Hall; employing new technology; and developing new forms of community
outreach. Wilburn created the Department of Marketing and Business
Management to consolidate the museum's revenue-making enterprises,
hoping to increase profits enough to support about 10 percent of the Institute's operating budget. He expanded the Development Department,
which took over membership responsibilities, and raised admissions fees
from two dollars to three dollars.

In 1985, Rand-McNally surprised the nation by naming Pittsburgh

     THE HIGH COMMAND

"America's Most Livable City," but ensuing local public discussions about what made the city so livable oddly ignored Carnegie Institute and Library of Pittsburgh. This disappointed Wilburn, especially since outside media, including the *New York Times,* the *Boston Globe,* and the *London Times,* always identified Carnegie Institute and Library as the single outstanding feature of the Pittsburgh cultural scene. He identified the crux of the problem as the Carnegie's fragmentation in the public mind—confusion over the names of the Scaife Gallery, Carnegie Museum (natural history), Carnegie Library of Pittsburgh, Carnegie Museum of Art, Carnegie Music Hall, and Carnegie Institute. The Carnegie was a general presence in Pittsburgh, but no one agreed on its constituent parts or the centrality of its role in the city.[27] Wilburn quickly perceived the danger this raised for fund-raising: if the institution's identity and services were not understood, public and private support would surely diminish.

Determined to change this situation, Wilburn, working with outside consultants and the Board of Trustees, changed the institution's name for marketing purposes to "The Carnegie"—a simple title, easily remembered, that reaffirmed Carnegie's original mission to promote art, science, literature, and music. In 1986, he wrote in his annual report, "we became The Carnegie"; the public were invited to "Explore All Four," the building itself, with its four iconic sculptures, reinforcing the new sense of synergy.

Ironically, this ambitious rebranding led to conflict with the great achievements of Wilburn's tenure: the additions of Carnegie Science Center (formally Buhl Science Center) and the Andy Warhol Museum. Some trustees argued that the public would never understand that they too were part of The Carnegie, for The Carnegie seemed to be centered in the magnificent Oakland building. During the next presidential administration, under Ellsworth Brown, the name was changed again, this time to "Carnegie Museums of Pittsburgh." These name changes were costly, demanding new logos and published materials for the institution and all its component parts, and required a long-range marketing effort. Unfortunately, the public was once again confused about the organization and its makeup. The public and the media had easily adopted the concept of "The Carnegie" and called the institution that long after "Carnegie Museums of Pittsburgh" became its new name.

Wilburn's accomplishments saw him named Pittsburgh's man of the year in 1992, and soon afterward he left Carnegie to lead first Colonial Williamsburg and then the Gettysburg National Battlefield Museum Foundation. Staying long in one position did not suit his temperament, and he wanted above all to avoid complacency, preferring to tackle new challenges.

<h1 style="text-align:center">ELLSWORTH H. BROWN,
1993–2004</h1>

The search for the next president was led by the chair of the Board of Trustees, Konrad M. Weis, a long-time supporter of Pittsburgh's cultural life. From a group of over one hundred candidates, the board chose Ellsworth H. Brown on February 4, 1993, the retiring president of the American Association of Museums and the twelve-year head of the Chicago Historical Society. Brown was an experienced analyst of museum practices, focused on the organization of museums rather than their subject matter, and he came with a strong set of convictions and an agenda that would unfold over the eleven years of his tenure.

Brown's preeminent goal as president was the "deevolution" of the "corporation": returning decision-making authority back to the various museum directors, rather than keeping it in the hands of the central administration. Thus, whereas Wilburn had consolidated the diverse interests of the museums and libraries under one entity called "The Carnegie," Brown moved in the opposite direction by increasing directorial responsibility and, on the advice of outside consultants and in keeping with his own beliefs, renaming the institution "Carnegie Museums of Pittsburgh" in 1996. "I spent eight years devolving the organization," Brown remarked upon his 2004 retirement, "putting the risks and rewards and authority back into the hands of the directors. I looked at the museums from the four corners, thereby multiplying the leadership energies fourfold."[28] This devolution, of course, was simpler in theory than in practice. Services and staff for each museum were now duplicated rather than centralized, so that each of the four museums and the library was as independently staffed as possible, and costs increased as a result.

Brown's approach was heavily influenced by the philosophy of museum guru Stephen Weil, whose 1992 book *Making Museums Matter* had challenged the profession by arguing that museums could only remain relevant in the modern world if they abandoned their traditional top-down culture of management. Weil argued for the reverse: a bottom-up approach in which the public, through their attendance and support, showed the museums what was most culturally relevant and important. By Weil's standard, then, high attendance at Carnegie Science Center, with its child-friendly activities, was a mark of community relevance, while smaller attendance at the other quieter museums implied weakness. To help each museum be more competitive, Brown expanded the institution's Marketing Department and increased its budget.

Many museum administrators and more traditional board members

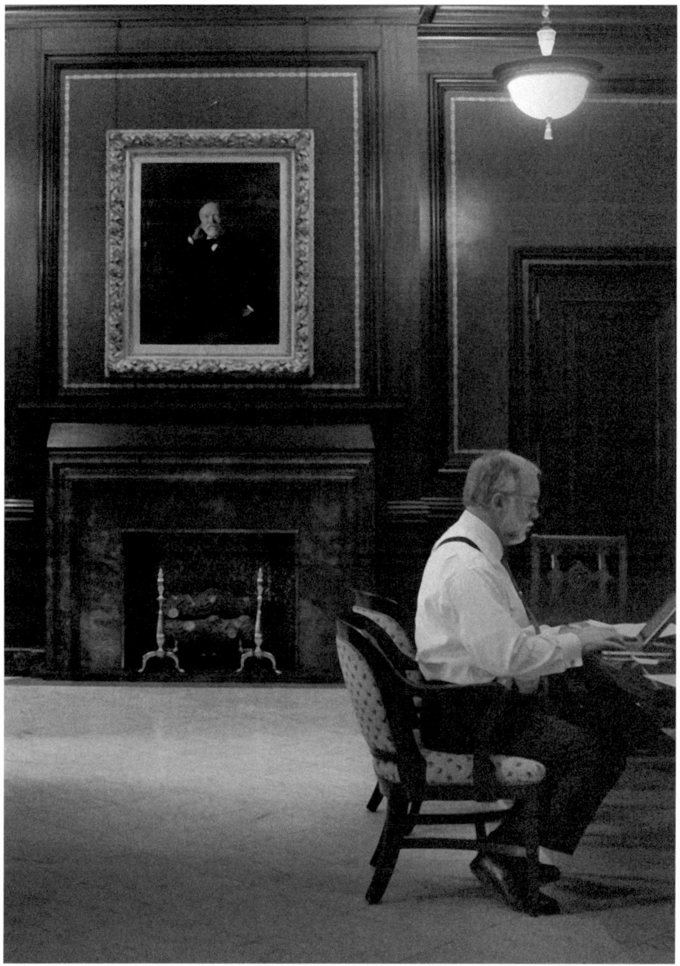

*Ellsworth Brown, president from 1993 to 2004, promoted a policy of
returning management decisions to the individual directors.*

resisted Brown's policies, some because of the uses of the endowment and
others because of top-level appointments that did not work out. The museum directors as a group resented the well-funded Marketing Department,
charging that its large staff needs had essentially made it a fifth museum.
Within a few years a new bureaucracy of middle management arose, with
"directors" for such activities or corporate communications, membership,
and group tours. So many directors made decision making increasingly
complicated; simply choosing the logo for each museum took two years.
William F. Neil, Carnegie's long time controller, summarized the skepti-

cism many felt: "If Marketing was to bring people into the building, they could practically have made the Institute free again, and raised attendance that way, instead of spending millions on marketing."[29]

Under Brown, from 1999 to 2001, the salaries of top executives increased dramatically, along with benefits such as company cars, bonuses for meeting quotas, and personal financial consultants. These changes were in line with those typical for executives of large for-profit corporations, but when a newspaper revealed the rising executive salaries at a time when the endowment continued to shrink, the Institute's financial management was challenged by critics.[30] Further, while financial responsibility had been transferred to each museum, the authority to devise an appropriate financial system had not. Thus, the sales shop at Carnegie Science Center, for example, could not be open during evening hours, even though the Omnimax Theater and Buhl Planetarium were busy. Doreen Boyce, the president of the Buhl Foundation and a long-time supporter of the Science Center, found such restrictions hopelessly antiquated: "The whole corporate organization of Carnegie Museums became a fascinating example . . . of a system that was too complex to work efficiently."[31]

By 2000, the stock market decline was affecting the endowment of museums nationwide, and over the next three years, the Carnegie's dropped by 20 percent, from $250 million to $180 million.[32] In late 2002, Carnegie Museums of Pittsburgh disbanded its large centralized Marketing Department, and Brown announced that in 2003 marketing funds would no longer be a "special draw" on the shrinking endowment. Budgets were reduced for all the museums, which were now again responsible for their own marketing, and cutbacks were made to centralized services, some disappearing entirely. The building's post office closed. The Natural History Museum cut its budget across all its departments, while the Museum of Art eliminated one entire department, the Section of Film and Video. Morale among the museum's staff now reached a new low, and a union was formed for service workers. To some people, the institution seemed to have lost its soul.[33]

In April 2004, Ellsworth Brown resigned as the president of Carnegie Museums of Pittsburgh, his agenda for deevolution incomplete. Still, Brown felt he had successfully redirected the institution's priorities and that it was time to move on: "The job of president had become a job of sophisticated coordinating instead of being creative, and I found this, to be honest, not as interesting."[34]

After Brown's resignation, Suzy Broadhurst, a successful restaurateur and chair of the Board of the Trustees, served as the institution's acting president, making no institutional changes of direction. After a year's search, the Search Committee recommended David Hillenbrand, who had just retired from the Bayer Corporation at age fifty-eight, an experienced executive with a history of supporting the arts in Pittsburgh. He was appointed on May 6, 2005, and the *Journal of Philanthropy* ran a story about him entitled "Globetrotting Executive Lands Dream Job at Carnegie Museums."[35]

One of Hillenbrand's strengths was immediately clear: his easy, comfortable way of explaining complex financial issues. Thus, while he did not share Brown's crusading desire to reorganize the museums, he was well equipped to pursue deevolution by applying sound business policies. Despite his reservations, he oversaw the more complete financial separation of the Institute and Library, a process already begun by the Brown administration and advocated strongly by two library directors. The two institutions stopped sharing services wherever possible—human resources, building and grounds, maintenance, security, and information technology. Hillenbrand saw Carnegie Museums as very different from Carnegie Library, which was totally dependent on public money and thus on economic factors beyond its control. The museums' endowment, on the other hand, provided 25 percent of its total operating expenses, and it could develop as a private corporation in different ways. Likewise, the overlapping board structure created by Carnegie was an anachronism, with lifetime trustees serving on both boards and public officials serving ex officio on the board of this private institution. Old disputes over space surfaced between the library and the Institute; the internal doorway in the corner of Architecture Hall was now closed, and the public was no longer allowed to pass freely within the building between the two institutions. Hillenbrand, however, remained clear about change: "I don't want to be nostalgic about the past. I don't believe that the model that Andrew Carnegie established for a late Victorian Pittsburgh society is the model we should aspire to today."[36]

Hillenbrand further insisted that the museums live within their means, not spending more money than they generated: "There are institutions— great and small—falling off the board every day, nationally, whether it's for lack of relevance or lack of funding, or the ability to attract in a declining demographic." The museums were asked to present a five-year budget and a strategic plan, extra endowment draws to be used only for long-term, strategic initiatives. If any one museum needed more than was budgeted, it could borrow against next year's allocation at 7 percent interest, under

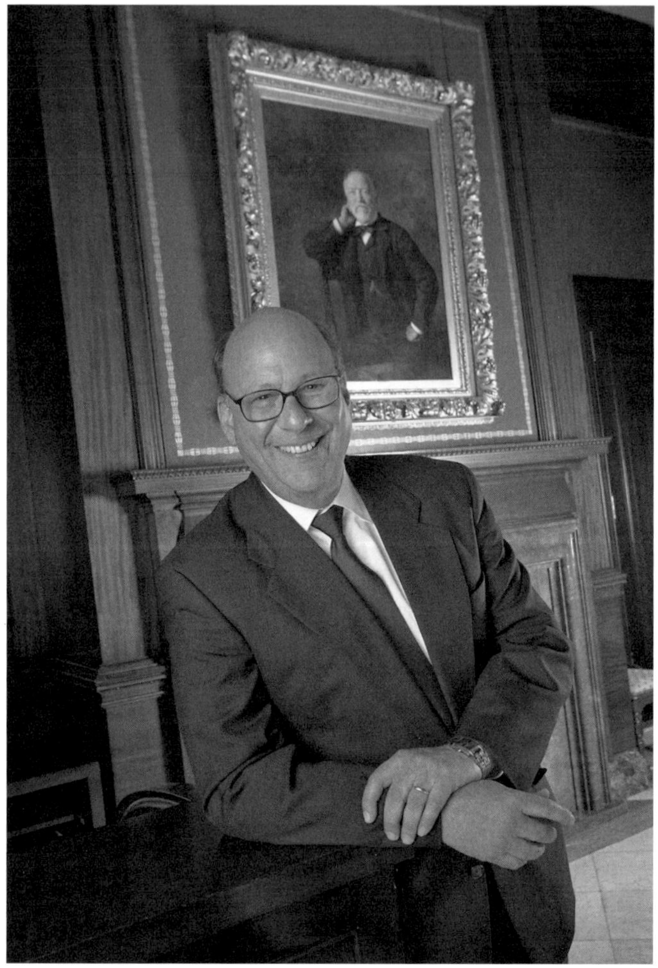

*David Hillenbrand, president from 2005 to 2011, restored the financial
stability of the corporation during a national economic decline.*

the condition that the loan be paid back the next year. "I've had a successful business career," he later reflected, "because I realized early on that my
success depends totally upon the result of other people's efforts. I'm there
to help them focus and give them structure and the tools they need to do
their job. At the end of the day I feel that's what leadership is about. One
man cannot deal with the complexities of this institution alone."[37]

Hillenbrand was focused on the museums' financial survival and raised
museum admission costs, from twelve to fifteen dollars for an adult, and in
2008 he ended Museum of Art sponsorship of the large annual Three Rivers
Arts Festival, instead placing it under the aegis of the Pittsburgh Cultural

  THE HIGH COMMAND

Trust, which had become a force in managing downtown cultural events. He also wrapped up the largest fund-raising drive in the Institute's history in February 2008. The "Building the Future" capital campaign, begun in 2002, had reached $161 million, erasing much of the debt incurred during the Brown administration. This brought the endowment to roughly $300 million, and all four museums benefited as a result.

Hillenbrand retired after five years, and John Wetenhall, an art historian, administrator, curator, and scholar, was named in January 2011 as the ninth president. Wetenhall had a distinguished career in museum management, including eight years at The John and Mable Ringling Museum of Art in Sarasota, Florida, and the Miami Art Museum. His international perspective as well as his accomplishments in handling multiple institutions and fund-raising were praised by his former associates and valued by the Carnegie search committee.

BEYOND THE HIGH COMMAND

Viewing Carnegie through the administrations of its presidents is helpful, but it ignores much of the institution's significance to the Pittsburgh community. Carnegie Institute, symbolic when it opened in 1895, remained a symbol. From the beginning, citizens of Pittsburgh, whether desperately poor or from one of the country's wealthiest families, felt it an honor to be part of the Carnegie, to advance its goals in small or large ways. Volunteers worked devotedly: writing small specimen labels in the scientific departments, giving tours of the art galleries, working as trustees. For many, the Carnegie was their entrée into the world of art, literature, music, and science, and they needed to be part of that world.

Pittsburgh had long had an inferiority complex—the dark side of its industrial power. A classic six-volume study, *The Pittsburgh Survey,* published in the early twentieth century, had revealed Pittsburgh as the worst urban environment in America, marked by raw sewage, industrial pollution, typhoid fever, and slum housing. When H. L. Mencken visited Pittsburgh, he wrote, "Here was the very heart of industrial America, the center of its most lucrative and characteristic activity, the boast and pride of the richest and grandest nation ever seen on earth—and here was a scene so dreadfully hideous, so intolerably bleak and forlorn, that it reduced the whole aspiration of man to a macabre and depressing joke. . . . One expects steel towns to be dirty. What I allude to is the unbroken and agonizing ugliness, the sheer revolting monstrousness, of every house in sight."[38] Such indictments typified the old view of Pittsburgh as "hell with the lid off," and the city's leaders spent much of the twentieth century struggling to change it.

The poor and wealthy alike always understood the importance of Carnegie Institute and Library, and donors responded by giving generously, the major gifts memorialized in the names of art galleries and natural history halls: the Sarah Scaife Gallery, the Heinz Galleries, the Ailsa Mellon Bruce Galleries, the Heinz Architectural Center, the Hillman Hall of Minerals, the Walton Hall of Ancient Egypt, and the Benedum Hall of Geology, to name a few. Carnegie Science Center features the Henry Buhl Jr. Planetarium and the Rangos Omnimax Theater, while the Andy Warhol Museum could not have existed without the generosity of the Andy Warhol Foundation and the Dia Art Center in New York. Carnegie Library also sought private support, despite its historic dependence on public money. In the 1970s and 1980s, Carnegie Institute began printing annual lists of gifts and donations, requiring dozens of pages of small type.

The Institute experienced the changes and trends that shaped other museums and libraries in the twentieth century. These were sea changes, marked by shifts in technology, politics, society, and the maturing museum and library professions. Such changes were visible at Carnegie by the 1970s, and when the Worldwide Web gained prominence in the 1990s, Carnegie's operations changed dramatically. Museums were once stand-alone facilities relying on local catalogs and collection records, but now they were part of a world arena of standardized record keeping. Modern database systems changed management policies, and both the Institute and the library invested in costly new equipment, creating departments of information technology.

The computer age dawned at Carnegie Museum of Natural History in 1975 with a Data Services Department. Each of the museum's estimated thirteen million specimens or artifacts was accompanied by information about its type or species, place of origin, and the person who had collected it, and Data Services began digitizing this information, succeeding after four years in digitizing 350,000 records—only a fraction of the whole. Each scientific section began to inventory and standardize all its collection information— the first step toward international databases. Carnegie Museum's first database manager, John Sutton, predicted what lay ahead: "In the not too distant future, museums will each have small computers which can be linked into a network for information exchange. This possibility will allow one museum to directly interrogate a database at another museum in search of pertinent information." Within twenty-five years, this prediction was reality.[39]

The Museum of Art was not driven by the same technological imperatives. It began to develop computer files in the 1980s to inventory and track the location of its approximately thirty thousand art objects, some of which moved around for exhibition and conservation purposes. In 2002, it adopted an internationally marketed system of software and removed its records from the Institute's centralized system. Digitized images existed for about one-third of the museum's holdings by 2001—some twelve thousand paintings, decorative arts, works on paper, and photographs, displacing the traditional and expensive printed color catalog.

The computer revolution also held some potential threats to the museums' well-being: twentieth-century technology led toward the privatization of leisure time, and audiences could now find entertainment and information while never leaving home. In 2007, the U.S. Census Bureau estimated that Americans spent more than eight hours a day watching television, using a computer, or listening to the radio. Such routines had the net result of diminishing museum visits as essential cultural experiences, especially since museum admission costs, nationally, kept rising.[40]

But even as personal and family recreation was becoming more isolated in some ways, the world of museums also saw a new internationalism, thanks in part to the easy global reach made possible by technology and to the end of the Cold War and the subsequent Glasnost, or "openness." With the official end of the Cold War in 1989, both the Soviet Union and Communist China ended the fifty-year stalemate that had kept Western scientists from exploring historical and fossil-rich sites in Asia and countries that made up the former Soviet bloc. Carnegie paleontologists began to collaborate with Chinese partners in the rich quarries of northern and central China to uncover new evidence of the earliest mammals and reptiles from the Age of Dinosaurs. Carnegie Science Center worked with China to lease the programs created in the Henry Buhl Jr. Planetarium for worldwide distribution and sent experts abroad to advise counterparts who were developing ambitious new science centers. In January 2000, the Andy Warhol Museum sent Warhol's pop art on a world tour under the diplomatic sponsorship of the U.S. government, a traveling exhibition that was very popular in twelve cities formerly within the Soviet sphere.[41]

The new globalism also drew the museums of Carnegie Institute into the politics of returning artifacts to their original owners and countries of origin. Carnegie Museum of Natural History agreed that pottery and artifacts uncovered by Carnegie anthropologists should stay in the Caribbean, and that valuable fossils discovered by Carnegie paleontologists should stay in China. New species of insects captured by Carnegie entomologists in the rainforests of South America or the Caribbean now required higher levels of clearance if they were to leave the country. New politically correct policies also influenced the Natural History anthropological exhibits—in Polar World, for example, and the Hall of Native Americans.

The Carnegie was also challenged by serious competition from the culture of entertainment—attractively designed zoos, botanical gardens, theme parks, art galleries, history museums, and theaters. The new Children's Museum on Pittsburgh's North Side (2004) drew families with young children away from traditional museums, while the Frick Art Museum in Point Breeze (1970) competed with Carnegie Museum of Art. The Heinz History Center in downtown Pittsburgh (1996) expanded dramatically, staked out a claim to regional history, and allied with the Smithsonian to showcase nationally traveling exhibits.

By the 1990s, the Institute had become the venerable dowager queen of Pittsburgh's cultural life, facing aggressive competitors that sought the same grants from government agencies and private foundations and gifts from the same donors who had once been loyal to the Institute. Some local foundations had widened their organizational goals: the Mellon Foundation now focused on buying and preserving environmentally threatened tracts of land, and the Heinz Foundation concentrated on global environmentalism. Carnegie Corporation of New York had long ago redefined its priorities on an international scale. Pittsburgh's stature as an American city had also diminished. It now had lost much of its industrial base and had reduced population and political power, and the city struggled to maintain its schools, hospitals, and cultural institutions. The Carnegie's administrative plan had been made in the days of Pittsburgh's industrial might, when the promise of the city's new millionaires seemed sufficient to secure its future. One contemporary cartoon showed Carnegie operating a machine, feeding templates of people (his partners) into its hopper, while little Pittsburgh millionaires were spewed out the other side, carrying away bags of money. Carnegie's idea of Pittsburgh as a mecca for the arts was based on a Victorian vision: future millionaires would perpetually donate paintings to the "Department of Fine Arts" and give "the Museum" their personal collections of coins and stamps, or watches and carved ivories, and buy for it valuable natural history collections and specimens as they came up for sale. By the 1920s, however, the limits of the Institute's resources and growth were clear, despite the gifts of generous patrons who loved the institution as much as the founder had. For most of the twentieth century, the Institute was engaged in a battle for financial survival, embroiled in the currents of technological, political, and social change that were altering American society.

CARNEGIE MUSIC HALL

"Music, Sacred Tongue of God"

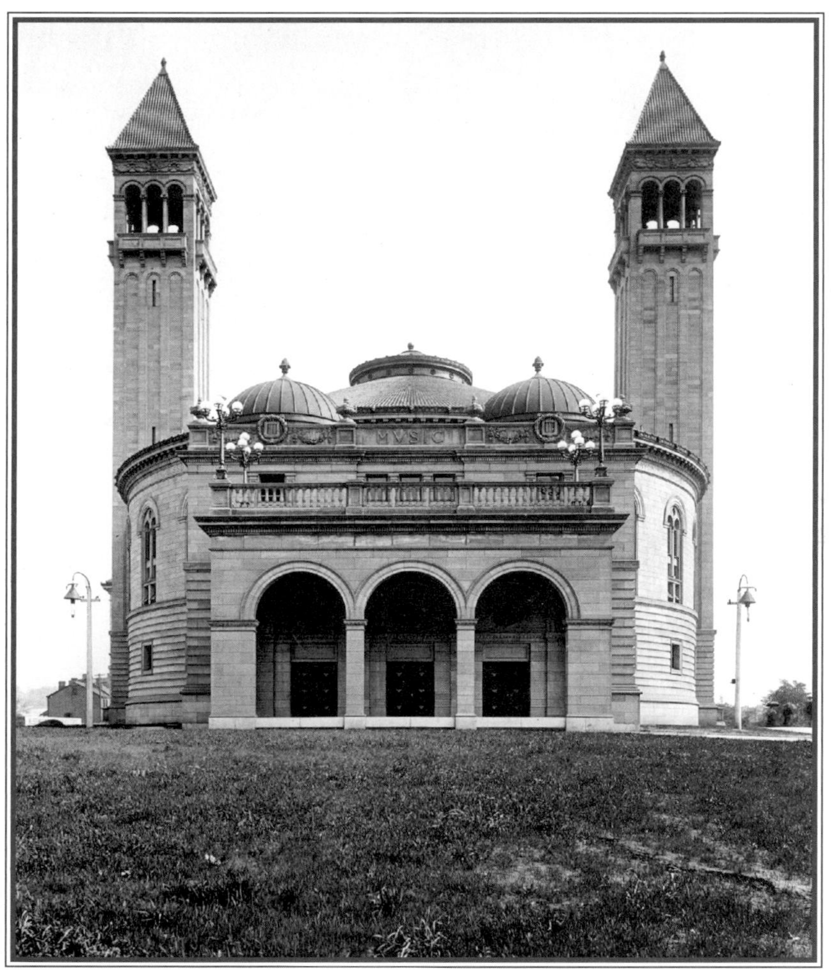

The entrance of the Music Hall in 1895, with the Florentine towers that Carnegie
called "donkey's ears."

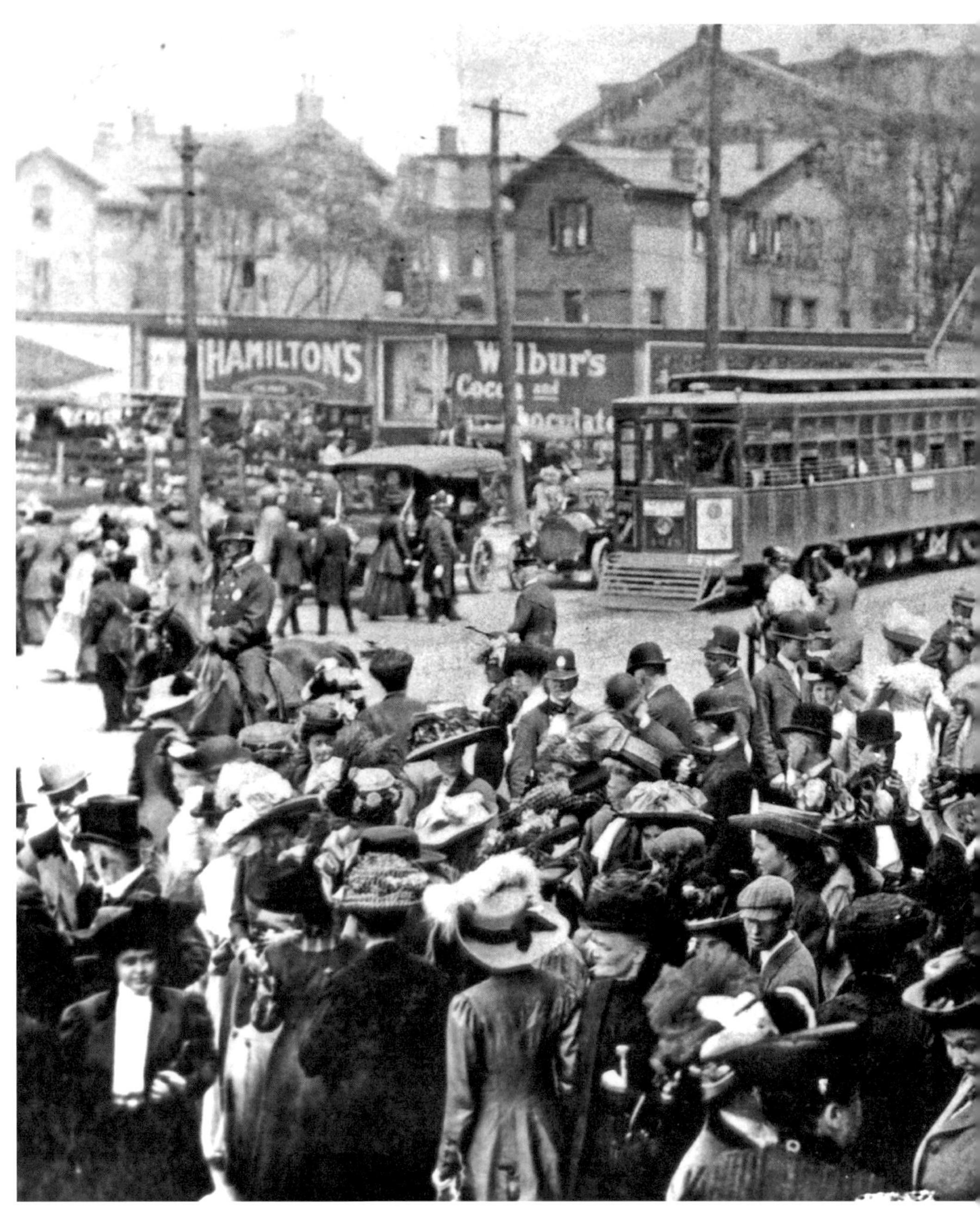
HAMILTON'S
Wilbur's
Cocoa and
Chocolate

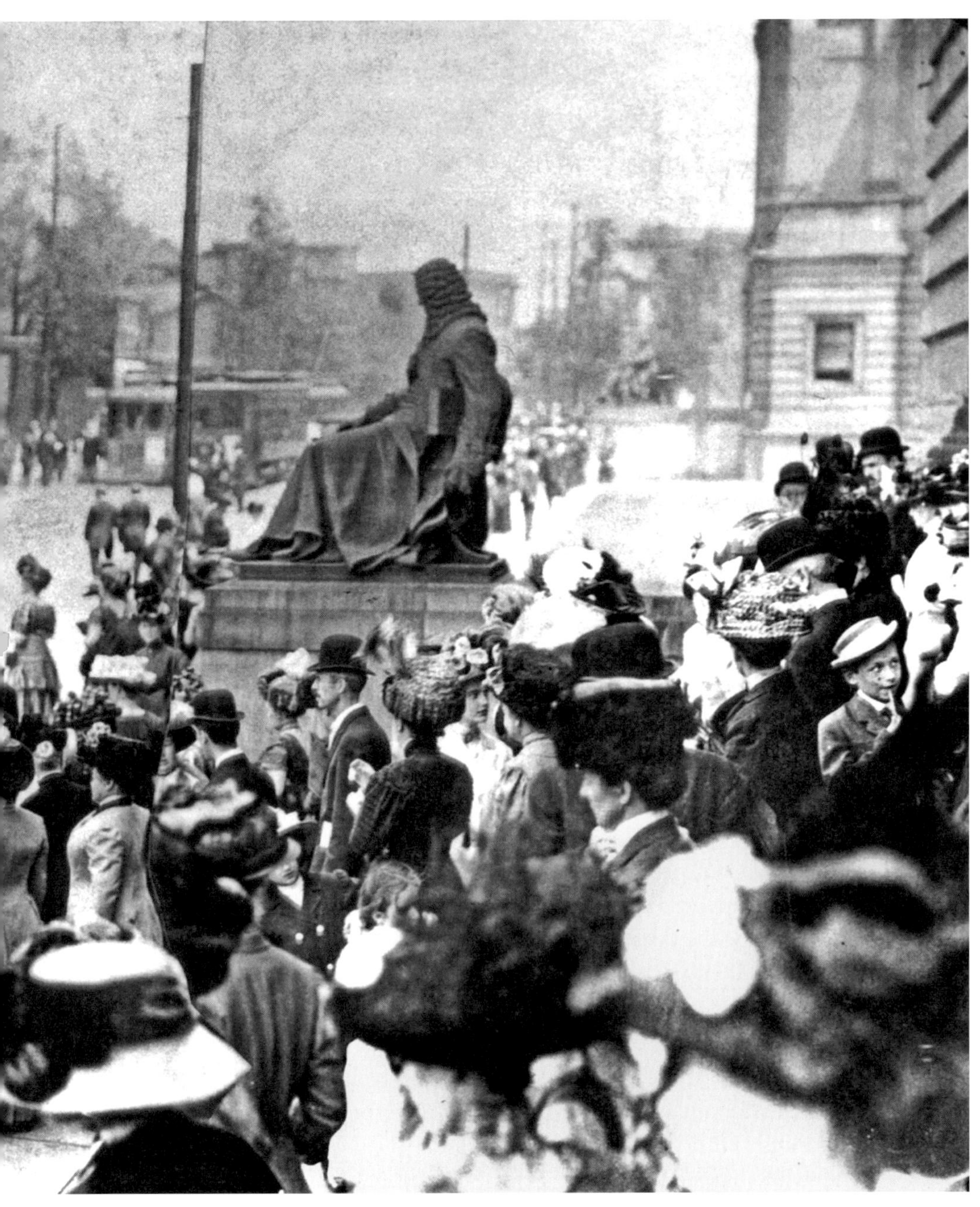

Crowds wearing their Easter Day finery leave the Music Hall after a program on Easter Sunday, 1910. This was the last year the Pittsburgh Symphony performed in the hall before a long hiatus due to lack of funds. When it returned after sixteen years, it performed at the larger Syria Mosque.

Straight roads lead from music to everything good.
Andrew Carnegie, 1895 dedication, quoting Goethe

LISTENING TO MUSIC delighted Carnegie but did not match his passion for literature and libraries. While he donated music halls to Pittsburgh, Allegheny City, Braddock, and other communities to which he felt indebted, his friend Walter Damrosch, the conductor and composer who persuaded him to build New York City's Carnegie Hall, later noted that Carnegie's "admiration for music in its simpler forms never crystallized into as great a conviction regarding its importance in life as that he had regarding the importance of science or literature, and though always generous in support, his benefactions never became as great as in other directions.... He always insisted that the greatest patronage of music should come from a paying public rather than from private endowment."[1] Carnegie generally felt music halls should be self-supporting, and in New York, for instance, the top floors of Carnegie Hall were designed with studios for rent. Acoustically, Carnegie Hall (1892) was a gem, designed by the architect William Tuthill, who was also a singer in the Oratorio Society. Still, when Tuthill refused to compromise his original design by adding a revenue-producing addition holding yet more studios, financial need won out: Carnegie simply hired a new architect.

Like Carnegie Hall, Pittsburgh's Music Hall, which seats nearly two thousand, is renowned for its acoustics. Indeed, members of the Juilliard String Quartet, preparing for the twenty-first season of the Pittsburgh Chamber Music Society in 1981, deemed it acoustically the world's most ideal hall for the performance of chamber music.[2] "You will not have as perfect a hall as we have in the Music Hall here [New York]," Carnegie wrote James Scott in 1893, "but you will have the best hall in Pittsburgh, [and] people will think it perfect."[3] Beyond acoustics, both halls were built with the traditional stone and wood construction techniques of the late nineteenth century, just before the advent of structural steel led to ever larger buildings and skyscrapers; both music halls were expanded a few years later with structural steel additions. Alexander W. Longfellow, the Music Hall's chief designer, had studied at Paris's Ecole des Beaux Arts from 1879 to 1881, and he thus drew many of his ideas from neoclassical examples, especially Parisian ones. The hall was compared to Charles Garnier's Paris

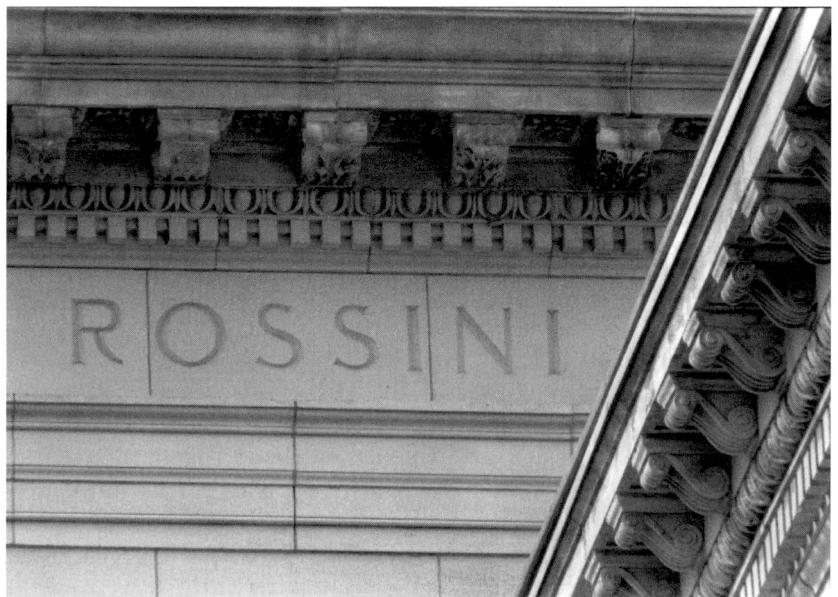

"Rossini" is one of the many composers' names carved in stone outside the Music Hall.

opera house and to Gabriel Davioud's semicircular Theatre Lyrique and his Trocadero Palace.[4]

Dedicated on November 5, 1895, Pittsburgh's Carnegie Music Hall was immediately, as Carnegie had predicted, the greatest public space in the city. Longfellow and his partners, Alden and Harlow, had designed the hall's interior to bring the audience "within easy seeing and hearing distance of the performers." The low, domed ceiling is ornamented "so as to preserve lightness and detail and yet be sufficiently broken up for acoustical properties. . . . The handsomely decorated proscenium arch, the most elaborate piece of decoration in the building, forms a worthy setting for the towering organ. . . . The stage has been planned to accommodate large choruses and an orchestra."[5] Carnegie's goal was to make the hall the center of musical culture in Pittsburgh—the home of the Pittsburgh Orchestra and a place where the public could hear free organ recitals—the best and most economical way to present music to "the masses." In his 1895 dedication speech, he said, "That this Hall can be and will be so managed as to prove a most potent means for refined entertainment and instruction of the people and the development of the musical taste of Pittsburgh, I entertain not the slightest doubt, and Goethe's saying should be recalled, that 'Straight roads lead from music to everything good.'"[6]

During the five-day dedication ceremonies in 1895, the British organist-conductor Frederic Archer—the first director of Carnegie Music Hall, its organist, and the conductor of Pittsburgh Orchestra—gave four organ recitals and was a soloist at one of three concerts performed by the New York Symphony Orchestra, under the direction of Walter Damrosch. Archer's stated goal was to elevate the public taste gradually, by "the interspersion of music of lighter character" with "more solid items of the musical feast." Toward this end he proposed a four-point plan: organ recitals twice a week; concerts featuring madrigals, glees, and church music by a select choir of twenty-four mixed voices; musical lectures of a popular, nontechnical character; and concerts by a symphony orchestra, the advent of which would "mark a new era in the musical history of the city."[7]

At the dedication, the first of the three concerts under Damrosch's direction began with the commissioned "Dedication March," by the locally famous Pittsburgh composer Adolph Foerster (1854–1927). Foerster represented the musical class that was expected to flourish after the Music Hall opened in Pittsburgh, a city whose musical tradition was linked to its most famous composer, Stephen Foster, and that was the home of such societies as the Mozart Club, the Tuesday Musical Club, and the Bohemian Club. Raised in a German family, Foerster, first taught music by his mother, embraced the German tradition of choral singing and romantic art songs, or *leider,* featuring lofty musical themes.

Thus, when he was chosen as a native Pittsburgher to compose a song for the dedication of Carnegie Music Hall, he understood the solemn, high purpose of the occasion. One of Foerster's principles of composition was to use familiar pieces of music for special effect, so for the "Dedication March," he used the familiar strains of Foster's "Old Folks at Home" and sweet Scottish airs to allude to Andrew Carnegie's Scottish-American origins. Today this triumphant march seems bombastic and mannered, with its heavy processional theme, its base in the keys of A and C (Carnegie's initials), and its musical tapestry weaving Foster's popular song with Scottish melodies. But at the time it captured perfectly the multilayered significance of this watershed event—the dedication of a noble home for the arts and sciences in the hive of working-class Pittsburgh. Performed by the New York Symphony Orchestra under Damrosch, the "Dedication March" encapsulated the cultural ambitions of the city.

Less than two months after the 1895 dedication, the inaugural concerts of the newly formed Pittsburgh Orchestra took place in the Music Hall. Frederic Archer led the orchestra in a rousing interpretation of Felix Mendelssohn's *Scotch Symphony,* a tribute to Carnegie. The lengthy and varied program also included orchestral favorites and vocal works by Beethoven,

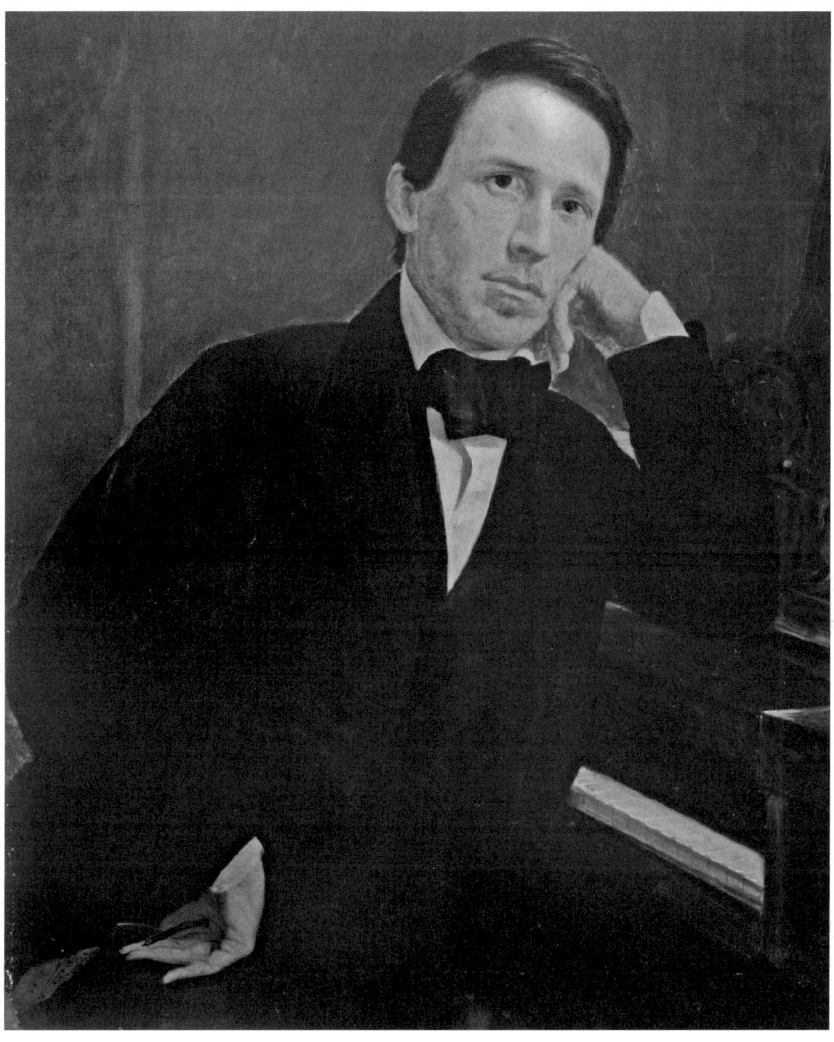

A portrait of Pittsburgh composer Stephen Foster, donated by Carnegie, was installed in the Music Hall Rotunda to inspire the public.

Wagner, Saint-Saens, Liszt, Wagner, and Anton Rubinstein. By 1897, however, the orchestra was already experiencing financial difficulties, and the *Pittsburgh Leader* reported, "Orchestra May Disband."[8] Fortunately, a group of wealthy businessmen (headed by Institute president William Frew and including Henry Clay Frick) became "guarantors" by pledging up to one thousand dollars for each of three seasons to staff the orchestra and eliminate the debts. Carnegie noted in his 1898 Founder's Day address, "There is no such thing in the world as a permanent orchestra maintaining itself.

Those of Boston and Chicago are subsidized, and we owe to a body of public-spirited citizens a guarantee fund which has had to be called upon yearly."[9]

George H. Wilson, the manager of the hall, interviewed in the *Pittsburgh Dispatch,* was emphatic about the Institute's devotion to music:

There is nothing like it in the country. It is unique in its position and standard. No other city is as rigid. The Boston Music Hall takes cat shows, dog shows and prize fights, poetically termed "sparring matches"; even poultry shows are, on occasion, admitted within its portals. It is not strictly a music hall, but rather a large hall open for rental to any one who can pay the price demanded, and is not reserved for entertainments of a high grade.... Carnegie Music Hall in New York is let for miscellaneous purposes, such as Salvation Army meetings, political rallies, etc. The art standard there is not as high as the purpose of the edifice calls for. When speaking of Chicago, the first hall to enter the mind is, of course, the Auditorium, the home of the Chicago Orchestra and of the Apollo Club.... It is opened to all sorts of entertainments. Charity balls are given therein, also the performances of any extravaganza company which can afford the rental asked. Besides these considerations, it is too large for a music hall pure and simple.[10]

When asked whether he thought that Carnegie Music Hall was managed to a higher musical standard than halls elsewhere, he replied:

No, I do not think that. I know it. I know it as no other man could, save perhaps those who have acted with me since I was placed in charge. It was opened with the best aim in view and so far in its career this aim has never for a single moment been lost to view. I know of no other parallel.

THE PITTSBURGH ORCHESTRA

Music historian C. Hax McCullough traced the roots of the Pittsburgh Orchestra to 1873–74, when a group of thirty-five men calling themselves "Germania" began to give concerts. In 1878, this group changed its name to the "Symphonic Society" and continued to perform for the next fifteen years, often with the large Mozart Club chorus. In time, it became the Art Society, with many distinguished subscribers, and founded the Pittsburgh Orchestra, which flourished at Carnegie Music Hall from 1896 through 1910 under three conductors: Frederic Archer, Victor Herbert, and Emil Paur.[11]

Frederic Archer (1838–1901) was the head of the orchestra for three seasons, until his contract expired in 1898, after which he continued as organist in residence until his death three years later. Archer held strong convictions about the importance of bringing music to the masses through popular free organ recitals; this made him a good choice as the orchestra's

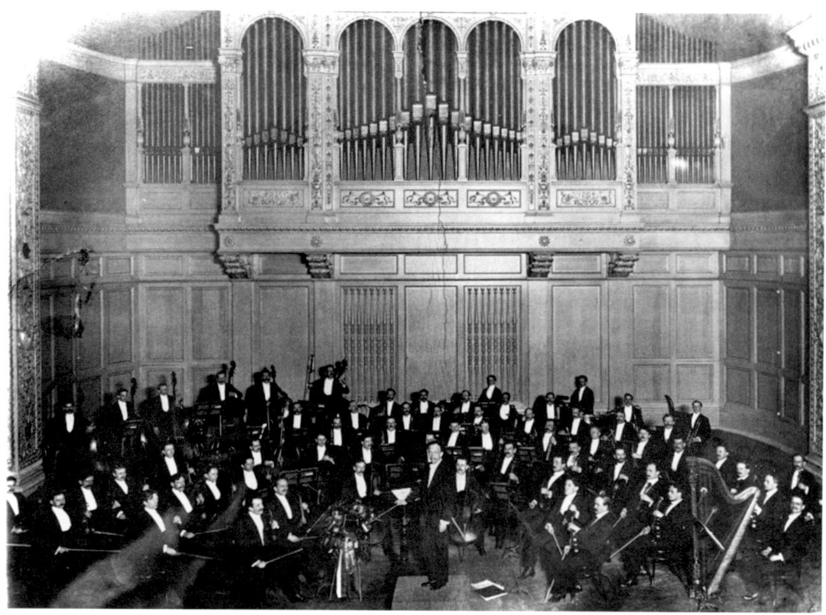

The Pittsburgh Symphony Orchestra performs with Emil Paur conducting.

first director and conductor. But he was also subject to complex internal politics, managing a staff and musicians under the supervision of the Orchestra Committee of the Art Society, whose patrons actually paid for the musicians and voted on management decisions. The Pittsburgh Orchestra, then, actually "belonged" to the Orchestra Committee. This left Archer in a difficult position, whatever public success the orchestra might have. He faced disagreement over who should be the concert master, for example, after dismissing an orchestra manager who had ingratiated himself with the music patrons. He confronted controversies over how much the musicians should be paid. Patriotic music lovers passionately debated the orchestra's repertoire, particularly how much American versus European music should be included in the programs.

There was also disagreement over whether the orchestra's musicians had to be residents of Pittsburgh. In its early years, under Archer, most of the Pittsburgh Orchestra's eighty musicians came from other cities for the twelve-to-fifteen-week season, but they did not live or remain in Pittsburgh. To establish a musical culture in the city, many believed that only musicians based in Pittsburgh should be hired. Nevertheless, Archer, focused on the music and sometimes overbearing, irritated the Art Society by contracting soloists without gaining permission from his governing board. He seemed

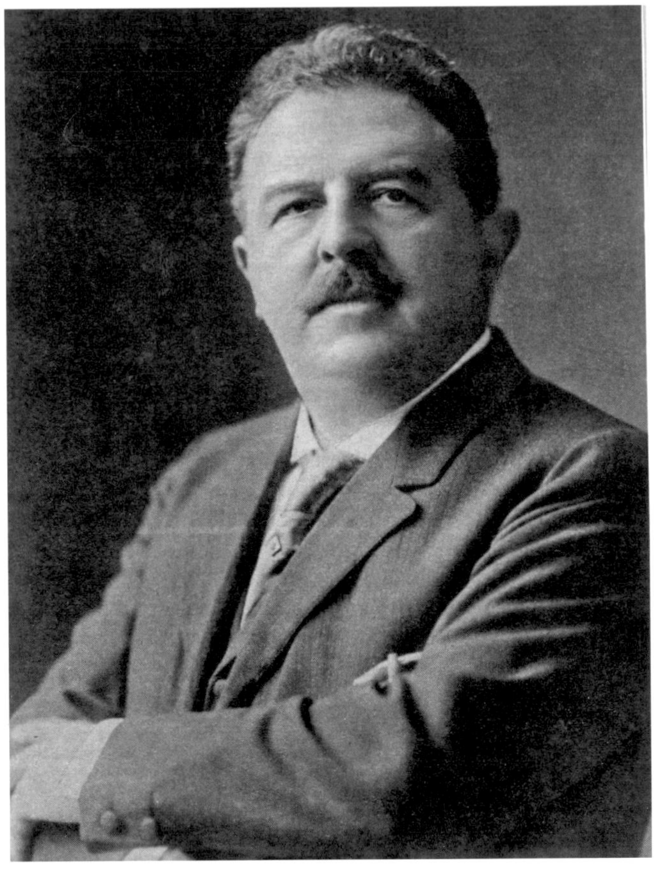

*Victor Herbert served as director of the Pittsburgh Symphony
Orchestra from 1898 to 1904.*

surprised when his contract was not renewed in 1898, although he probably
should not have been.

Archer's successor, Victor Herbert (1859–1924), was a flamboyant,
Irish-born conductor who brought a complete change of pace to the orchestra when his term began in 1898. For his Pittsburgh debut on Founder's
Day, November 3, 1898, a grand audience assembled in the Music Hall,
including Carnegie, Frick, their wives, and music critics from New York,
Boston, and elsewhere, doubtless brought at Carnegie's expense. After
the concert, the *Pittsburgh Times* proclaimed "Victory for Herbert," and
the orchestra became a social phenomenon in the city. The next year,
125 carriages lined the streets in front of the Music Hall for the start of the
1899–1900 season.[12]

While working in Pittsburgh, Herbert composed "Babes in Toyland"

(1903) and played many of his other compositions with the orchestra, and the city's audience for popular, accessible orchestra music began to expand. Carnegie was proud of Herbert and the success of the orchestra: "I think it is the best orchestra, with the exception possibly of the Boston Symphony, in the United States."[13] He was so enthusiastic that he twice paid to bring the Pittsburgh Orchestra to New York's Carnegie Hall to show it off; at one of these concerts, he noted with pleasure, three thousand people were in attendance, including the fashionable New York "four hundred." Reviews of the concert were generally favorable, although one music critic declared the wind, string, and brass players mediocre—"and yet the band plays like a house on fire."[14] Musical purists always held Herbert's success with band music and light opera against him, expecting more gravitas from serious orchestras. Shortly before he died in 1901, the ousted Archer published his sour opinion of Herbert's Pittsburgh orchestra: this "specimen of the modern colossal orchestra," he wrote, "may be accessible to the 'groundlings,' but it is calculated to make the judicious grieve."[15]

As a leader, Herbert was "one of the boys," inviting his players out to drink German beer after their concerts. The sacralization of symphony music as a high art, with concomitant strict codes of behavior for performers and audience alike, had not yet fully taken hold in Pittsburgh. William Nimick Frew, however, then the president of the Institute and mindful of the orchestra's importance to Pittsburgh's cultural reputation, kept a watchful eye over the musicians' behavior. He wrote Archer that musicians at afternoon concerts should wear "white shirts, black neckties, black frock or cut-away coats and dark trousers," and that they should not leave the platform while a concert was in progress, finding that practice "very objectionable . . . and I think annoying to the audience." "The talking and laughing among the players," he insisted, "should, by all means be stopped." He later reprimanded Herbert for an unfortunate "relaxation of discipline" among the players, pointing out the behavior of one obnoxious musician who was unsuccessfully trying to gain the attention of two ladies in the audience.[16] Herbert left Pittsburgh in 1904 to continue his career with his own Victor Herbert Orchestra, presenting programs of light music on tour and at summer resorts for many years, even as he continued to produce operettas such as *Naughty Marietta.*

The next music director brought yet another change of direction—a commitment to strict interpretation of the classical repertoire. Emil Paur (1855–1932), the former conductor of both the Boston Symphony Orchestra and the New York Philharmonic, brought exacting standards to Pittsburgh, remaining until the orchestra disbanded in 1910. The theatrics of Herbert's leadership were missed by some, but connoisseurs appreciated the orchestra's new sound; it had lost a "certain acidity," wrote one, but gained "plasticity, unison, spirit and sonority." Others found Pauer's repertoire too heady. Mrs. Taylor Allderdice, the head of the Symphony Committee, remarked, "Pauer was a man of high ideals who refused to slip down to the audience's level. After Herbert, the contrast was too great and he knocked the love of music out of a number of people. He played too far over their heads. He played to the musicians and took the people to the music while Herbert brought the music to the people."[17]

The orchestra's fifteen years at the Music Hall had many highlights. At the second concert, Edward MacDowell, then America's foremost composer, appeared as a soloist in his *Piano Concerto No. 1*. In 1904, guest conductor Richard Strauss introduced *Till Eulenspiegel* to Pittsburgh, joining his wife, Pauline, in performing groups of his songs with orchestral and piano accompaniment. His Bavarian sense of humor provided a quaint gag: a pair of photos of the orchestra in which Strauss and Victor Herbert have exchanged places, taking turns posing on the podium and behind a bass fiddle. At the Pittsburgh Orchestra's final concert, in 1910, Emil Paur played Brahms's *Piano Concerto No. 2* and conducted his own symphony *In der Natur*. A program note on that occasion extolled the orchestra for being "ranked by musical critics and patrons of arts as third in artistic importance in America."[18] There was no hint that this concert was its swan song.

Soon the newspapers were publishing reports about the orchestra's need for a $1 million endowment, which would guarantee $50,000 per year for operations. After fifteen years, however, Pittsburgh's old-guard businessmen had exhausted their willingness to pay for a superb orchestra, and new donors were needed. By midyear the fund-raising efforts were seen to be woefully short, and the Arts Society voted to suspend concerts for a year, a strategy that doomed the orchestra, since its musicians needed to take jobs elsewhere.[19] The one-year suspension of concerts led to the termination of the orchestra. The historian C. Hax McCullough noted that the orchestra had played 260 concerts in Pittsburgh and 190 in other cities (usually more lucrative). It had played Carnegie Hall in New York and in Boston, Chicago, Cleveland, Cincinnati, and other major cities.

The next sixteen years saw the outbreak of World War I in Europe in 1914 and America's eventual entry into that war. During this period, the Music Hall featured traveling orchestras from other cities under the aegis of the Pittsburgh Orchestra Association. When the Pittsburgh Symphony Orchestra finally revived in 1926, it launched its program in the much larger auditorium at nearby Syria Mosque, built in 1915 with thirty-five hundred seats. The acoustics were not of the same standard, and the musicians initially had to accept very little pay, but the orchestra survived, eventually growing to a size that the Music Hall could scarcely accommodate. When the Pittsburgh Opera finally formed, it too made its home at Syria Mosque, which provided the staging facilities the Music Hall lacked.

Still, even without the orchestra, the Music Hall was the venue for many musical events. By 1927, Charles Heinroth's free organ recitals had attracted strong community interest, while other concerts and recitals also drew large audiences. The crowd attending a performance by Fritz Kreisler that year led hall manager Roy Ambrose to say the hall needed to expand its seating capacity. Attendance in 1927 reached 223,698, and the next year Ambrose reported, "This is the real crowning achievement in the matter of musical service to the public of Pittsburgh. In this day of radio transmission, jazz music, and high speed transportation, there is yet a place where the inspiring classics of old masters may be heard and without cost."[20]

ORGAN MUSIC FOR THE MASSES

Charles Heinroth's popular organ recital marked the culmination of one of Andrew Carnegie's long-term interests. He had become a donor of organs by chance, after donating a pipe organ in 1873 to the small Swedenborgian church his father attended in Allegheny City. Through the years, incessant requests from other churches followed. At first he enjoyed having Presbyterian churches swallow their pride and ask him for an organ, but he was inexorably drawn into an interdenominational whirlpool of churches that needed free organs. By 1901 he had a system that required a church to fill out a questionnaire and show its financial resources; if it were not deeply in debt, he would have his business secretary, Robert Franks, and his investigative assistant James Bertram (who devised the library-giving system) grant the request. He once wrote an applicant for a charity that he must refuse her request, saying, "It would be a case of Organs over again"—a task that took too much of his assistants' time in correspondence and research.[21] Eventually, he donated 7,689 church organs, distributed throughout the English-speaking world. Organ music always brought him pleasure, and he had pipe organs in both his New York home and his castle at Skibo, where he would begin the day and energize his guests with rousing music and soothing spiritual strains. Pittsburgh's mammoth pipe organ was a grand symbol of public music, its pipes defining the background of the stage, its concealed console rising up before the audience so all could see and admire the organist at work.

The Music Hall's organ enjoyed its heyday around the turn of the twentieth century, when theater organs evolved from the pipe organs that had been designed for liturgical use. In motion picture theaters, these organs became surrogates for a full-scale orchestra that could emulate the sounds of the trumpet, clarinet, flute, violin, drums, castanets, tom-toms, gongs, and so on. At one point, there were orchestral organs all over the United States, with famous ones in Portland, Maine, and San Diego, but theater organs began to disappear with the arrival of the "talkies" in 1927–28. Today the Carnegie Music Hall has one of the few large examples still to be found, with 130 stops and 8,600 pipes. The organ took shape in 1918, when the original Ferrand and Votey organ was rebuilt by the Aolian-Skinner Organ Company. The organ was reconstructed in 1933–34, when it was modernized with a new console and a player's keyboard and about one-third of the pipes were replaced. Two new concert grand pianos were also ordered in 1933, one of which could be played from the organ keyboard. The system was improved again in 1950 through a gift from the H. J. Heinz Company. Today the large antique is seldom played, since its construction of wood, leather, and other materials is expensive to restore and maintain.

Still, for a time, Pittsburgh, with its many churches, was known as the organ capital of the world. Over the years, millions attended the free organ recitals at Carnegie Music Hall, which continued into the 1970s. At a typical recital, the music ran from Bach's *Passacaglia* and Batiste's *Song of Hope,* to Saint Saëns's *Omphale's Spinning Wheel,* Grieg's *Peer Gynt Suite,* and Elmore's *Donkey Dance,* to Handel's *Largo,* Schubert's *Ave Maria,* and the *Londonderry Air.* The audience frequently sang along with well-known tunes.

The art of transcribing orchestral music for organ performance was a special skill. The organist-composer Edwin H. Lemare, who took over for Frederic Archer as director of the Music Hall in 1902, was excellent at crafting such organ arrangements, including such favorites as Wagner's *Ride of the Valkyries* and the *William Tell Overture.* Charles Heinroth took over as organist and director of music in 1907, serving for twenty-five years, until 1932, when he resigned to become head of the Department of Music at the City College of New York. Heinroth's concerts regularly filled the Music Hall, and when he left, many were saddened: "On the street, in streetcars, he is accosted by men—plain men, simple men, working men—who tell him of the pleasure they have had in his playing and the sorrow they have in his going away."[22]

Marshal Bidwell succeeded Heinroth in 1932, winning an organ recital competition against seventeen other enthusiastic applicants. Bidwell promised to be a crowd-pleaser, declaring, "There must not be a single dull moment, either from the standpoint of the material or the manner of its performance."[23] Bidwell lectured about the history and development of the organ, employing stereopticon slides, and brought in students from Carnegie Tech to perform a cappella concerts. When Bidwell died in 1966, after thirty-four years of service, the audience for free organ recitals had been declining for a decade. Leon Arkus, the director of the Museum of Art, once observed in a candid moment, "If I had to listen to Marshall Bidwell play the 'Flight of the Bumblebee' one more time, I would commit suicide."[24]

In 1974, Paul Koch, director of music at St. Paul's Cathedral, became the Music Hall's organist-in-charge. He revived the free Sunday-afternoon organ recitals at Carnegie Music Hall, continuing a tradition that still appealed to some but that gradually faded as the audience dwindled and the aging organ became unplayable. Pittsburgh was one of the last major cities to perpetuate the free municipal organ-recital tradition in a public hall that was not affiliated with any church or religion.

THE HALL THROUGH THE DECADES

The range and caliber of musical events that took place at Carnegie Music Hall over more than a century would have pleased Andrew Carnegie: Harold Bauer, Ferruccio Busoni, Pablo Casals, Lynnwood Farnam, Virgil Fox, Fernando Germani, Percy Grainger, Jascha Heifetz, Myra Hess, Hans Kindler, Fritz Kreisler, John McCormack, Nathan Milstein, Mme. Lillian Nordica, Sigrid Onegin, Vladimir de Pachmann, Luciano Pavarotti, Gregor Piatigorsky, Ezio Pinza, Rosa Ponselle, Sergei Rachmaninoff, Eugene Ysaye, and on and on. The hall hosted recitals by the world's best string quartets and the Pittsburgh Chamber Music Society, as well as famous poets and readers, brought to Pittsburgh by the International Poetry Forum. A few operas were staged there, and the Carnegie-Mellon Philharmonic Orchestra, one of the best university orchestras in the country, used the hall for decades. The hall has also offered jazz and folk music from such musicians as Maynard Ferguson, Ella Fitzgerald, Arlo Guthrie, and Chuck Mangione.

Since the 1970s, the Music Hall has had three managers: Bernita Mills, Fred Sereno, and Eileen Twigger. For a time, its space was increasingly given over to lecture series, award ceremonies, private speaking engagements, school graduations, and wedding parties, but Twigger maintains that the hall "is at its greatest in intimate musical performances, whether that be string quartets, recitals, contemporary classical or soft rock music."[25] Institute president David Hillenbrand restored the hall's service spaces in 2005 and began the process of returning the hall to its original beauty. By 2007, the carpeting on the first floor had been replaced, and the seats on the main floor had been recovered. The "Star's Dressing Room" had been upgraded, the windows sealed, the walls restored. The auditorium, though still very much a Victorian hall, no longer seemed neglected, but fresh and inviting.[26]

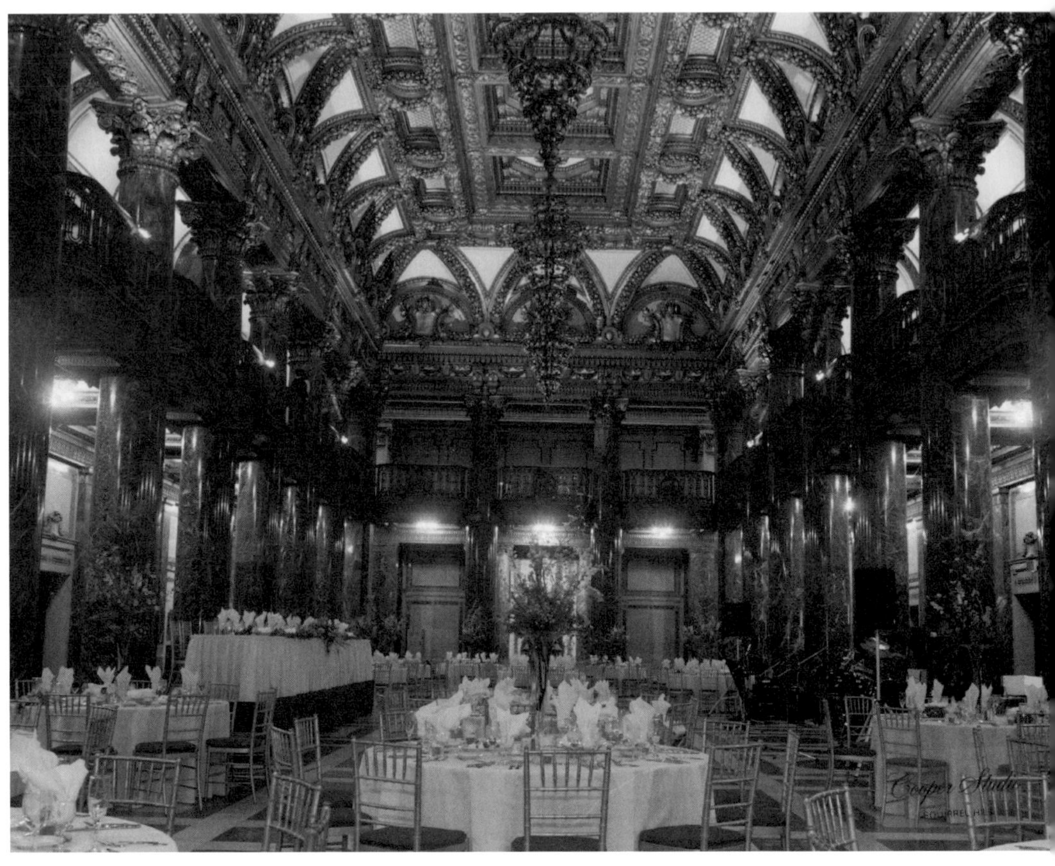

The ornate foyer of the Music Hall has been a spectacular setting for countless private and public events for more than a century.

Challenges remained. The hall needs to be air-conditioned if it is to be used in hot weather. Better lighting would allow visitors to more easily see the portrait gallery of past presidents and other notables that lines the marble corridor outside the auditorium. By 2010, the storied pipe organ could scarcely be played, giving off squeaks and howls in addition to music. Periodically, lovers of classic organs approached Twigger and offered their services to work on the instrument, but she was reluctant to have anyone "tinker with an instrument of that value and antiquity," holding out for the day that will bring a proper full-scale restoration, along with a maintenance plan or endowment that will keep the organ playing well into the future.[27] Such a restoration—and the further renovation of Carnegie Music Hall itself—awaits major funding, board advocacy, and grassroots support.

     CARNEGIE MUSIC HALL

CARNEGIE LIBRARY OF PITTSBURGH

"Free to the People"

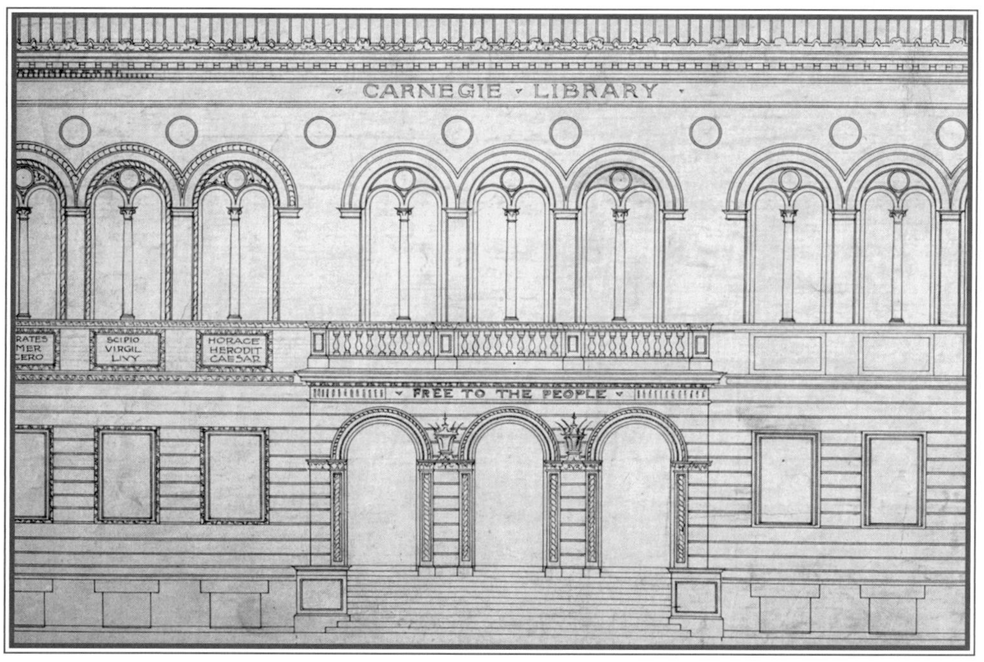

Detail of the blueprint of the Carnegie Library of Pittsburgh, as designed by Longfellow, Alden and Harlow in 1895.

"FREE TO THE PEOPLE" is carved in stone over the entrance to Carnegie Library of Pittsburgh and the doorways of many of the 2,509 libraries Andrew Carnegie donated. Carnegie donated the buildings only and required the community to support them. Typically, a community would be asked to annually provide one-tenth of the amount of his own gift; the public would thus benefit from a 10 percent return on the initial donation in perpetuity. "This was not philanthropy but a clever stroke of business," he joked, viewing himself as a businessman striking a bargain for the public.[1]

Competitor that he was, Carnegie was well aware of other benefactors who had given free libraries: Ezra Cornell in Ithaca, New York; George Peabody in New England and London; Walter Newberry in Chicago; Charles Bower Winn in Massachusetts; Enoch Pratt in Baltimore. Such nineteenth-century donors saw themselves as patriarchs of an extended family of readers—those people fortunate enough to enjoy access to their libraries. Such paternalism was typical of the social reform of the late nineteenth century, and library architects found ways to acknowledge patrons in their designs. A library would have private meeting rooms for trustees, symbolic fireplaces and hearths, colored glass, and a place of honor reserved for a portrait or bust of the donor.

Like other benefactors, Carnegie saw his libraries as a way of doing good work for the community. He started by erecting libraries in places with which he had personal associations, such as Allegheny City, where he had lived as a boy. The 1890 dedication of the Allegheny Free Library was a national event, President Benjamin Harrison delivering the keynote address. Eight years later, Carnegie asked William Nimick Frew, president of Carnegie Institute, to oversee erecting a monument to James Anderson in front of the library, which was dedicated before enormous crowds in 1904.[2] Popularly called "The Reading Workman," the bronze sculpture depicts a seated laborer next to an anvil, reading a large book, while behind him on a pedestal is a bust of Colonel Anderson. Carnegie's autobiography repeats the inscription Carnegie penned for this monument:

To Colonel James Anderson, Founder of Free Libraries in Western Pennsylvania. He opened his library to working boys, and on Saturday afternoons acted as librarian, thus dedicating not only his books but himself to the noble work. This monument is erected in grateful remembrance by Andrew Carnegie, one of the "working boys" to whom were thus opened the precious treasures of knowledge and imagination through which youth may ascend.

He continues in his autobiography:

This is but a slight tribute and gives only a faint idea of the depth of gratitude which I feel for what he did for me and my companions. It was from my own early experience that I decided there was no use to which money could be applied so productive of good to boys and girls who have good within them and ability and ambition to develop it, as the founding of a public library in a community which is willing to support it as a municipal institution. I am sure that the future of those libraries I have been privileged to found will prove the correctness of this opinion. For if one boy in each library district, by having access to one of these libraries, is half as much benefited as I was by having access to Colonel Anderson's four hundred well-worn volumes, I shall consider they have not been established in vain.[3]

Carnegie outfitted many western Pennsylvania towns with libraries: Braddock (1889), Allegheny City (1890), Johnstown (1891, replacing the library destroyed by the 1889 Johnstown Flood), Homestead (1896), Duquesne (1901), Carnegie (1898; formerly Mansfield: the town changed its name in appreciation). The Braddock, Homestead, and Duquesne libraries were owned not by municipalities, but by Carnegie Steel, which constructed them, maintained them, and delivered coal for their heating systems. These were mill-town community centers, with showers for workers, pools and gymnasiums, bowling alleys, barber shops, billiard rooms, and meeting rooms, exceeding in both style and cost most of his later libraries. A board of U.S. Steel executives ran these libraries until the 1960s, when the company decided to get out of the library business, "selling" the Braddock, Homestead, and Duquesne libraries to the local school districts for one dollar each. The Duquesne library could not be supported by the community and was demolished in 1968 to make way for a housing development; it was far too grand and expensive for the community to support.

The Allegheny Free Library had established the pattern for municipal governance that Carnegie typically followed. Responsibility for this library fell to a commission comprising six members, three appointed by the city and three by Carnegie. Allegheny City held an architectural competition, inviting seven firms to compete. The winning design, by Smithmeyer and Pelz, the architects of the new Library of Congress building in 1886, lavished upon the Allegheny Library the customary signs of paternalistic opulence: a massive fireplace with a portrait of Carnegie on the mantel, a stained-glass skylight that gave the interior a religious atmosphere, mosaic floors,

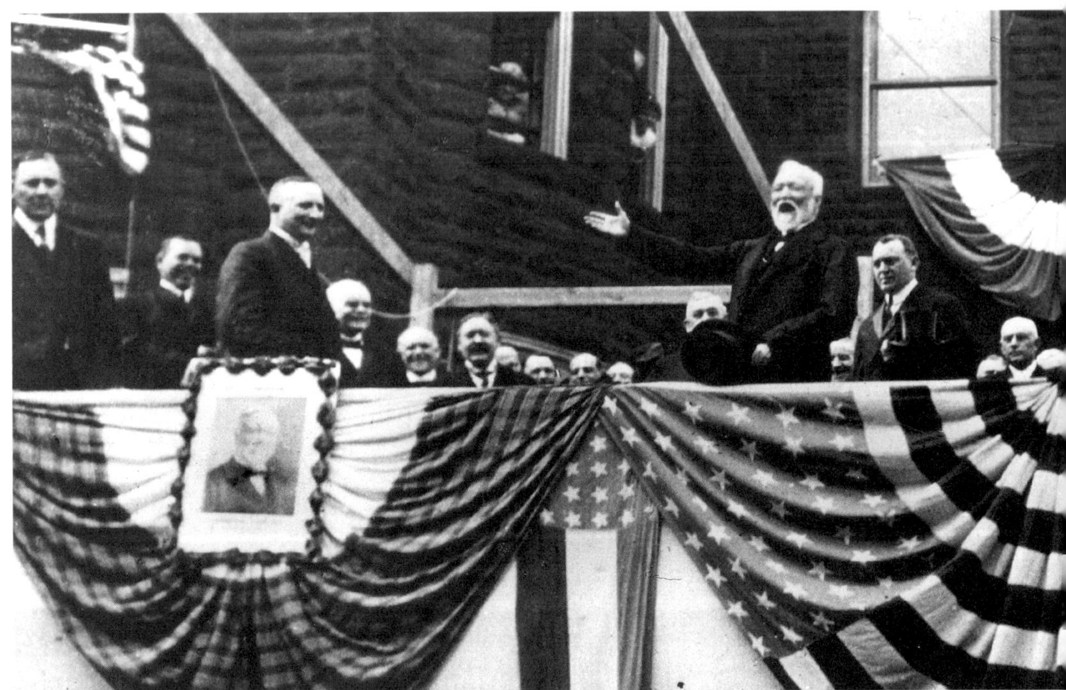

Carnegie delivers a speech in 1914, on the twenty-fifth anniversary of the Braddock Library. Built in 1889, the Braddock branch was Carnegie's first American library in the United States.

a frieze featuring the names of twenty-six American authors, a wainscoted Trustees Room, a sweeping staircase.

By the time Carnegie Library of Pittsburgh was being planned, the 1892 Homestead strike and Carnegie's role in breaking the steelworkers' union had triggered a national debate over whether communities should accept his "tainted money."[4] Carnegie, sensitive to criticism, shifted to the second phase of his library giving after erecting the central library in Pittsburgh and developed a more objective program for awarding libraries. With an eye on costs and a desire to delegate decision making, he moved from what he called his "retail" to his "wholesale" system of giving libraries. In 1897, he hired a personal secretary, James Bertram, to oversee the dispensing of libraries. Bertram streamlined the process: when a town asked for a library, Bertram, famously sharp-eyed and testy, acted as the bad cop while Carnegie remained above the fray. Bertram's position was difficult: he knew that many requests for libraries were not really about libraries at all, but about obtaining free money from Carnegie to erect multipurpose civic buildings. In response to a proposal from Anthony, Kansas, he wrote: "It is all very well for you to plan your building as a dance hall, club, YMCA, dining room, kitchen, etc, but remember Mr. Carnegie is paying for a Library Building and not for this kind of miscellaneous general convenience."[5]

Whenever a letter requesting a library came in, Bertram sent the applicant a detailed questionnaire asking the size of the town's population, whether it had any other libraries, what the size of its book collection was, and what its circulation figures were. If initial requirements were met, Bertram asked the amount the town was willing to pledge for the library's annual maintenance, whether a site was being provided, and the amount of money already available. At the same time, the buildings themselves became more austere. Pittsburgh, with its eight branches built between 1898 and 1910, was the proving ground for this strategy. Bertram had a formula in which Carnegie offered two dollars per capita, as of the last census, to erect a building. He continuously challenged town officials about money wasted on pretentious architecture and useless space. Efficiency minded, he was drawn inevitably into architectural design, and his familiar response to elaborate plans was, "This will not do."

The foremost architect of the multipurpose library building, typical of an earlier era, was Henry Hobson Richardson, whose Winn Memorial Library, in Woburn, Massachussetts (1876–79), was in a Romanesque style, its design drawn from medieval monastic libraries, including a row of two-story alcoves with bookshelves facing the common central hall.[6] The fledgling American Library Association (ALA), however, founded in 1876, was in agreement with the new austerity espoused by Bertram. The ALA discouraged alcoved book halls with high shelves requiring a ladder, as well as sheltered galleries and niches, reminiscent of sixteenth-century Europe, largely because modern librarians could not supervise such spaces efficiently.

Thus, the first Pittsburgh branch library, built in Lawrenceville by Alden and Harlow in 1898, signaled a break from the Richardsonian style. The famous "Carnegie library style" was reflected in Bertram's pamphlet "Notes on Library Buildings" (1911), which codified his architectural criteria for libraries, especially smaller ones, recommending a lecture room, reading rooms for adults and children, a staff room, a centrally located librarian's desk, twelve-to-fifteen-foot ceilings (in an era before air conditioning), and large windows six to seven feet above the floor (at a time when electric lights were limited). Contrary to popular lore, no architectural style was recommended for the exterior, nor was it necessary to put Andrew Carnegie's name on the building. In the interests of efficiency, fireplaces were discouraged, since that wall space could hold five to six hundred books. Using Carnegie's "reformed" English spelling, Bertram declared his mission

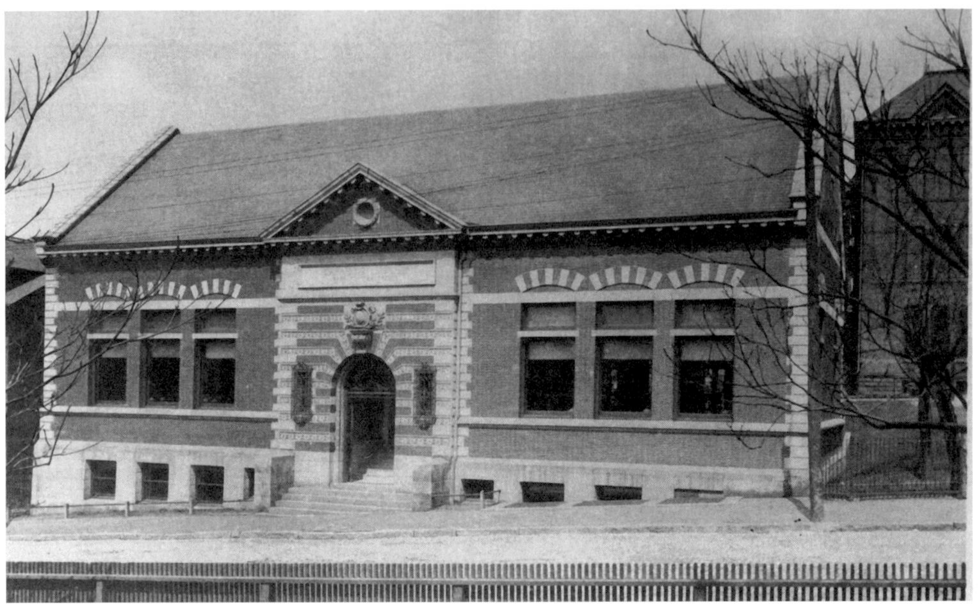

The Lawrenceville branch of Carnegie Library, completed in 1898, was the first branch built in Pittsburgh and a model for free branch libraries in other cities.

"to obtain for the money the utmost amount of effectiv accommodation, consistent with good taste in bilding."[7]

There were no strict requirements about furniture, but most of it came from the Library Bureau, established by Melvil Dewey in 1888, which sold standardized chairs, tables, catalogs, and bookshelves. Victorian bentwood chairs were an early recommendation, but the Library Bureau, sensitive to high-minded artistic trends, after 1897 endorsed the Arts and Crafts aesthetic in furniture such as tables, card catalogs, and file cabinets; the material was oak, the bases massive and square—a style thought to bridge the gap between basic function and classic design. The round-backed Windsor chair was promoted for comfort and durability. The catalogs also offered a full range of office supplies, making it easy for a library to buy everything it needed from one supplier.

The public library system in Pittsburgh was a force for civic stability and social change, and librarians often had a missionary zeal. In its early years, Carnegie Library sent "Library Visitors" into homes to tell stories and help children learn to read, offering classes in English and "Americanization" to immigrants. During the Depression, in the midst of economic and social chaos, the library was a place where civility still reigned. In 1938, the

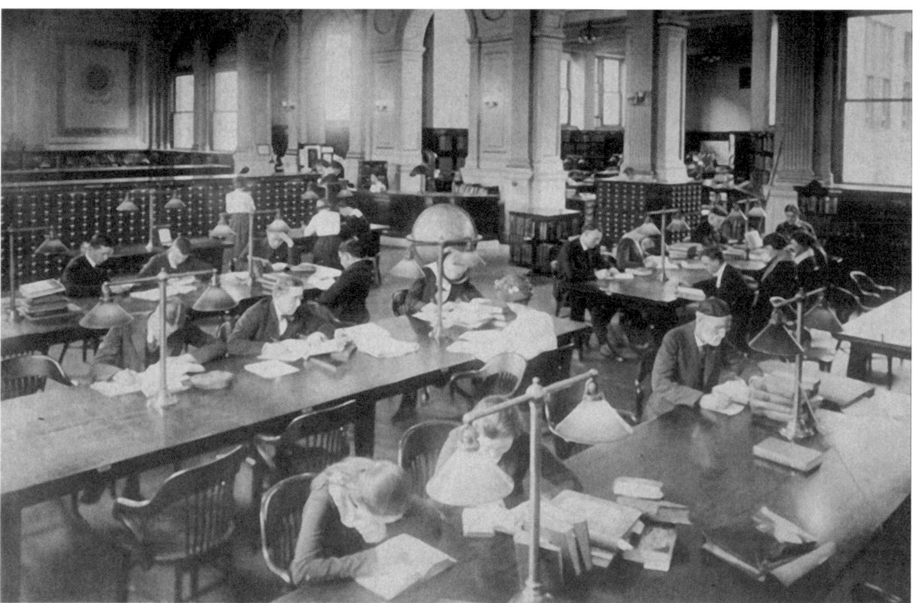

The large second-floor reading room of the Pittsburgh branch as it looked in 1907. Melvil Dewey's Library Bureau furniture gave it the same ambience for more than a century.

Gillespie Room was opened—the first "browsing room" in a public library, where the public could enjoy the librarians' choice of three thousand of the library's most attractive books in a fine room with expensive chairs and reading lamps. During World Wars I and II, the library was where people gained the technical skills they needed to work in the war economy. Social change was debated in the meeting rooms of many branch libraries, especially during the Equal Rights Movement of the 1960s. Carnegie Library began to serve the blind and the physically handicapped in 1907, taking steps toward normalizing participation in society by the blind and physically handicapped long before federal legislation required it. The Pennsylvania Division's genealogical collection and its classes in genealogical research promoted pride in family and ethnic traditions. The Oakland branch became the home of the International Poetry Forum and its popular series of public readings and developed an excellent library of contemporary poetry. In the 1980s, the library began offering family counseling and helped individuals learn how to prepare their taxes. With the advent of personal computers, the library offered classes in computer literacy, serving as a place where citizens could access the Internet without buying personal computers.

A famous example of the Carnegie Library's importance is how the playwright August Wilson used it as a youth. Upset by a high school teacher's unfounded charges of plagiarism, Wilson dropped out of high school as a teenager, in the 1960s, but continued his education by reading books and magazines at his local branch library. At age fourteen, he walked into the Hazelwood Branch of Carnegie Library "and changed my life: I discovered the Negro section with its 30 or so books. . . . That gave me the proof that it was possible to be a writer. . . . I wanted to see my book up there too."[8] His cycle of ten plays about the black experience in America, which sets all but one play in Pittsburgh, became a national phenomenon. Wilson later said that his favorite honor—outweighing his two Pulitzers and scores of other awards—was the high school diploma he received in 1999 from Carnegie Library of Pittsburgh.

RUNNING THE LIBRARY

For most of the twentieth century, the library's funding depended primarily upon the precarious financial condition of the city of Pittsburgh, which owned the buildings Carnegie had donated and annually allocated funds for staffing, maintenance, and improvements. For its first half century, the library survived on the basis of the missionary values Carnegie had set down, administered frugally by directors who faced continually expanding services, the financial struggle ironically masked by the palatial home of the Central Branch in Oakland. After World War II, the trend toward regional and state services became greater, and funding began to come from government sources beyond the city, including the county and the commonwealth. In 1994, the primary funding strategy finally changed, when the Allegheny County Regional Assets District (ARAD) was formed to support nonprofit organizations annually through a 1 percent county tax. This expanded support is appropriate: the library's importance to the region was fully revealed by a 2004 economic study that pointed out that more than half of the city's residents, and one out of every five of the county's residents, had a Carnegie Library card. In two separate independent 2004 studies, Pittsburgh was ranked third in "literacy" and fourth in "library services."[9]

Its strong position in the community is due in large part to the fact that, from its early days, Pittsburgh's Carnegie Library has been blessed with a series of distinguished directors. Several rose high in the national ranks of the American Library Association, including Edwin Anderson, Ralph Munn, and Keith Doms. Many had international renown. Munn was asked to design the library systems of Australia and New Zealand. The eighth Carnegie Library director, Robert Croneberger, noted, "When I went to New Zealand I was treated like a king because of Ralph Munn."[10]

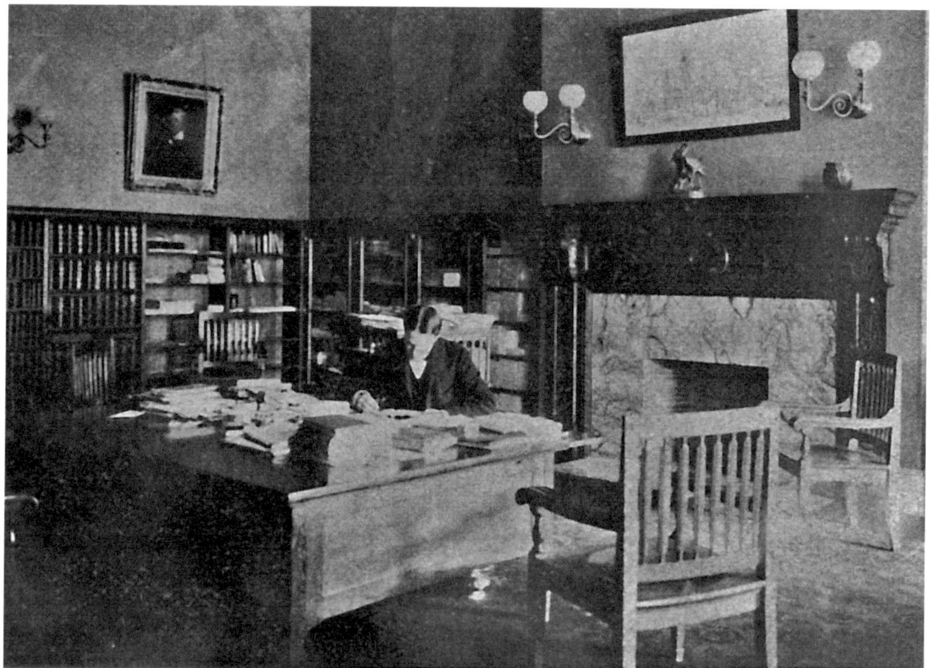

*Edwin Anderson, first director of Carnegie Library of Pittsburgh, developed
ambitious programs from 1895 until 1904.*

One deputy library director reported that international colleagues "treat
you with a kind of reverence for working at Andrew Carnegie's library."[11]
Barbara Mistick, the tenth director, echoed this perception: "People look to
this Library for a leadership position, because we were the first. So much is
known about the Library and the Institute globally. That should make us
think twice about how we evolve and the leadership we project. We can't
lose the history that made this all possible."[12]

That history began with the first director, the energetic thirty-four-
year-old Edwin H. Anderson, a trusted administrator drafted from Carnegie's library at Braddock to direct the new facility in Pittsburgh from
1895 to 1904. A workhorse, Anderson opened six branch libraries during his
tenure and developed home libraries, reading clubs, summer playground
services, and book loans to schools in neighborhoods without branches. The
book collection grew from 27,000 held in the Central Branch to 222,000
held throughout the system, the staff from 19 to 113, and city appropriations
grew from $65,000 to $158,000.[13]

While library apprentices were initially taught the "library hand" for
keeping legible records, soon Melvil Dewey's Library Bureau was producing

standardized library cards, on which information could be typed. Card catalogs had been created for each branch by 1898. Pittsburgh was the first large U.S. city to have a fully organized Children's Department with centralized supervision over the entire system, and it was the first to offer a "training class" for children's librarians, beginning in 1900. Anderson endorsed the belief of the U.S. commissioner of education, William T. Harris: "Give me the child.... The state shall have the man."[14]

In his 1904 "Annual Report," Anderson explained the social activism and moral reform he had tried to inculcate: "The public schools of our country teach the children to read; they cannot teach them what to read. Knowing how to read, nothing can keep them from reading. We have plenty of evidence to show what sensational and injurious stuff they do read if better is not provided. Scattered throughout this city are innumerable shops where the most debasing and sensational literature is daily sold to children. Is it not a wise expenditure of effort for a free library to enter vigorously into competition with these purveyors and place within the reach of every child of our city all the clean and wholesome literature it can secure?" In poor neighborhoods, he installed "home libraries"—small bookcases housed in homes where children could meet each week. A "library visitor," usually a volunteer, came to the home libraries to talk about books, read aloud, and tell stories. If a home library could not be established, the library sponsored "reading clubs" that met at school in the evenings. By 1905, there were thirty-one home libraries, thirty-seven reading clubs, and fifty-six "school stations," where books could be borrowed. By 1914, some twenty-four adult stations had been established in fire stations, seven in department stores, and three in factories.

Anderson's training class for children's librarians enjoyed similar success. It was established on October 1, 1900, with five students in a two-year class. Soon, however, other libraries wished to send experienced staff to receive specific training, and a special one-year course was developed in 1906 for those with library experience from a recognized library school. Carnegie himself supplied more funds for the Training School for Children's Librarians. From 1901 to 1915, the Training School for Children's Librarians was a department of the library, funded in part by Carnegie himself, but in 1914 the newly formed Carnegie Corporation of New York, granting what would become an annual appropriation, required that it become a department of Carnegie Institute. It subsequently changed its name to Carnegie Library School, with an increased endowment. Then, in 1930, it moved to the Carnegie Institute of Technology, training most of the librarians in the region; in 1962, to maintain accreditation with the American Library Association, which required association with a liberal arts university, it became part of the University of Pittsburgh. At that time it had about fifty students, half of them part time. It grew rapidly at the University of Pittsburgh, from 50 students in 1962 to 397 by 1965. It eventually became one of the few schools in the country to offer a doctorate in library science, later evolving into the highly ranked School of Library and Information Science.[15]

Anderson also oversaw the founding of the library's Department of Science and Technology, launched in April 1900 when Harrison W. Craver, a chemist and metallurgist, joined the staff of the Reference Department. He also established a significant architectural library in Pittsburgh, a city visibly without physical grace, through a bequest of Julius D. Bernd (1830–92).[16] This type of specialized collection (only Boston and New York had architectural holdings of similar significance) helped make the library so important to the city. In his 1894 dedication speech for the library, Carnegie recognized the import of Bernd's gift and expressed his hope that it would set an example: "His name will be first upon the tablet at the entrance which is to record for all time the names of our benefactors."[17] To ensure the success of the new collection, Anderson made the library the home of the newly established Pittsburgh Architects' Club, which held its organizational meeting on December 9, 1896. Three years later, he helped the club secure "permanent and commodious rooms in the Carnegie Institute" and exhibition space for surveys of contemporary architecture. He asked local architects to advise the library about which books to purchase and instituted the library's publication of annotated lists of architecture books, increasing the audience for architecture materials. Eventually, the costs of maintaining a comprehensive collection exceeded the resources of the Bernd legacy, but the architectural collection still exists, an indication of the Institute's fostering of local societies and special interests.

Anderson resigned on December 1, 1904, just as the library embarked on a major expansion. Upon his resignation, his successor, Anderson Hopkins, wrote, "To have built up an institution of such magnitude and excellence is a great work, and to have done this in less than even the brief space of a decade is the safe mark of a master hand. . . . In the departure of Mr. Anderson not only this library but the whole library profession has lost . . . one of the strongest men who has ever engaged in this work."[18]

Hopkins, an experienced librarian from Chicago's John Crerar Library and the Louisville Public Library, took over on January 1, 1905, but retired because of ill health after only three and a half years. Still, he directed the Central Branch through the physical drama of its expansion. Another of Hopkins's legacies was the library's provision of services to the blind, beginning in 1907, with a home teacher teaching the blind how to read embossed books. He also tried to raise the city's appropriation to support the library's

expanding services, but the myth of a generous Carnegie "endowment"—
encouraged by the magnificent building that housed the library—hampered this attempt and, indeed, lived on in the minds of the public and
local politicians for most of the twentieth century. Thus, between 1904 and
1907, even while the enlarged library and Institute were being constructed,
library services themselves declined. No funds were available to pay for a
full staff when the library reopened in April 1907, and the Central Branch's
Children's Room operated under reduced hours for years. In 1909, library
hours of operation were reduced, staggered to cast the widest net possible
to serve the public.[19]

Harrison Craver, the chemist and metallurgist who had been central
to the founding of the library's fledgling Science and Technology Department, took over as the third head librarian on December 1, 1908, inheriting
a system with seven branches and 163 other outlets. City financial crises in
1915–17 city forced budget cutbacks for library operations, and fifty staff
members—about one-fourth of the total—had to be dismissed. Book purchasing and binding funds were cut to the bone, and eighty-one children's
agencies were closed. The last of the original eight branches, and by far
the largest, opened in Homewood on March 10, 1910, thanks to Carnegie's
willingness, in this one instance, to pay for land as well as a building (he
had lived in Homewood for a time before moving to New York). Craver
resigned on March 31, 1917.

The Board of Trustees now decided that whenever possible it would
promote the library's chief executive from within the Institute's staff, changing the position's title to "director." Accordingly, it appointed John Hopkins
Leete as the library's first director. Leete, the former dean of the School of
Applied Sciences at the Carnegie Institute of Technology, had no training
as a librarian, but established a pattern that would be seen in later years.
While later some of these skilled business executives without library training were criticized internally as being unsuited to the role, Leete was sensitive to the role of the library in the educational framework of Pittsburgh,
and he created standing committees to run a multitude of library agencies.
While World War I slowed library building nationally, it also triggered a
need for auxiliary libraries for servicemen in camps, on ships, and overseas.
The American Library Association and the Red Cross administered over
$1.6 million raised by public subscription to fund libraries for the armed
forces, and Pittsburgh's library participated wholeheartedly, its home city
a key producer of war materials and a barometer of patriotic feeling. "Win
the war" was the library's motto in 1918, and many employees left to assist in
the war effort. World War I also underscored the need to recognize foreign
languages and to serve immigrants; "Americanization" became central to

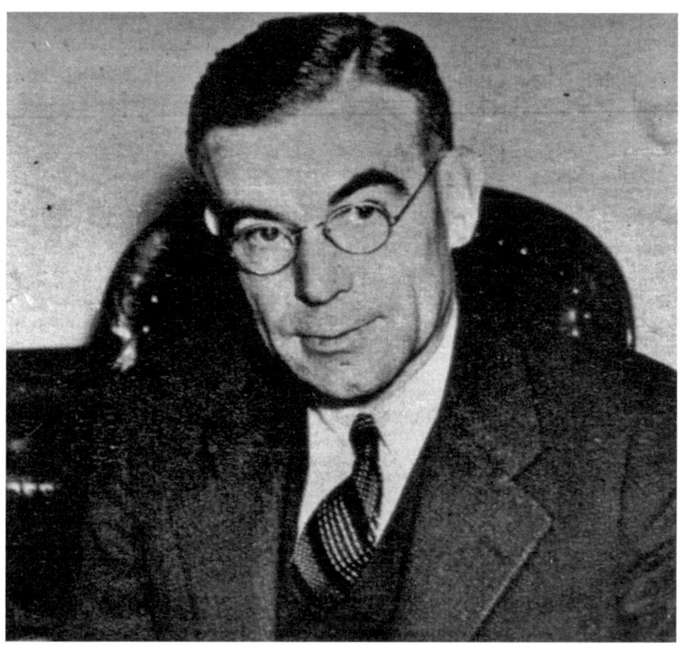

*Director Ralph Munn led the library for thirty-six years,
from 1928 until 1964.*

social policy in Pittsburgh. In 1921, the city's Chamber of Commerce opened an Immigration and Service Center, and the Carnegie Library developed foreign- and English-language book services.

When Leete resigned on June 7, 1928, because of ill health, Ralph Munn took over as director. Munn's thirty-six-year tenure would shape the library's policies for decades. A graduate of the University of Denver's law school and of the New York State Library School, Munn would later become the president of the American Library Association and develop the library systems of Australia and New Zealand. Munn took a philosophical view of libraries as educational centers, criticizing Carnegie's venerated policy of donating libraries to small communities, a policy that he felt kept the library movement in a "small-town" mode, hampered by a sense of comfortable neglect. When he took over in 1928, he found "matters which seemed to call for prompt attention" and proceeded to institute many changes to such library operations as ordering and cataloging books and binding publications.[20] Disciplined and conservative by instinct, he undertook a study of the entire system in 1929, concluding that circulation per capita was low compared to other cities. He found the reference services superior and the staff excellent, but he called for more downtown branch services and more county services.

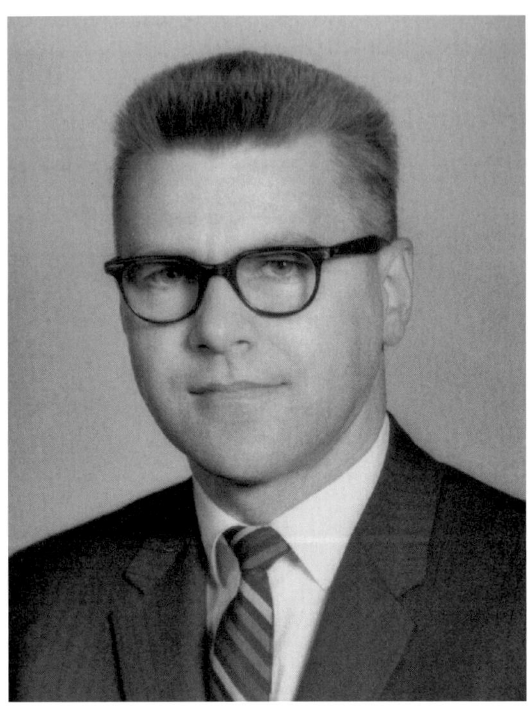

Keith Doms, library director from 1964 to 1969, scouted potential library sites in Allegheny County as services became more regional.

The Art Reference Division opened in 1930, with a strong collection in architecture, and the Music Division opened in 1938, with local musicians assembling funds to buy private libraries. These donors later became the Friends of the Music Library, devoted to expanding the library's musicology resources. The 1930s were also the Golden Age of Radio, and many library patrons now opted for hearing stories via soundwave, rather than borrowing "light reading"—romances and detective stories—from the library. The library chose to move toward more selective purchasing, focusing on books with literary merit or historical and social themes. The 1940s, because of World War II, saw constant turnover in the library's professional staff, as some enlisted, others became civilian librarians in army and navy facilities, and many left to work in industrial libraries that paid higher salaries. By the end of the war, the movement toward more regional services was under way, and in 1956 the library began lending materials free of charge to all residents of Allegheny County.

When Munn retired in 1964, Keith Doms, a graduate of the University of Wisconsin Library School and Munn's assistant director, took over. Like his predecessor, he was a student of library management, and he also went on to become president of the American Library Association. His Carnegie tenure witnessed the library's expanding role within a comprehensive state library system, as Carnegie Library became one of four state "resource centers," along with the Free Library of Philadelphia, the State Library in Harrisburg, and the Pennsylvania State University Library.

Following Doms, Anthony Martin served as director, from 1969 to 1986. Under his leadership, several new library branches opened: the new East Liberty Branch (1969), Squirrel Hill (1972), Sheraden (1980), and the new location for the Hill District Branch (1982). His attention to local issues resulted in the library becoming the home of the new International Poetry Forum (1969) and of the Martin Luther King Jr. Regional Reading Center (1970). Carnegie Library of Pittsburgh also became the first library to participate in the computerized cataloging services of the Ohio College Library Center (OCLC) (1973) and started shifting from the traditional Dewey Decimal System (DDS) to the more complex Library of Congress (LC) system, more appropriate to wide-ranging and scholarly research. Oddly, the library's transfer from DDS to LC cataloging was never completed, leading to the puzzling use of two systems, criticized by future director Herb Elish as an example of how unresponsive libraries were to readers' needs.

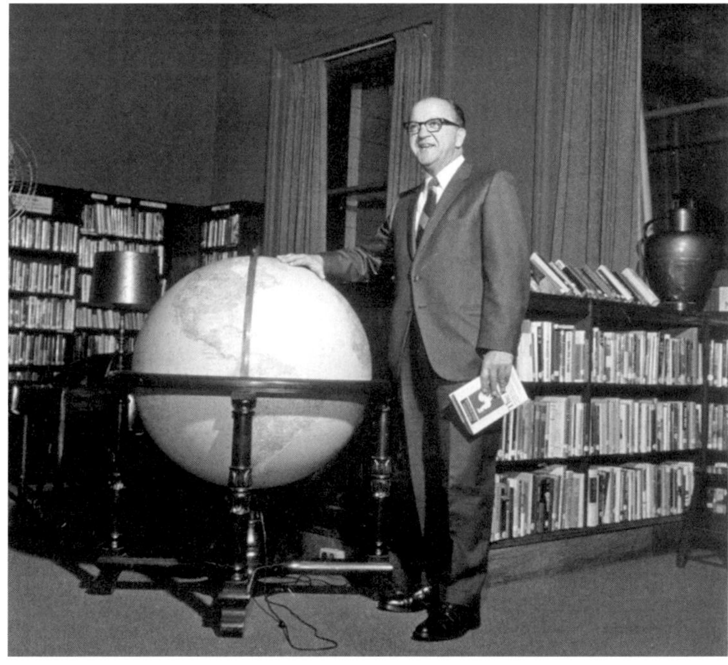

Director Anthony Martin ushered in a long period of stability in management from 1969 to 1986.

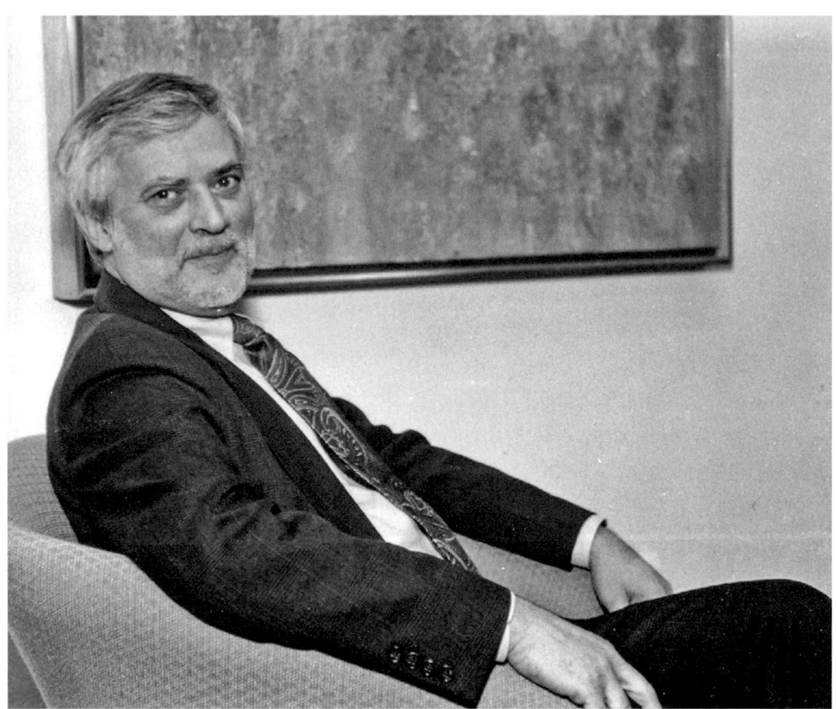

Robert Croneberger, director from 1986 until his death in 1998, advocated for libraries as centers for new social services.

During Martin's tenure, the presidency of Carnegie Institute and Library passed to Robert C. Wilburn, who wished to reshape the role of the library within the orbit of one unified institution called "The Carnegie." This meant that the library lost some of its autonomy and independence, and Martin, who believed the library's larger civic role was eroding under the new strategy, resigned in 1986 after sixteen years. After a six-month national search, Wilburn chose Robert Croneberger from among fifty applicants. At age forty-nine, he became an important part of Wilburn's new team of directors. Croneberger, a spirited thinker shaped by the social radicalism of the 1960s, believed in the fundamental right to free information, especially for the poor. He "saw the library not as a passive dispenser of information but rather as an active information advocate for all those who lack ... information, ... [whose] lack of power deprived them of an equal share of society's offerings."[21] A former seminary student, Croneberger, in the words of the president of the Urban Library Council, "chose a secular institution but he brought to it a sacred passion."[22]

In Pittsburgh, Croneberger initiated many library and community partnerships, including the Pittsburgh Mediation Center, focused on conflict resolution, and an early intervention literacy program called "Beginning with Books." He also developed the Electronic Information Network (EIN), which linked all the libraries in Allegheny County and marked the library's first major effort at local computer and networking technology.

Struggling with the library's perpetual lack of funding, Croneberger was shocked when he took a group of visiting librarians to Mayor Richard Caliguiri's office, where a spokesperson told them that Carnegie Library of Pittsburgh did not cost the city very much, since Andrew Carnegie had endowed it: "I was stunned. There is no endowment from Carnegie. People in the city thought we were hoarding this endowment and had lots of money."[23] Croneberger publicly criticized Governor Robert Casey in 1992 for a $2 million cutback in state funds for cultural organizations, and he created the Friends of the Library program to facilitate individual donations. An activist administrator, Croneberger was also admired by leaders in his profession for his stand on intellectual freedom. At the height of the "culture wars" of the 1990s, when artists and institutions throughout the country were threatened with censorship and cuts in funding from the National Endowment of the Arts and National Endowment of the Humanities, he testified before the U.S. Supreme Court on behalf of the American Library Association and a coalition of other groups. His eloquent opinions were cited three times in the Supreme Court's decision in favor of intellectual freedom.

Croneberger died in office in 1998 after a heart attack, and spurred by the Insitute's move toward more efficient business practices, the search committee appointed a business executive, Herb Elish, as the next director. Elish had no experience running libraries, but the search committee was focused on the need to streamline management and revitalize the system. Elish promptly launched a capital campaign, hoping to make the branch libraries more popular by incorporating some of the patron-friendly features found in major bookstore chains. By the time he retired, in 2004, the library had raised $25 million but had spent nearly all of it upgrading the Central Branch and a number of the more aging branches, each redesigned by a different Pittsburgh architectural firm. Elish reversed Croneberger's social policy agenda, instead funneling money into the library collections and staff, trying to bring salaries up to market level. He had senior staff take a course in modern management techniques at the Katz Graduate School of Business at the University of Pittsburgh, so that they might become more skilled in business and marketing decisions. The collections and traditional departments at the Central Branch also underwent change, the high-profile divisions of Science and Technology, and Music and Art, reduced to the status of other subject areas. Elish later noted, "It was hard for some staff

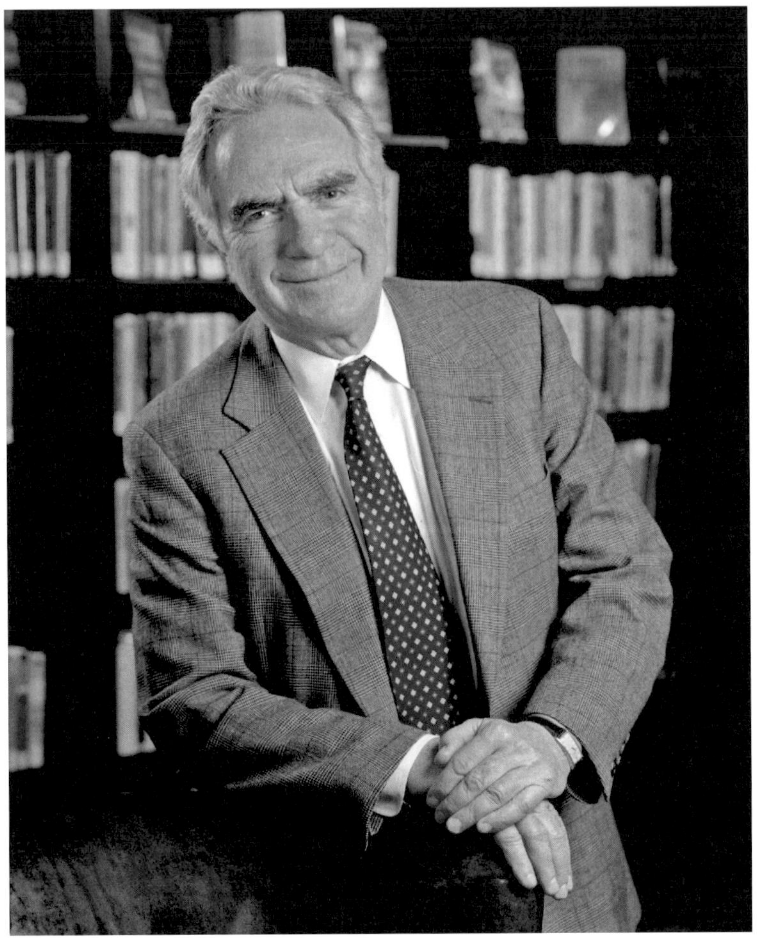

*Director Herb Elish served from 1998 to 2004, and renovated the Oakland
building and several branches by using different architects for each building.*

to reorganize the Central library. It was a big culture shock for many, but
it had to be done. . . . We don't have the depth of expertise we once had, but
neither do we get the depth of questions we once had, especially in science
and technology."[24]

In spite of the initial controversy, Elish's tenure was evaluated posi-
tively. Frank Lucchino, the chair of the library's executive committee, remarked on Elish's retirement, "The risk we took in hiring somebody with
a business degree has paid off in spades."[25] The executive director of the
ARAD Board, David Donohoe, agreed: "Herb Elish brought a different
perspective to the library. He thought libraries should be customer-friendly
and brought those ideas directly to the library staff and to the operations.

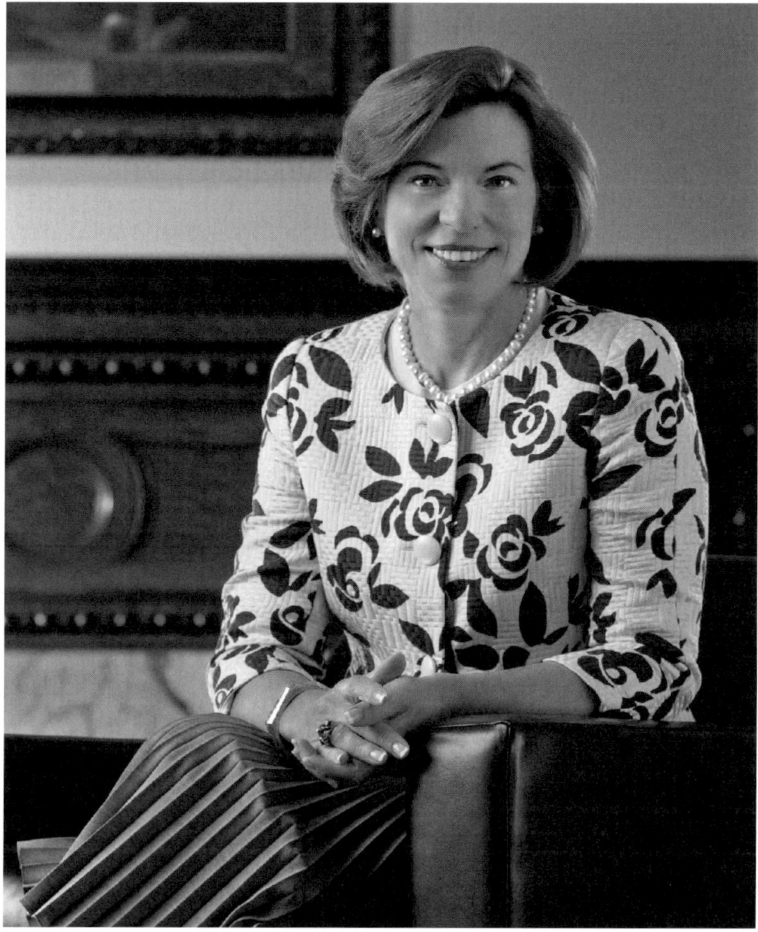

Barbara Mistick, director from 2005 to 2011, raised the profile of the library as one of the most significant cultural assets in Allegheny County.

He was sure that the library could attract more users if it were more comfortable and easier to use and now it seems the physical improvements are paying off. More people are borrowing books and more people are getting library cards."[26]

The Search Committee, hoping for a new director to carry on Elish's business-savvy approach, found one in Barbara Mistick, hired on June 1, 2005. Like Elish, Mistick saw the library as institutionally separate from the Institute. She felt, further, that the library was handicapped—precluded from museum fund-raising and without the right to fund-raise on its own. One of her first moves as director, then, was to commission a study by Carnegie Mellon's Center for Economic Development that evaluated the impact of the number of jobs directly and indirectly generated in the community by the library. The results were overwhelming: the library was revealed to be one of the most widely used and economically important services in the region; community members depended on it for literacy and learning, quality of life, and children's services.

Mistick saw this as a mandate for the library to operate more boldly: "In the community the library is seen in a benign way. Nobody ever gets mad at the library. Despite the things we've done wrong they still love us. The problem with benign thinking is it's not too far away from benign neglect.... We have facilities that aren't ADA compliant ... [and] some without air-conditioning. We're making progress slowly, but it's the product of neglect over time."[27] After reading Ralph Munn's 1967 report, she felt that the library had long been financially vulnerable: "Those four words that haunt me every day: 'Free to the People.' They aren't true. It's never free. There is always an associated cost."[28] In 2009, when an economic analysis forced Mistick to announce the closing of several branch libraries, a public debate erupted, a long-overdue confrontation between the library and city government in which the city was faulted for not providing enough tax support. Carnegie's initial 1895 request that the city provide $40,000 annual tax support was still paid by the city at that rate. When Mistick announced in 2011 that she was leaving, a long-term solution to sustainable annual funding was still needed.[29]

CARNEGIE'S LEGACY

The historian Abigail Van Slyke detected an ambiguity in Andrew Carnegie's enthusiasm for branch libraries, arguing that it was at odds with his distrust of working-class readers, especially after the Homestead strike. Since Carnegie believed only a few people had the strength of character necessary to improve themselves, how could he preach about helping workers change their fortunes through reading?[30] Her unsympathetic conclusion typifies academic historians' distrust of Carnegie's motives, but in fact, the Pittsburgh branches, and the free libraries Carnegie funded in urban centers all over the United States, had a profound and positive effect on American society.

The Pittsburgh libraries, in effect, were a training ground for the families of workers, familiarizing them with middle-class behavior and etiquette and preparing them to fit in socially, whether at school, at work, or in church. There was no spitting on the floor or shouting. At the Mount Washington branch, a basin in the corner of the room allowed librarians to supervise the washing of children's hands and faces. This emphasis came through in the architecture itself: Frank Alden and Harlow, for example, built open stacks in five of the branches to allow readers to retrieve their own books, the stacks radiating outward from the librarian's desk to allow the librarian to monitor the aisles. The branches in Hazelwood, West End, and Mount Washington had a variation on this design—small reference rooms in the center of the rear of the building. The librarian was an all-seeing presence: low, glass-topped partitions made supervision over patrons easy.

Carnegie's libraries and service centers eventually blanketed the city, in response to the community's needs. Some neighborhood services operated for years out of existing storefronts and buildings, while construction had begun by 1930 on separate branches in Brookline and Carrick. In 1956, the Allegheny Regional Library, with its Woods Run Branch, became part of the Carnegie Library system. President Lyndon Johnson's Great Society Initiative (1964) brought new funds to libraries, and Pittsburgh, like many U.S. cities, began to see a surge in urban branch development, new buildings erected for Woods Run (1964), Knoxville (1965), Beechview (1967), East Liberty (1969), and Squirrel Hill (1972). In older neighborhoods, relocated branches reflected the city's physical and population changes: a branch opened in Sheraden in 1980, and the Hill District moved from Wylie Street to another location in 1982. The Martin Luther King Jr. Reading Center was built in 1988 and lasted until 2005, when services were reorganized in a new location.

However fine the branches were when they opened, the original ones had to survive much of the twentieth century without extensive changes. By the end of the century, library director Herb Elish looked with a reformer's eye on their poor condition, saying of Lawrenceville, "The rugs are held together by masking tape. I was struck by how dingy it was, like someone had taken a vow of poverty."[31] The creature comforts of 1900 were clearly inadequate to modern life: single-pane windows and old casements let cold air in during the winter, and the lack of proper air-conditioning meant the rooms sweltered in the summer. Most libraries were in violation of the Civil Liberties Act, with no elevators available to patrons with disabilities. Elish began upgrading as many branches as possible, using different local architects to breathe new life into each branch. The refurbished libraries, now equipped with the latest amenities and suited to their particular surroundings, were revived as the local showplaces and centers of attention they had been a century before.

Carnegie Library's evolution into a regional resource has, of course, extended its reach well beyond Pittsburgh's borders. Beginning in the 1990s, under the umbrella of the Allegheny County Library Association (ACLA), county library services were federated into one system, which meant that a patron could use a Carnegie Library card to borrow a book or order material from any of the regional libraries. Pittsburgh's Electronic Information network (eiNetwork) served as a national model, establishing a common automation system for libraries throughout the county, including forty-three independent libraries and the eighteen branches of Carnegie Library of Pittsburgh.

Still, in spite of the library's clear importance to the region, it remained hampered by the stubborn myth that Carnegie had endowed the library in perpetuity. In 1994, to address the library's financial needs more aggressively, the Board of Trustees expanded to include twelve new term trustees, and this eventually led to increased tensions between the library and the institute. The Economic Impact Study commissioned by director Barbara Mistick in 2006 confirmed that the 110-year-old system had evolved with the times, remaining a central force for education and literacy in the region, bringing "more than $91 million to the economy of Allegheny County, which equals $6 for every dollar of local public funding, and $75 worth of annual benefits per person in the County."[32] Mistick had proved that Carnegie Library of Pittsburgh deserved to be the largest recipient of funds from the Allegheny Regional Asset District.

6

CARNEGIE MUSEUM OF ART

"The Moral Mission of Art"

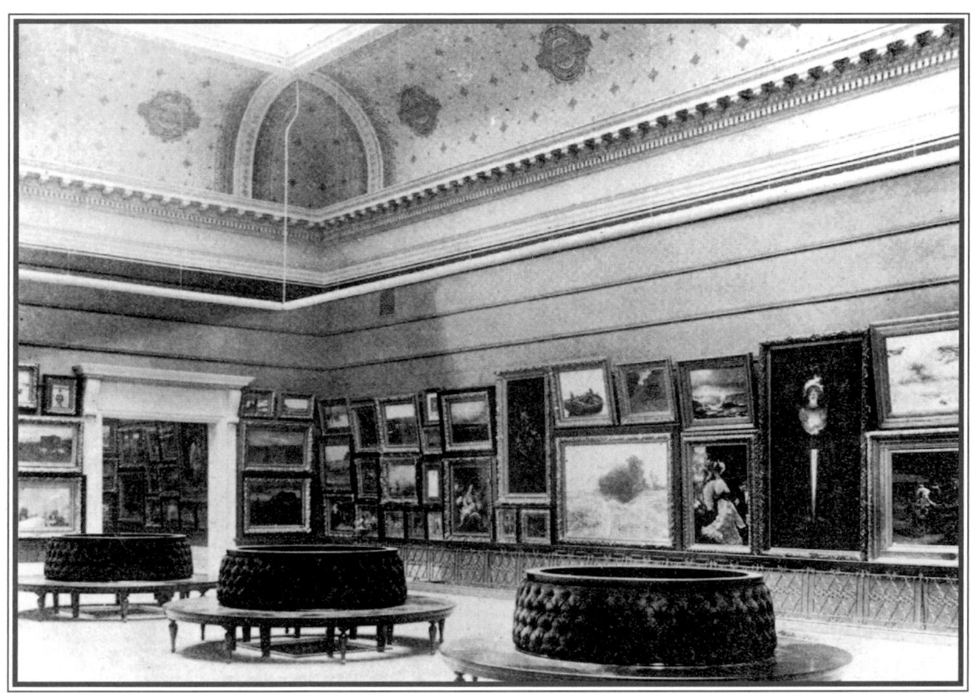

*The first annual exhibition took place in 1896, when the art galleries were housed
in the north wing of the library.*

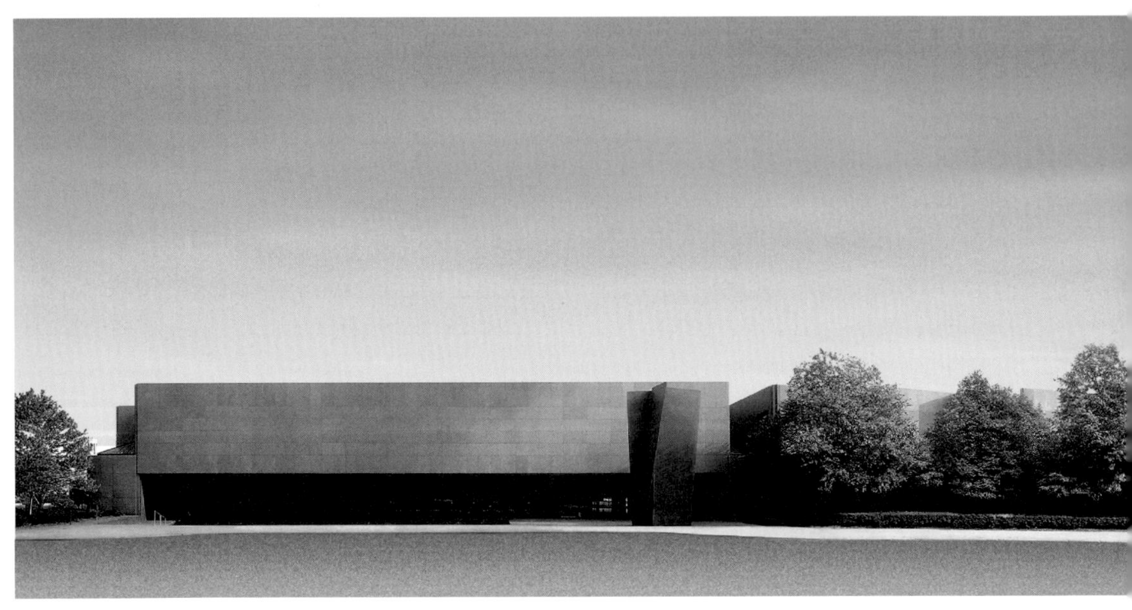

CARNEGIE RARELY rhapsodized about the visual arts, but he did so in his 1895 dedication speech. The rapt Music Hall audience of Pittsburgh's business and intellectual elite applauded in appreciation as Carnegie declared his resistance to artistic fads and outlined his hopes for the new Department of Fine Arts:

I remember, as if it were yesterday, when I first awoke to the sense of color, and what an awakening it was and has been. A child, sitting in a cold, barren little church, the only relief to the dull white walls and plain ceiling being one inch of a border of colored glass around the edge of the principal window, and yet that narrow line of little square pieces of different colors was the first glimpse I ever had of what seemed to me the radiance of heaven. . . .

I am firmly convinced that no surer means of improving the tastes of men can be found than through color and the sense of beauty. The cant of art, indulged in most by those who are least under its influence, is not, perhaps, to be altogether

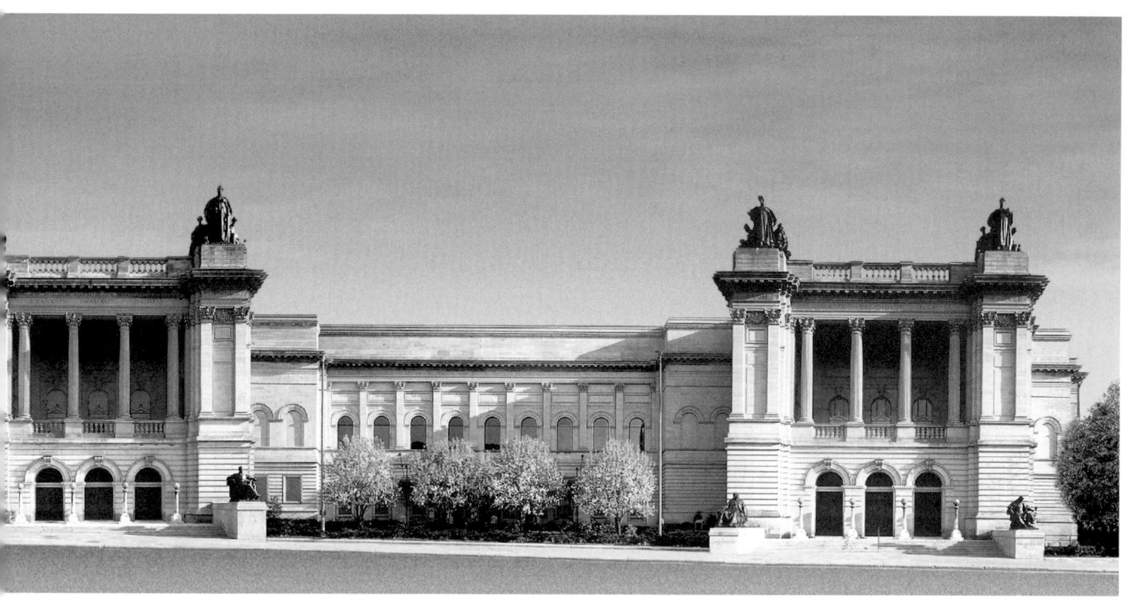

A panorama showing the Institute including the Sarah Scaife Gallery, added in 1974. No one looking at the immense facade of this building on Forbes Avenue can stand far enough away to photograph this subject as one picture, so four images had to be blended together to create this view for the 1995 Centennial.

deplored, for it keeps interest alive. Each petty school calls aloud that it has the truth, the whole truth, and nothing but the truth, but no school can embrace the whole, since art is universal, and the judgment of the masses of the people is finally to prove the truest test of the supreme in art, as it is admittedly in literature. . . . Let us hope that the pictures exhibited here from time to time will be of all schools, and reach both extremes—the highest critic and the humblest citizen. . . .

One of the most important objects in view in endowing it with annual revenues is that this Gallery should eventually contain a chronological collection of American painting and sculpture. It is provided that the commission shall each year purchase at least three works of American artists exhibited in that year, preferably in this Gallery. . . . It will not much matter historically, as you will observe, whether these pictures are invariably of surpassing excellence; if art in the United States has its periods of decadence and revival, it is proper that a historical record should show this clearly. . . .

. . . There is a great field lying back of us, which it is desirable that some institution should occupy by gathering the earliest masterpieces of American painting from the beginning. But the field for which this Gallery is designed begins with the year 1896. . . . Some day, perhaps, and that may not be remote, the artists of the United States will strive to have one of their productions selected as the best of its year, and placed in the historical collection of this Gallery, as today they strive to be admitted to the Luxembourg. . . If this fond hope be realized, then Pittsburgh will be famous for art as it is now for steel.[1]

Like the manufacturer he was, Carnegie extolled the systematic production of great art, the best annual examples to be displayed in his gallery. He would not compete with other collectors for overpriced art when the "masterpieces of tomorrow" were available at bargain prices. His plan to document U.S. art from 1896 onward should demonstrate that America was the equal of Europe in artistic matters. In addition to the museum's permanent collection, Carnegie wanted to mount an annual Pittsburgh exhibition that, like Chicago's Columbian Exposition of 1893 and the Venice Biennale, started in 1895, would be international in scope, not like other American annual exhibitions that focused only on American art.[2]

Carnegie's notions of art were clearly Victorian and paternalistic. In 1894 he had declared himself against the display of nudity in classical sculpture in his library and galleries, fearing that it would offend ordinary citizens. He saw art as a means to uplift the struggling masses, providing spiritual inspiration and moral tales, and indeed, Victorian paintings did regularly provide uplifting messages and religious content to match his views. Henry Clay Frick was in just this frame of mind when he donated the first religious painting he ever bought to the Department of Fine Arts in July 1898: *Christ and the Disciples at Emmaus,* by Pascal-Adolphe-Jean Dagnon-Bouveret (see color plate). Local ministers hailed this large canvas for revealing "the surpassing glory of the divine spirit," expecting that it would "do as much for humanity in this city as any pulpit."[3]

Carnegie was as opinionated about art as he was about everything. He complained to Institute president William Frew about the choices of great artists whose names would be carved in stone at the library: "Among painters Perugini out and Rubens [*sic*] in, the latter only a painter of fat, vulgar women, while study of pictures of Raphael will show anyone that that he was really only a copyist of Perugini, whose pupil he was."[4] He later reminded Frew that transient fashions in art were not to be trusted and that the experts were often wrong: "Let me say . . . that the last men I should appoint to manage business, are experts. The expert mind is too narrow. For this reason, painters of the day ridiculed Millet as vulgar; the musicians of the day, Wagner as insane; writers of the day, Shakespeare as bombastic.... I wish to trust my fund to a committee dominated by men of affairs, who have within reach the expert element with which they can confer. Besides this, I wish a larger number of officials directly from the people in the committee, as I am satisfied that unless the institution be kept in touch with the masses, and therefore popular, it cannot be widely useful."[5] But there was a difference between placing his Institute in the hands of businessmen and installing a committee of such businessmen as art critics. Inadvertently, Carnegie was planting seeds of discontent among important artists, who felt they were being asked to submit their best work for the approval of Pittsburgh businessmen.

Nevertheless, Carnegie continued to dote on the unpredictability of the judgment of average Pittsburghers and businessmen. He elicited applause in his 1907 dedication speech when he spoke approvingly of Carnegie judges having "skied" the work of the famous French artist Edouard Detaille (1848–1912)—that is, having placed it high on a gallery wall where it could not easily be seen, since it was considered not of the first quality:

There is a lesson in it for all of us.... When the gentlemen of the jury were informed they had skied Detaille the reply was superb. Mr. John Caldwell's jury said: "We can't help that; we don't regard names here, but art. It would have been the same if it had been painted by Rembrandt." ... I congratulate Pittsburgh upon this example of triumphant democracy.... Pedigree does not count in the Pittsburgh Institute, and the manner in which we elect our jury is thoroughly democratic.... I am bound to say it is not always satisfactory to all the exhibitors. Yet, I remark, you do not hear any of their complaints through the omnipotent press. They are silent.[6]

Carnegie saw personal collections of expensive art as a wasteful self-indulgence, but he considered donations of art to a public institution to be in the spirit of his Gospel of Wealth. In the years after his gallery opened, he monitored and influenced its progress, tinkering with its reputation by providing prize money to attract the best artists, arranging to buy art from the annual exhibition when Pittsburgh art patrons failed to do so, and providing funds for the gallery to acquire works for the collection. His personal gifts of art to the museum included items such as teapots, probably acquired during his travels to Japan, as well as less expensive works on paper—etchings, woodcuts, engravings, lithographs, mezzotints. Carnegie was no art collector: Henry Adams noted that "his most prized painting, which hung in his bedroom, was one he valued purely for its subject—a portrait of Captain Bill Jones, the madly driven booster of production quotas, who had died in an explosion while working beside his men to clear a blocked stack at the Edgar Thompson works."[7] Still, he did donate two paintings to the Department of Fine Arts. The first, a portrait of Pittsburgh's famous composer Stephen C. Foster, was put in the rotunda of the Music Hall after the 1907 building opened. The other, *The Mill in Winter: A Sketch,* was an unfinished work by John Twachtman, a regular contributor to the annual exhibitions who had served on the jury in 1898.[8]

Carnegie's specific plans for the Department of Fine Arts had to be modified almost immediately, although directors, curators, and trustees were always careful to honor his general principles. His notion that the collection should start only in 1896 was simplistic, and mounting an annual juried exhibition proved impractical. The permanent collection began to extend the museum's reach back into history, and the museum, like other art museums, became more comprehensive in its mission. Significant gifts from donors, and eventually from facilities such as the Sarah Scaife Gallery, the Ailsa Mellon Bruce Galleries of Decorative Arts, and the Heinz Architectural Center, pushed the museum in a new direction. Art itself was to change dramatically during the twentieth century, paintings losing their early preeminence, while collections of sculpture, decorative arts installations, photography, and prints and drawings developed. The question of whether to develop a costly permanent collection or stage an expensive international exhibition bedeviled directors throughout the twentieth century, but the Carnegie International remained the museum's signature feature, lifting it from its status as an interesting provincial museum to the world stage of contemporary art. For five decades its collecting habits at the Internationals earned it a reputation as a conservative museum in a conservative city, but in the 1950s the museum finally embraced Modernism, and Pittsburgh began to open itself more fully to the vigorous challenges of contemporary art.

The twentieth century also saw changes to the museum's name, reflecting the political agendas of Institute presidents, the realities of the museum's changing role in Pittsburgh, and the maturing of the museum profession. The Department of Fine Arts, Carnegie Institute, became the Museum of Art, Carnegie Institute (1963), and eventually Carnegie Museum of Art. In 1963 President Bovard (with the approval of the director and the trustees) changed its name from the Department of Fine Arts to the Museum of Art, Carnegie Institute, to distinguish it from the College of Fine Arts at nearby Carnegie Institute of Technology, with which it was regularly confused, and to clarify its independence as a public art museum serving western Pennsylvania and the tristate area. In 1986 President Wilburn renamed it Carnegie Museum of Art, as a way of emphasizing its role as one of the four museums of "The Carnegie." Thus, the art department and staff adapted to three different name changes in twenty-three years.

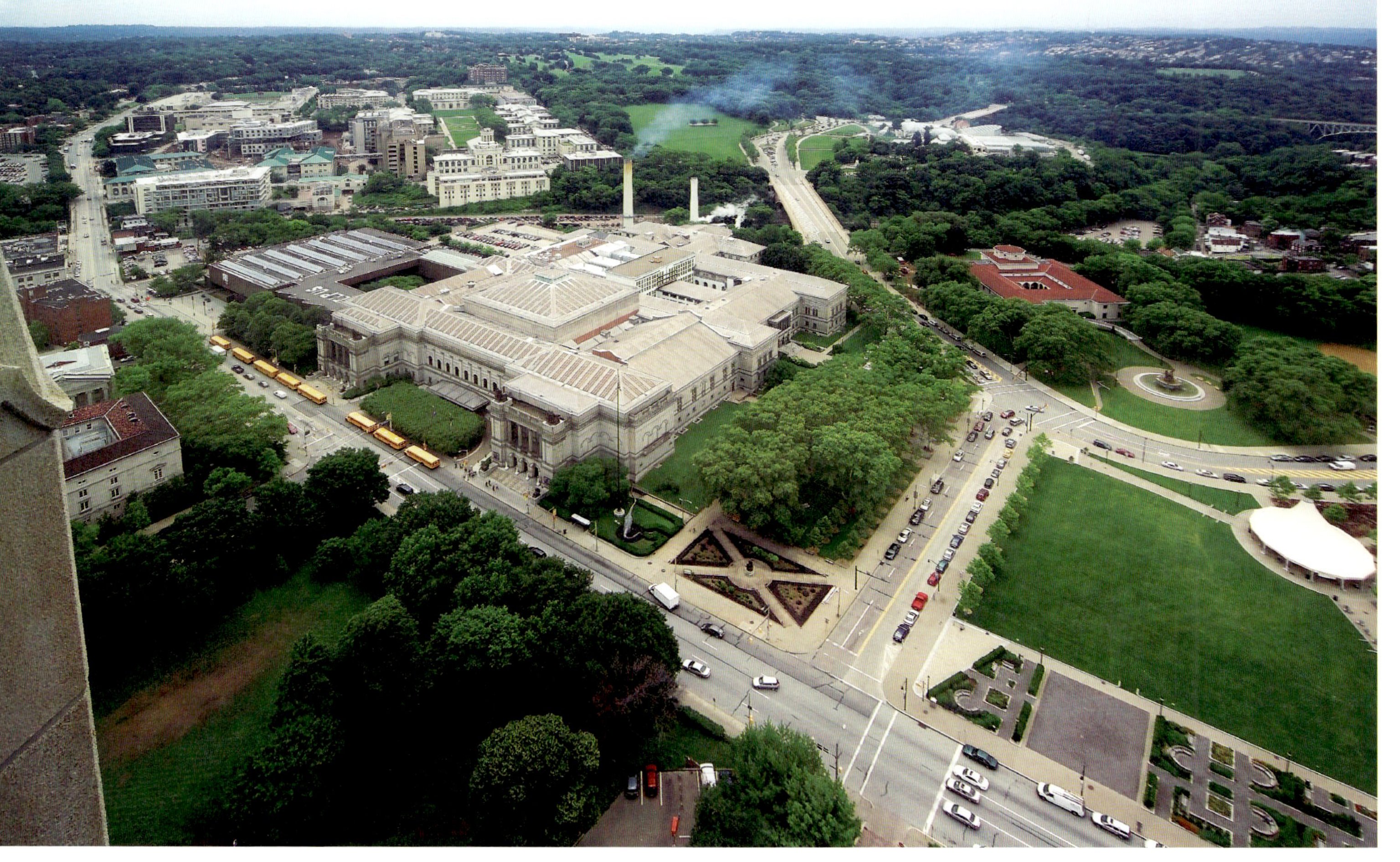

The Carnegie Institute and Library complex in 2010. The line of yellow school buses on Forbes Avenue is common in late spring, when thousands of students attend the museums on field trips. Carnegie Mellon is in the background, left. To the right is Schenley Plaza, the formal entrance to Schenley Park, and above it is the Mary Schenley Fountain. Behind that is the Frick Fine Arts Building of the University of Pittsburgh, an Italian renaissance-style villa. Phipps Conservatory and Schenley Park are in the distance.

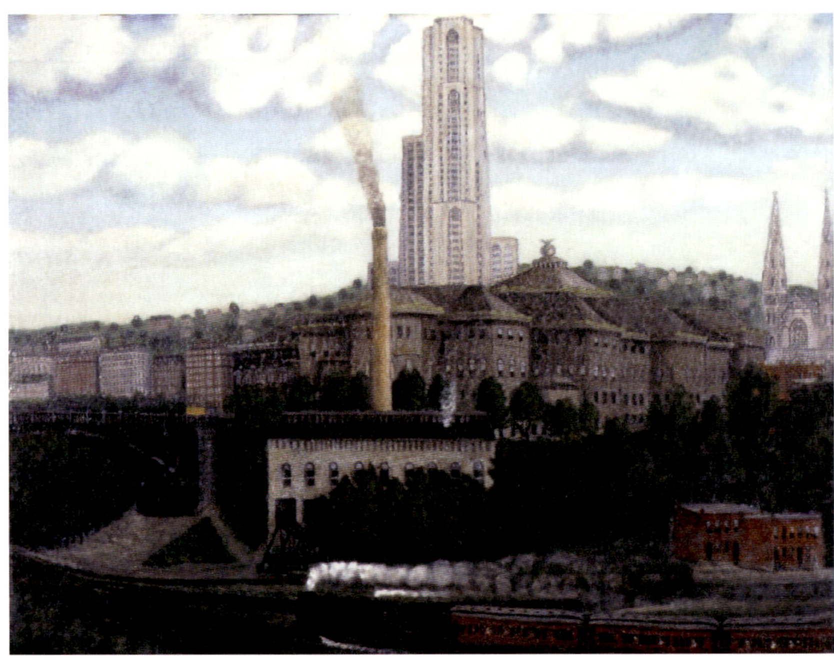

John Kane, The Cathedral of Learning, *1930. Pittsburgh laborer and self-taught artist John Kane became famous when one of his paintings was unexpectedly included in the 1927 International. He loved his city and often painted it.*

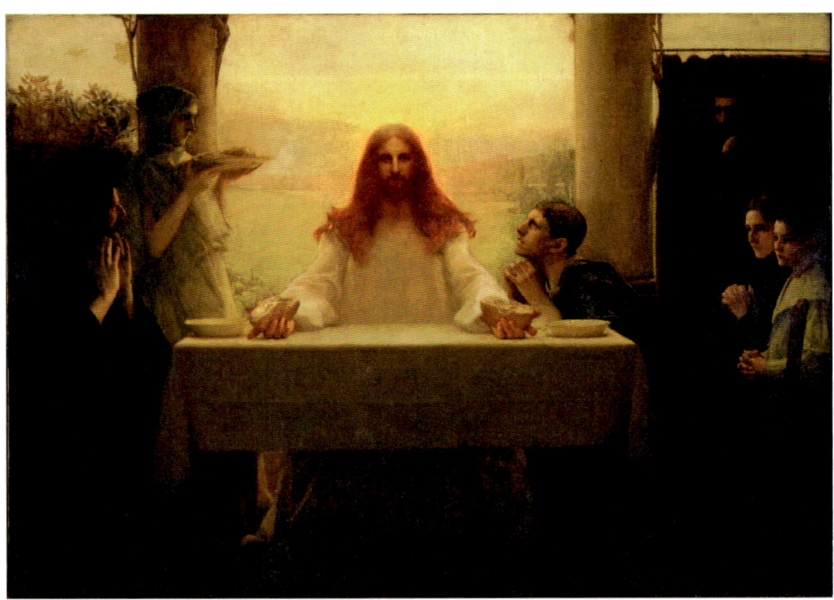

Pascal-Adolphe-Jean Dagnon-Bouveret, Christ and the Disciples at Emmaus, *1896–97. This painting, exhibited in the 1898 Carnegie International and given to the museum by Henry Clay Frick, depicts the New Testament narrative in which the resurrected Jesus appears to his disciples and breaks bread with them. Dagnon-Bouveret said that the three figures on the right reveal the modern era: the woman is unswervingly faithful, the child accepts without understanding, and man in the shadows has doubts and anxieties caused by modern philosophy and science.*

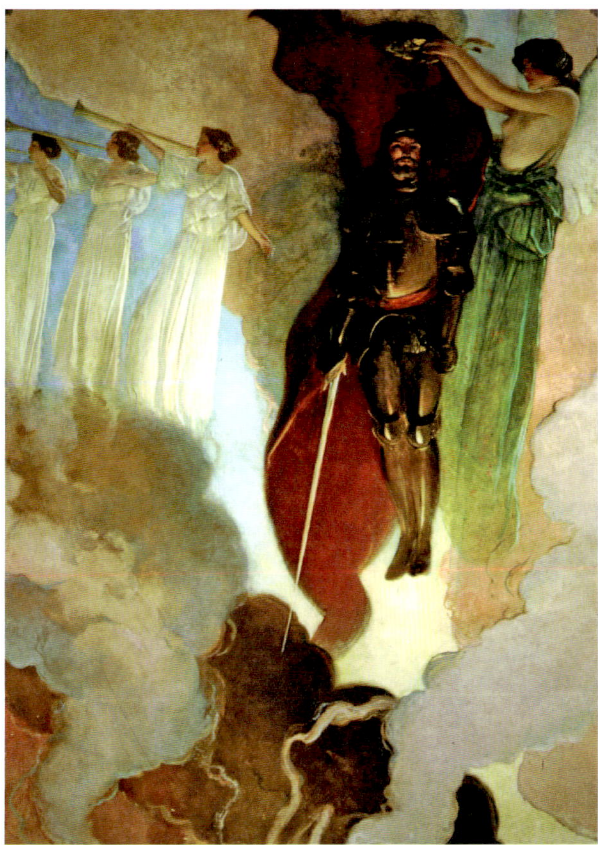

John White Alexander, The Crowning of Labor. *The lower level of murals depict workers in the steel mills. The smoke rises up, and on the second level, female spirits bring the fruits of labor to the black knight wearing steel armor. The knight resembles Andrew Carnegie.*

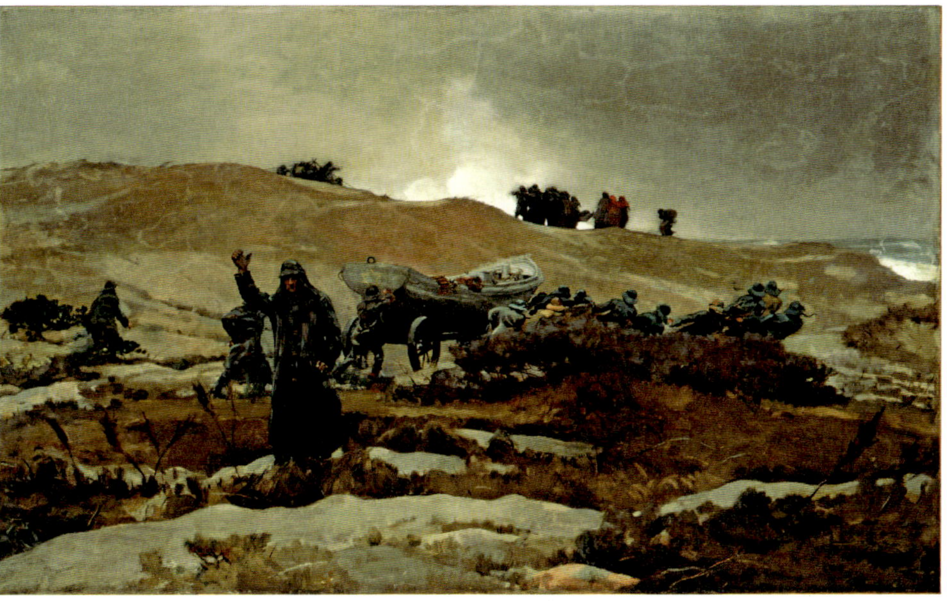

Winslow Homer, The Wreck, 1896. One of Homer's last interpretations of rescue at sea, the painting won the first Carnegie Chronological Medal in 1896 and the purchase prize of five thousand dollars—the highest price Homer ever received for a single work. It was the first painting acquired for the permanent collection. Homer exhibited at nine more Internationals and served twice on the jury of award.

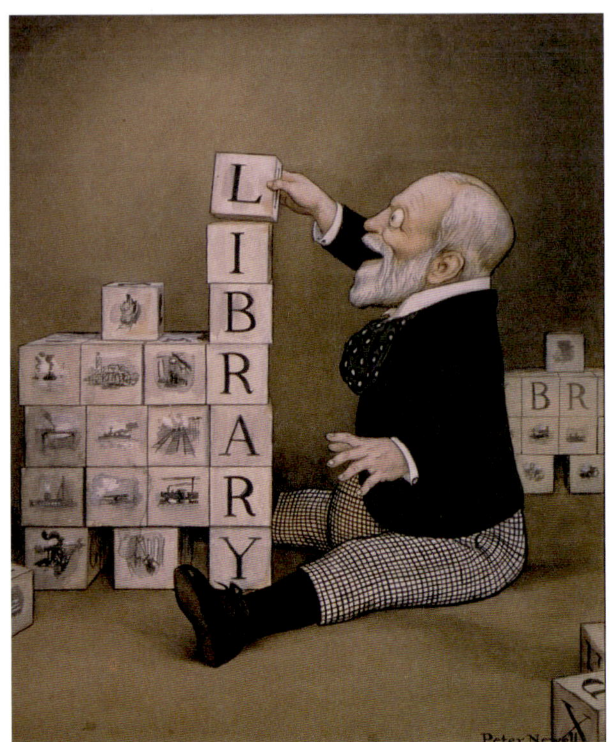

A famous 1901 cartoon by Peter Newell in Life magazine captures Carnegie's enthusiasm for building libraries.

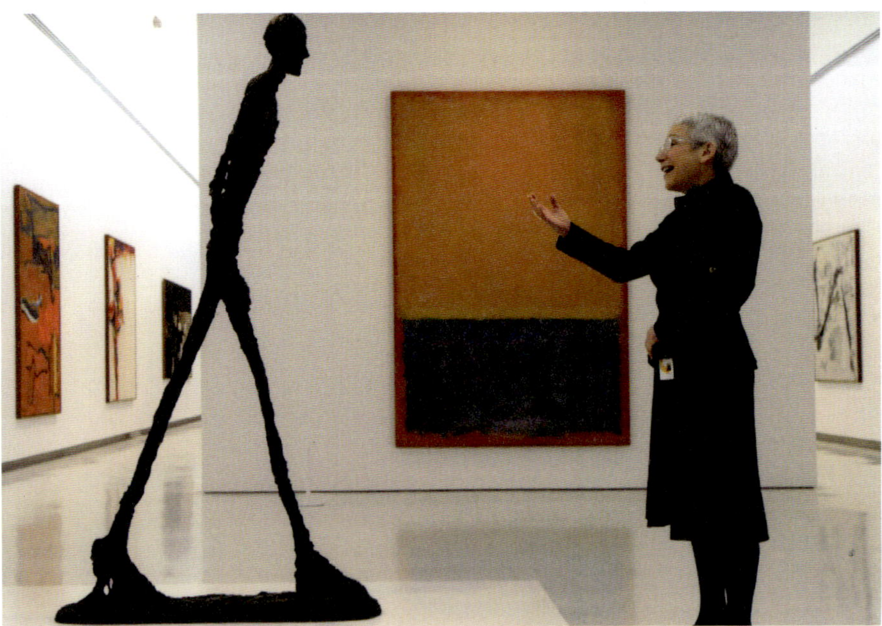

Lynn Zelevansky, director of Carnegie Museum of Art since 2009, pictured with Alberto Giacometti's 1960 bronze figure Walking Man I, which won first prize for sculpture in the 1961 International. That year the Patron's Art Fund purchased for a relatively modest sum this first cast in the artist's edition of six copies. In 2010, Sotheby's of London sold one from this edition for over 100 million, and set a record-breaking price for a single work of art.

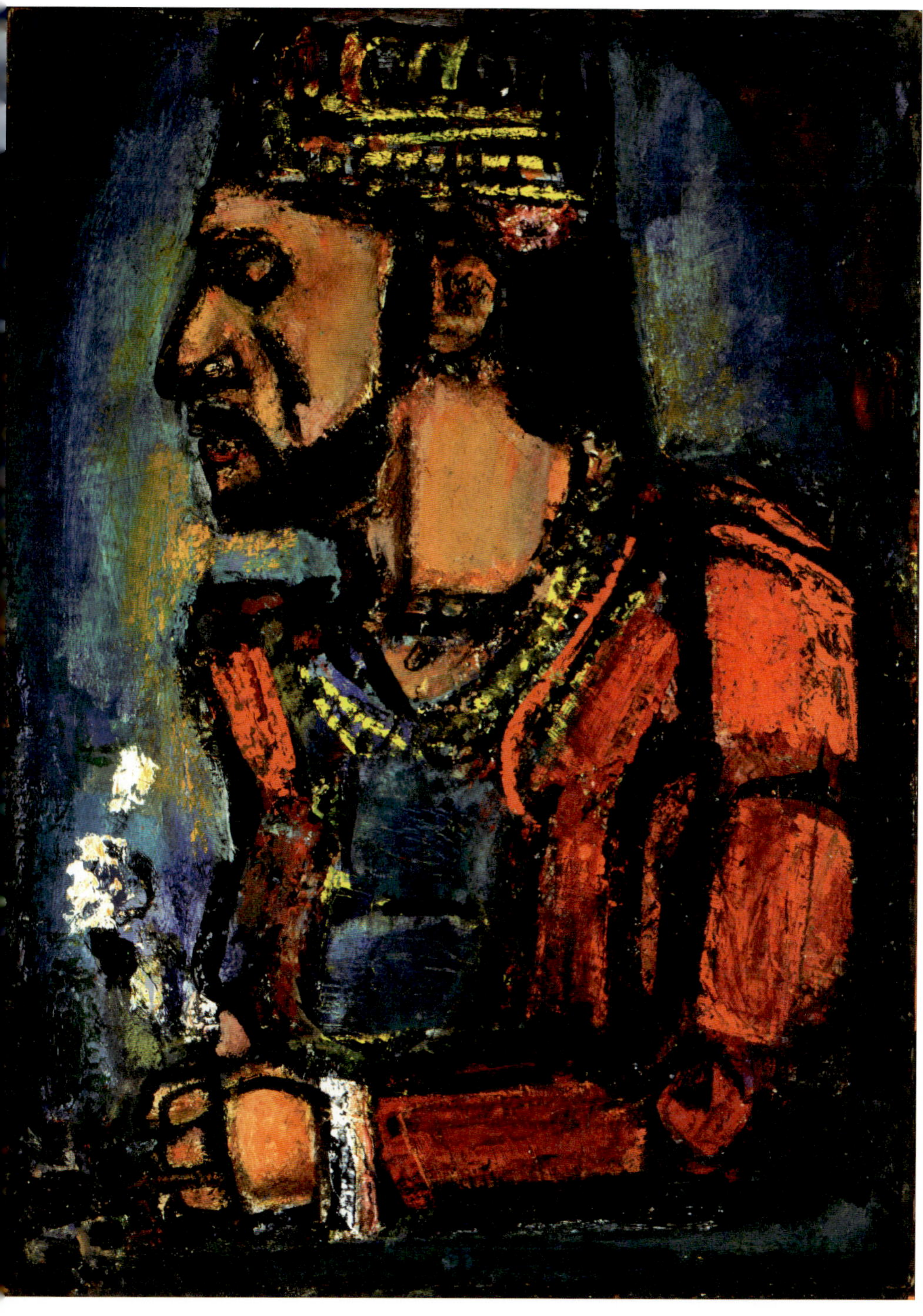

Georges Rouault, The Old King, *1916–36. Exhibited in the 1939 International and bought in 1940 by the Patron's Art Fund. Director Leon Arkus said this celebrated expressionist work was the one painting other museums wanted to borrow, and a rare example of European modernism to enter the collection before the 1950s. An ancient king, as if in stained glass, has had his scepter of power replaced by flowers, symbolizing a hoped-for peace after Europe was devastated by World War I.*

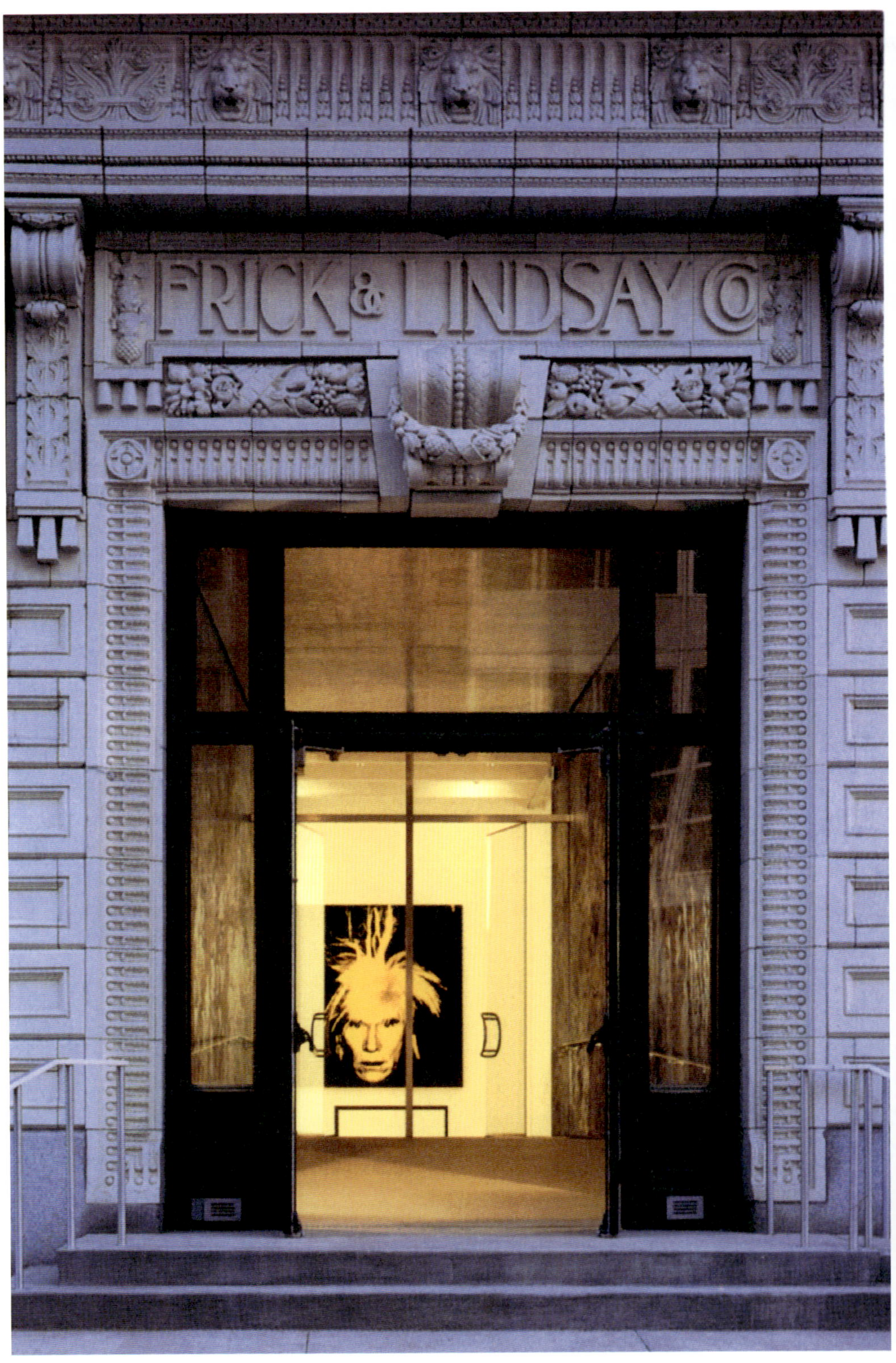

The entrance to the Andy Warhol Museum is a door to the artist's world.

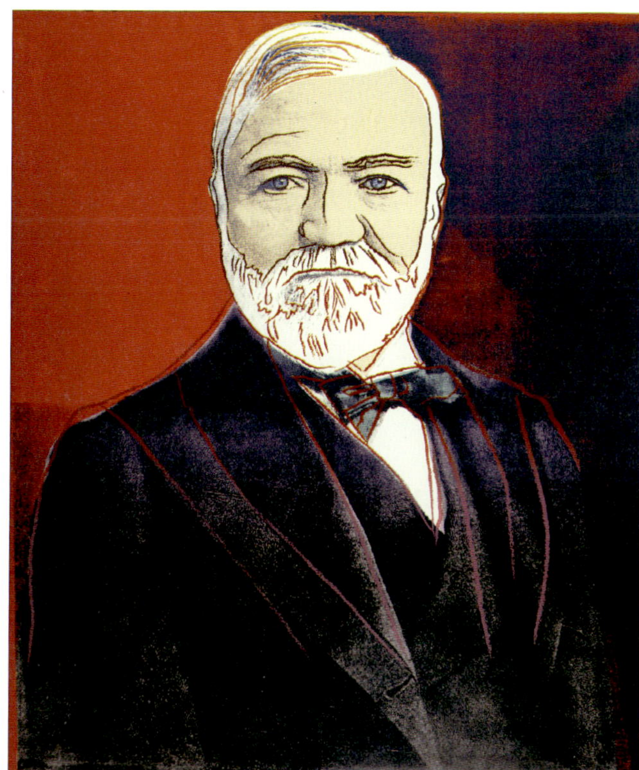

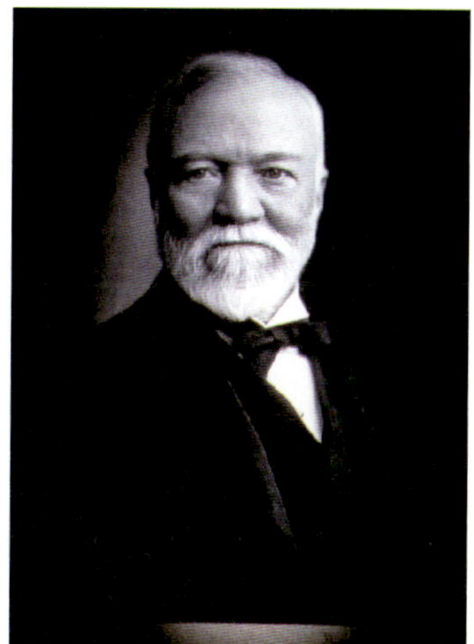

The 1896 photograph (above) of Carnegie was sent to Andy Warhol in New York. In 1981, he used it as the basis for two large color portraits, both simply titled Andrew Carnegie, and now owned by the Carnegie Museum of Art.

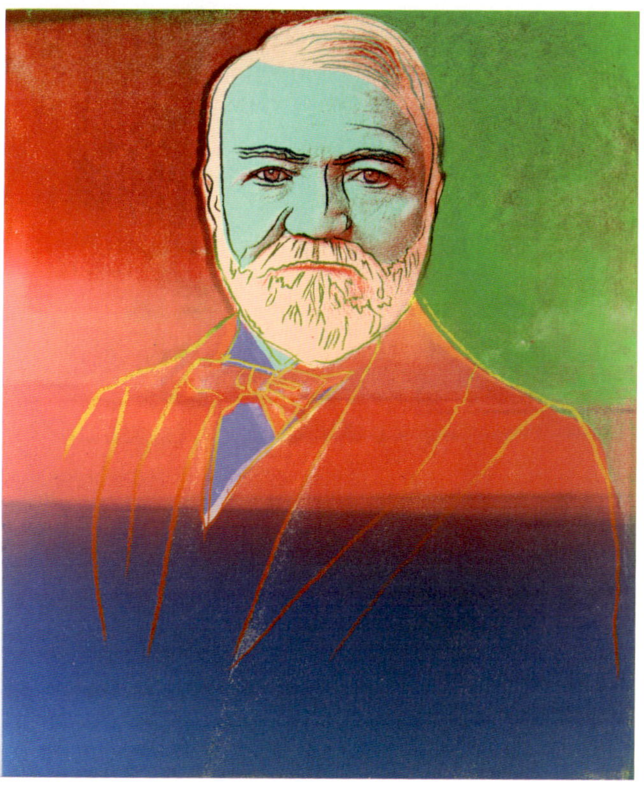

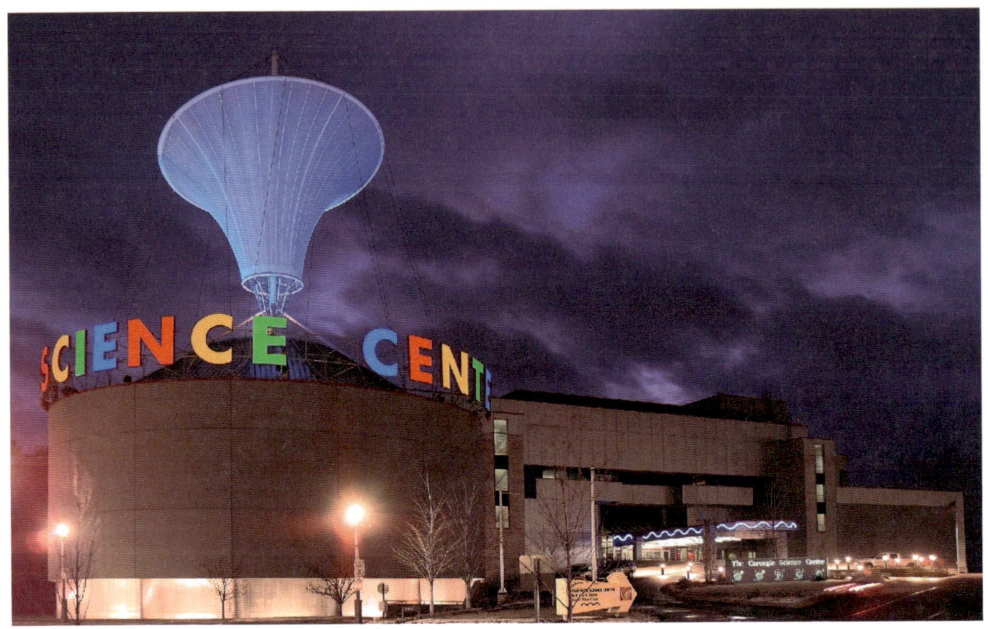

Carnegie Science Center is lit up for the evening.

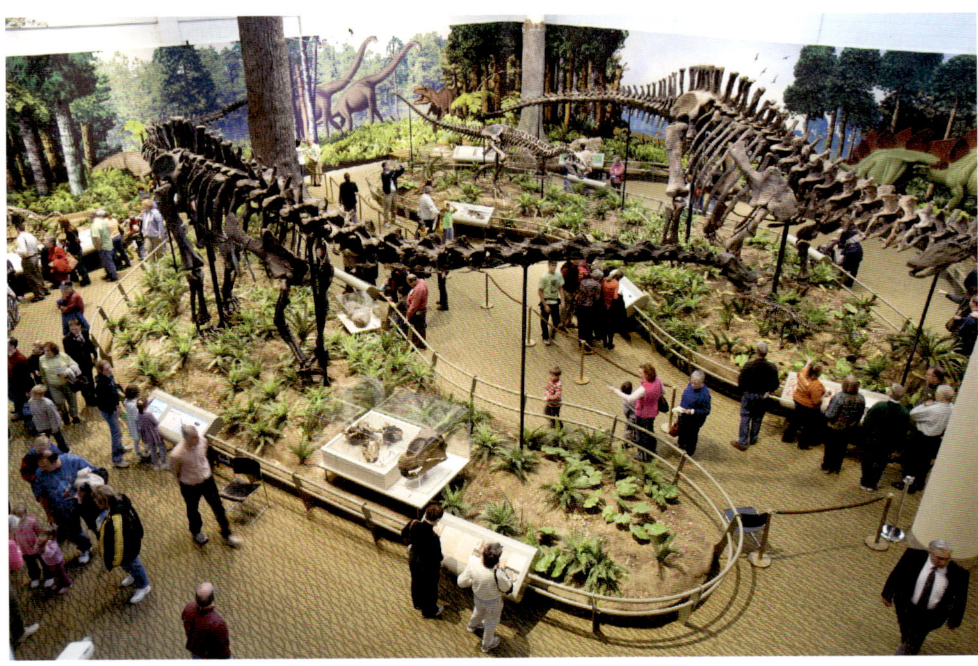

Dinosaurs in Their Time, emphasizing the environmental context of the Age of Dinosaurs, is a vast exhibit that in 2007 changed the way Carnegie Museum of Natural History appealed to the public. It was conceived as a first-day attraction for tourists in Pittsburgh.

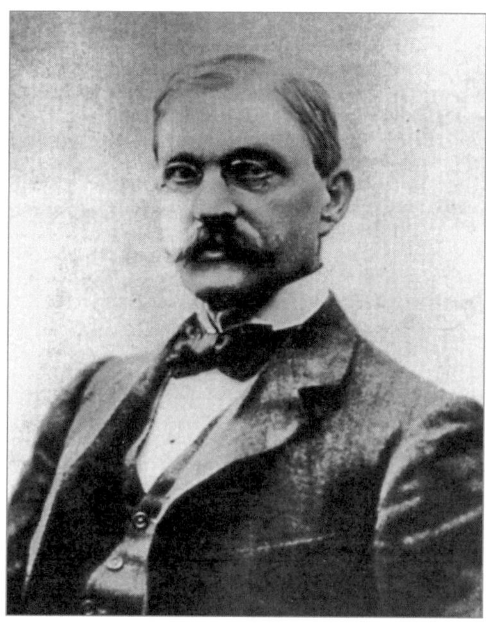

Director John Beatty set the direction and style of the Department of Fine Arts from the museum's opening in 1896 until 1922.

"THE ARTISTIC CLASS"

The art museum's first director, John Wesley Beatty (1896–1922), exemplified the approach of the successful businessman. A devout Methodist, he was at home in the clubrooms and offices of Pittsburgh's business leaders and joined them for golf and fishing. His office at the Institute was spare, with no symbols of his artistic vocation and little evidence of his passion for producing art exhibitions.

But Beatty was an artist by temperament and training, who started as a silver engraver in Pittsburgh before going to study at the Royal Academy in Munich in 1876. He returned to Pittsburgh to become the city's most conspicuous art educator, serving as the secretary of the local Art Society and the director of the Pittsburgh School of Design. He was working as an illustrator just as American print technology began to feature dramatic illustrations in newspapers and magazines, covering assignments such as the Johnstown Flood and the violent Pittsburgh Railroad strike. Many of his paintings showed men and horses working the land. He had also served on the advisory committee of the 1893 World's Columbian Exhibition in Chicago and knew many of the European-trained artists working in the

American mainstream. He seemed a natural choice to manage the new Department of Fine Arts.

Beatty was one of the Institute's early public-education-oriented directors, like Edwin Anderson at the library and William Holland at the Natural History Museum, and the department's educational outreach flourished under his leadership. He personally gave tours of the galleries and developed an ambitious program of lessons for eighth-grade students in painting, sculpture, and architecture. Art historian Henry Adams notes that the museum under Beatty "led the nation in developing art programs for local schools and in bringing schoolchildren to the museum" and quotes Beatty's assertion that "the influence of the permanent gallery and the annual exhibition ... has been more noted among the great mass of people than the few whose wealth and education had given them the opportunities for previous cultivation of taste and knowledge."[9] Beatty explained his goals as a teacher to the Association of Urban Universities, meeting in Pittsburgh in 1917: "The purpose of this is to give the students the true point of view with reference to some of the essential qualities of art. The average young person, indeed the average old person, sees in painting only the story told, and this is of very slight importance; or they note the merely technical quality ... while the essential qualities secured by the artist—character, tone and harmony—few people understand or appreciate."[10]

As a curator, Beatty did not separate artists by nationality. He believed that the annual exhibition's mission was to intermingle American work with paintings from Europe, underscoring Carnegie's goal of making American art equal to European art. The Institute's 1896 exhibition, however—its first—immediately raised problems that would continue to frustrate Beatty and other directors. That year, Beatty exhibited 312 paintings, from England, France, Germany, Scotland, and the United States. The first medal went to Sir John Lavery's portrait *Lady in Brown* (location now unknown), and Winslow Homer's *The Wreck* (see color plate) also won a medal and was subsequently purchased. Another great work also entered the collection that year: James Whistler's *Portrait in Black: Senor Pablo de Sarasate*—a dark, dramatic portrait of the violin virtuoso, the first Whistler to be bought by an American museum. But Whistler's work, painted in 1884, clearly predated Carnegie's proposed 1896 starting point.[11] Further, only three paintings were purchased from the first annual exhibition, an expenditure of $6,400—a disappointment to participating artists, who had wrongly assumed that the $50,000 Carnegie had donated to his art gallery would be used solely to buy paintings. Artists, as noted earlier, were also unhappy with Pittsburgh's "businessmen's jury," a group of laypeople empowered to judge their work. Some artists felt resentful and cheated and vowed never to send another painting to Pittsburgh.[12]

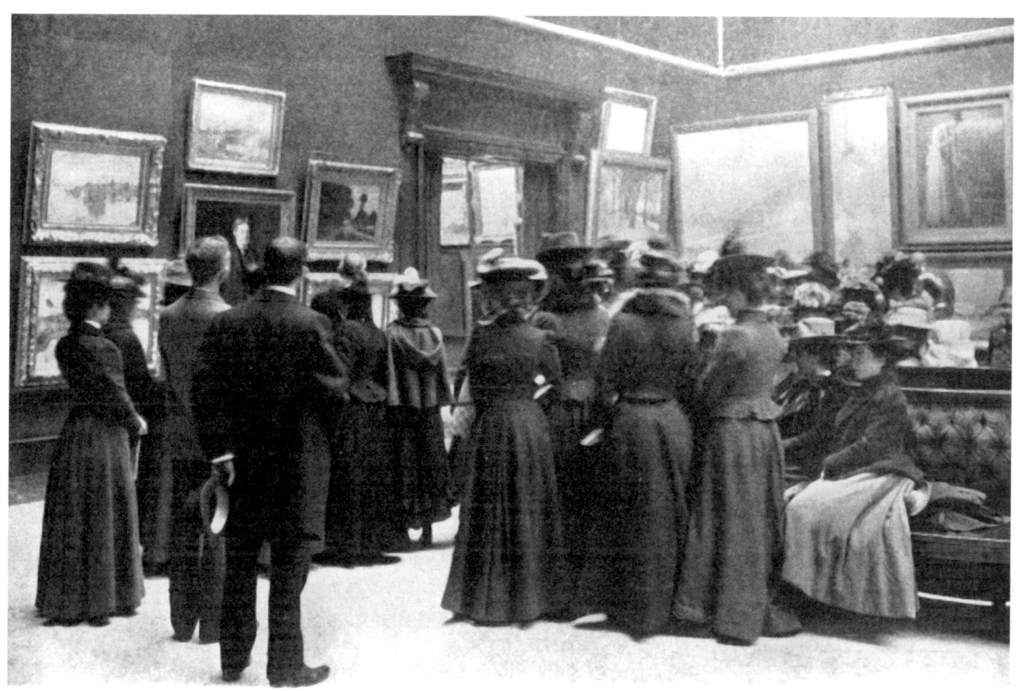

Beatty gave personal guided tours of the exhibitions, such as this one in 1896.

In addition, the Fine Arts Committee and Beatty himself made an embarrassing mistake in applying the rules. Gari Melchers's powerful realistic painting *The Shipbuilder* was initially given a $3,000 award, but John White Alexander, Beatty's liaison in Paris, discovered that it had been previously exhibited in Paris at the Champs-de-Mars Salon—an exhibit that Beatty himself had attended. Melchers confessed that he had only casually read the rules for submission to the Pittsburgh show and thought the restriction against previously exhibited work applied only to exhibition in the United States. The mistake was unintentional, but the committee, having failed to catch it, had to rescind his $3,000. In 1898 Melchers submitted *A Sailor and His Sweetheart,* which the Department of Fine Arts bought, perhaps as a belated attempt at damage control.

While the first International was deemed a success, refinements in the rules of submission and the distribution of prize money were clearly needed. Carnegie, sensitive to any criticism, suggested some revised rules at an 1897 meeting held at the home of Henry Clay Frick. Hearing, for example, that the artists disliked the businessmen's jury, he "suggested that the best way to overcome this was to require the painters themselves to select a jury from among the greatest names in the world, from all countries." Painters, he said, should return home from Pittsburgh saying, "How wonderful it was!"[13]

During Beatty's tenure, oil painting was considered the supreme form of artistic achievement, and thus the Internationals, with minor exceptions, showed only paintings. Beatty, adhering to the principles of late nineteenth-century art, set a tone that one critic regarded as standardized: "During the seventeen years which have elapsed since the inauguration of this splendid series of exhibitions there have been no surprises, no brusque departures from precedent, and no signs of retrogression."[14] Certainly, the Fine Arts Committee did not select art that portrayed violence or passion, social conflicts or economic injustice. Such topics were considered errors in taste, without the high virtue of conveying aesthetic pleasure. Most of the early prizewinning paintings depicted the changing seasons, or people in old age or childhood, or landscapes, or figure studies (rarely nudes). Even Homer's famous painting *The Wreck* keeps the wrecked ship out of sight, beyond the beach dunes.

Beatty's approach was conservative; art, he argued, should be essentially imitative of nature, not creative in its own right. Thus, while French Impressionism was represented at the Internationals with paintings by Claude Monet, Camille Pissaro, Auguste Renoir, and Alfred Sisley, and Symbolism with works by Pierre Puvis de Chavannes, such works were not early Pittsburgh favorites. In Beatty's view, while an art lover might relish Impressionism, Tonalism, and Symbolism as various approaches to reproducing nature, aggressive forms of abstraction such as Cubism were excessive, more faddish than permanent. He rejected artists then coming into fashion such as Van Gogh, Cezanne, and Gauguin, who he felt overemphasized some technical quality or eccentric style, rather than maintaining the ageless principles of beauty, harmony, and grace. While many derided Beatty's conservatism, a Boston critic, writing in 1913, reminded his readers that the Carnegie's mission was specific: "The Carnegie is primarily an educational institution and . . . citizens of Pittsburgh look to it for guidance in matters of art."[15]

Art world politics were of course unavoidable when mounting such an exhibition. While cash prizes were attached to the medals awarded—$1,500 for gold, $1,000 for silver, and $500 for bronze—winning did not guarantee a painting would be sold. Many successful artists found medals irrelevant, preferring cash and sales. Further, Beatty and his staff had to persuade European artists to send their works to faraway Pittsburgh with no guarantee of a sale or a prize. And in 1897, when control of the exhibition passed to a jury of ten artists, rather than businessmen, controversy increased.[16] Eight of the ten jurors were to be American artists living in the country, no more than three from the same city (essentially New York); the other two could

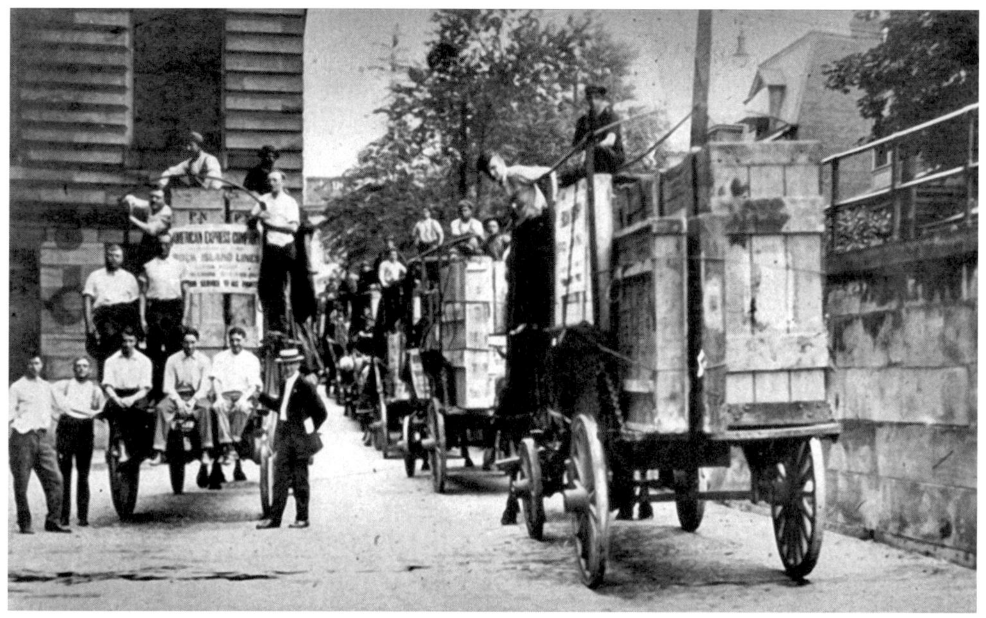

American Express delivers boxes of paintings for an early International at the expanded Institute. The need to ship so many paintings from Europe to Pittsburgh on a regular basis forced the Institute to develop new standards for transporting works of art, and other museums took notice.

be European nationals or American expatriates. The rules also left the local art community feeling slighted or even excluded.[17] And even artists who were loyal to the city could be temperamental. The expatriate Mary Cassatt wrote Beatty a vehement letter in 1909, refusing to send a photograph of herself for the catalog: "It would be very disagreeable to me to have my image in a catalogue or in any publication.... What has the public to do with the personal appearance of the author of a picture or statue? Why should such curiosity if it exists be gratified?"[18]

In spite of the difficulties, Beatty staged annual exhibitions from 1897 to 1905 but broke his pattern in 1902 by exhibiting only loaned works that spanned a 300-year period and by changing the annual exhibition into a biennial one. There was no exhibition in 1906, because of the expansion to the art wing of the library, but the tradition resumed in 1907. World War I put a halt to the international exhibitions for five years, from 1914 to 1919, while the international scene was in political confusion. The 1920 show was the last one organized by Beatty alone. From Beatty's final exhibition the museum bought John Singer Sargent's *Venetian Interior* (c. 1880–82) and Claude Monet's *Water Lilies Beneath the Bridge* (1899, deaccessioned in 1953).

Beatty, throughout, felt that the tremendous energy that he, his agents, and his staff devoted to creating this one exhibit could be better expended by building a finer permanent collection. In 1904 he began to expand the collection modestly, acquiring drawings, and in 1906 he started to acquire Japanese woodblock prints. By 1911, he had added etchings and engravings, by 1916 original bronze sculptures, and by 1919 marble sculptures. His last published checklist of the collection, created in 1917, finds ancient art represented by plaster casts and marble copies, old masters by etchings and engravings, modern art by drawings and paintings, and non-Western art by Japanese prints.

When Beatty retired in 1922, his health and eyesight failing, he had set the museum's course for decades and acquired works the museum still prizes. His successor, Homer Saint-Gaudens (1922–50), whose long tenure matched Beatty's, shepherded the museum through turbulent times, organizing Internationals amid the global chaos of World War II, the rise of Soviet Communism, the Cold War, and a depressed local economy. By this point, Carnegie's original endowment barely covered the museum's

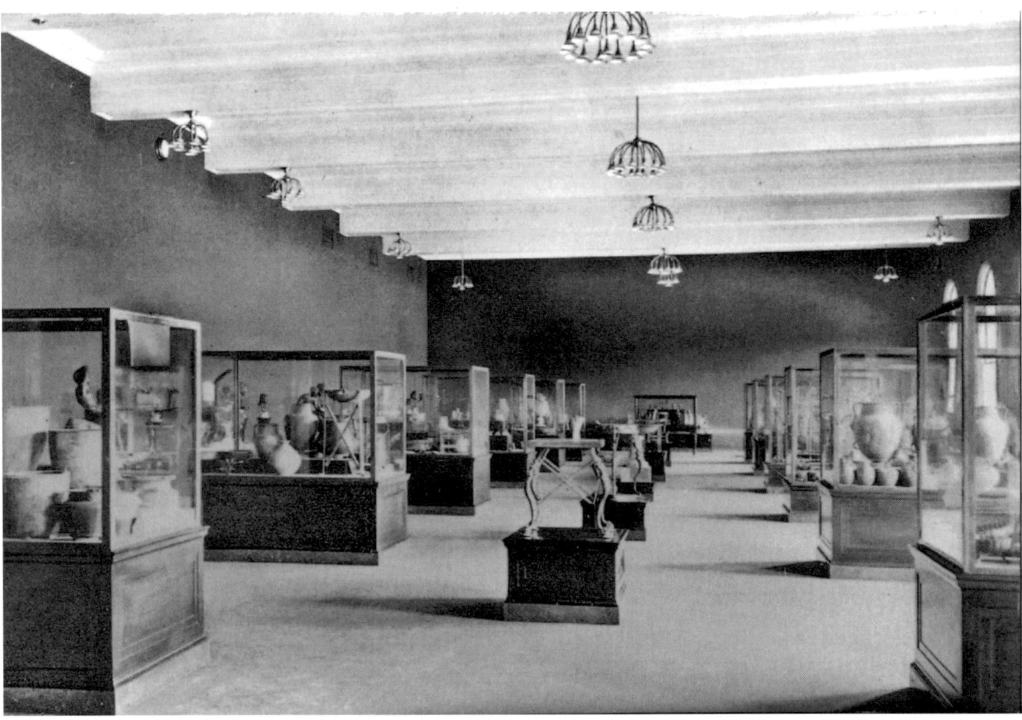

The Hall of Bronzes: Carnegie bought replicas from ancient Herculaneum to install in the large 1907 gallery, now the Ailsa Mellon Bruce Galleries for Decorative Arts.

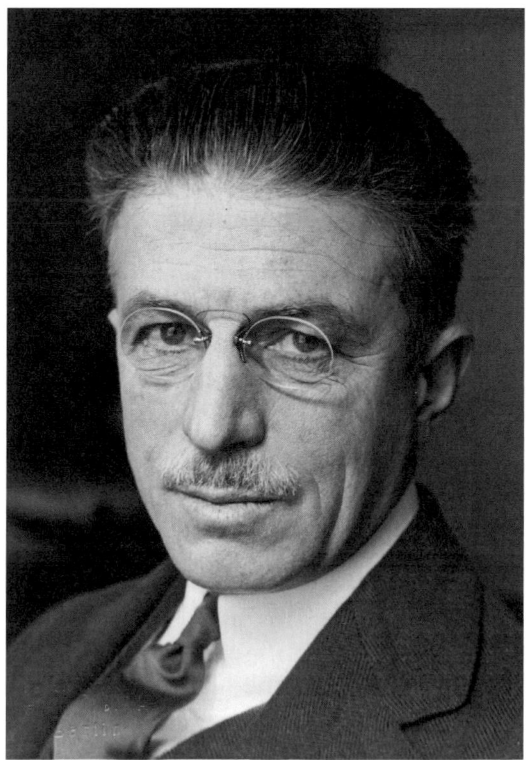

*Homer Saint-Gaudens, director of the Department
of Fine Arts from 1922 to 1950, created programs in the
spirit of a free community arts center and guided
the museum through tumultuous times.*

operating costs, so one of Saint-Gaudens's early moves was to establish the
Patron's Art Fund to develop the permanent collection even further. Like
Beatty a careful, conservative director, Saint-Gaudens was also a master of
clever deals that ensured the museum's survival, a gambler on the outcome
of international politics, and a quiet proponent of Modernism who cautiously introduced new works to his conservative Pittsburgh constituency.[19]

The son of America's most famous sculptor, Augustus Saint-Gaudens,
Homer Saint-Gaudens held an automatic passport granting him access to
the art world. He had worked as a journalist in New York, been an editor
of several art-focused magazines, and served as the stage manager for the
celebrated actress Maude Adams as she crossed the country giving one-
night performances in American cities. During World War I, he was the
director of the U.S. Army's first camouflage units, a role that he reprised

in World War II, when he was chief of the Camouflage Section in Europe from 1941 until 1945. Just before coming to Pittsburgh in 1921, he was working as a theatrical director on Broadway, with three shows to his credit.[20] Thus, when he was appointed assistant director to the aging John Beatty, he was skilled at staging events, managing the press, and giving the public what it wanted.

Not an art historian, Saint-Gaudens had imbibed the genteel conservatism of his New England family and personally favored academic art, although as a showman he understood the need to bring Modernism—in its less objectionable forms—to the public. Carnegie's death in 1919 gave him a freer hand in interpreting the founder's wishes. A veteran traveler, he went regularly to Europe, diplomatically choosing the number of art works to represent each country at the International and persuading famous artists like Matisse to come to Pittsburgh to serve on juries. He also understood that controversy captures public attention, and in 1931, during the Great Depression, he succeeded in securing heavy attendance at the International by displaying Franklin Watkin's *Suicide in Costume,* a puzzling painting of a suicidal clown that might be a comment on the fractured, self-destructive social trends of the era. Saint-Gaudens was used to mockery from the press and cartoonists for even his restrained presentation of Modernist art, but his exhibitions remained popular.

During the decades of his tenure, Saint-Gaudens was confronted with the political and racial upheavals that fractured the art world. He had to protect his European agents (some of them Jewish) from harassment, but he tried to delicately balance the artistic scales by exhibiting official Nazi art, as well as work by Jewish artists, and conducting and publishing an interview with Benito Mussolini. One year the Carnegie prize went to the American Jewish artist Leon Kroll, an indirect protest of Hitler's racist policies. The paintings shipped to the prestigious Carnegie International from Madrid in 1939 were carried out of the city in the same truck that was smuggling the treasures of the Prado out of the city for safekeeping. They remained in Pittsburgh until after the war, along with other paintings from Europe, and eventually returned to their stabilized countries of origin. Throughout all this turbulence, the Carnegie International carried on while other museums cancelled exhibits, and Pittsburgh survived as an important venue. In the 1940s, while Saint-Gaudens was in the army, the museum staged annual exhibitions of American art, managed largely by assistant director John O'Connor. Saint-Gaudens's final International was staged in 1950, with funding from the Andrew Carnegie Foundation. This show included more abstract art than ever before: Pittsburgh was turning the corner on Modernism.

Saint-Gaudens was hampered by budget shortfalls that sometimes allowed him to purchase only one painting a year, and while he wanted to modernize the galleries, there were usually no funds available. He felt the museum's mission was to make art accessible to the Pittsburgh public, and admission remained free. The first concern of the Department of Fine Arts, his populist philosophy held, was to convince the public that "the artists of today are, as were the artists of the past, the friends and associates of the public, different from the public [only] in that they possess clearer seeing eyes and more skillful fingers."[21] During the Great Depression and World War II, the galleries became a refuge for the public, a place removed from the cares of daily life.

In keeping with his desire to make the museum relevant and accessible to the public, Saint-Gaudens operated museum programs in the spirit of a free community arts center, moving away from the academic gallery concept promoted by Beatty. While he did not acquire controversial works for the permanent collection, during the 1920s and 1930s, individual works and even entire collections were donated to the museum, as a passing generation of collectors—their aesthetic literacy perhaps enhanced by their exposure to great art in Pittsburgh's galleries—began to settle their estates. Saint-Gaudens purchased John Kane's *Scene from the Scottish Highlands* from the 1927 International, the first painting by a self-taught Pittsburgh artist who would go on to astonish the art world. He also added work by the Pittsburgh artist David Blythe (1815–65), a formerly obscure figure whose reputation had been revived by exhibitions at the Carnegie Institute (1932) and the Whitney Museum of American Art (1936). Today Pittsburgh holds the largest collections of the works of these two self-taught Pittsburgh artists.

Saint-Gaudens's retirement in 1950 led to the appointment of Gordon Bailey Washburn (1950–62) and a shift in course. Washburn challenged the conservative outlook so long espoused by his predecessors. Elegant and articulate, he was the former director of the Rhode Island School of Design Museum and the Albright Art Gallery in Buffalo.[22] He was a conspicuous Pittsburgh leader during the city's first renaissance, his influence reaching well beyond the museum's walls. He helped develop the concept of the Three Rivers Arts Festival and served on the City Art Commission and on the advisory committee of the Pittsburgh Plan for Art. Experienced with the media, he helped create educational television programs for public broadcast through WQED; at the museum, he helped develop the Women's Committee and the Junior Council of the Department of Fine Arts.

Washburn's establishment of the Women's Committee was no small feat, and it has had significant results for the museum and the Pittsburgh community. Indeed, this group of about 215 volunteers, over half a cen-

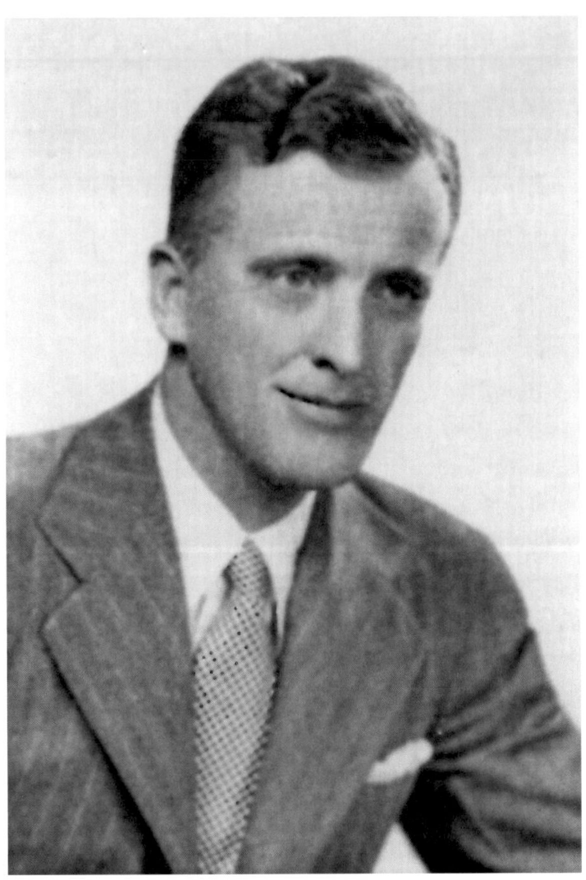

*Gordon Bailey Washburn, appointed director in 1950,
was the first head of the museum to collect controversial
contemporary art.*

tury, has raised more than $4 million to buy art for the permanent collection and to fund museum restoration and remodeling projects. It founded Pittsburgh's Three Rivers Arts Festival and went on to sponsor an annual antiques show and the Decorative Arts Symposium. Its members serve by invitation only, working as volunteer docents, staffing the museum gift shop, and organizing fund-raisers. President David Hillenbrand, on the group's fiftieth anniversary, remarked that he was amazed by what its members had accomplished: "If the Women's Committee did not exist, the void could not be filled—not because of any one woman, but because of its collective commitment to the Museum of Art."[23]

Washburn also organized four Internationals that showcased over three hundred works of art: In 1952, the exhibit featured work from Latin

America. In 1955, the collector G. David Thompson served as a juror, while in 1958, Marcel Duchamp and the actor-artist Vincent Price were on the jury. In 1961, the exhibit yielded a number of works that are still in the collection. In 1958 and 1961, in particular, Washburn moved away from the long dominance of painting, and in those years the Internationals displayed more than a hundred contemporary sculptures. To some extent, Washburn was swimming against the city's institutional current, and art historian Donald Miller, for example, wrote of Carnegie Institute president James M. Bovard ordering Washburn not to include the work of "that communist" Pablo Picasso in one International.

Washburn pressed on, however, preaching the virtues of contemporary art to his Pittsburgh audience, pointing out that innovations in art are like innovations in business; this new art could grasp the complexities of a chaotic world. In 1961, he made a classic argument in support of contemporary art:

Modern art, like modern science, is largely concerned with truths that are not outwardly visible. The artist seeks to make visible for you—as well as himself— various ideas, concepts, images, or visions. He must externalize these, calling them up from their hiding places within the heart and mind, not drawing them directly from outer life. Since his art no longer mirrors things, academic training in the copying of things is beside the point. . . .

No longer guided by the conventions of his immediate time and place, our contemporary artist feels at liberty to make his creations out of any material whatsoever and even to mix together the traditional categories such as painting, modeling, stonecutting, wood carving, and the rest. No kings, churches, national academies nor governments (except behind the Iron Curtain) tell him what he must or must not do, and so he chooses to do whatever he likes. . . . It is, as we may see, a veritable artistic emancipation and, as we may also see, the artist revels in it and fully explores its possibilities.[24]

In spite of his advocacy, the International was perpetually plagued by financial instability, and it changed from a biennial to a triennial exhibition in 1952. The 1958 exhibition was saved only because Allegheny County made it part of the city's bicentennial celebrations.[25]

At the same time, Washburn increased the collection's holdings of important works, hoping to ensure its future success. Businessman G. David Thompson donated Henry Moore's *Reclining Figure* to the Carnegie Institute, a work that had won second prize in sculpture in 1958. Thompson also bought the sculpture that took first prize, Alexander Calder's mobile *Pittsburgh,* donating it to the Pittsburgh International Airport, where it continues to revolve slowly before thousands of travelers. In 1961, a series of one-artist shows featured a group of modern artists whose work remains vital to the collection, including Pierre Alechinsky, Richard Diebenkorn, Grace Hartigan, Carl-Henning Pedersen, and David Smith. Also during the early 1960s, Sarah Mellon Scaife, Andrew Mellon's niece, began to buy European art for the collection, launching an effort that her family continued after her death in 1965. One of her purchases was Monet's *Nympheas (Waterlilies)*, in 1962. Washburn added works by Perugino, Hals, Degas, Renoir, Vuilliard, Monet, and Matisse to the permanent collection, his espousal of abstract art not excluding the forerunners of Modernism, whose interests in color, line, and form had laid a foundation for the work of later artists.[26]

Nevertheless, Washburn—in spite of his support for contemporary artists—was increasingly criticized for not being sufficiently au courant: he was charged with failing to keep up on the treadmill of art trends promoted by leading national art critics. At the other end of the critical spectrum, his own trustees disapproved of his plan to cover up the John White Alexander murals in Staircase Hall, which to him symbolized the sentimental, old-fashioned art he wanted to move beyond.

Perhaps Washburn's pursuit of contemporary art had exhausted both himself and his trustees, for after the 1961 International he began searching for another position, finding it at the Asia House Gallery in New York City. His resignation came as a surprise to Institute president James Bovard and other community leaders, but the next two scheduled Internationals—in 1964 and 1967—had already been funded by the A. W. Mellon Educational and Charitable Trust, and Washburn pledged that he would continue to do "spadework" to ensure they were mounted. His successor, Gustave Von Groschwitz, called "Von" by his friends, seemed well qualified to take over the reins. As chief curator at the Cincinnati Museum of Art, he had mounted six international biennials of lithography and had strong contacts among international artists, collectors, and dealers. A quiet, scholarly man whom many found more accessible than Washburn had been, Von Groschwitz organized the 1964 and 1967 Internationals with the help of Washburn's long-time associate Leon Arkus (now the museum's associate director) and European correspondents whom he called informal cojurors.[27]

As a specialist in prints, Von Groschwitz expanded the print collection but also continued to collect paintings, as Washburn had done with Arkus's help. He began to fill out the collection with more French Impressionist and Post-Impressionist paintings, and Howard Noble's 1964 bequest of sixty-four paintings by the "old masters" was a major gift to the museum. Thus, the abundance of American art accumulated in the museum's first half century now began to be balanced by more traditional European art in the core collection. Von Groschwitz had no passion for collecting the sometimes scan-

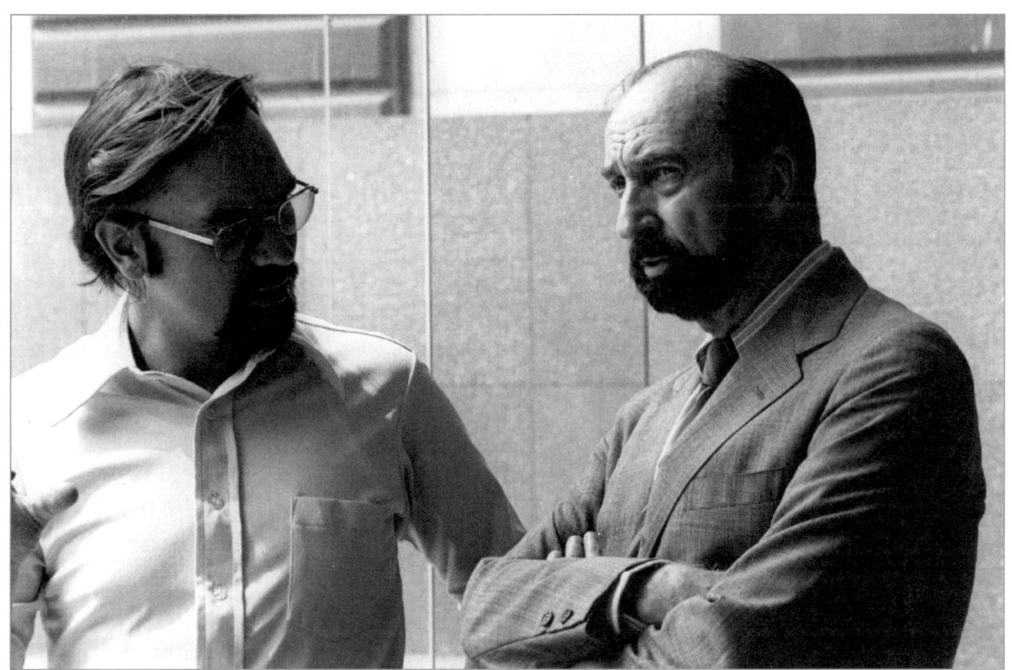

Robert Gangewere interviewed director Leon Arkus in 1974 about the opening of the Scaife Gallery.

dalous and disreputable work of the 1960s avant garde, with its rebellious artists who sometimes rejected prizes offered by the established art world.

Von Groschwitz resigned in 1968, the same year James Bovard retired after twenty years as president. Washburn's protégé Leon A. Arkus (1968–80), who had worked at the museum since 1954, first as assistant director and then as associate director, took over as the new director. Carnegie Institute itself was now under new leadership, and the new president, James Mellon Walton, took a strong interest in the Museum of Art. Arkus served as the museum's director during the significant expansion of 1974, when the new Sarah Scaife Gallery opened thanks to the generosity of another Mellon family member, Richard Mellon Scaife, tripling the exhibition space and offering new facilities, including a theater. Pittsburgh's art museum, with its new Scaife Gallery designed by the celebrity architect Edward Larrabee Barnes, was now more visible in the world of art museums, a world that was rapidly changing and becoming more competitive.

The larger spaces of the Scaife Gallery also meant that Arkus had to operate a more active exhibition program. Convinced that the Museum of

Art should develop a better permanent collection to complement its spectacular new gallery, Arkus proposed that the International be retired. There were philosophical as well as practical reasons for doing so. Arkus agreed with those art critics who felt that the International was an outmoded venue and that selecting one work of art as the best in any given year, and also one artist, led to very arbitrary selections. Great artists often had decades of productivity behind them, and there were compelling reasons to give awards for a career of artistic achievement, not simply one performance.

Arkus had managed concerts in New York and run the Masters of Art exhibition at the 1939 New York World's Fair, and he had an impresario's instinct. He and Gordon Washburn had met in New York, part of the circle surrounding the art connoisseur and "gentleman dealer" Stephan Bourgeois. Washburn and Arkus both subscribed to the Bourgeois creed: "When looking at a painting for the first time do not concern yourself with period or style, but concentrate on the painting itself as a work without ties to anything you have seen before."[28] Indeed, Arkus was famous for the "eye" he brought to exhibitions, a sensibility that came into play in the new spaces in the Sarah Scaife Gallery—all white, filled with natural light, the paintings hung in isolation to help the viewer avoid visual interference while contemplating each work. Arkus himself was so passionate about contemplating art that he regularly began his day by walking alone through the galleries, saying a silent good morning to the great works in the collection.

This collection was beautifully displayed in the gallery designed by architect Edward Larrabee Barnes. Barnes, an astute Modernist, relished function and form and avoided ornamentation. Barnes planned the ground floor of the gallery as an entrance to the whole Institute complex. The ground floor, as an extension of the exterior plaza, had "a rugged street-like quality," designed to serve as "a place for social exchange as well as the display of sculpture."[29] The galleries above, in contrast, provided space for quiet contemplation, skylights admitting light whose intensity shifted with the clouds and the seasons, showcasing the collection. Another striking feature of the design is the forty-foot-high glass wall that leads visitors up to the second floor, revealing changing views of the outdoor sculpture court. John Russell, in the *New York Times,* called the Scaife Gallery an "unflawed paradise," while Hilton Kramer declared that henceforth art lovers would have to put Pittsburgh on their museum itineraries.[30] Arkus hoped the Scaife Gallery would be considered a gem: "What is important is making sure that everything we have is of shining quality. And that is our direction. We have arrived at the point where the world regards us as a significant museum. And now that we have a beautiful new space our next step is to become a great museum. What that means is acquiring more, over

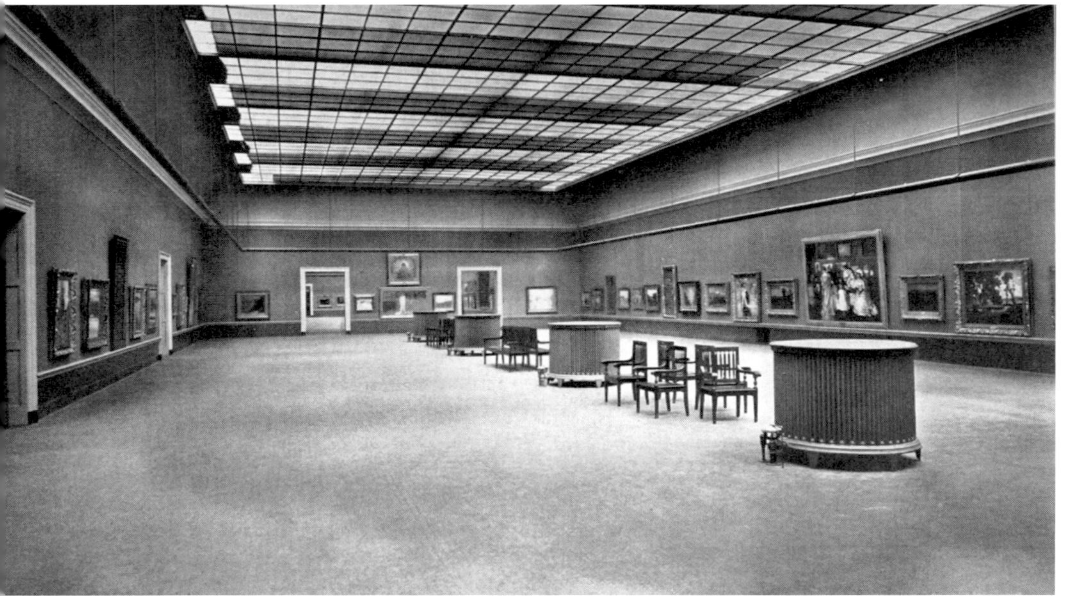

The third-floor galleries were sky-lit until the 1950s, when leaking glass panes and the need for better temperature control forced the roof of the building to be sealed with Pittsburgh-made aluminum.

time, that lives up to the quality of what we already own. For us the last twelve years has been our coming of age."[31]

Indeed, building the museum's core collection was Arkus's central project from the 1950s until his retirement in 1980. Under Washburn, Arkus advised Sarah Scaife on which works she might purchase for the museum's permanent collection, her generosity and their eventual friendship laying the foundation for a solid Impressionist collection. After acquiring the "core" permanent collection with funds from Sarah Scaife and other donors, he assembled the traveling exhibition Twelve Years of Collecting, featuring major acquisitions—notably French Impressionist, Post-Impressionist, American, and contemporary works. The collection now seemed worth talking about nationally: it was hailed in the *New York Times* as "a delectation of masterpieces." Arkus noted in his memoirs that before this exhibition, Georges Rouault's *The Old King* (1916–36; see color plate), acquired in 1940 by the Patron's Art Fund, was the only picture that any other museum wanted to borrow.[32] For his own 1970 International, Arkus gathered largely abstract paintings and sculptures by past International artists. Unlike his hero Washburn, Arkus didn't like making cutting-edge selections: he had little interest in pop, minimalism, conceptualism, earth art, and installation, and he showed none of them.[33] When he retired the Internationals after the Scaife Gallery opened, believing that a more powerful perspective is provided through artists' whole careers than through individual works, he introduced the International Series, which featured the work of a few significant artists in depth: Pierre Alechinsky in 1977, Eduardo Chillida in 1978, and Willem de Kooning in 1979. Some trustees believed that the Museum of Art without the Carnegie International was diminished, and lacking international cachet, but everyone celebrated the museum's improved permanent collection and a magnificent modern gallery that other cities would envy.

When Arkus retired in 1980, at age sixty-five, Institute president James Mellon Walton wrote that "in addition to the physical transformation of the museum, he has seen a 50% increase in the size of the permanent collection, a guarantee that the museum will always possess fine art for exhibition." Arkus, he noted, had been the "key to the emergence of the museum as an important, permanent art institution on the international scene."[34]

Despite this assessment, however, Leon Arkus's successor, John (Jack) R. Lane (1980–87), was specifically charged with instituting a dramatic shift in course, reviving the Carnegie International and moving the collection forward into the realm of contemporary art. Lane, who had a Ph.D. in fine art from Harvard and an M.B.A. from the University of Chicago, was assistant director at the Brooklyn Museum. He had no specific training in contemporary art but was an effective manager, and he lost little time in making changes in Pittsburgh. He quickly eliminated nearly all the existing curatorial staff, bringing in people with whom he was comfortable. He hired Barbara Phillips as his assistant director, charged with managing the museum's financial affairs and daily operations, and in 1981 he appointed Karen Crenshaw as the museum's first full-time conservator.

Specifically charged with restoring the Carnegie International, Lane asked a New York colleague, Gene Baro, a senior curator in prints and drawings, to oversee the revived exhibition. Baro worked hard, selecting a group of sixty-three artists from twenty-seven countries whose work reflected his own tastes and, together with Lane, inviting some of the world's leading art critics to Pittsburgh to review the exhibition. Baro, however, died several weeks before the show opened, and when the invited panel of critics rendered their opinions, they were uniformly hostile. The critic Roberta Smith observed crushingly, "There isn't a single object in this exhibition that I would wish to see again in my life."[35] By any measure, the revived 1982 International was a failure.

Lane felt he might be fired at that point, but the trustees gave him a

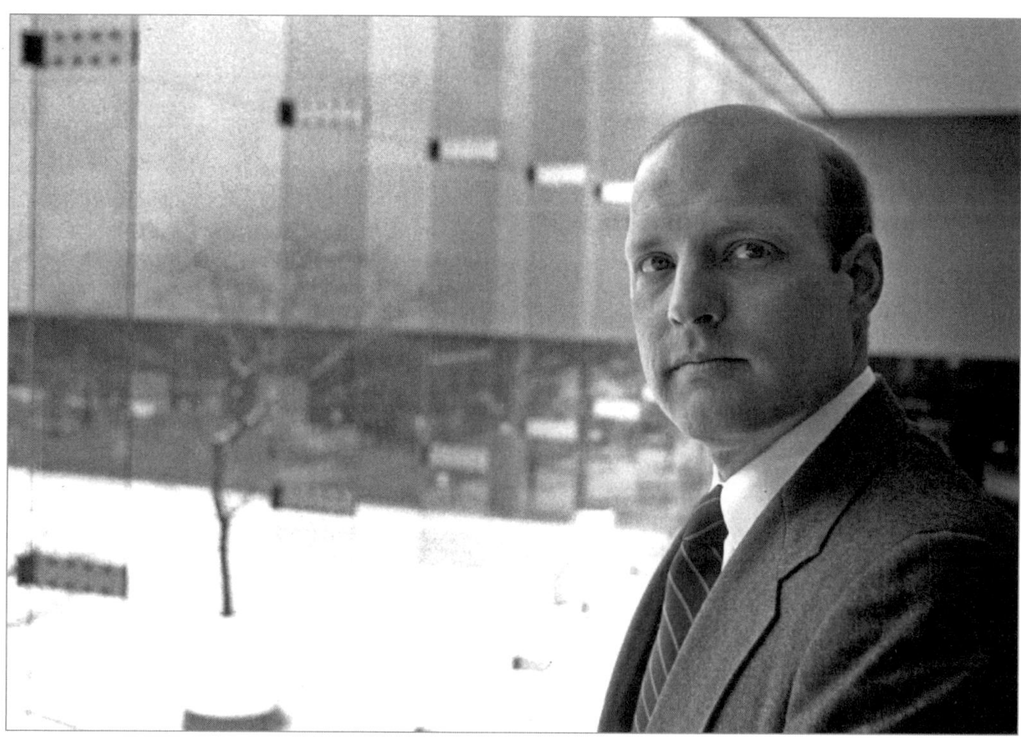

*After 1980, museum director Jack Lane restored the traditional, multi-artist International
exhibitions that had stopped after the opening of the Scaife Gallery.*

second chance, and Lane brought in yet another friend from New York,
John Caldwell, to work on the 1985 International. Together canvassing European experts for opinions and assistance, Lane and Caldwell were struck
by the residual goodwill Europeans felt toward the Carnegie International:
in the 1950s and 1960s, Pittsburgh had been one of the few places in North
America to take European art seriously. Because European art had been
unrepresented in major American shows for so long, Caldwell and Lane had
decades of artistic accomplishment to choose from, and the resulting show
was ambitious in scope—and a success. *New York Times* critic John Russell
noted the show's "exhilarating quality" and the prevailing "atmosphere of
goodwill that verged on euphoria," one that "has not been rivaled at any
international exhibition of its kind."[36] The 1985 International also led to
some notable purchases for the museum's permanent collection: Richard
Serra's prizewinning *Carnegie,* a giant sculpture of tilting corten-steel plates,
and Anselm Keifer's *Midgard.* Jack Lane had reached the goal set for him
by the trustees.

In 1987, Lane moved on to direct the San Francisco Museum of Modern Art. Now a career museum director, he later went on to transform the Dallas Museum of Art. Much later in his career, in 2004, Lane defended the Carnegie International as a tradition worth keeping. The original Carnegie vision—populating the collection through purchases from the Internationals—was in fact a brilliant strategy, Lane said, resulting in a museum collection with a special character. Further, the International attracts exceptional talent and forges lifelong relationships among future leaders in the art world: "It's hard to overestimate the value of that to this city, and to this institution and to this exhibition." The International, Lane said, "is America's only visual arts event of an international contemporary art character that rivals the Venice Biennale or Documenta in Kassel, Germany. . . . Looking at it as a museum director involved in other institutions of contemporary art, I would say the Carnegie International is a treasure and a tradition that all of us would kill to have."[37]

The next director, Phillip M. Johnston (1988–96, acting director 1987), had been hired by Jack Lane in 1982 to be the curator of antiquities and oriental and decorative arts. Jack Lane had been hard-driving deal maker, but Johnston brought a more collegial pace, consulting carefully with his other curators and steering the museum cautiously through the fundamental changes implemented under the Institute's new president, Robert C. Wilburn, particularly the advent of the new Andy Warhol Museum as a nascent institution under the wing of Carnegie Museum of Art.

Johnston's tenure saw extensive renovations to the Institute building. It also saw administrative challenges, entering into agreements in 1989 with the Andy Warhol Foundation for the Visual Arts and the Dia Art Foundation to establish the Andy Warhol Museum in Pittsburgh. The year 1990 brought yet another opportunity, when the Henry J. and Drue Heinz Foundation funded the Heinz Architectural Center with $10 million and established an endowment for the director's position at the art museum. Phillip Johnston became the "Henry J. Heinz II Director of Carnegie Museum of Art."

Under Johnston's direction, John Caldwell brought off the 1988 International successfully, and when Caldwell left to join Lane in San Francisco, Johnston hired British curator Mark Francis and arts writer Lynne Cooke to mount the 1991 International. Francis and Cooke's International, which used the entire Institute and library as exhibit space to anticipate the approaching Centennial, asked participating artists to honor the Carnegie tradition by designing work for these different spaces and to place installations throughout the city. In response, one artist cast enormous numbers of dinosaur bones, while another worked in the Hall of Architecture, installing

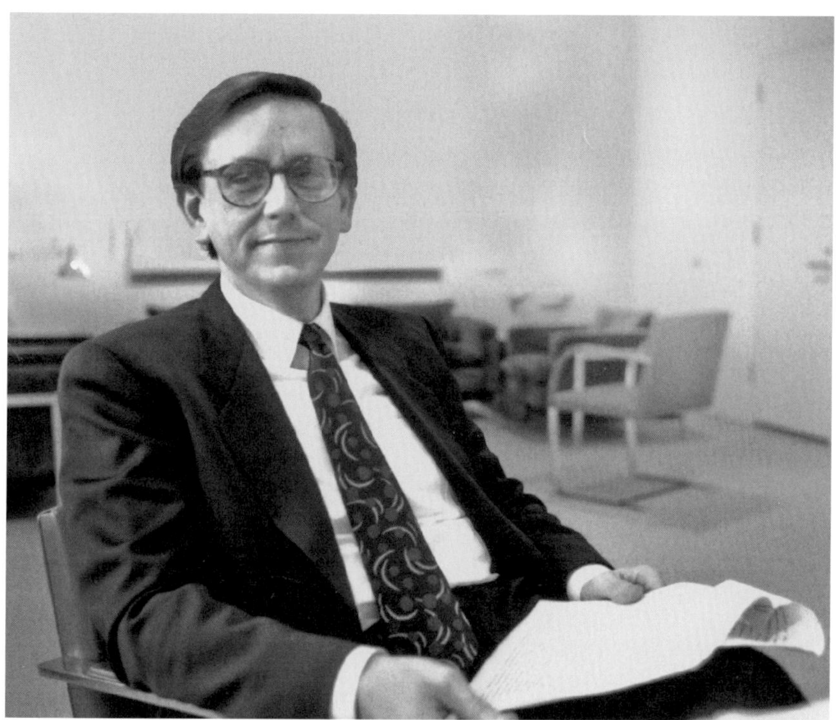

During Phillip Johnston's tenure as director, the museum added the Heinz Architectural Center and became responsible for the new Andy Warhol Museum.

plaster acronyms representing organizations that advocate for people who work in dangerous industries. In the library, a Chinese artist had surplus books pulped into papier-mâché and reinstalled them on the shelves. But the stench was so great the library staff refused to work, so the material was dessicated and installed in Plexiglas boxes. Off-site projects were varied: Ann Hamilton transformed a little house on the North Side with a collection of small wax heads that were heated, dripping wax onto the floors below. Another artist planted trees in Point State Park, in cooperation with the Western Pennsylvania Conservancy. The 1991 International also honored several senior artists, such as Louise Bourgeoise.

Beyond the International, Johnston confronted the ever-shifting boundaries of the contemporary art world by clarifying curatorial responsibilities between contemporary art and fine arts, marking the dividing line between the two as the year 1945, following World War II, and hiring Louise Lippincott, from the J. Paul Getty Museum, as the new curator of fine arts. Johnston hired Richard Armstrong, formerly of the Whitney Mu-

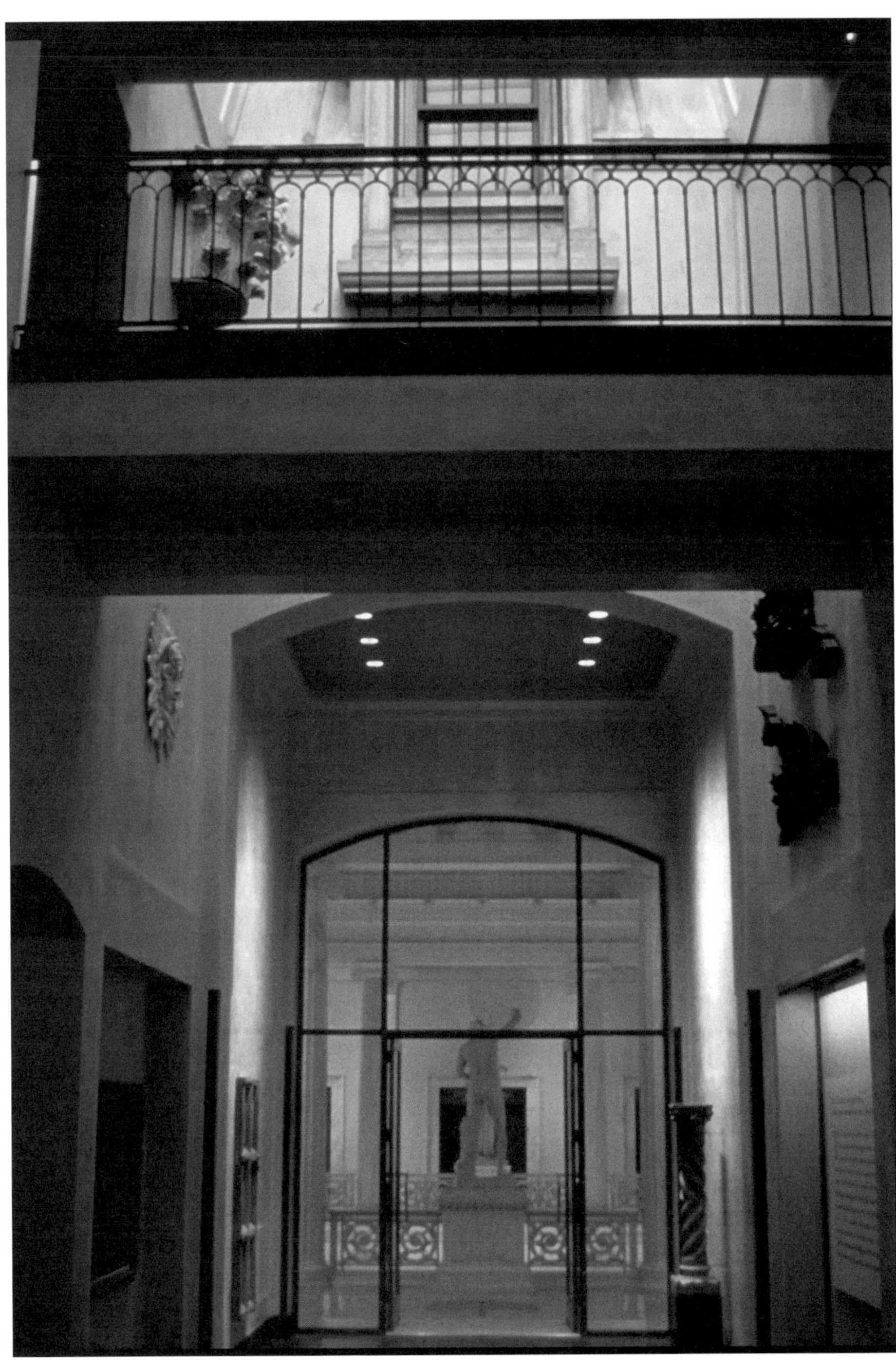

The Heinz Architectural Center, opened in 1993, ushered in a new era of architectural expertise at the museum. A building within a building, it has three floors. Above the entrance from the Hall of Sculpture is a dormer from Carnegie's mansion in New York City.

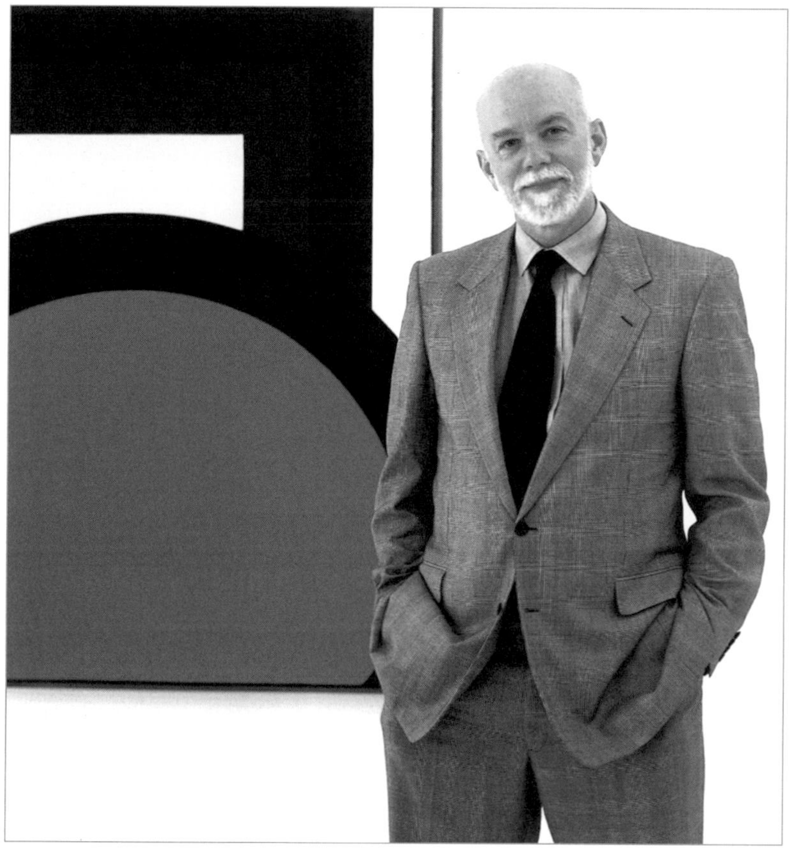

Richard Armstrong, director from 1996 to 2008, was a skilled administrator admired by his staff.

seum in New York, as the curator of contemporary art in 1992. Armstrong also served as the chief curator, acting as a liaison between the director and the other curators, and curated the International in 1995, Pittsburgh's centennial year. Armstrong spent much of his first two and a half years on the job traveling, first visiting twenty-seven countries on four continents, then narrowing the field to thirty-six artists from sixteen countries, and finally producing an exhibition of 272 works of art. His show was a popular success, capturing a particular moment in art history.

When Phillip Johnston resigned in 1996, Richard Armstrong (1996–2008) took over as the museum's director. Armstrong, in addition to being an experienced manager and an expert in contemporary art, was a smooth administrator and highly regarded by his staff. Attuned to the new agenda being advanced by Institute president Ellsworth Brown, Armstrong saw that the museum was faced with the demand to increase attendance: "I think trustees and staff feel that we must share the museum with even more people. The principal challenge facing us is to widen the audience and deepen the experience while here. Museums may be one of the few places left where imagination and intelligence are of comparable value. We teach, but we must encourage dreaming also."[38]

The budgetary crisis of 2003, falling endowment revenues, and shifting attendance demands forced Armstrong to eliminate one department, the Section of Film and Video, under curator William Judson, a highly regarded figure in the cultural scene of Pittsburgh. The Internationals went on as before. Madeleine Grynsztejn, in 1999–2000, mounted an exhibit featuring the work of forty-one artists from around the globe, while Laura Hoptman's 2004 International showcased thirty-eight established and emerging artists from five continents. In 2008 Douglas Fogle selected art under the rubric "Life on Mars," for the first time giving the International a thematic title. The most recent Internationals have continued to showcase art that reflects the moment. While Victorian expressions such as those Andrew Carnegie used ("the moral mission of art") are seldom heard today, contemporary artists do in fact often dwell upon global injustices and ethical dilemmas. After 1995 the missions of the International became philosophically more ambitious and pretentious. Madeleine Grynsztejn, discussing the disturbing work of the South African artist Kendall Geer, cited Geer's anger as a response to the philosophical question the exhibition posed: "What becomes of the self in the face of a reality that is perpetually subjected to the dynamic emergence of new relations, and to the dissolution and reconfiguration of the models?"[39] Laura Hoptman, too, showed, in Richard Armstrong's words, a "willingness to probe through art the central issues of life." Hoptman pursued "the Ultimates," such subjects as "the nature of free will, immortality, the existence of God, and the extent of the universe." Ethics, she believed, "is the engine that fires some of the most consequential art of the past five years."[40] Douglas Fogle, likewise, mounted a show that posed ethical questions: "Are we alone in the universe? . . . Or are we, ourselves, the strangers in our own worlds?" "To me," Fogle said, "contemporary art is as much about coming to terms with our own world as it is about creating a set of worlds parallel to those that we walk in every day."[41]

Richard Armstrong resigned in June 2008, at age fifty-nine, accepting a position as the director of the Solomon R. Guggenheim Foundation in New York and observing that it was atypical for an art museum director to remain at one institution for a dozen years. Praised by his curators and colleagues in Pittsburgh for his strategic and intelligent decisions, Armstrong left the museum in as good a shape as it had ever been, financially and physically.

After a lengthy search, the museum board appointed Lynn Zelevansky as the next director in May 2009. A respected curator from the Los Angles County Museum of Art, she was admired in the field of contemporary art and enthusiastic about her move to Pittsburgh, having visited it often during recent Internationals. In appointing Zelevansky, Institute president David Hillenbrand and the board broke the century-long pattern of hiring only men as directors of the art museum. Pittsburgh's Palace of Culture was seldom first in breaking traditions of museum administration, but it was usually not far behind.

ART EDUCATION

Public education at Carnegie's Department of Fine Arts began early and developed according to Andrew Carnegie's hopes. The first museum director, John Beatty, personally gave public tours of the paintings in the collection and in 1901 began working with the Pittsburgh public schools to schedule groups of students to take the art appreciation courses that were offered every year. In his 1917 annual report, Beatty noted that the Pittsburgh school board had sent five thousand eighth-graders to the Institute for art instruction, authorizing trolley fare for all the students—a more liberal plan than could be found in any other city. Giving children an understanding of the basic qualities of art, rather than technical skills, was Beatty's goal, helping them define the subtle qualities that characterize good art.[42]

After Beatty's retirement, the famous Saturday Art Classes for Children were instituted in 1928, under Margaret M. Lee, the museum's first director of fine arts education, who supervised two classes: Tam O Shanters (fifth-, sixth-, and seventh-graders) and Palettes (eighth- and ninth-graders). She kept this role for some thirty years, declaring, "Today, in fostering the three C's—character, culture and citizenship—art is fundamental."[43] Public school art teachers recommended students to the museum program on the basis of artistic talent and intelligence, and they were constantly reminded of the honor of being chosen. Classes were free, and so were art supplies—paper, drawing boards, crayons. For poor attendance a child could be dropped from the program. Lee emphasized children's spontaneity and creativity, using public school teachers to develop their technical skills. Museum teacher Elmer Stephan, director of art for the Pittsburgh public schools, described these classes in 1932, noting that he had first faced 25 talented boys and girls in a museum class with some trepidation. However, he soon realized that they had a "fearless attitude towards freedom of self-expression"; the talent was there if he had enough sense to let it alone. These students were determined and eager: "One little boy ten years old

came to class soaking wet. He had walked four miles to the Institute without
car fare." The next year Stephan added 10 more pupils, and by 1932 he was
teaching 450 "eager children of special ability." The yearly program would
eventually reach 25,186 students, drawn from 151 of the city's elementary
and junior high schools.[44]

Stephan followed a formula: he stood on the stage and drew, often tell-
ing a simple story. Then he asked students to draw—to reproduce the lines
and forms he had sketched. After this he asked them to make an "applica-
tion" of the drawing techniques they had rehearsed, searching out subjects
in the galleries that illustrated the lesson. He emphasized technique and
realistic draftsmanship. His was a Depression-era approach to art, in which
discipline in regimented and authoritarian classes was thought to encourage
creativity and individuality—a seeming paradox. Students, while asked to
reproduce techniques, could not copy another's work. When Stephan drew
a house with smoke curling out of the chimney, for example, students were
asked to draw their own houses, not to copy his.

The line of students outside the Institute on Saturdays was so long that
it took thirty minutes for the Tam O Shanters to enter the building; print
their names on attendance cards; pick up their drawing boards, papers,
and crayons; and then take their seats. The older students gathered elsewhere with their teacher, Katherine McFarland, the director of art for the
Wilkinsburg Public Schools. McFarland had only two hundred students,
their lessons based on all the Institute's permanent collections, both natural
history displays and exhibits in the Department of Fine Arts. The students'
art education was very much a Pittsburgh experience: sometimes the class
went to Schenley Park or to the Phipps Conservatory for the annual flower
show.[45] She encouraged life drawings of people in costume and once organized a stained-glass project in which student designs were constructed by
master craftsmen.

Even though the students' experiences were rooted in Pittsburgh,
teachers used the Carnegie Internationals to demonstrate international
art trends. Students, for example, were asked to explore their own faces
with their fingers, finding the hollows and ridges, and then translate that
into abstract art. McFarland had her students draw and paint in the balcony
of Architecture Hall, where the great skylights provided excellent light.
They were to think of themselves as artist-critics, aware of the collection's
masterpieces; the cornerstone of their season's work would be the International exhibition. Her goal was "to cultivate the child's ability to choose
and discriminate; to encourage him to look, to see, to remember; to help
him build an art vocabulary; to give him many art experiences through
Carnegie Institute's endless resources."[46]

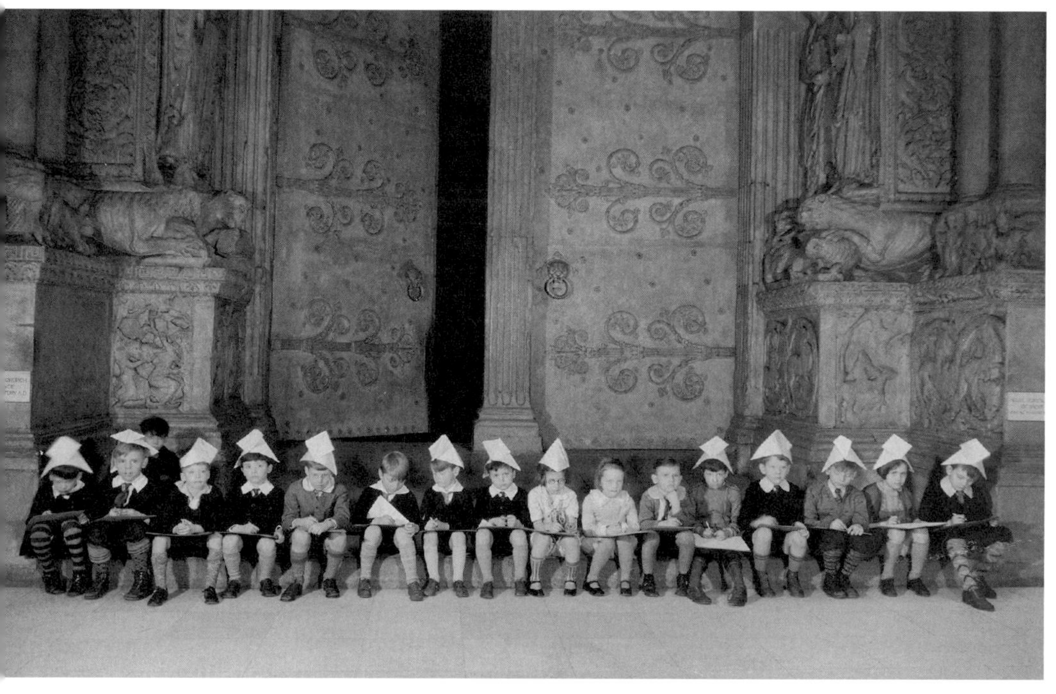

From the time Saturday art classes started in 1928, instructors used the Institute's dramatic surroundings to inspire children.

Another memorable teacher, Joseph Fitzpatrick ("Fitz"), also the Pittsburgh public school art director, developed an astonishing following of young students, adhering to Lee's mantra of "to look, to see, to remember" in his own style. Future art critic Donald Miller, one of his students, later recalled not only his charm but the fact that "he was the first person of style we knew who could discuss aesthetics.... We knew we had talent. Our selection assured it. We burned to learn. And, beauty of all beauties, our teacher treated us like *adults*.... We would have walked through fire for him."[47] Fitzpatrick took a holistic view of art education: "It was important that the students should come to a place where the environment was magnificent, and where they could learn without someone taking a club to them and insisting upon it." He wanted them to pass through the doors and feel at home. In the foyer of the Music Hall, they might study the colonnade and the marble inlays on the wall or the "tremendous rococo business" on the ceiling. Or he would take them outside to look at the statues: "I think this kind of attention helped teach young people to care for their public buildings, and be interested in the environments in which they lived in their communities."[48]

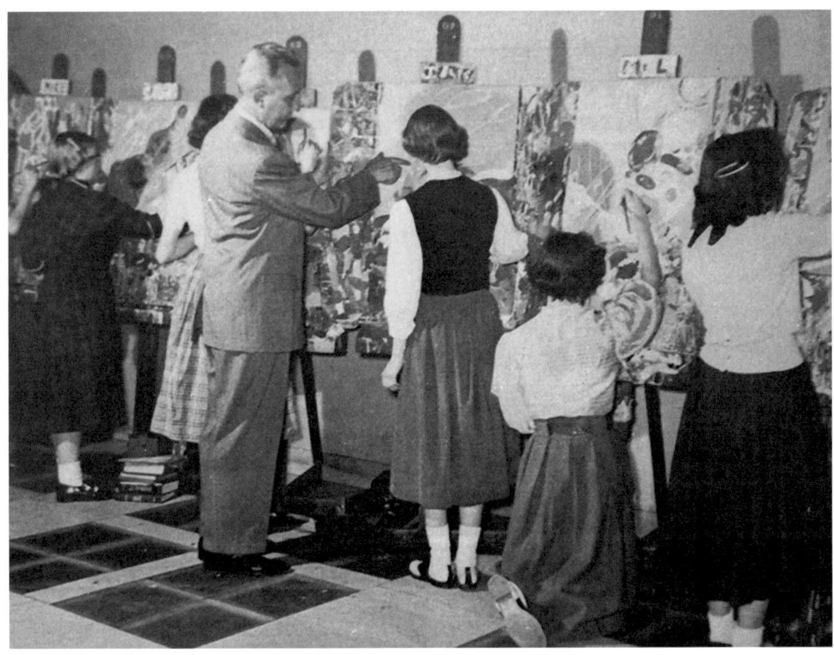

Joe Fitzpatrick teaches young art students on the sky-lit balcony of Architecture Hall, where classes have been held for more than a century.

In 1948, art education at the Institute united with natural history education in one department, the Division of Education—a rare example of administrative unity between the two museums. Arthur Twomey, a well-traveled ornithologist, was the head of the department, which lasted until 1976, when the Scaife Gallery art classroom initiated a new era. Art education at Carnegie throughout the 1940s, 1950s, and 1960s nurtured an amazing pool of talented children, including Andy Warhol, Phillip Pearlstein, Mel Bochner, Jack Butler, and Raymond Saunders. But more important, this exposure to the arts enriched generations, influencing their lives even though most never became professional artists.

Annie Dillard, a Pulitzer Prize–winning author and a museum student in the 1960s, wrote tellingly of her experience in *An American Childhood*, describing her first sight of the sculpture *Man Walking (Walking Man I)*, by Alberto Giacometti (see color plate), which won first prize at the 1961 International:

I saw the sculpture: a wiry, thin person, long legs in full stride, thrust his small mute head forward into the empty air. Six feet tall, bronze. I read about the

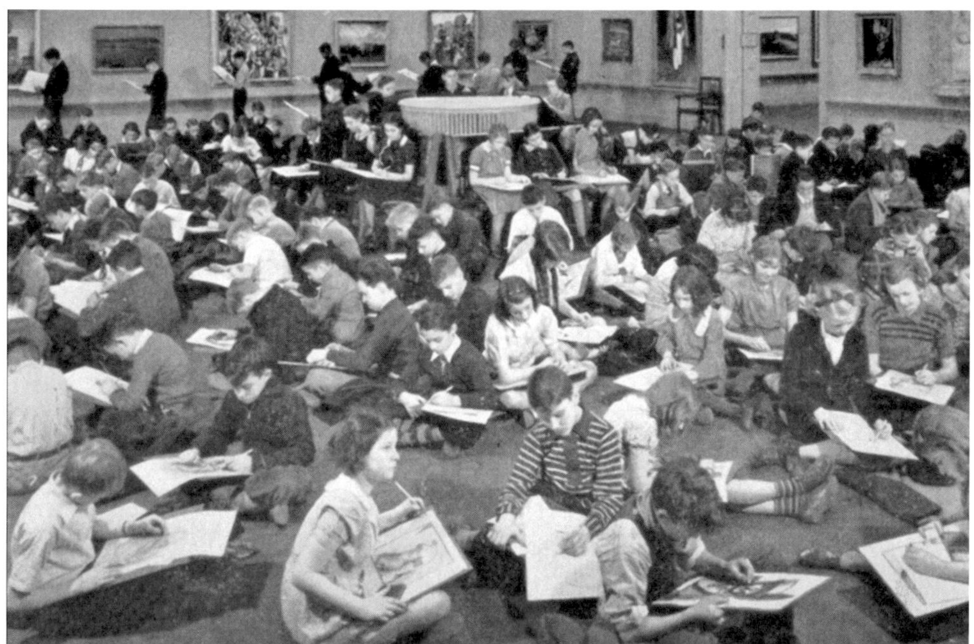

After 1950, art students took classes through the Institute's Division of Education, which combined the resources of the art and natural history museums.

sculpture every time I opened the paper; I saw its picture; I climbed the marble stair alone to look at it again and again. To see *Man Walking,* I walked past other abstract canvases by Robert Motherwell, Franz Kline, Adolph Gottlieb.... At school I began to draw abstract forms in rectangles and squares. But more often, then and for many years, I drew what I thought of as the perfect person, whose form matched his inner life....

... *Man Walking* was pure consciousness made poignant; a soul without a culture, absolutely alone, without even a time, without people, speech, books, tools, work, or even clothes.... *Man Walking* was so skinny his inner life was his outer life; it had nowhere else to go.... The sculptor's soul floated to his fingertips; I met him there, on *Man Walking*'s skin.[49]

Beginning in 1976 the Scaife Gallery art classroom initiated a new era, with the program reorganized and renamed the Saturday Creative Art Classes, and eventually the Art Connection. At the Scaife, smaller groups of about twenty students were now taught by young professional artists and teachers. For the next thirty years, the museum's Art Education Department, its directors including Anthony Landreau, Vicki Clark, and Marilyn

Russell, oversaw a more focused program, true to the more modern tenets of art education, but without the armies of children trooping through the building in disciplined groups.

DECORATIVE ARTS

Every museum defines the vast field of decorative arts for itself, taking into account its own mission and vision for the future. Should the museum collect mass-produced objects or focus on the limited edition, the one-of-a-kind? Should it collect forms that relate to its other historical collections when it buys furniture and lighting, or should it collect in new areas such as sports equipment and computers? Newer objects are often exquisitely designed and say as much about society today as an elaborate tea caddy says about eighteenth-century social life. Each curator and museum must address such questions, the passions of different curators and donors giving each decorative arts collection a distinct personality.[50]

The Carnegie's collection was created in 1953 under director Gordon Washburn with a $75,000 grant from the Sarah Scaife Foundation and a great deal of later support from other foundations. Each curator of the collection over the last half century—Herbert Weissberger (1953–61), David Owsley (1968–78), Phillip Johnston (1982–92), Sarah Nichols (1992–2006), and Jason T. Busch (2006–)—has worked to develop a permanent collection that relates to the museum's other strengths. In spite of gaps in the line of curatorial appointments, which reflected the museum's financial condition and the priorities of different directors, the department has been consistently supported by the Women's Committee of the Museum of Art, which has raised funds to buy objects and sponsored panel discussions and antique shows since its founding in 1957.

Herbert Weissberger (1953–61), the first curator of decorative arts, oversaw the initial transfer of objects from the Anthropology Department of the Museum of Natural History, which formed the core of the collection. Highlights included Herbert DuPuy's collection of miniatures and other precious objects (three hundred American and European portrait miniatures and over three hundred snuff boxes, enamels, ivory and wood carvings, fans, and gold and silver objects from the sixteenth, seventeenth, and eighteenth centuries). Henry J. Heinz gave exquisitely detailed Chinese and Japanese ivories, many collected in 1902 and 1913 during Heinz's visits to China and Japan as the president of the World's Sunday School Association. Weissberger, tasked with establishing a rationale for maintaining a permanent collection, pursued his goal through exhibitions, publications, and acquisitions. With substantial help from the Sarah Mellon Scaife Foundation, the department bought Meissen porcelain from the famous Swan service, establishing ceramics as an important area of the collection. The Hearst newspaper empire owned a Pittsburgh newspaper, and the Hearst Foundation donated several large late seventeenth-century French tapestries to the department in 1954, a magnificent gift to a department that was not yet one year old. The tapestries proved a catalyst: over the next few years, the museum continued to receive gifts of tapestries, forming the core of a small but choice collection.

After Weissberger resigned in 1961, however, the acquisitions program declined, and there was no full-time curator of decorative arts until 1968. Still, significant gifts continued, laying the groundwork for future developments: Mrs. John Berdan, for example, donated eight pieces of American furniture to the museum in 1966 and 1967, eventually shifting the collection's direction from European toward American decorative arts. In 1968, when Leon Arkus became director of the museum and James M. Walton president of the Institute, decorative arts was revived, and David T. Owsley was appointed curator. Owsley, an independent and knowledgeable collector himself, promptly began to expand the collection's range and overall quality. He was a purist and disdained Carnegie's plaster replicas, secretly attending to the destruction of some of the lesser casts and dreaming of filling the entire Hall of Architecture with an environmentally controlled boxlike room where the public could view the treasures of decorative arts.[51] While this dream was never realized, his leadership did lead to several dramatic developments. In 1970, Owsley's enterprise secured for the museum a substantial acquisition of objects from the estate of Ailsa Mellon Bruce, who had died in 1969. The Ailsa Mellon Bruce Collection became the core of a notable eighteenth-century collection, including over twenty-eight hundred European works of art, much of it ceramics, as well as furniture. Then, in 1972 and 1973, the distinguished art historian Walter Read Hovey of the University of Pittsburgh donated his Chinese, Persian, and Indian art to the museum, significantly expanding its non-Western holdings and nearly doubling the size of its Chinese collections. In 1973, and again in 1981, the gifts of Mr. and Mrs. James Drain moved the collection into yet another area: regional furniture produced in Pittsburgh and western Pennsylvania.

Owsley resigned in 1978, and the next four years saw another gap in appointing a curator for the collection, which was managed by departmental assistant Susan Johnson. Museum director Jack Lane finally appointed Phillip Johnston in 1982. A careful and thoughtful administrator who would eventually direct the entire museum, Johnston concentrated on two main areas of the decorative arts collection: the eighteenth century, thus strengthening an already notable collection; and objects that complemented the museum's paintings and sculpture collections. Strategically, since the

Carnegie Museum of Art's historic mission was to collect contemporary art, he shifted decorative arts toward objects that had been created since 1850.

Johnston's personal area of expertise was silver, and the museum thus acquired silver made by Tiffany and Company, the world's leading producer of fine silver from the early 1860s to the late 1880s, reinforcing the new emphasis on collecting objects created after 1850. Johnston began to develop a collection of chairs—affordable for a smaller-scale museum and easily stored, giving the museum flexibility in changing its exhibits. Unlike Owsley, Johnston directed positive attention toward the Hall of Architecture, having it cleaned and renovated, its sculptures repaired, its vast walls painted a classic museum green and ivory to enhance the displays.

Sarah Nichols, the assistant curator of decorative arts under Johnston, took over leadership of the department in 1992. She followed Johnston's lead by continuing to collect chairs and developing the department's collections of more contemporary work and of pieces related to Pittsburgh. Under Nichols, the museum developed a collection of works in aluminum that is one of the finest in the world, celebrating one of Pittsburgh's basic industries.[52] She collected ceramics by Pittsburgh's contemporary artists, including Edward Eberle, thus working to heal the historic breach between local artists and the museum. She also established a relationship with collectors Bill Block and Maxine Block, who focused on contemporary glass, and their 2002 gift moved the department into yet another new direction.

Nichols, like David Owsley, occasionally deaccessioned pieces to build a better collection: "I am a great believer in museums being allowed to deaccession, so long as all the money goes back into acquisitions. We would never deaccession art just to pay the bills."[53] While many museums were forced to deaccession "just to pay the bills" after 2003, as endowments were weakened nationally by stock-market reversals, Carnegie Museum of Art never moved in that direction.

When Nichols retired after seventeen years at the museum, the museum, in her honor, acquired an 1897 armchair by the Glasgow-based architect Charles Rennie Mackintosh, a pioneer in the modern design movement. Her successor, Jason T. Busch, had been the associate curator of architecture, design, decorative arts, craft, and sculpture at the Minneapolis Institute of Arts and the Wadsworth Atheneum Museum of Art, in Hartford, Connecticut. A $3 million gift from the Alan G. and Jane A. Lehman Foundation established a fund to purchase decorative arts and other works of art and to endow the curator's position in 2008, and Busch became the first Alan G. and Jane A. Lehman Curator of Decorative Arts. Jane Lehman was a founding member of the Women's Committee. When Busch arrived, the Bruce Galleries had been closed for years, used for storage while other galleries were renovated. In November 2009, under Busch's direction, the Bruce Galleries reopened, featuring a sophisticated display that captured the collection's strengths. One highlight was a large and long-neglected 1842 portrait of Mary Schenley, rolled up in storage since 1931 but now restored. Andrew Carnegie would have approved.

FILM AND VIDEO

Film and video flourished at the museum for thirty-two years, before the department was eliminated at a time of financial stress. The museum's interest in film as an art form began in March 1970, under director Leon Arkus, with a screening of international films made between 1895 and 1960, presented in Carnegie Lecture Hall. Initial funding was provided by Richard Scaife and the Allegheny Foundation, allowing Sally F. Dixon of the Women's Committee, the force behind the film program, to develop a program that paid avant-garde filmmakers a five-hundred-dollar honorarium.[54] Dixon, appointed the first curator of the Section of Film and Video at the Museum of Art, also developed a film-equipment center at the museum that eventually became Pittsburgh Filmmakers, with Robert Haller as its founding director. The result was that Pittsburgh, with the Museum of Art initially operating as a nonprofit umbrella, emerged as an experimental filmmaking center, along with New York and San Francisco. In 1974, the program moved to the new theater in the Sarah Scaife Gallery, which included an office for the film curator.[55] A grant from the A. W. Mellon Educational and Charitable Trust seeded both the workshop and film programs and the Pittsburgh Filmmakers. The list of filmmakers who visited Pittsburgh to teach and make films during the 1970s was a who's-who of the avant-garde. For three decades, film and video at Pittsburgh built a national reputation and was in the vanguard of the independent film movement, bringing many directors to Pittsburgh to speak, teach, and sometimes make films.

Dixon left in 1975, drawn to national film programs and administrative roles in other cities, and her assistant William R. Judson (1975–2003) was appointed as the second curator of the section. He was a film expert from Oberlin College with an art history background, had studied in France, and had a more academic turn of mind. The transition was relatively seamless, and the values and passions remained the same, even with some programmatic changes. A professor in the Fine Arts Department at the University of Pittsburgh, Judson brought the skills of an interlocutor to the museum: "He was academic but never didactic, he most often introduced visiting artists with the curiosity of his public audience."[56] Over his twenty-seven-year tenure, Judson attracted many film experts from the mainstream film world, but the program gradually evolved into a different kind of venue.[57]

Curating film presented special challenges. As a replicable medium, films were not as unique or collectible as paintings, and this necessitated some adjustments to the museum's acquisition program. In addition, running the program was demanding—films in, films out, and a great deal of processing to handle a hundred or even two hundred screenings a year. Locating prints could be difficult: "They might be in Teheran, or in Chicago, or New York, because somebody else is showing them."[58] Judson had to keep in touch with dozens of centers around the country because Pittsburgh could often share the costs and trouble of obtaining the films.

When Jack Lane became director of the museum in 1980 and installed his own team, Judson was the only curator who remained. Judson told Lane that he would like to increase the section's emphasis on video, which was becoming the medium of choice for many artists. Video art appealed to Lane, who shared Judson's interest in cutting-edge art and had witnessed the medium's growth in the New York gallery world. The name of the department was subsequently changed to "Section of Film and Video." When Lane resigned, Phillip Johnston supported the department, nurturing all his curatorial staff, as did Richard Armstrong until financial troubles beset the museum.

In 2002, the Museum of Art, like many museums, was facing a newly bleak financial picture, as the stock market and endowments dropped. Major funding now went to the centralized Marketing Department, which was aggressive in arguing the importance of higher attendance figures. While the Museum of Art struggled to increase attendance, film and video's numbers remained relatively low: in 2002 it screened ninety independent and foreign films with an attendance of eleven thousand.[59] The museum deliberated carefully over what to do with the section, the internal debate involving the museum's entire senior staff. Nevertheless, the decision to eliminate the section seemed sudden, shocking many inside and outside the museum. Art critics, stunned, lamented the loss of a major arts program in the city, one that had served as a major forum for international issues and culture.[60] John Hanhardt, the senior curator of film and media arts at the Guggenheim Museum, described Judson as an extraordinary curator, a scholar who had done much to advance the history of the moving image. While Hanhardt was not surprised that the museum had been forced to make cutbacks, he noted that "one doesn't expect there to be vulnerability for a program that has such a long history and is obviously providing so much to its city."[61] For his part, Judson felt that the decision ignored cultural and ethnic diversity in the city, seeing the cut as the price that mainstream marketing typically exacts upon nonprofit educational agendas. There was

widespread feeling in the local arts community that had the museum really
wanted to preserve film and video, it could have found a way to do so. Still,
Armstrong and Institute president Ellsworth Brown remained adamant,
arguing without much evidence that other Pittsburgh programs would
pick up the section's work. Eventually, the Andy Warhol Museum, under
curator of film Geralyn Huxley (formerly Judson's assistant), agreed to
accept and preserve the existing archive of film and video materials from
the Carnegie Museum of Art.

WORKS ON PAPER

When Henry Adams, the museum's curator of fine arts (1982–84), published
a catalog entitled *American Drawings and Watercolors in the Museum of Art,
Carnegie Institute* (1985), he described the collection as having two parts: first,
material from the John Beatty years (1896–1922), drawings that inclined toward the moralistic, conservative, and academic work of the late Victorians;
and second, modern and contemporary drawings, collected beginning in
the 1950s under director Gordon Bailey Washburn. Adams, however, was
providing an overview of American drawings and watercolors, not all of
the museum's "works on paper," which included photographs, "old master" prints from Europe, and an outstanding collection of Japanese prints.
"Works on paper" refers to any art that is drawn, printed, or reproduced on
paper as a medium. Carnegie Museum of Art does not have a department
with that title, instead hiring various curators of prints and drawings or
assistants who work with the collections—an ad hoc approach that leaves
control with the curator of fine arts. Louise Lippincott, the current curator
of fine arts, notes that the varied collection of prints, drawings, watercolors,
and photographs is administered by two modern departments: Fine Arts,
for works created before 1945, and Contemporary Arts, for works created
after 1945.[62] Important subdivisions, of course, remain within this broad
chronological division, notably Japanese Prints, Pittsburgh Photographs,
and the Teenie Harris Photographic Archive.

In a smaller museum such as Carnegie Museum of Art, curatorial
responsibility is as much a matter of available expertise as it is of artistic medium or chronological timeline. The additions of works on paper
thus usually came about as fortuitous gifts, not necessarily because of the
museum's efforts. Thus, the collection of works on paper developed in a
protean fashion, never fully emerging as a separate department (except in
the case of photography).

Drawings were first collected under the director John Beatty, himself
an illustrator and artist, who took advantage of opportunities to buy excel-

lent drawings at prices his Fine Arts Department could afford; acquiring drawings cost much less than buying paintings from the Internationals. Beatty thus worked to deepen the collection on a limited budget. He followed Andrew Carnegie's mandate to collect American art, enlisting the help of Sadakichi Hartmann, a New York art critic and connoisseur who agreed to alert Beatty to whatever drawings by contemporary American artists he could ferret out. This collaboration between the conservative Methodist businessman and the cosmopolitan aesthete was an odd one, but it produced significant results. Fine drawings by William Glackens, John Sloan, Winslow Homer, Eastman Johnson, James McNeill Whistler, Childe Hassam, John LaFarge, Frederick Remington, and many others all joined the collection in Beatty's time, along with a few drawings from before the mid-nineteenth century. The second period of collecting American drawings came in the 1950s, when director George Bailey Washburn appointed his assistant director Leon Arkus as curator of prints and drawings, and the museum began to collect modern art. Between Beatty and Washburn, the collection from the 1920 to the 1950s had grown only sporadically, through the efforts of unpaid trustees such as the connoisseur Edward Duff Balken, who donated some thirty works to the collection. Washburn and Arkus now sought to modernize the collection with abstract expressionist art, acquiring drawings by such figures as David Smith, Franz Kline, Ellsworth Kelly, and Sam Francis.

Along with the museum's collection of drawings, the print collection benefited from gifts from major collectors during the tenure of Homer Saint-Gaudens. The first "old master" prints came to the collection from Pittsburgh collector and museum trustee Kenneth Seaver during the 1930s and 1940s.[63] A second large gift came in 1974: the bequest of Charles J. Rosenbloom, which added three hundred prints to the collection. Rosenbloom's rich gift represented every period from medieval times to the modern era, including prints by Albrecht Dürer, Rembrandt, Jacques Callot, nineteenth-century satirists such as Honore Daumier, and twentieth-century artists such as George Bellows. To curator Linda Batis, the gifts of Rosenbloom and Seaver formed "the crux of the old master collection" in works on paper.[64]

Yet another major donor of prints was James B. Austin, a U.S. Steel executive who confessed in 1959 that he had been "incurably afflicted with the collecting virus" after seeing Japanese wood block prints in Japan.[65] Austin, whose regular meetings with his business counterparts in Japan meant that he could read the text on the classical Japanese prints and speak to Japanese dealers, had gradually amassed one of the finest collections in the United States, including the much desired *ukiyo-e* ("pictures of a fleeting world") and the more modern *sosaku hanga* (contemporary creative prints). By the time he died in 1988 at age eighty-three, he had shifted toward buying the

Buddhist prints of earlier centuries. The exhibition and catalog *800 Years of Japanese Printmaking* (1976), and Austin's bequest of twenty-six hundred prints in 1989, immediately gave the museum prominence as a national repository of Japanese prints.

Also in the 1980s, the museum began to acquire Pittsburgh photographs more methodically. There were the "classics" of Pittsburgher Luke Swank and others; photos of the Industrial Age; pictures of Carnegie Institute by Ralph W. Johnston and of Carnegie himself by B. L. H. Dabbs; moody scenes by Hugh Torrance; photographs from the Pittsburgh renaissance of the 1940s and 1950s by artists such W. Eugene Smith, Elliott Erwitt, Clyde Hare, and Harold Corsini; and works by modern photographers such as Duane Michaels and Mark Perrott. The photography collection's largest and most original acquisition was the archive of work by Charles "Teenie" Harris, the photographer from 1936 to 1975 for the *Pittsburgh Courier,* one of the nation's most influential black newspapers. When Harris retired, he had an archive of some eighty thousand negatives that recorded a lively history of Pittsburgh's Black neighborhoods over four decades of the twentieth century, forming probably the most complete photographic documentation of one American city's Black community.

In 1993 Louise Lippincott hired Linda Batis as the prints and drawings assistant to the Fine Arts Department. To Batis, it was clear that the print collection had many gaps: "It's a good collection, but far behind that of the Met, which has over a million objects, or the National Gallery, or Boston, or Chicago.... They have been systematically working on their print collection for perhaps 40 years, through the careers of three curators." She discovered further that prints were scattered throughout the Carnegie system: the library and the Natural History Museum had wonderful Audubon prints, and the Andy Warhol Museum also had print collections. But these resources were never combined into one collection under the Museum of Art.

Then, in 2008, Richard Armstrong, in one of his last acts as director, created a separate department of photography and appointed Linda Benedict-Jones as its curator. Works on Paper had thus reached a critical point: it was being subdivided for curatorial control.

THE HEINZ ARCHITECTURAL CENTER

When the Hall of Architecture opened in 1907, Carnegie Institute presented architecture to the public in the spirit of the late nineteenth century, relying on architectural casts. Today, the hall is administered by the Heinz Architectural Center, which opened on Founder's Day in 1993, a gift of the Drue Heinz Foundation and of Mrs. Drue Heinz, the widow of Henry J. (Jack)

Heinz, initiating a new era of architectural focus at the Carnegie Museum of Art. The founding curator was Christopher Monkhouse, a distinguished scholar hired in 1991, before the center itself opened to the public.

The center, designed by Cicognani Kalla Architects, is a three-level building within a building, located off the Hall of Sculpture, on the second floor, with its own galleries, study room, offices, and elevator. The concept of a "center," rather than another museum department, evokes the facility's role as a library of resources, with a resident scholar and a mission of public service different from that of a typical exhibition gallery.

Physically, the center's stylistic synthesis of classicism and Modernism alludes to the original design of the Institute without copying it. The architectural fragments displayed on its walls include a section of the original Carnegie Institute copper cheneaus, which adorned the building until the 1950s, and two window dormers from Andrew Carnegie's mansion in New York, now the Cooper-Hewitt Museum of Design. Phillip Johnston, director of the art museum, described the center's collection in a 1993 article, particularly its emphasis on the creative process: "In forming an architectural collection ... the museum is focusing on the drawings and models which are two- and three-dimensional representations of architect's concepts, from preparatory sketches in which ideas are being worked out, to highly finished presentation renderings made to capture clients' enthusiasm and elicit their commitment. What is exciting is that, through them, viewers are invited to participate, vicariously, in the architect's creative process."[66]

Christopher Monkhouse, who left when director Phillip Johnston resigned in 1996, was succeeded by Dennis McFadden, who left in 1999. Tracy Myers served as acting curator for eight months, until Joseph Rosa was appointed. Rosa, however, stayed for only two years, leaving at the end of 2001. These frequent shifts in leadership made it difficult to develop the Heinz Architectural Center's long-term programming and mission, a situation that museum director Richard Armstrong attempted to redress in 2002 by appointing two cocurators, Tracy Myers and Raymond Ryan.

Throughout the shifts in leadership, the center has been educationally oriented toward the general public, a place for studying the meaning of architecture. Curator Myers observes, "You could conceivably go through life without being much influenced by painting or sculpture, but you could not do that with architecture. You have to interact with your environment."[67] Thus, the center walks a careful line, straddling the local audience, the regional architectural community, and the larger world. It stages at least three exhibitions a year, their subjects ranging from the highly theoretical, such as "Lebbeus Woods: Experimental Architecture," to contemporary trends and traditional topics, such as "Vernacular Architecture of the Western Pennsylvania Barn," curated by resident scholar and historian Lee Donnelly. And indeed, the emphasis on public outreach seemed immediately justified after the exhibition on Pennsylvania barns, as some people who had seen the exhibition now sought and obtained conservation easements on their farms and barns, to preserve them from being destroyed someday by development.

CARNEGIE MUSEUM OF NATURAL HISTORY

"Museum Science"

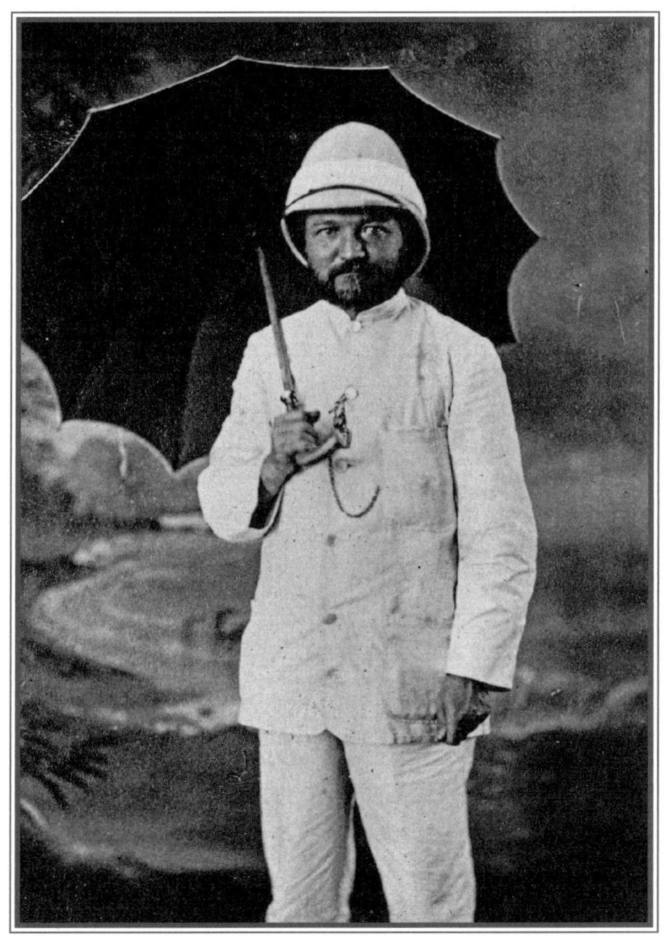

Andrew Carnegie's 1879 world tour took him to Ceylon, where he learned about taxidermy. This eventually led to his own museum's displays of mounted animals.

❧❦❧

"CARNEGIE MUSEUM" is arguably the most famous component of Carnegie Institute. It is far larger, wider, and deeper in its collections than Carnegie Museum of Art; has more curators than the art museum; and with its twenty million objects considers itself among the top half-dozen natural history museums in the United States. It is the elephant in the room in terms of research and collections, completely dwarfing the other three Carnegie Museums of Pittsburgh. To its staff and the public, it was originally "the Museum" in Pittsburgh.

It is not to be confused with Carnegie Institution of Washington, D.C., which Carnegie founded six years later, in 1902, to pursue "pure science" and to serve all U.S. universities as a central agency for research and discovery and practical applications to benefit humankind. Carnegie Institution became a great multisite enterprise, a seminal force in astronomy, geophysics, embroyology, plant biology, global ecology, and terrestrial magnetism, its facilities including Mount Wilson in California and its staff including Nobel Prize winners. In a way, the popular success of Carnegie Museum in Pittsburgh produced a logical philanthropic offspring in the Carnegie Institution of Washington, which concentrates on its globally important scientific agenda without much public fanfare.

When Carnegie founded the Department of the Museum at Pittsburgh's Carnegie Institute in 1896, the Victorian idea of a science museum had evolved from the eighteenth-century "cabinet of curiosities" into large institutions like the British Museum and the Smithsonian, with collections that inspired scientific study as well as philosophical speculation. The late nineteenth-century natural history museum was a warehouse of "objects, rare, valuable, and historical" (as Carnegie described it), with collections that shed increasing light on earth history. This was close to the heart of Pittsburgh industrialists who had made their fortunes through extractive industries in coal, gas, and oil. It included evolution, since Carnegie was a stout believer in Darwin's theory and in the progress of civilization. The fascination with evolution soon led to a new category, anthropology (including archaeology). Carnegie often boasted about his enterprising museum in Pittsburgh and paid a great deal for its success, particularly in paleontology, which became a topic of enduring public fascination. He was especially proud of the museum's "scientific men," such as William Jacob Holland, his close friend and the museum's first director, and John

174

Brashear, a trustee whose telescope lenses advanced the work of astronomy.

The names of the museum's departments spring from traditional scientific classification: the familiar mammals, botany, birds, amphibians and reptiles, mollusks, and anthropology and the perhaps less familiar invertebrate paleontology (fossil animals without backbones), paleobotany (fossils of plants), invertebrate zoology (insects), and vertebrate paleontology (fossil animals with backbones) (VP). Within these broad categories, museum scientists apply a much more specific system of classification, developed by Sweden's Carolus Linnaeus. Linnaeus, confronted by the chaos that reigned when individuals from different cultures called the same species by different names, or lumped different species together under one name, established the new science of taxonomy in the mid-1700s, providing an orderly system of binomial Latin names that subdivides life into kingdoms, divisions (phyla), classes, orders, families, and finally genus and species. Museum scientists still scrupulously follow Linnaean principles, some even working in the field of "systematics"—the science of bringing order to classification systems. In the two and a half centuries since Linnaeus's time, biologists have given Latin names to about 1.8 million species of plants, animals, and microorganisms—still only about 10 percent of the total, according to biologist Edward O. Wilson, who puts the number of species remaining to be discovered between 10 million and 100 million.[1]

For curators, classification is the liberating force that takes the confusion out of the study of the natural world, providing a key to the mysteries of nature and a means of explaining how past species were related to each other and to the species of today. The classification efforts of twentieth-century scientists have been advanced immeasurably by new technologies for discovery, powerful microscopes, computers, DNA analysis, and CAT scans (computer-generated three-dimensional images and cross-sections), inviting a new perspective on the frontiers of evolution. New species can now be identified through minute traces of evidence, and questions such as whether dinosaurs were warm-blooded or cold-blooded can be answered. Twentieth-century scientists have discovered dinosaurs' relation to birds, that the museum's *Tyrannosaurus rex* and *Diplodocus carnegii* walked and ran differently than originally thought (and mistakenly shown in exhibits), and that mammals coexisted with dinosaurs millions of years ago.

Museum nomenclature has regularly been tuned and departments redesigned, reflecting the ferment within the greater world of science and politics. The "Section of Man," its title adopted in the 1950s, became the Section of Anthropology in the 1970s, reflecting advances in science but also the rise of political correctness in the use of the word "man." After more than half a century, many classic dioramas and exhibits were out of date and even inaccurate. The burgeoning global culture of the 1990s, and the digital age, brought new opportunities and pressures. China and the Soviet Union opened vast lands to Western scientists and invited more collaborative research, and natural history museums were challenged to bring the digital age to bear in interpreting and presenting natural science. Carnegie Museum of Natural History, like natural history museums throughout the world, gradually brought the digital age to bear in its interpretations and presentations of the natural world.

THE SCIENTIFIC STAFF

While Carnegie Museum of Natural History is a stand-alone public museum, museums are often connected to universities: New Haven's Yale Peabody Museum; Philadelphia's Museum of Archaeology and Anthropology (the University of Pennsylvania); New York's American Museum of Natural History (Columbia). Carnegie's situation is slightly different: although it is an independent facility, academic powerhouses such as the University of Pittsburgh and Carnegie Mellon University are nearby, facilitating collaboration, research, education, and exhibitions. Professors send students to do research at the museum, while curators regularly lecture at local universities and sometimes have appointments as adjunct faculty.

Curator John Rawlins argues that official university ties can limit a museum's mission: "Such ties," he notes, "are important to some departments, indifferent to most, and genuinely undesirable and not advisable for a few. Many museums have wisely avoided the burden of university ties."[2] Curatorial independence fosters devotion to the museum's collections, rather than to an academic department: historically, many of Carnegie's curators were homegrown, amateurs who rose through the ranks, earning relevant academic degrees along the way. Such independence also allows researchers to define their area of research, often for a lifetime of work; this is one reason why museum scientists often have such long tenures. Some researchers even leave full-time academia, choosing to work at the museum for personal and professional growth. Curator of mammals John Wible, for example, left a job as a full-time professor of human anatomy at a university in Chicago to work at the museum, where a collection that matched his interest in mammalian evolution waited right outside his office door. His assessment is straightforward: "I think that for most of the people that end up here, the primary attraction is the collection." Museums also allow scientists to be part of a small, important community. While a teacher at a large university can be one of thousands of faculty members, a staff member at Carnegie Museum of Natural History might be one of a dozen curators, with a higher profile. Wible cites this as another of his reasons for coming to the museum: "At the university you are unknown, but here, suddenly, people actually knew me within the institution. Clearly I think there are more opportunities to shape yourself . . . to shape your collection . . . to shape your career in a museum, than in any university."[3]

While curators are the museum's scientific leaders, their work would not be possible without collection managers, who keep materials active as a research resource, make acquisitions and loans, update the records and the library, supervise volunteers, and act as a liaison for educational and public projects. They take field trips, often coauthor scientific papers, and are in charge of their collection if there is no curator in place (which can happen for long periods of time).

The museum's first director, the Harvard archaeologist Frank H. Gerrodette, became famous for the wrong reasons, leaving after only a few months on the job. The controversy over the museum's digging up of ancient Native American burial sites at nearby McKees's Rocks in the summer of 1896 was so intense that Gerrodette resigned in December of the same year, leaving the museum field. Local rumors and inflammatory newspaper articles wrongly accused Gerrodette of digging up Christian graves as well as those of prehistoric people. His successor, Andrew Carnegie's friend William Jacob Holland, accepted the position when Carnegie himself pressed him to take it. Holland became the director of the museum in March 1897, although he still served as the chancellor of Western University of Pennsylvania until 1901. When he did resign as chancellor, it was at Carnegie's urging: "Mr. Carnegie, urged me to resign the Chancellorship and devote myself wholly to the interests of the Library and the Institute. . . . 'The University can find a Chancellor more readily than I can find a man to aid and advise me in the work I have undertaken, and I need your services. You will never need from this time forward,' he said to me, 'to worry about finances, and you can devote yourself unremittingly to your scientific pursuits." In a moment of what I often since have thought was weakness, I yielded."[4]

Holland's interests and areas of expertise were wide ranging. He published his *Butterfly Book* in 1898, and it sold five thousand copies in the first few weeks. He went on to publish *The Moth Book* in 1903, *To the River Platte and Back* in 1913, and the *Butterfly Guide* in 1915, establishing his fame as an entomologist. He directed the cast-making for the famous *Diplodocus carnegii* and traveled to museums in other countries to supervise the installation of replicas. One replica was presented to the trustees of the British Museum, including the king, in 1905. In anticipation of other royal requests, five additional replicas were produced, and requests followed from Kaiser Wilhelm of Germany, President Fallieres of France, Emperor Franz Joseph

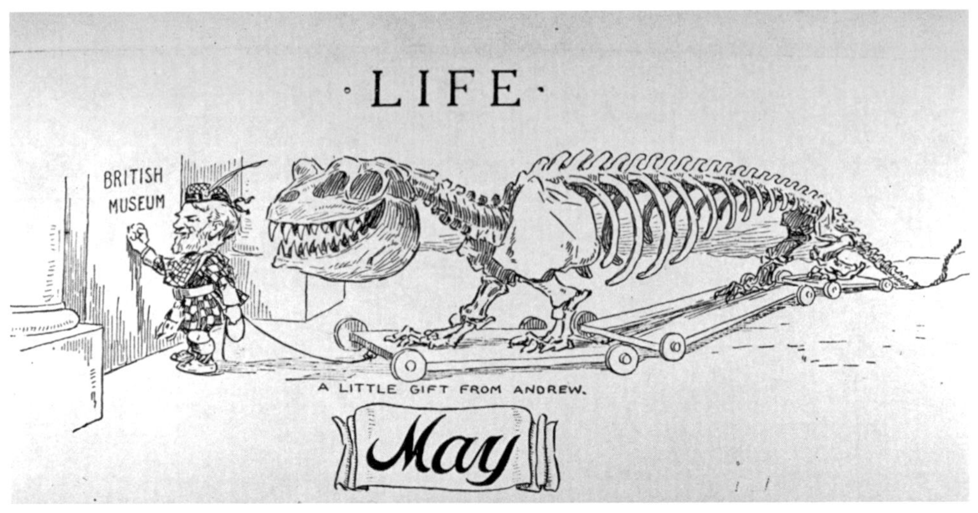

This 1905 cartoon from Life *magazine shows Carnegie delivering his dinosaur to the British Museum at the request of the king of England.*

of Austria, and King Vittorio Emmanuelle III of Italy. Holland, making the formal presentation in each country, was honored and decorated. This gratifying success, which flattered Carnegie's belief that he could influence U.S. foreign policy through his relationships with kings, presidents, and diplomats, led Holland to cast four more replicas.[5] In 1910 he traveled to Russia to give one to Czar Nicholas II and then to Spain to give one to King Alfonso XIII. He went to Argentina to give one to the National Museum at the request of President Rogue Saenz Peña; another was given to the Mexican National Museum in 1929 at the request of President Emilio Portes Gil.

As the museum's first successful director, serving for twenty-five years, Holland was the primary force in developing the first exhibits, collections, and scientific staff. He planned the exhibit halls, scientific offices, and preparation laboratories for the 1907 expansion. He was a forceful speaker who could give brilliant impromptu speeches, projecting his booming voice into the last row of the top gallery.

Holland retired reluctantly on July 1, 1922, at age seventy-seven, probably forced out by an equally strong-willed president, Samuel Harden Church. But he continued his research unabated as director emeritus, working on his collections until his death in 1932. He was followed by his assistant Douglas Stewart (1922–26), the son of one of Carnegie's partners. From 1901 until his death, Stewart—a hands-on and knowledgeable administrator—was the custodian of the mineral collection, and by 1917 he was responsible for collections including Archaeology and Ethnology, Numismatics, Art Work in Metal, and Textiles. Unfortunately, Stewart died after only three years and ten months as director. His wife donated two habitat groups to the museum as memorials to Stewart in 1927: a carboniferous forest showing Pennsylvania's plants and life of 250 million years ago, now in the modern Benedum Hall of Geology, and a remarkable group showing a composite of several Pennsylvania caves (a fine exhibit that unfortunately was demolished).

Stewart was succeeded by Andrey Avinoff (1926–45), a former member of the Russian aristocracy who "embodied those refinements which come only from generations of good breeding," according to his friend the art professor and collector Walter Read Hovey.[6] "He spoke seven languages, read another ten, and exuded erudition," wrote his grand-nephew Alex Shoumatoff.[7] Before the Russian Revolution, Avinoff, who was in charge of receiving gifts to the czar, had financed forty-two collecting expeditions into remote territories such as Tibet, in search of new species of butterflies. By 1917 he had ninety thousand specimens, 90 percent of the known species in Central Asia—the largest collection ever amassed by a private individual.

He found himself marooned in America at the age of thirty-three, unable to return to Russia because of the Russian Revolution, which had taken possession of all his collections and property. As an émigré, "he could have had a career in any number of fields—law, diplomacy, piano, art history, entomology."[8] He was working as an artist in New York in 1922 when he met Holland, whose classic *Butterfly Book* had fascinated him. Holland quickly invited him to be associate curator of entomology. He came to Pittsburgh in 1923 and began sorting out and classifying the species and varieties, discovering new varieties in the process. He returned to New York, perhaps because the salary was so modest, but when Holland's successor, Douglas Stewart, died unexpectedly, Avinoff was offered the job of director and returned to Pittsburgh.

Avinoff was a great hit in Pittsburgh, a city hungry for signs of Old World culture. "He descended on our city like a fabulous creature from another planet," said a man who would later take a course in fine arts from him at the University of Pittsburgh. "He was the idol of my youth."[9] For twenty years, he was a familiar sight on Forbes Avenue—an elegant, sparrow-boned man, with pince-nez and natty bowtie, reading as he walked. John Walker, who later became director of the National Gallery, recalled him well: "I've never known anyone with the universal knowledge he had. I thought it must have been a fake—I thought he was a phony—so I probed and probed when I would see him at parties. I wanted to show him up, but never could, because it was all sound, he was all there, he really *did* know.

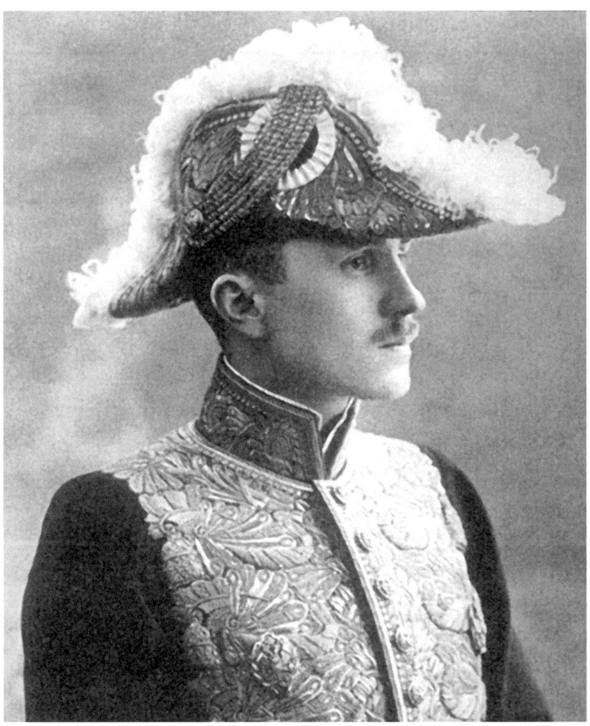

*The gifted, Russian-born Andrey Avinoff was a courtier to the
czar and a noted entomologist before the 1917 Russian Revolution.
He became director of Carnegie Museum in 1926.*

And whenever he came out with an extraordinary erudite fact or something
you wouldn't expect him to know . . . he always did it deferentially, as though
he were apologizing for his brilliance."[10]

Throughout his tenure as the museum's director, Avinoff continued
to pursue his artistic interests. During the flowering season of 1940–41,
Avinoff illustrated 351 species of native and naturalized wildflowers gathered and identified by Otto Jennings, then the curator of botany (and later
briefly the museum's director). Years later the Western Pennsylvania Conservancy published Avinoff's spectacular illustrations in its annual cal-
endars. He privately illustrated a poem by a Russian friend entitled "The
Fall of Atlantis," using esoteric symbolism. Museum employee John Bauer
posed in the nude for the pure young male figure that dominates the series,
while Avinoff attended the life drawing class at the Carnegie Institute of
Technology to sketch the female figure.[11] He also continued his research
on butterflies, publishing several important articles. At the University of

Pittsburgh, he oversaw the development of the Russian Classroom in the Cathedral of Learning.

Tested economically by the Great Depression, he took pride in getting things done cheaply and keeping everyone on his staff. He was a quick, cerebral man, involved in all the details of the museum and interested in the lives of his staff. This intensity perhaps took a toll, and in 1945 he had a heart attack at the age of sixty-one. He resigned to recuperate and resumed his painting career, widely regarded as the best flower painter of the age. He was preparing for a series of lectures at the Metropolitan Museum of Art, to be featured in *Life* magazine, when he died at age sixty-four.

Otto E. Jennings, Avinoff's close associate and the most influential botanist in western Pennsylvania, was made acting director for a year after Avinoff's departure, before becoming director himself in 1946 and serving until 1949. Jennings took over just after World War II, and he brought continuity and stability to the museum as the city worked to resurrect itself after the exhausting war effort. Widely known for his collaboration with Avinoff on the brilliantly illustrated *Wildflowers of Western Pennsylvania,* Jennings, as the museum's botanist, for decades had spent his weekends in the field, leading Botanical Society trips or taking classes, colleagues, and community leaders to ecologically significant areas of western Pennsylvania.[12] He also played a key role in preserving many of the region's tracts of land, including Presque Isle, Ohiopyle, Cook Forest, Bear Cave, McConnells Mill, Linn Run, Pymatuning, Raccoon Creek, and Blazing Star Prairie. Today, appropriately, the Jennings Environmental Education Center is named after him.

After Jennings retired at age seventy-two, civic leader Wallace B. Richards was appointed as the next director (1948–53). An imaginative public figure who was instrumental to the civic revival known as Pittsburgh's "renaissance," Richards brought new energy to the museum. He was the first director who was not a naturalist or museum trained; like later directors, he saw the value of promotion. (One of his ideas, to outline the dinosaur bones with fluorescent paint, was fortunately never pursued.)[13] Richards helped unify the art and natural history educational programs under one Division of Education, expanded adult education, and promoted the idea of membership in the Institute. He resigned because of failing health after just five years, dying after a lengthy illness in 1959. His obituary said, "His imprint upon Pittsburgh and the museum is splashed in color, poured in concrete, built into exhibits, and fibered in the hearts of those privileged to have labored with him for community betterment and human ennoblement."[14]

After Richards's tenure, the museum turned back to one of its own for leadership. Graham Netting, who had started working at the museum

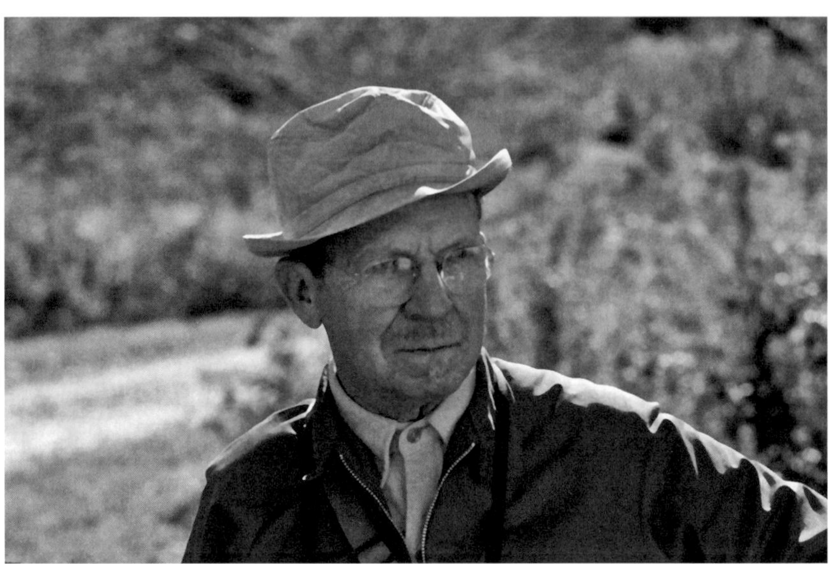

Graham Netting, director of the museum from 1954 to 1975, retired to Powdermill, where he continued to band turtles for the rest of his life.

as a volunteer in herpetology, served as the director from 1954 to 1975, a twenty-one-year span that made him one of the museum's longest-serving administrators. One of Netting's great assets as an administrator was his probity and meticulous attention to detail. He pinched pennies in the budget, although he slightly increased the size of the museum's scientific staff. Still, it fell to him to report that the long tradition of free admission was over, and a small admissions fee now had to be charged. Significantly, the Netting years returned the museum to its regional roots with an emphasis on local archaeology and fieldwork and close associations with groups such as the Western Pennsylvania Conservancy. Like Jennings, he worked to preserve the region's large tracts from development, including Powdermill Nature Reserve and the new Moraine State Park. One of his last innovations was to appoint a curator of environmental studies to address environmental problems in the tristate area. Netting hoped to retire in 1974, but his successor was not chosen for another year, and he remained in place until 1975.

The museum appointed yet another of its own as the next director: Craig C. Black (1975–82) had begun his career as associate curator and then curator of vertebrate fossils at Carnegie Museum, before leaving to be a curator elsewhere. Upon his return to Carnegie Museum, Black took a broad view of the profession and became the president of the American Association of Museums, a role that led him to delegate authority for daily museum management. He was cognizant of national trends in museum management, and like directors across the country, he focused on broadening the museum's education programs and modernizing its exhibits and collection areas. Significantly, under Black, the museum undertook a massive reorganization of its collections in a new, expensive storage system. During his tenure, Pittsburgh was steadily losing its corporate base, and corporate contributions decreased accordingly. Black began deaccessioning the museum's holdings and tried selling off the coins and stamps collection to raise funds for a new annex that would relieve the crowded storage conditions in Oakland. This effort triggered a public dispute, a tug-of-war between the museum, which wanted to deaccession the collection to ensure the museum's broader good, and the local Historical Society of Western Pennsylvania, which wanted to save it as a public patrimony. The dispute lasted for years and eventually ended up in court, the museum, in the final compromise, retaining representative examples of the collection. The incident highlighted the conflict between the autonomy of museum directors and the financial control held by the Institute's centralized business department and remained a sore point for the next twenty-five years.

The next director, Robert M. West (1983–86), stayed less than three years, although he undertook several important innovations, including a reorganization of the scientific sections to reflect a modern approach to research and an accelerated program for developing new exhibit halls. West's reorganization grouped research areas into three divisions: Earth Sciences, Life Sciences, and Anthropology, each with its own chair. West, like Black, struggled with the fact that the Institute's financial authority over the museum left him without the power to enforce lasting change, even though the director was expected to assume responsibility for the museum's operations. West felt himself hampered: true control, he felt, instead lay with Carnegie Institute's chief financial officer; there were no financial incentives a museum director could present to his staff in terms of salaries, new facilities, or innovative or costly programs.[15] He resigned after only two years and seven months, making him one of the museum's shortest-term directors.

His successor, James (Jim) Edward King (1987–96), was yet another experienced museum professional, a paleontologist by training who projected an easy sense of authority, comfortable with himself and museum management. Hired by Institute president Robert Wilburn, he enjoyed supervising, administering, and providing creative public services, and he did not see his primary role as fund-raising. Under his tenure, a number of new exhibit halls opened in the museum, after years of preparation, while Carnegie Science Center and the Andy Warhol Museum joined the institution that was now, under President Ellsworth Brown, calling itself

Carnegie Museums of Pittsburgh. The historic primacy of the Natural History Museum was now diminished, as a quartet of equally powerful museum directors emerged. When Ellsworth Brown took over as Institute president, King decided to avoid the budgetary and administrative stress that would mark the deevolution of power from the central administration back to the four equal museums. He resigned to become director of the Cleveland Museum of Natural History.

Jerome (Jay) Apt's short tenure as director (1997–2000) had a major impact on the reordering of the museum's priorities. Jay Apt, a celebrated astronaut and NASA scientist, was from a Squirrel Hill family that was noted for its support of the arts. Experienced in finding funding for his own research, he believed that although funding was tight, "in Pittsburgh if you have a plan that excites people you can get it to happen. That is our job here—to get people's attention riveted on the exciting ways that we can present to the public the wonderful information within these walls."[16] He wanted to quicken the flow of information through the museum, hoping the public would feel as if they were missing something if they did not visit the museum every month and take advantage of interactive exhibits. To reach his goals, he raised funds, introduced technology-driven exhibits, and focused on the staff's scientific performance.

However, despite his lofty goals, strong credentials, and enthusiasm, Apt made some significant missteps as an administrator. His technology-driven innovations occasionally misfired. For example, Apt promoted robots to replace docents in giving tours of the museum's halls, but while the technology might have been groundbreaking and was devised by Carnegie Mellon University, children visiting the museum found the talking robots a distracting novelty rather than an educational experience. His focus on high scientific standards for the staff also led to some discontent. He appointed an academic dean of science to evaluate the scientific work of his curators. While such evaluations were important, the museum had no more than a dozen curators, so appointing one of them on a rotating basis to evaluate the work of colleagues stirred up resentments. Such evaluations also focused more on a curator's ability to find research funding than on service to the community. The abrupt dismissal of two longtime curators in botany was felt by many to challenge the museum's traditional culture. Staff members and some key trustees felt alienated by Apt's top-down, military style of decision making, and their opposition increased when he proposed selling Powdermill Nature Reserve as irrelevant to the museum's "real" mission. Under increasing pressure from trustees and the administration, Apt resigned. But he paved the way for new technology and forced the museum to face the new realities of presenting museum science.

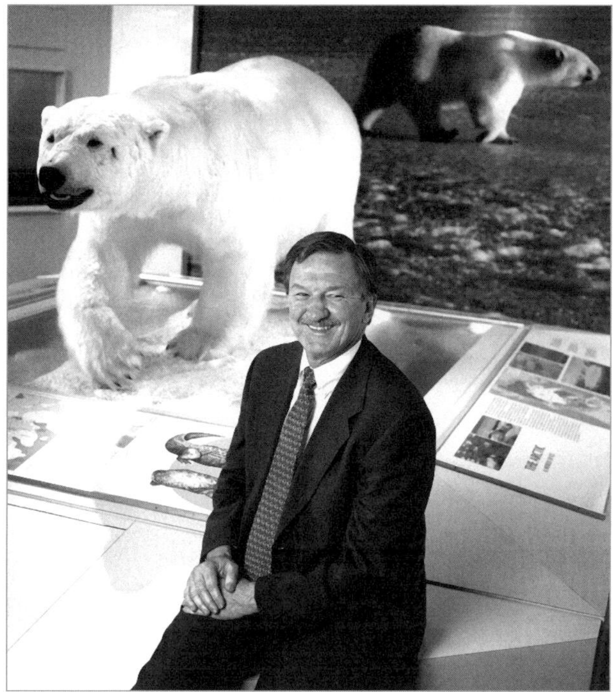

*Billie (Bill) R. DeWalt, director from 2001 to 2007, oversaw the
many renovations required by the large new exhibit Dinosaurs
in Their Time. Here he is seen in Polar World.*

Billie (Bill) R. DeWalt (2001–7) took over from Jay Apt, and his collaborative personality, sympathetic intelligence, and academic background were reassuring to the staff. Faced with a staff alarmed by recent decisions to replace time-honored exhibits and displays with technology, to destroy old dioramas, and to ignore important collections in creating new exhibits, DeWalt set a new course, deciding instead to feature museum science by drawing upon the Carnegie's deep collections to create exhibits that focused on evolution, ecology, biodiversity, and cultural diversity.[17] Over five years, DeWalt oversaw renovations of Hillman Hall of Minerals and Gems and facilities at Powdermill Nature Reserve and the creation of new education classrooms and a new museum scientific library. He also raised $32.5 million for the exhibit Dinosaurs in Their Time, although he left the museum in February 2007, several months before the opening of the much-publicized exhibit.

At this point, the financial pressures on the museum were steadily increasing, and the prospect of dismissing curators and staff seemed likely.

The vaunted new dinosaur exhibit, with its hefty price tag, focused attention and funding on Vertebrate Paleontology and diminished attention to other scientific areas. Carnegie Institute's president and board faced a familiar dilemma: trying to balance resources between largely invisible research and highly visible exhibitions that increased museum attendance.

To confront these considerable challenges, the museum appointed Samuel M. Taylor as the next director in February 2008. Although he had served as a young education specialist at Carnegie Museum of Natural History twenty years earlier, he had gone on to become a marine biologist and museum scientist with a national profile. His first priority on taking over the museum's reins was rebuilding the curatorial staff, which was now reduced to twelve. He believed that the "research engine runs the museum," and he wanted Carnegie scientists to play a public role, explaining evolution and analyzing environmental issues such as global climate change and habitat loss. He also believed the museum, given its scientific reputation, could be more aggressive in its search for support, and he broadened fund-raising efforts accordingly.[18]

All museum scientists ultimately depend upon their collections, and Carnegie Museum presents its collections through exhibits in an evolutionary sequence: first Earth Sciences, then Life Sciences, and finally Anthropology. That is the sequence followed here. While the museum-speak of scientific language is generally avoided in the discussion that follows, the proper names of departments are used. Thus, dinosaurs are to be found in Vertebrate Paleontology, and insects in Invertebrate Zoology. Part of the charm of understanding a natural history museum is learning how it looks upon the world systematically.

THE EARTH SCIENCES
Invertebrate Paleontology

Andrew Carnegie and the other Pittsburgh businessmen who made their fortunes in extractive industries, mining for coal and ore and drilling for gas and oil, saw earth science as central to Pittsburgh's industries, crucial to the city as a whole and thus a proper subject for the new museum.[19]

Modern geology started about 1799 when William Smith, the "Father of English Geology," created the first geologic maps. From that point scientists understood that layers (strata) of rocks in different geographic areas could be related on the basis of common fossil animal and plant content (stratigraphy). Significantly for Pittsburgh, twentieth-century efforts to discover oil led scientists to the notion that fossils in rocks could be used as indicators of rock layers that might be drilled profitably to discover oil, leading to the subdiscipline of biostratigraphy and, more broadly, to the transformation of an academic pursuit into a modern industrial science. By the late 1960s, geologists were also beginning to understand that invertebrate fossils were distributed through the rock record not only in time but in space—that certain genera and species recurred within certain rock types—and thus began paleoecology: the idea that organisms lived in biological communities that were captured in time in the rock record. This led further to the subdiscipline of paleobiology—part biology and part geology. From this point the scientific literature began to explore major extinction events in Earth history and how the biosphere had changed in relation to these catastrophic periods and to explain the relations among ecology, biogeography, and the tempo of animal evolution—all information trapped and recorded within the planet itself.

For the museum, such heady speculations can be traced to Andrew Carnegie's 1903 purchase of Baron de Bayet's famous fossil collection for one hundred thousand francs. The Bayet Collection, featuring more than 130,000 "spineless wonders," has long entranced visitors. One curator described the collection in poetic terms in 1973, decades after its assembly and purchase and long after the kinds of information it held had been put to practical ends: "The superior preservation of some of these fossils is incredible in organisms that lived 140 million years ago: squids and cuttlefish with ink sacs preserved and tentacles outlined in the lime mud; flying insects with almost every detail of their wings pressed into the mud in which they were buried; crabs and shrimps that almost make one salivate; and many other kinds of beautiful creatures as well."[20] The Bayet Collection was one of the museum's early treasures, and it led to the hiring of the museum's first geologist, Percy E. Raymond, in 1904. Raymond, appointed assistant curator in the section of Paleontology—Division of Fossil Invertebrates, immediately began unpacking, organizing, and identifying the thousands of fossils in the collection, an analytic chore that continues to this day. He also studied the regional geology of western Pennsylvania, added new collections to the museum's holdings, and accompanied the dinosaur-fossil hunter Earl Douglass on early field collecting expeditions to Minnesota and Montana. He left in 1910, after his request for a raise in salary was denied, but he continued to donate valuable fossil collections to the museum, from such important formations as the Burgess Shale and the Mazon Creek Shale.

For a dozen years after Raymond left, the museum, under director William Jacob Holland, did not hire another curator, even though the collections continued to increase in scope. When Holland's successor, Andrey Avinoff, hired the scholarly I. P. Tolmachoff, a fellow Russian émigré, to take over as curator in 1922, Tolmachoff and his graduate students continued to expand the museum's holdings until Tolmachoff's retirement in 1945, donating the collections they had gathered during fieldwork in western Pennsylvania and nearby states. Much of this material also remained uncurated.

Tolmachoff was followed by one of his students, Eugene Rudolph (Rudy) Eller, who remained at Carnegie for twenty-five years. Eller did much to advance the new field of biostratigraphy, funded by an aggressive oil industry, and added collections from the Devonian rocks of New York, Michigan, Ontario, and the Silurian of Wales. His greatest achievement in public education was developing Paleozoic Hall (*paleozoic* meaning "ancient life"), begun in 1961 with a grant from the Richard King Mellon Foundation. Occupying six thousand square feet on the museum's first floor, it covered a tremendous span of time, from the Precambrian period of more than 550 million years ago, when life began, to the time of the great dinosaurs, the Mesozoic ("middle life") period, only 200 million years ago. Over this stunning stretch of time, North America was largely covered by shifting seas, seeing great physical changes and climatic extremes. During the Pennsylvanian period in geology, for example, vegetation flourished that formed Pennsylvania's vast coal deposits. For Eller, Paleozoic Hall was the fruition of a thirty-year quest, his dream to create "a dramatic presentation that would impress upon every viewer the population explosions of aquatic organisms that laid down their skeletons to build the limestones of the world."[21] The hall was logically placed at the entrance to Dinosaur Hall, its dioramas depicting ancient life in the teeming seas to illuminate the period's tremendous span of 350 million years. Paleozoic Hall at the time was considered the world's finest presentation of life before the rise of the great dinosaurs.

In the late 1960s, Eller developed a vision problem and took a leave of absence, eventually retiring in 1970. In 1972, John L. Carter, an expert on carboniferous brachiopods, was appointed as associate curator and began to consolidate the physically scattered invertebrate fossil collections into one location, a task that took nearly two years. Carter, who remained at the museum until 1999, like his predecessor added major collections to the museum's holdings, including 110,000 Mississippian specimens from Iowa; 8,900 specimens from C. Germain; and 54,000 Pennsylvanian specimens from David K. Brezinski, who took responsibility for the section in 2002 but agreed to delay his arrival at the museum in the face of intense budget constrictions. Brezinski, then, became an associate curator-adjunct, an arrangement that continued for years, since the budget never improved. His first priority was to bring greater visibility to the section in the region and within the museum. In keeping with Andrew Carnegie's priorities, he and collection manager Albert Foller developed educational programs, including one at Powdermill Nature Preserve, and established a support group called the PAlS (Patrons and *lauradanae* Supporters—*lauradanae* being a common form of trilobite). PAlS activities were geared toward helping nonscientists understand important geological and paleontological principles by studying the rocks of the tristate region, including those in the Pittsburgh city parks.

After decades of collecting and displays, the modern Benedum Hall of Geology opened in 1988, with the support of the Claude Worthington Benedum Foundation, founded by Pittsburgh oilman Michael Benedum in memory of his late son. Today Benedum Hall presents the dynamic, ever-changing nature of the planet itself, including what we might think of most quickly in relation to invertebrate paleontology—the study of fossils of ancient life forms without backbones—and also the theory of plate tectonics—the notion that the outer layers of the earth are organized into "plates" that move slowly and constantly, their interactions leading to volcanoes, earthquakes, and the formation of mountains.

While Invertebrate Paleontology has a checkered history as a section and did not always enjoy strong institutional support, it often benefited from the leadership of respected scientists. Since 1977 its public-oriented collections manager, Albert Kollar, has kept the section highly visible through tours, courses, and pamphlets, and the public thus continues to view invertebrate paleontology as an active scientific discipline.

For museum visitors today, Invertebrate Paleontology illuminates a long-invisible period of the earth's history, including the organisms that fueled the region's economic development. From the Benedum Hall of Geology, today's visitor moves into the dramatic Hillman Hall of Minerals and Gems, before entering into the science of Vertebrate Paleontology.

Minerals

Mineralogists, looking at human history, see mineral deposits as the prime mover behind the growth of civilization. Marc Wilson, today's head of the section, sees the Roman conquest of Great Britain as a consequence of Rome's need to gain control over the "Tin Isles"—Britain's tin mines in the south; consequently, the Romans built a wall to seal off raiding barbarian tribes from the north. Likewise, the silver mines of ancient Greece were pivotal in the rise of Greek civilization, and the overwhelming greed for gold that marked sixteenth-century Europe led the Spanish and Portuguese to explore and colonize Central and South America. Closer to home, oil and coal deposits in nineteenth-century Pennsylvania triggered the American

Industrial Revolution. Wilson notes further that the Korean War was linked to the fact that the United States obtained 100 percent of its tungsten from South Korea and that part of the U.S. rationale for going to war in Iraq centered on the control of oil supplies in the Middle East.[22]

In spite of their clear relevance to the history of humankind, minerals as a museum discipline are challenging to describe and exhibit: the earth is over 4.5 billion years old, and its prolific minerals can only be captured through a scientific nomenclature that often baffles the public. Richard Souza, the second head of the section, described the collection in 1990: "Marvelous silvers, proustites, acanthites, stibnites and anglesites have been recently acquired. Additionally, fluorites, rhodochrosites, pyromorphites and vivianites, topazes and apophyllites have all been significantly upgraded. Also newly acquired species of molybdates and tungstates such as wulfenites, scheelites and powellites have been added to the collection"[23] The obvious linguistic barrier to public understanding means a good minerals exhibit must emphasize popular education, displaying the properties of minerals in a way that will strike and move the public.

The six-thousand-square-foot Hillman Hall of Minerals and Gems, from its opening in 1980, set a gold standard in this regard, making the museum's holdings in this area relevant and exciting to the lay public. Funded by the Hillman Foundation, the hall is arguably the most original exhibit ever created at Carnegie Museum of Natural History, its appeal both experiential, with interactive devices and systematic cases arranged like giant crystals against a mirrored wall, and overwhelmingly aesthetic, its mineral "masterpieces" glowing in quiet splendor. The hall introduces visitors to the planetary processes that create rocks and minerals and explains the fundamentals of igneous, sedimentary, and metamorphic rock and unusual mineral properties such as fluorescence, phosphorescence, and radiation; it provides a spectacular introduction to crystallography—the study of mineral crystals.

The impetus for this spectacular and educational display came directly from philanthropist Henry Hillman, who had graduated from Princeton with a degree in geology and understood from his family's mining investments how important minerals were to Pittsburgh's industries. It took eleven years for the Hillman Hall of Minerals and Gems to open its doors, Hillman Foundation president Ronald Wertz working closely with the museum to acquire the best specimens, endow the hall, and guarantee it had the finest mineral displays. After thirty years Hillman Hall was commonly acknowledged as the greatest mineral hall ever developed for the public.

But long before anyone had even dreamed of such a spectacular showcase as Hillman Hall, minerals were integral to the museum's holdings.

Indeed, Andrew Carnegie, about a century earlier, had imagined a Pennsylvania minerals exhibit. The museum assiduously collected the materials of Pittsburgh's industries—ores and manufactured products made of tin, lead, copper, antimony, and bismuth; specimens of oil-bearing rock and crude petroleum and of coal, coke, and graphite; and local steel products. When the Department of the Museum opened its doors to the public in a wing of the 1895 library, a few private individuals had already donated mineral specimens; Gustave Guttenberg, curator of the Academy of Science and Art of Pittsburgh, had loaned his entire personal collection. When Guttenberg died in 1896, Carnegie purchased his mineral collection of some five hundred specimens, and it formed the nucleus of the museum's permanent mineral holdings.[24] The collection continued to grow through regular gifts and bequests of personal collections, including a series of iron ores presented by the Carnegie Steel Company. In 1905, the museum bought one of the finest private mineralogical collections available, that of William W. Jefferis, a banker whose passion for mineral specimens led to a collecting spree that lasted over sixty years. Early in the twentieth century, the museum also obtained twenty-six hundred gem specimens from John L. Lewis, leader of the United Mine Workers.

All of these specimens were curated by a museum committee under the leadership of Douglas Stewart, who worked at the museum from 1901 to 1926, first as the custodian of the mineralogical collections and later as director of the museum. When he died unexpectedly in 1926, the minerals were grouped with related areas such as geology and paleontology, and honorary curators from the local universities were placed in charge, including Charles Fettke of the Carnegie Institute of Technology and Henry Leighton of the University of Pittsburgh. Fettke served as a consultant for ten years, while Leighton served for twenty, retiring in 1947. I. P. Tolmachoff, the curator of invertebrate paleontology, was named the acting curator of mineralogy in 1937 and then the curator of geology and mineralogy in 1943. He was followed by his assistant David Seaman from 1945 to 1949 and then by Eugene Randolph Eller, another notable figure from Invertebrate Paleontology, who worked at the museum until 1969.

In the 1950s, the old exhibit hall was dismantled, and the collecting philosophy shifted toward exhibit-quality specimens. In 1969, Institute president James M. Walton asked Henry Hillman to contribute to a Capital Fund for Carnegie Institute; the museum's annual report that year noted that the Hillman Foundation had agreed to provide "funds that will be applied toward the development of a new Hall of Minerals in the Museum." Research associate Delbert Oswald, beginning in 1969, worked to catalog and analyze the museum's holdings. The 1970 inventory showed sixteen thousand cataloged specimens, divided into four different collections: minerals, meteorites, gems, and geological materials. By 1972, Oswald's analysis indicated where the study collections were deficient, a list that served as a guide for future acquisitions. After Oswald retired in 1980, the same year Hillman Hall opened, Richard L. Souza was appointed to oversee both the new hall and the collection's education program. The collection itself now included some twenty-three thousand specimens, and Souza worked with the Hillman Foundation's Ron Wertz to develop it even further, launching one of the most active specimen acquisitions programs of any North American natural history museum.

Souza left in 1990, and after another hiatus, mineralogist Marc Wilson was hired in 1992. Wilson's passion for minerals, shared by his family, had a touch of the spiritual: "Crystals to me represent a microcosm of the order of God's creation. They are so perfect, so ordered, so beautiful. Each one is unique, and the best are of a beauty that cannot be matched by anything humans can try."[25] Wilson increased the emphasis on hands-on investigation and added organic materials that are popularly regarded as minerals, such as amber and copal, to the collection's holdings. Visitors could now see amber and copal both in their rough forms, some samples including fossilized insects, and as beautifully polished freeform specimens and jewelry. After the fall of communism in 1989, world markets opened up, and Western buyers, including Hillman Hall, could finally purchase significant mineral specimens from behind the former Iron Curtain. In 1996, Wilson added a display of pseudomorphism—one mineral that takes the shape of another mineral, the transformation caused by changes in the conditions under which crystals are growing.

Mineralogy at the Carnegie Museum of Natural History is a various object of study, suited to Pittsburgh's industrial history but perhaps most notable because of the extraordinary beauty of the specimens in its collections. Indeed, most mineral acquisitions here are made on the basis of beauty, of sheer magnificence, and fall into one of three categories: masterpiece specimens—large, unique pieces that cause visitors to gasp in amazement; systematic specimens—top-quality examples of as wide a range as possible; and reference and research pieces—filling in gaps in species and creating suites from important localities. In size, the Hillman's collections are not as extensive as those at the world's largest mineral museums, but in terms of specimen quality and interpretation, Hillman Hall of Minerals and Gems is without equal.

When Hillman Hall was renovated in 2007, the two-thousand-square-foot Wertz Hall: Gems and Jewelry was added, capturing the ambience of one of the exclusive viewing rooms at Tiffany's in New York and concentrat-

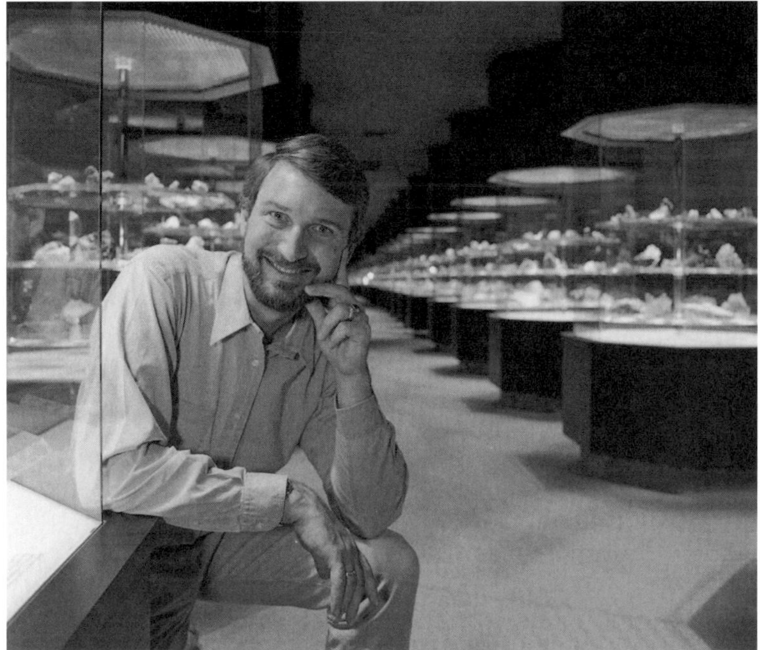

Marc Wilson became head of Hillman Hall of Minerals and Gems in 1992.

ing all the lapidary art and gems, such as birthstones, in one section. Marc Wilson for a long time ran an informal "thumbprint" test on Mondays after a busy weekend, to see which glass cases had the most fingerprints, showing popular appeal, and the birthstone exhibit always won.

Vertebrate Paleontology

By far the most famous exhibit at Carnegie Museum of Natural History is the dinosaurs, and the section of Vertebrate Paleontology has often been in the news, beginning with Andrew Carnegie's expensive 1899 commitment to bringing to Pittsburgh the largest fossil dinosaur ever found. Carnegie would go on to spend a quarter of a million dollars on fossil collecting before he was through, the storied collection of fossils a boon to the museum and to paleontology itself. Vertebrate paleontology is devoted to the fossil records and preserved bones of animals with backbones—mammals, reptiles, amphibians, and birds, as well as dinosaurs. Clearly a vast field, it has brought millions of visitors to the museum—some five hundred thousand a year while it was still housed in the library building.

Vertebrate Paleontology differs from the museum's other sections in requiring trained fossil preparators, since bones fossilized in rock are fragile, difficult to identify by species, and need to be exhumed by painstaking laboratory work, in recent times with the help of electric tools and digital scanning equipment. It took decades to work through the crates of massive fossil-rich rocks brought back from the West in the early twentieth century and stored in the museum basement; a century later the task is not yet finished. More recently acquired skeletal material, such as the intermingled bones of many species that died in Ice Age caves tens of thousands of years ago, also demands the painstaking work of skilled technicians. Thus, the section has always depended on a cadre of dedicated preparators, from Arthur S. Coggeshall in 1899 to Norman Wuerthele a century later. Joseph Yarmer, who retired in 1973, prepared fossil specimens for forty years. Every skeleton on exhibit is a testament to the skills of preparators. Early exhibits also testify to the work of Pittsburgh's creative iron and steel workers, who crafted graceful mounts to hold the fragile bones.

While this section's appeal to the public is obvious, it has also gained international scientific attention. Fossil remains from different geological ages have made possible a better understanding of the environments in which species evolved. Scientists could correlate rock beds containing fossils across distant sites, setting up time sequences to detail the global processes that controlled life on earth. As the study of fossils became increasingly refined, evolutionary patterns became ever clearer, and entire lineages of life forms could be traced, often for millions of years. The vertebrate paleontology collections now include approximately 103,000 fossil specimens, with 376 primary types—the original examples that define a species, including *Tyrannosaurus rex.*

How did it all start in Pittsburgh? In 1898, Andrew Carnegie wrote a now famous note to museum director William Holland, scribbled in pencil on a newspaper clipping cut from the *New York Post:* "Dear Chancellor, Buy this for Pittsburgh." Pictured on the newspaper's front page was a drawing of a giant dinosaur peering into a skyscraper window, the headline declaring, "MOST COLOSSAL ANIMAL EVER ON EARTH JUST FOUND OUT WEST." Carnegie followed up on his initial enthusiasm by establishing a businesslike ten-thousand-dollar annual budget for fieldwork to collect dinosaur fossils, and his personal support lasted until his death.[26]

At Carnegie's initial request, Holland promptly dispatched a field expedition to Laramie, Wyoming, in the spring of 1899, including J. L. "Jake" Wortman, a ten-year veteran of dinosaur hunting for the American Museum of Natural History; Arthur S. Coggeshall, a preparator formerly with the same museum; and the local Wyoming prospector W. H. Reed, a knowledgeable cowboy turned bone hunter. The first advertised site at Medicine Bow proved unfruitful, yielding only one limb bone of the animal

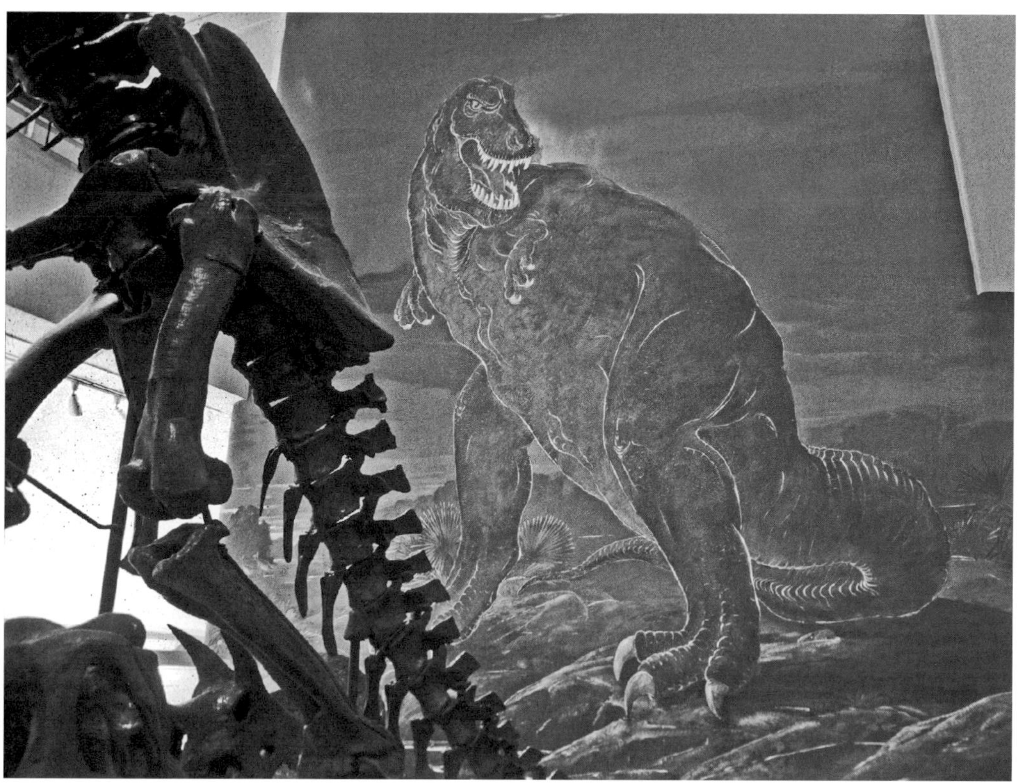

This iconic 1951 mural of Tyrannosaurus rex *reflected the tail-dragging look of the Godzilla movies of that era as well as the mounted specimen. In the 1990s, scientists who understood that the animal was a more agile, bipedal predator removed the mural and rearranged the pose of the fossil specimen.*

fully pictured in the New York newspaper. Coggeshall reported, "Discouraging? Yes it was, but bone hunters, like prospectors for gold and silver, have to take discouragement in their stride."[27] Two months later, at a site called Sheep Creek, some thirty miles away, the dinosaur prospectors discovered a large dinosaur skeleton, nearly intact, in the mud of an ancient stream or lake from 120 million years ago. Discovered on July 4, 1899, the specimen Coggeshall promptly deemed the "Star Spangled Dinosaur" was inspected the next month by Holland himself. Some of its bones had weathered away, but another specimen discovered nearby furnished more, and by 1901 the species was described in scientific literature as *Diplodocus carnegii,* an eighty-four-foot-long reptile.

When Wortman resigned in 1900, he was followed by John Bell Hatcher, an experienced scientist who had made three expeditions to Patagonia for

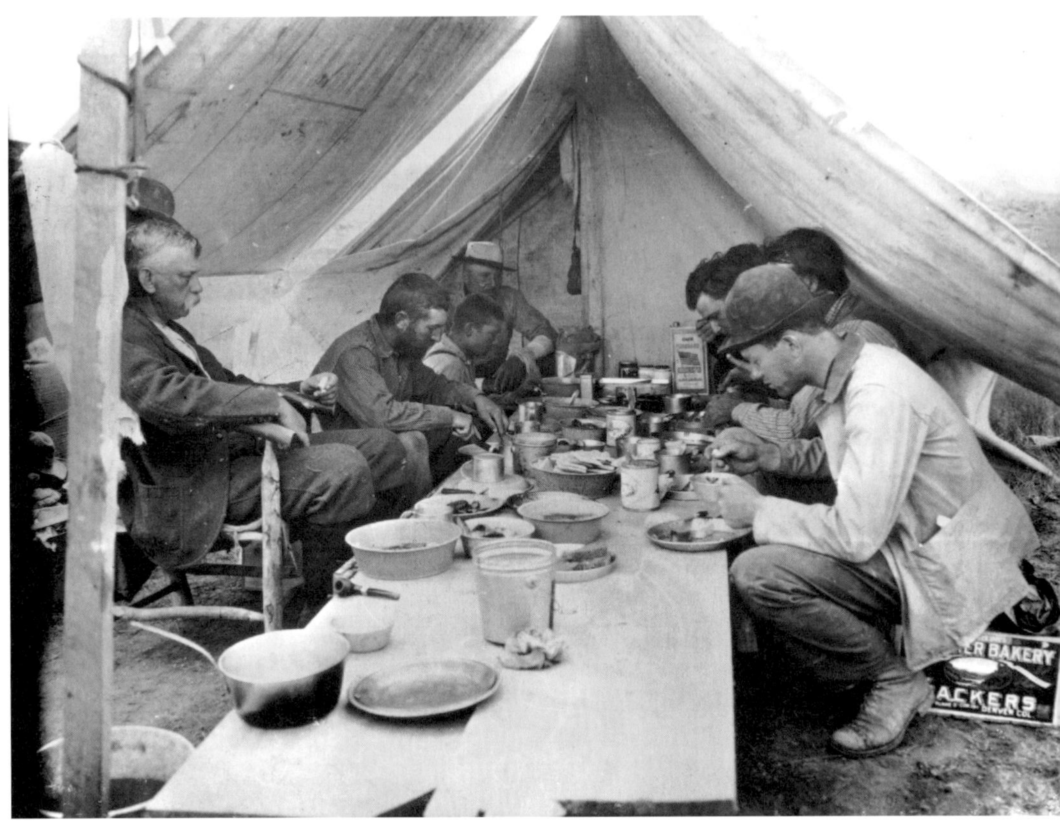

Director William Holland (seated in chair), joins the bone hunters for dinner at the "Camp Carnegie" quarry in Wyoming in 1899.

the U.S. Geological Survey. Tragically, Hatcher died of typhoid in Pittsburgh at the height of his career in 1904, at age forty-three. His brother-in-law and associate Olof Peterson took over, launching a thirty-two-year career with the museum that would make him one of the country's most renowned vertebrate paleontologists. Earl Douglass, another long-time museum figure, came to Carnegie in 1902 and remained for twenty-two years. In 1909, Douglass discovered the most outstanding of all dinosaur deposits, holding dozens of the immense creatures, their fossil bones intermingled, high on a Utah desert ridge. The largest quarry of Jurassic period dinosaur bones ever discovered, this find would eventually become part of the two-hundred-thousand-acre Dinosaur National Monument. Douglass worked at this site for thirteen years, sending large crates of bones still in the matrix (rock) back to Pittsburgh via freight wagon and rail. These specimens gradually joined *Diplodocus,* displayed in lonely splendor since

     CARNEGIE MUSEUM OF NATURAL HISTORY

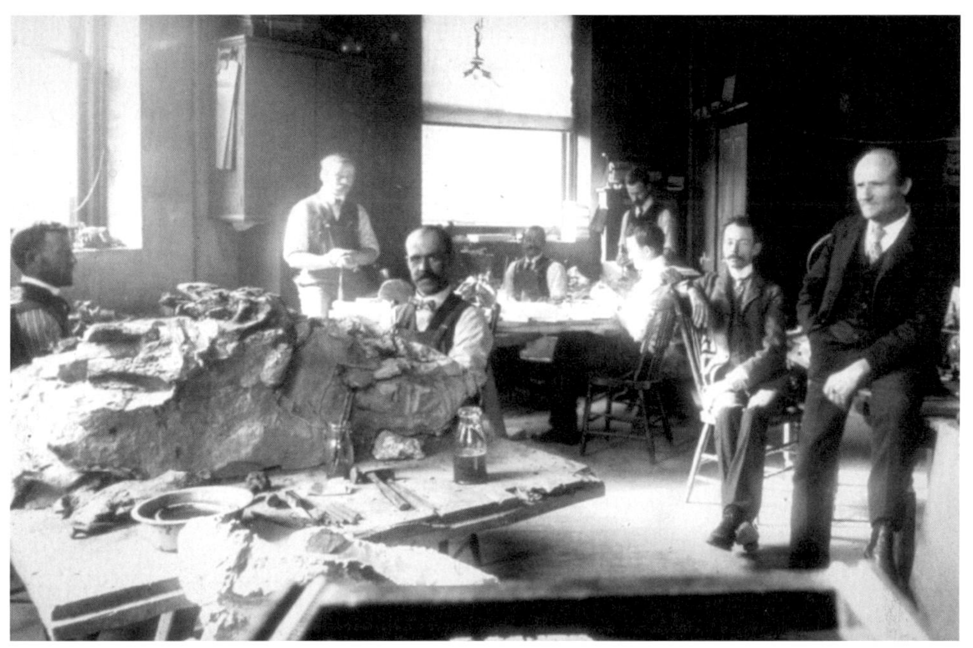

The brilliant paleontologist John Bell Hatcher (right of photograph) directed dinosaur research from 1900 to 1904, but died of typhoid in Pittsburgh at the height of his career, when he was forty-three years old.

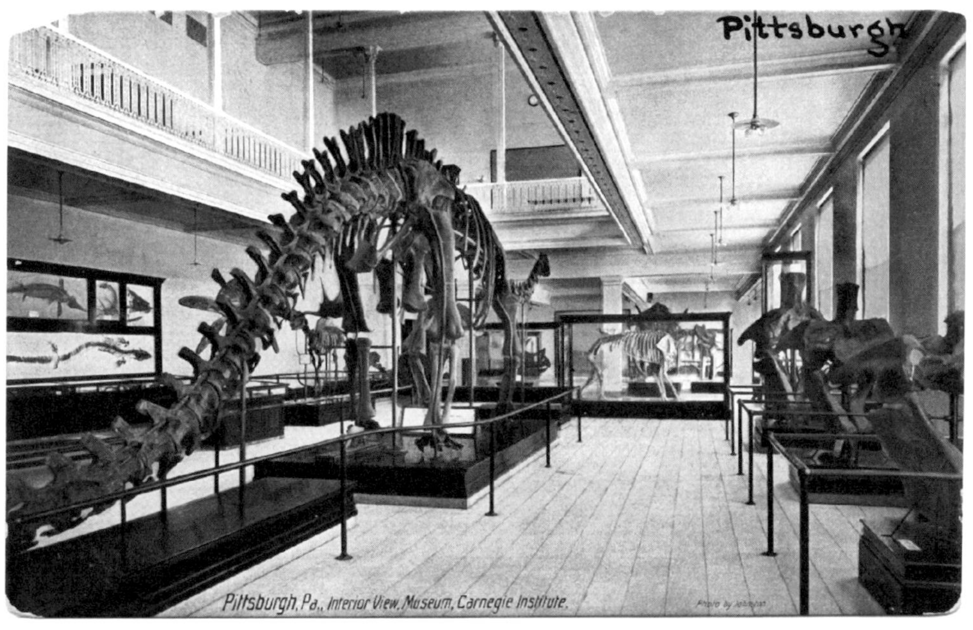

This postcard shows Dinosaur Hall's main attraction after 1907, the giant Diplodocus carnegii; in 1915, the second large dinosaur, Apatosaurus louisae (named after Mrs. Carnegie), was added.

1907: *Apatosaurus* in 1915; *Camarasaurus* in 1924; the flesh-eating *Allosaurus* in 1938; *Camptosaurus, Dryosaurus,* and *Stegosaurus* in 1940. Douglass's finds, which remain some of the museum's greatest treasures, took decades to identify scientifically and prepare for display.

Carnegie's investment in fossil collecting was remarkable: no institution today could mount an independent program of such magnitude. For over twenty years, three or four separate field parties explored the badlands of the Dakotas, Nebraska, Wyoming, Montana, Colorado, Idaho, and Utah, a research effort that ended with Carnegie's death in 1919. During these early days, too, a system developed for sharing fossil materials with other institutions; tons of dinosaur bones were sent to less generously endowed institutions in exchange for fossil materials that helped Pittsburgh build its collections. When storage facilities could no longer keep up with the growing collections in the early years, a catalog system, tailored to the collection's immediate needs, was begun. Over time, this catalog was computerized, and new techniques provided better storage. While fossil dinosaur bones may seem ponderous, they are in fact as fragile as glass, and today they are cradled on beds of plastic foam.

When Carnegie died, the museum's prospecting for fossil dinosaurs came to an end. In subsequent decades, museum preparators continued to discover and remove specimens encased in tons of solid rock. Beyond dinosaurs, Holland had persuaded Carnegie in 1903 to purchase the incomparable Bayet Collection, which includes fossil plants, invertebrates, and vertebrates and has continued to draw researchers for over a century. Early exploration brought the collection interesting examples of fossil mammals from Montana and Nebraska. In 1905, curator and field collector O. A. Peterson found incredibly rich deposits of Miocene mammals in western Nebraska, a site that later became the Agate Springs Fossil Beds National Monument. From the 1930s through the 1950s, fieldwork continued primarily in Montana and Utah, where curator J. Leroy Kay pursued a great diversity of Eocene and Oligocene vertebrates. Among his assistants was John E. Guilday, one of the nation's experts on cave-deposited materials. In 1982, the year before Guilday died of polio, he described the remarkable preservation of bones in caves: "Caves have a constant internal environment that varies little with the seasons, so that any surface object that finds its way into them may remain there, unchanged for millennia.... Lying far beneath the weather and erosion, and undisturbed by surface scavengers, skeletons of bears, jaguars, mountain lions, American cheetahs, saber-tooths, dire wolves, and peccaries have been found in Appalachian caves under circumstances that would suggest that the animals must have lost their way at some fateful turn many thousands of years ago."[28] In 1983, the

John Guilday Caves Nature Preserve, near Franklin, West Virginia, was named in Guilday's honor.

The era's staff curators and paleontologists were remarkable. J. Leroy Kay, fondly called "Pop" by the staff, worked in the Carnegie's section of Vertebrate Paleontology from 1925 until 1957, spending years prospecting in the Tertiary fossil beds of Montana, Utah, Colorado, and Wyoming. He remained an emeritus curator from retirement until his death in 1971. Craig Black joined the staff in 1960 as an associate curator, becoming the curator of vertebrate paleontology two years later and—after a brief hiatus at the University of Kansas and Texas Tech—eventually the director of the museum, renewing paleontology's support. Mary Dawson worked at the museum over more than four decades; her research, concentrating on fossil mammals, produced fossil evidence that North America and Europe had at one point been linked, thus validating the plate tectonics theory of continental evolution. She served as curator of vertebrate paleontology from 1970 until 2003. Leonard Krishtalka worked at the Carnegie for twenty years, from 1975 until 1995, writing the column "Missing Links" for *Carnegie Magazine,* as well as a popular book on dinosaurs, *Dinosaur Plots and Other Intrigues in Natural History.* David S. Berman, who began working at the museum in 1979, resolved an old conflict about which skull should be attached to the famous *Apatosaurus louisae* (named after Carnegie's wife, Louise), discovered by Earl Douglass in 1909, long (and incorrectly) known in popular culture as a "Brontosaurus." Berman, working with his colleague John S. McIntosh, scientifically identified the correct skull for the species, whose type specimen at the Carnegie had long been headless and then mismatched with a *Camarasaurus* skull. The correct head was installed with great publicity on "Dinosaur Day" in 1979.[29] During the 1980s, Berman excavated remains of the small bipedal dinosaur *Coelophysis* from a quarry at Ghost Ranch, New Mexico, and in 1992 his work with German colleagues at the Bromacker Quarry in central Germany produced the fossils of many primitive amphibians and reptiles from approximately 290 million years ago, long before the Age of Dinosaurs, irrefutably reinforcing the theory that North American and Europe had once formed a continuous landmass.

In 1989 a new generation of paleontologists began with the appointment of Christopher Beard, who became one of the rising stars in vertebrate paleontology, receiving a MacArthur Foundation "genius" award in 2001, worth $500,000, and becoming the curator of vertebrate paleontology when Dawson retired in 2003. Beard was a world authority on the evolution of early primates, his research shaping debates about the evolutionary and geographical origins of mammals. Scientists had long known from the fossil record that humans had evolved from apes in Africa, some five to ten

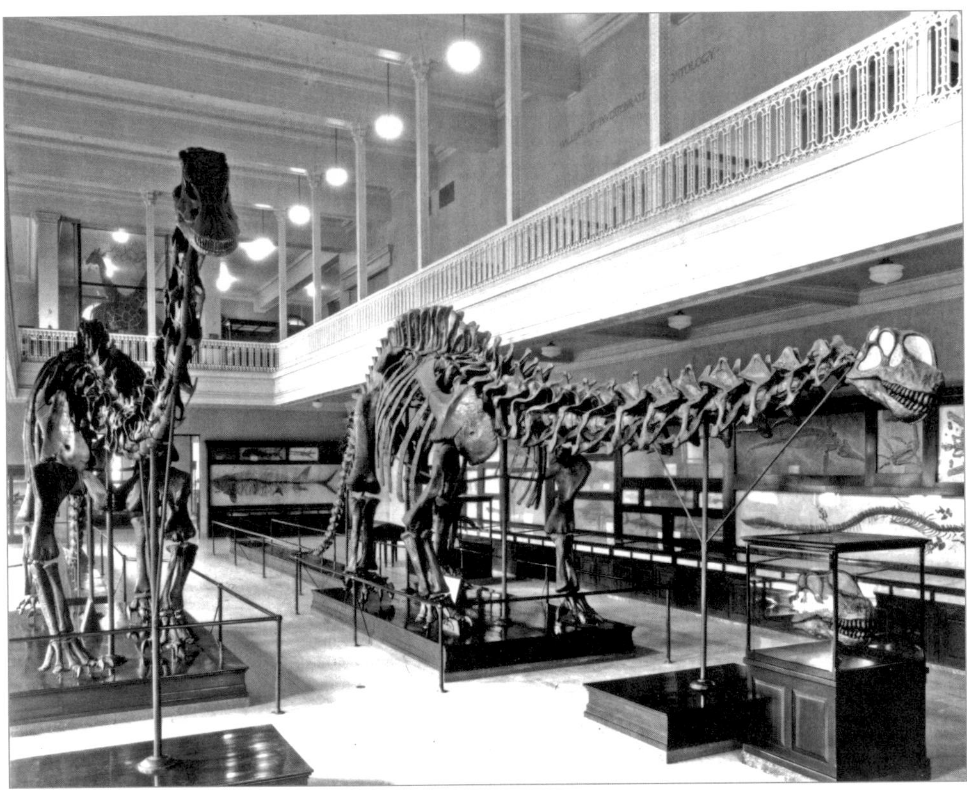

Apatosaurus louisae *lacked a head for twenty years because scientists could not agree on the correct skull. In 1932, after Holland's death, the wrong blunt-nosed skull shown here was attached, and the correct long-snout skull that Holland advocated was displayed as an alternative in a box beneath it. In 1979, Carnegie scientists proved Holland correct and installed the right skull.*

million years ago, but paleontologists still had little information about the transitional mammal species that existed between the lower primates—the animals that foreshadowed humans, such as the nocturnal, tree-dwelling lorises, lemurs, and tarsiers—and the higher primates—those that most resembled *Homo sapiens,* such as monkeys and apes.[30] In 1992, while digging in middle Eocene soil deposits in Jiangsu Province, near China's east coast, Beard and his colleagues unearthed distinctive fossils, including a portion of a tiny lower jaw containing parts of three molars. They appeared to be Eocene primates, unlike any primitive species seen before; the paleontologists named this previously unknown species *Eosimias sinensis,* or "dawn monkey."

Yet another distinguished scientist joined the staff in 1996, Zhe-Xi Luo, who quickly established himself as one of the world's authorities on Mesozoic animals. In 1997, his collaboration with scientists from the Insti-

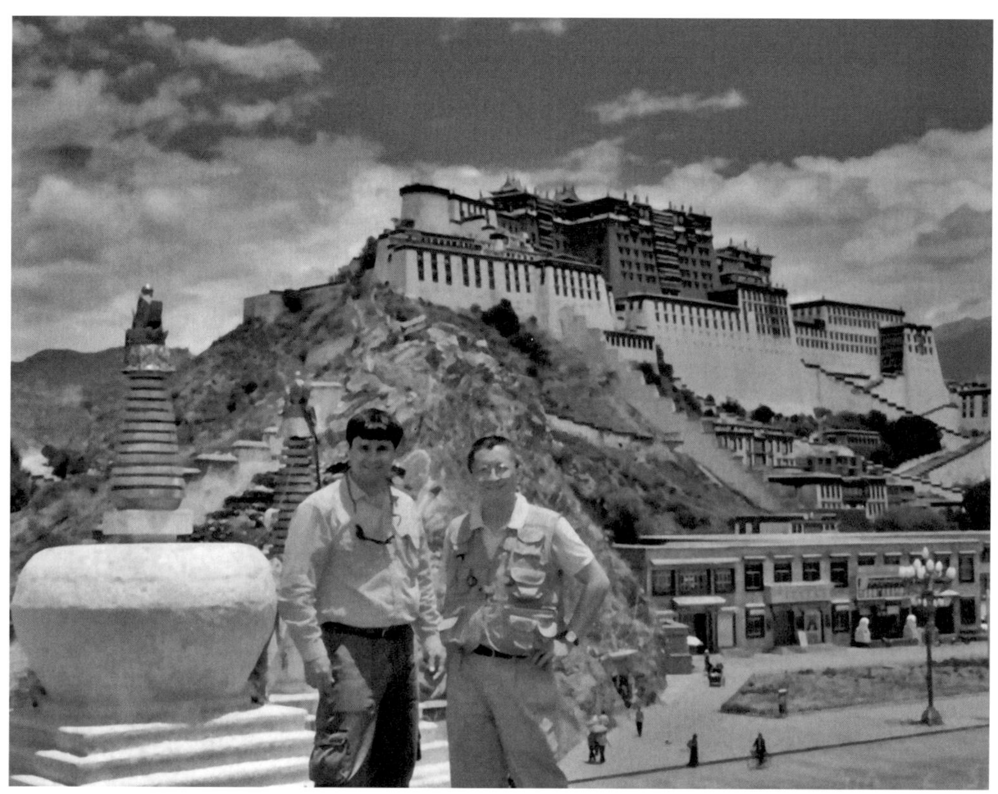

A new generation of Carnegie paleontologists, including Christopher Beard and Zhe-Xi Luo, began to dig in China in the 1990s.

tute of Vertebrate Paleontology and Paleoanthropology in Beijing yielded what was at the time the most complete mammal ever found from the period 120 to 140 million years ago, filling yet another important gap in the understanding of how humans evolved from ancient mammals. One of his newly identified species was a small insect-eating mammal he and his team called *Jeholodens,* which lived during the time of the dinosaurs. It had a mobile shoulder girdle that allowed its front legs to move dexterously, like later mammals would. Very few skeletons of such early mammals had been found, and scientists had only vague ideas about their lifestyles; the discovery of this species showed that early mammals could walk with an almost erect gait. Luo also studied the evolution of hearing in whales and published findings from China's famous Liaoning Province that yielded evidence of the first feathered reptiles, alive during the time of the dino-

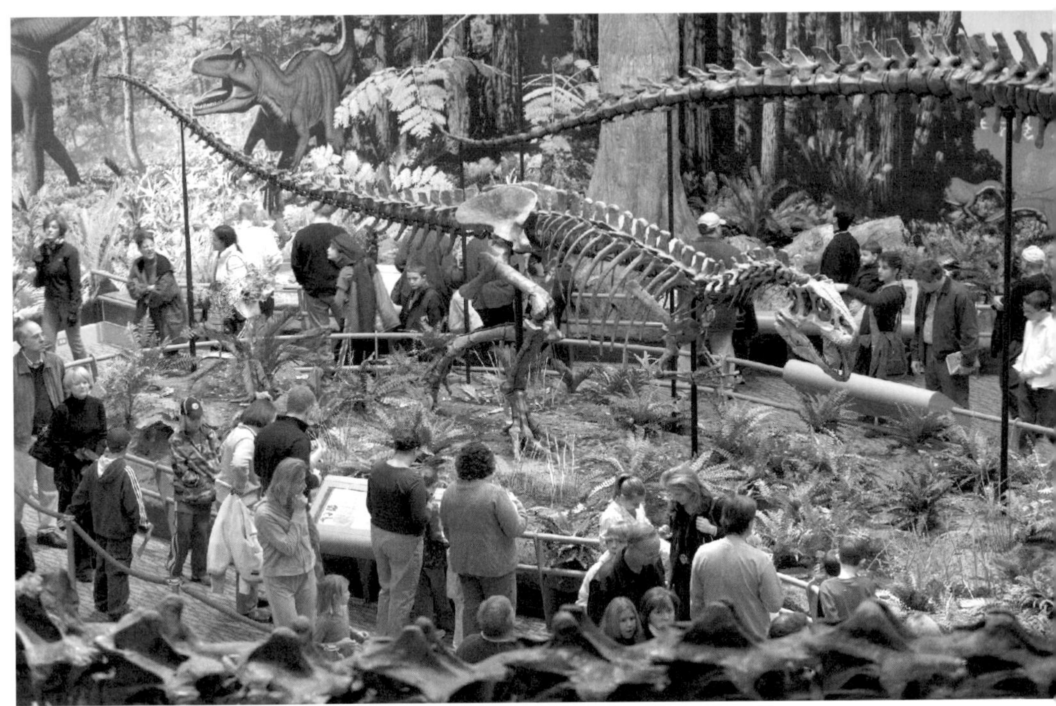

*Dinosaurs in Their Time opened in 2007 and was the largest exhibit ever
and created by the museum.*

saurs, some 145 million years ago. Luo's research marked him as a standard
bearer for scientific initiative, and he was eventually appointed associate
director for research and collections at the museum and acted as one of
the museum's two interim directors when Bill DeWalt resigned in 2007.

Yet another notable researcher is Matthew Lamanna, hired in 2004.
Lamanna had gained fame in 2000 for the discovery of *Paralititan* in Egypt,
then considered the largest dinosaur ever discovered, a sauropod eighty feet
long and weighing between forty and fifty tons. Beginning in 2004, he began
work on a series of digs in China, in 2006 publishing an article about the
discovery of *Gansus yumenensis,* a missing link in the early evolution of birds.
Significantly, Lamanna's appointment demonstrated a renewed curatorial
commitment to dinosaur research, just as the museum opened what was
billed as the best hall of dinosaurs in the world, Dinosaurs in Their Time.[31]

This $36 million hall, opened in 2007, had been years in the planning;
museum officials hoped the exhibit, the most expensive one the museum
had ever mounted, would be a "first-day destination" for visitors to Pittsburgh. Dinosaurs in Their Time, which worked to establish a stronger link

between paleontology and environmentalism, modernized the old dinosaur exhibits, innovatively re-creating aspects of dinosaur environments from millions of years ago and emphasizing the fossils' accurate positioning. The new exhibit was so large it required the demolition of halls and rooms that had not changed since 1907, and it filled the open-air atrium between the Institute and the library's book stacks. The renewed exhibit, unveiled in two phases, set a new standard for environmental interpretation and scientific accuracy.

THE LIFE SCIENCES
Mollusks

From the earth sciences and paleontology, we move to the sciences of living things, beginning with one of the ancient life forms, mollusks. The public, in the opinion of curator Timothy Pearce, often overlooks mollusks because of the way the animal world is commonly viewed, divided into vertebrates (animals with backbones) and invertebrates (animals without backbones). This division, says Pearce, is vastly unbalanced: "People are stubborn, and they love their charismatic megafauna [large life forms]. Ask a random person to name any animal, and chances are extremely high that they will show their bias by naming a vertebrate animal (only 1 percent of all animals), and chances are still high that within that they will name a mammal (a mere 0.1 percent of all animals)." Pearce also attributes public indifference to the fact that no popular guidebook literature is available to help people understand mollusks. While birds and plants enjoy shelves full of handsome field guides, mollusks have nothing comparable. Pearce says he suffers from bird-book envy: "Bird books tell us what birds eat and show range maps, and not just where they occur, but where they occur in summer, winter, where they breed. For the vast majority of snails, we don't know what they eat, and our range maps are woefully incomplete."[32] North America also has comparatively few mollusk researchers (especially for terrestrial species), in comparison to the many land snail researchers in Europe. When Pearce became curator of the mollusks section in 2002, he noted that in Pennsylvania only Beaver County had a regional record of the smallest land snail in North America, *Punctum minutissimum,* in a 1985 map showing species distribution. Yet it is regarded as the most common snail in western Pennsylvania; people simply never searched for this species.

Given this lack of public knowledge, it might be best to begin with a definition: within the world of invertebrates, mollusks are a separate, large group including animals such as oysters, clams, and snails. These animals typically have soft, unsegmented bodies, a mantle, and a hard protective shell, although some species, like slugs and squids, do not have a hard shell. This is a vast, ancient, widespread life form: marine mollusks live in the sea, freshwater mollusks populate rivers and streams, land snails live in the soil, and some species even live on trees. After insects, mollusks are the largest group of living animals in number of species known, with estimates ranging from fifty thousand to two hundred thousand species.

Mollusks affect human life in many ways—as ingredients for medicines, as pests, as hosts for disease, as parasites that impact livestock and humans—and we ignore them at our peril. For example, one newly introduced foreign species, the zebra mussel (*Dreissena polymorpha*), emerged in the late 1980s as a billion-dollar economic threat in the Great Lakes and related rivers, aggressively clogging pipes and water filtration plants. This species can wipe out mussels and other native species by smothering them and competing for food and changing the habitat. Their invasion of North America is considered disastrous. Mollusks' extreme sensitivity to their surroundings makes them a key indicator organism for ecological change; the return of native freshwater mollusks to the rivers of western Pennsylvania, for instance, is a welcome sign of the rejuvenation of the watershed in the postindustrial age. Educators also find that freshwater, marine, and terrestrial invertebrates may be used to explain concepts such as evolution, adaptation, and conservation in a way that is easy for students to understand.

From the evolutionary point of view, all the invertebrates are very old, and the fundamental group, the phylum, has not changed in hundreds of millions of years. Famous popular examples include the "chambered nautilus" and the common horseshoe crab of the eastern U.S. shores (actually a relative of the spider). A few species of the living nautilus are the last representatives of a group that was formerly abundant throughout the seas, related to the giant extinct ammonites.

For most of its existence, the Section of Invertebrates (excluding insects) was, according to former curator J. José Parodiz, "a one-man section, in which the curator must toll the bells, conduct the choir, and preach the sermon all at the same time."[33] The first specialist for this section was naturalist Herbert Huntington Smith, who made collecting trips to South America starting in 1870, long before the museum opened. When Smith became the curator in 1896, he added to the section's collections until his retirement in 1903. The second curator, Arnold Ortmann, gave the collection its notable status as a scientific baseline for regional streams. A pioneer in documenting the change that pollution caused to rivers and streams during America's industrial age, Ortmann (1903–27) was born in Prussia in 1869.

He immigrated to the United States in 1894 and came to the Carnegie as the curator of invertebrate paleontology in 1903. An experienced collector in Africa and the Arctic region, he was an expert in the study of freshwater mussels and was said to have collected from every river in Pennsylvania and West Virginia, as well as throughout Ohio, Kentucky, Tennessee, North Carolina, and Virginia. One of his admirers described his typical collecting technique: "His weapon is a long handled rake with a light attached. This instrument is dragged over the shell bank and the disturbed mussels catch on the prongs as they pass and are lifted up to shore for inspection. If the catch is not what is needed it is thrown back into the water unharmed. If a new specimen, or a comparatively rare shell is found it goes into the bag to come up to town for indexing and study."[34] In 1920, he formulated "Ortmann's Law of Stream Position," suggesting that one species of mussel can take on different appearances depending on where in a river system the individuals live.[35] This discovery helped simplify the taxonomy, or identification, of mollusks: up to that point researchers had assigned different names to the same species because of their varied body forms.

Ortmann's fellow collector the trustee George Hubbard Clapp enjoyed a scientific reputation in his own right. While Clapp collected many things, shells were a particular passion, an interest he had inherited from his grandfather. He collected in "lots," any one of which could include two to ten thousand specimens. One individual specimen might be "only a millimeter long or as large as a kitchen roaster"; the smallest specimens were valuable because they were hard to find: one vial of shells in the Clapp collection could contain more than six thousand specimens, all minute but all adults.[36] The first gift he made to the section was a collection of sixty species of shells; the largest was a collection of shells from the Florida Keys. Clapp was an Institute leader from the time he was appointed to the original board in 1896; for more than half a century, he symbolized Andrew Carnegie's belief that private citizens would support science at the Institute.

While researchers have used the collection to study marine life, its unique strengths are in freshwater and terrestrial mollusks. Shellfish can have long lives, some living for fifty to sixty years or more. Once they settle, they stay in one place and can filter up to a liter of water an hour, sorting out the algae and bacteria and digesting what they need, thus cleaning the water. They establish population beds that can stabilize stream bottoms and provide continuity to environmental life in their proximity. This symbiotic relationship between freshwater mussels and shellfish and fish habitats is a timeless feature of freshwater systems. The United States east of the Mississippi has one of the richest populations of freshwater mollusks in the world, in number of species as well as individuals. Pennsylvania once had sixty-seven species of large, freshwater mussels, most in the western rivers. More recently, shellfish habitats have been affected by changes to their environment, including locks and dams, which limit the migration of fish and keep mollusks from easily repopulating regions and tributaries that lie upstream. Still, by the 1990s, native freshwater mollusks were making a comeback in western Pennsylvania rivers like the lower Allegheny. Above the Kiskiminetas River, a tributary laden with acid-mine drainage that joins the Allegheny near Freeport, the upper Allegheny is still relatively unpolluted. French Creek, which enters the Allegheny at Franklin, has long been an outstanding example of a pristine Appalachian mountain stream with abundant native mollusk populations, a living environmental model from long before the era of industrial water pollution. Nevertheless, stream pollution such as acid-mine drainage has made a number of species of mollusks extinct, while surviving species are sometimes difficult to identify because of ecological variation.

A new era began in 1952 when J. José Parodiz, from the Argentine Museum of Natural History (Buenos Aires), took charge of the section, soon becoming the curator. In Pittsburgh, he continued Ortmann's work on land and freshwater fauna of Pennsylvania, but he continued to collect from South America, and the museum's collection of South American naiads became the largest of its kind in the United States. Parodiz retired in 1982, and for two decades the section came under the control of other museum curators: Clarence J. (Jack) McCoy, of Amphibians and Reptiles, and John Rawlins, of Invertebrate Zoology.

In 2002, however, the museum once more tapped a mollusk specialist to curate the section, Timothy Pearce, who renamed the section Mollusks, reflecting both the long tradition of collecting at the museum and the importance of freshwater mollusks for charting environmental change. Like Parodiz, Pearce found he operated a one-person section and depended largely upon volunteers. In a given six-month period, this section, one of the most active for volunteers, has about twenty-five volunteers. They come to Carnegie for different reasons—some with degrees in biology, scientific skills, or secretarial skills; others because they see volunteering at the museum as a privilege, a way to advance museum research. The mollusk collection in particular depends on volunteers because it has a backlog of uncurated material going back nearly a century. Volunteers routinely process larger shells donated by Ortmann, for example, or unwrap specimens from newspapers with dates from the early twentieth century. Volunteers also work on "orphaned" collections—donated collections without sufficient data to realize their scientific value. One collection of some twenty thousand shells, for example, had been collected and numbered over thirty years, but the matching inventory records of the sites where they were found were lost when the library was dispersed.

In spite of continuing struggles to make its worth more obvious to the public, the mollusks section, with some three million specimens, is one of the fifteen largest collections in the United States, with some of the most precise locality data of any major mollusk collection in the world. The collection is divided into some 120,000 lots, of which more than 63 percent have computerized records. Nevertheless, a backlog of more than 15,000 lots awaits preparation, identification, and curation.

Botany

Unlike the collections in mollusks, those in botany have been more thoroughly and uniquely cataloged. Each leaf, twig, or flower is carefully preserved—not pinned in place like insects; not arranged in drawers like samples of birds, mammals, or shellfish; not bottled in alcohol like snakes. Instead, botanical material is preserved in an herbarium: an unbound library of dried plants, each "page" containing a pressed plant specimen that has been identified and filed. Historically, herbaria documented local collections of dried plants, glued on the blank pages of huge books; copies with duplicate sets of specimens were frequently exchanged between botanists from different regions. In this way, collections grew with the addition of volumes of plants from wider and distant areas. The museum's collection includes several older bound herbaria, the oldest that of the Englishman William Paine, which dates to 1728.[37] The labors of early botanists, forced to compare specimens held in bulky books, finally led collectors to unbind their pages and instead keep them as loose sheets. Today these pages are usually kept to an international standard, so that sheets documenting different species can be kept together and used easily when making comparisons to other species. Thus, all the sheets of the American "great rhododendron" (*Rhododendron maximum L.*) might go on a shelf that has some seventy-five sheets of specimens, collected during the past 150 years between Maine and Alabama; these sheets can be easily compared with samples of the same species collected from Nepal or Lapland. Botany at Carnegie has approximately five hundred thousand plant specimens from all over the world, from all major plant groups, ranking in the top twenty-five of the twelve hundred herbaria in the United States. It is particularly rich in specimens from the upper Alleghenies and western Pennsylvania, both past and present flora.

The herbarium's plants from western Pennsylvania set an environmental baseline by which to judge the rare or endangered status of local plants. Carnegie's herbarium is a National Regional Depository, akin to a national landmark or art treasure—the primary resource for identifying the region's poisonous and medicinally useful plants and for determining invasive new species. Researchers also use it regularly to study such topics as pollination ecology; hybridization experiments; and the anatomical, chemical, and chromosomal makeup of plants.

In the field, botanists collect several specimens of each plant, one for the collection and the others for exchange, eventually developing sets that range from one hundred to three hundred different species, a common unit for exchange with other herbaria. Each specimen is carefully arranged within a sheet of newspaper to reveal its taxonomically important parts and then dried in a plant press. When tied, a full press may be as tall as four feet; one to several days of low heat are needed for drying, since slow drying preserves the floral colors. Properly dried specimens may be stored for many years in newsprint before they are finally mounted. After a specimen is mounted on stiff white paper, the completed sheet is filed with those displaying other specimens in the correct taxonomic case. Each sheet includes a collector's label that indicates the scientific name, the date, the exact place of collection, and a stamped herbarium record number. In modern times, the need to trace environmental factors has led to additional field data being entered: population size, flower color, the pollinators that visit the flower, and soil pH and type.

Like any other systematic collection, the herbarium represents millions of hours of work in preparation and curation and relies heavily upon a loyal cadre of volunteers, as well as research associates and curatorial staff. The botanists in charge of the Carnegie's herbarium collected regionally and throughout the world, beginning with John A. Shafer. Shafer (1863–1918), a founding member of the Botanical Society of Western Pennsylvania and the first custodian of the herbarium, worked with N. L. Britton, the director of the New York Botanical Garden, to select duplicates for the new Carnegie herbarium. His successor, Otto E. Jennings, was an important figure in the life of the museum, starting as a custodian in botany in 1904, rising to curator in 1915, becoming acting director of the museum in 1945 at Avinoff's death and then the director from 1946 to 1948. For decades he was the most renowned botanist in western Pennsylvania, and he explored western Pennsylvania with the energy of a pioneer, discovering rare locales where specialized populations of plants survived. Millions of years ago, plant species were continuous throughout the northern regions of the world, but intervening geologic and climatic events produced modern isolation and evolutionary divergence. Western Pennsylvania, with its hills and valleys and microclimates that appeal to different plant species, has "relictual" (relict) floras that are almost identical to floras in distant parts of the northern hemisphere, from western North America to Europe, the Himalayas, China, and Japan.

Other notable botanists associated with the section include Edward Graham, whose publications include *Flora of the Uinta Basin* (1937) and *Flora of Kartabo* (1934), and LeRoy Henry, whose long association with the museum began when he was an undergraduate at the University of Pittsburgh. Henry, mentored by Jennings, eventually became the curator of botany in 1947. Like Jennings he discovered small natural areas that merited preservation and recommended them to the Western Pennsylvania Conservancy. When Powdermill Nature Reserve opened, Henry researched the plants of the reserve, publishing widely on regional plants, ferns, and fungi.

Frederick Utech became the associate curator in botany in 1976 and served as the curator from 1988 to 1999. He specialized in the lily family (*Liliaceae*) and added considerably to the herbarium through his fieldwork in North America, Europe, and East Asia. Utech's appointment also marked the beginning of a new era at the museum: by the 1980s, the modern environmental movement had taken hold, and educational activities in botany reflected this shift. Sue A. Thompson, who joined the section's staff in 1982 as assistant curator of botany, organized "BioBlitz" studies of all the species found in Pittsburgh's parks. These twenty-four-hour biological surveys, later lengthened to several days, drew scientists and local naturalists to the parks to find as many plants, animals, and microorganisms as possible within the parks' boundaries. At a site such as Riverview Park, amateurs and professionals "scanned the skies; set and pulled in traps, beat the bushes, watched the underbrush; looked under rocks, bark, and leaf litter, sampled plants; peered at pond scum; and walked through the forest and fields." They found 319 species of plants in Riverview Park and a total of 1,164 species in a twenty-four-hour period—far more than the original estimate of 500 to 700 species.[38] BioBlitz was the first collaborative effort in the country uniting a natural history museum, an urban park conservancy, and a city park system. In later years, the main Pittsburgh parks having been studied, the program moved to Powdermill Nature Reserve. Both Utech and Thompson left the museum under the troubled directorship of Jay Apt.

Throughout the administrative changes, botany was also undergoing changes in technology. Botany was the first section to have a fully equipped biosystematics laboratory, now considered essential to modern research and plant classification. Modern systems of classification use numerous characters in comparing different species, recording information about different levels of biological organization—from the community, population, and organism to the cell and subcell. In the laboratory, high-powered compound microscopes are used for chromosome observation to establish a species' karyotype—the arrangement of chromosomes in a cell. The laboratory was renamed the Fisher Scientific Biosystematics Laboratory after receiving support from the family of trustee James A. Fisher, which also donated a classroom to the laboratory.

Botany moved further toward laboratory science when Cynthia Morton was appointed associate curator and head of the section in 2002. One of her early projects at the museum was to complete botanical databases for several more counties in western Pennsylvania, thus providing an environmental baseline for remediation in areas that had been strip-mined. Morton also used technology to ensure that Schenley Plaza, the six-acre expanse in front of Carnegie Institute and Library, would enjoy a vibrant population of London planetrees in the future. In the 1920s, city officials had planted scores of these trees on the plaza, a hardy, pollution-resistant species. Eighty years later, when the plaza was restored in 2005, only 107 trees remained of the original planting of 212, the others having been killed by disease outbreaks.[39] With a $19,000 grant from the Garden Club of Allegheny County, Morton used DNA fingerprinting techniques to study the genetic diversity of the remaining trees in the plaza. She discovered that surviving trees were genetically diverse and resistant to damage from insects, fungi, and other pathogens, much more so than the planetrees normally sold at nurseries across the United States. This was because most nurseries today propagate trees by using available cuttings rather than seeds, thus preventing the trees from naturally diversifying by swapping DNA during reproduction. If the common nursery-grown trees had been planted, she concluded, they would have been wiped out if attacked by a common disease. The Pittsburgh Parks Conservancy thus replanted 93 new London planetrees in the plaza and will rely on cuttings from the existing disease-resistant trees for future plantings. Morton pointed out that this was an instance of genetic information being used to address an everyday problem: "There are a lot of interesting questions that people forget they can use molecular biology to answer."[40]

While botany has enjoyed consistent support from independent groups such as the Botanical Society of Western Pennsylvania and the dedicated labor of scores of volunteers, and while the section's researchers enjoy the benefits of the latest technology, Botany Hall was never updated to keep pace with changing ecological interests. The hall was originally planned by LeRoy K. Henry and Otto E. Jennings, who based their approach on the variable effects of heat and moisture on plants. Its dioramas beautifully depict a dry desert, a wet tropical jungle, spring flora, an alpine meadow, a bog. Later, the Lake Erie shore of Presque Isle was added, along with a scene from nearby Allegheny National Forest and one from Powdermill Nature Preserve.[41] Once the hall was completed, however, neither botany's curators nor the museum administration gave it high priority, and no new technology was added to draw the public or to bring out the collection's relevance to contemporary concerns. For example, the biodiversity it presented through myriad mammals, birds, and insects was never emphasized in relation to contemporary environmental issues. Tucked away in a corner of the second floor, it remained one of the museum's least trafficked halls and barely escaped destruction during the Apt administration and during the rearranging of exhibit space when Dinosaurs in Their Time was built. Thankfully, it was preserved, and the material it holds might still one day be technologically interpreted in light of modern concerns about biodiversity and global warming.

Amphibians and Reptiles

In 1999, fifteen green iguanas survived a two-hundred-mile trip in the Caribbean after being blown out to sea by a hurricane, clinging to a mat of uprooted trees, and were washed ashore on the island of Anguilla. The world responded to this story because it demonstrated that animals can successfully populate distant lands after making incredible journeys. But this example of modern environmental survival also shed light on how migrating populations may have moved throughout evolutionary history. Museum curator Ellen Censky, of Amphibians and Reptiles, was on the research team that documented the progress of Anguilla's new immigrant animals over the next three years. Weak and dehydrated at first, they soon recuperated. A pregnant female iguana led herpetologists to conclude that the Anguilla iguana population was healthy and had adapted to their new home. "Many scientists never believed such incredible journeys like this were even possible," said Censky, "but now we have concrete evidence."[42] "Just think of all the storms in all the millions of years—and there's a real probability of animals getting anywhere in the world," said evolutionary biologist Blair Hedges of Pennsylvania State University.[43]

During one week, Censky was interviewed for *Newsweek,* ABC News, Discovery News, National Public Radio, the *London Daily News,* Canadian Public Television and Radio, AAAS Radio, the *Hartford Courant, Science News, Book and Author,* the *New York Times,* and other news groups, including media outlets in Switzerland and Brazil.[44] For a scientific section that seldom made the news and often was without a curator in charge, this was rare visibility.

Iguanas belong to the group of amphibians and reptiles classified under "herpetology," a word from the Greek that means "to crawl" and includes other "herps" such as salamanders, frogs, lizards, snakes, turtles, and crocodiles. Amphibians were the first vertebrate animals to transition from aquatic life to a life fully lived on land, an ancient, time-consuming transformation that can be witnessed today whenever a tadpole metamorphoses into a frog. Animals in the scientific class Amphibia often lay eggs near or in the water, followed by an aquatic larval stage that can last months or even years and a transitional period during which the gill-breathing aquatic creature metamorphoses into a lung-breathing terrestrial one. But some species do not need water to breed and do not have a larval stage. And while amphibians and reptiles are usually grouped together, they do have some notable differences. Reptiles, for example, never lay eggs in water, and newly hatched reptiles resemble their parents. Curator Neil Richmond pointed out further that amphibians usually have soft and moist skin and that they have feet, but no claws. Reptiles always have scales, some modified for crawling (snakes) and some reinforced with bony plates (turtles, caiman).[45]

There are about one thousand species of amphibians and reptiles known in the United States, of which about seventy-six live in Pennsylvania.[46] Amphibians and Reptiles at the Carnegie maintains a collection of over 208,000 specimens, about the ninth-largest amphibian and reptile collection in the United States. It includes the largest and most complete collection of Pennsylvania amphibians and reptiles and a significant representation from nearby states such as Virginia, West Virginia, and Maryland, as well as specimens from all over the United States and most of the world. The section's notable historic collections are also rich in type specimens.

Of the specimens in the collection, 90 percent are preserved whole in fluid, while others are preserved as skeletons, skins, or mounts, or in cleared and stained slide preparations. The specimens were kept for decades in glass bottles in the "Alcohol House," a nineteenth-century "pickle house" holding snakes, monitors, and other creatures preserved in alcohol, giving the rare, unscientific visitor a grotesque thrill. But as in a library or herbarium, each bottle was identified and indexed by location, date of capture, and other critical information. Much of the collection, remarkably, remains in the Mason ball-top jars that Netting began using in the 1920s, although the even older nineteenth-century ground-glass jars, hand-crafted in Pittsburgh (but not as tightly sealed), were finally exchanged in 1997–98.

When the museum opened in 1896, the small but growing collection was in its beginning stages, overseen by volunteer curators such as D. A. Atkinson, a Pittsburgh physician and naturalist, and L. E. Griffin, a professor of biology at the University of Pittsburgh. Even without a full-time curator, it grew steadily, with material acquired from worldwide expeditions and contributions from a strong network of volunteers. Still, thirty years passed before the first staff herpetologist, Graham Netting, was hired in 1926, and he remained curator-in-charge for another twenty years. A meticulous administrator, Netting established modern curatorial standards and organized the early collection. Netting became increasingly preoccupied with museum administration, was eventually named the museum's director, and was replaced by Grace Orton in 1944. When she left in 1950, she was succeeded by Neil D. Richmond, an all-around naturalist. By this point, the collection had 57,796 specimens, and Richmond concentrated on completing the survey of Pennsylvania amphibians and reptiles Netting had started in the 1930s. In 1972, Richmond became the museum's first curator of environmental studies, a sign of how important amphibians and reptiles are to understanding environmental change.

Clarence J. (Jack) McCoy arrived at the museum to work as a collection assistant in 1964, beginning a specimen-exchange program with other museums and publishing, with Richmond, a list of the museum's type specimens in 1966. By the end of 1979, he had 119,192 specimens cataloged, with a backlog of another 20,000. By then the collection was among the ten most important in the United States, with some 60 percent of the material from the United States. When McCoy died suddenly of heart failure at age fifty-eight in 1993, he was followed by researchers John Weins and Ellen Censky. When Censky left in 1998, the collection came under the leadership of Stephen Rogers, a skilled and experienced collection manager who worked exclusively in herpetology from 2002 to 2005, and then became the collection manager of birds as well. A recent gift from the Heinz Foundation in memory of Ingrid and William Rea is intended to support the hiring of a curator for the section, in honor of the herpetological work and leadership of Graham Netting at Powdermill Nature Reserve.

Invertebrate Zoology

The building blocks of the Carnegie's great systematic collection in invertebrate zoology were laid with Andrew Carnegie's purchase of the Knyvett Collection of Indian butterflies in 1893 and later with the purchase of Henry Ulke's historic North American beetles collection in 1903. Private collections representing all parts of the world have continued to come to the museum throughout its history, and it now has over eleven million prepared specimens and millions more not yet prepared: it is by far the largest collection at the museum and among the largest in the New World.

To this day, the collection reflects the interests of the museum's early director William Jacob Holland, as well as other museum leaders; its historical strength in lepidoptera (butterflies and moths), for example, is the result of active lepidopterists serving as museum directors for half a century: first Holland, then Avinoff. Holland was America's greatest popularizer of butterflies and moths in the first half of the twentieth century, his

Butterfly Book (1898) and *Moth Book* (1903) still in wide use. He donated his private collection of more than 250,000 specimens to the museum and supported active collectors worldwide, between 1890 and 1930 obtaining major international collections through the efforts of many field collectors and associates.[47] During this era, international material came from many unlikely sources, such as missionaries Reverend A. C. Good and his son A. I. Good, who collected in the rainforests of Gabon and the Cameroon of West Africa. They sold collected specimens to advance the work of their mission in the jungle. Other collections also continued to pour in, from Japan, Buru, Manchuria, northern India, Assam, Cayenne, Bolivia, the Amazon, the American West, and many other locales.

When Holland stepped down as museum director in 1922, Hugo Kahl became curator of the section, then known as Insects and Spiders, and began to acquire even more prestigious collections, assisted for a brief time by Avinoff before Avinoff became the museum's director. When Kahl died in 1941, Avinoff served as the section's acting curator until 1943, when lepidopterist Walter Sweadner took over. Sweadner began the first comprehensive curatorial upgrading of the vast lepidoptera collection since Kahl and also conducted research on the geographic variation of species of wild silkworm moths in the Western United States. Hymenopterist (bees, wasps, ants) George Wallace was the primary steward of the non-lepidoptera collection from the late 1940s until 1979, focusing his research on parasitic wasps, some of which are so tiny that they can fly through the hole in a small button (the family Pteromalidae).

During this time span, from World War II until the mid-1970s, the collection grew relatively slowly, suffering from lack of space and from inadequate resources for expanding its holdings beyond butterflies. During the 1970s, the collection was rearranged in new storage cases, and research was aided by a grant from the National Science Foundation (NSF). Nevertheless, when Wallace retired in 1979, the section was left without a curator for more than a year. This was the collection's darkest hour. Holland's dream of a continuously flourishing collection was threatened by specimens precariously housed in drawers covered with Pittsburgh coal dust and old Schmitt boxes that were nearly inaccessible for research. Then, in 1980, coleopterist (beetles, weevils, fireflies) Ginter Ekis was hired as the section's new curator. Ekis at once sought more NSF funding and was rewarded with a grant to begin rehousing the collections in modern storage equipment and to hire assistants to oversee the reorganization.

Ekins left in 1983, and in 1985, lepidopterist John Rawlins became the section's new curator. Rawlins also asked for stewardship of the museum's large mollusk collection, which had no active curator at the time, and was responsible for the museum's collection of arthropods (insects, spiders, scorpions, mites, ticks). Reflecting these broader collection interests, the section's name was changed to Invertebrate Zoology (IZ) in 1985. Collection activities, renovations, and acquisitions increased dramatically during the 1980s and early 1990s. Storage space more than doubled when a 1995 NSF grant funded the purchase of a large state-of-the-art compactor system. Dipterist (true flies, mosquitoes) Chen Young was promoted to curatorial rank, and coleopterist Robert Davidson became the collection manager. The staff size continued to increase until IZ became one of the museum's largest scientific sections. NSF grants in 2000 and 2005 funded the continued curation and rehousing of the lepidoptera collection, a clear acknowledgment of the section's national and international scientific importance.

Field collecting in the section continued to be a priority: while some museum collections, such as birds or mammals, have a largely complete inventory of existing life forms, insects exist in a bewildering variety that offers many new species. Insects, indeed, have evolved into an incredible number of species during their 350 million years on earth. Some 1.5 million species are known, and an estimated 10 million remain to be discovered, making invertebrate zoology a science that will be actively discovering new species and life histories for years to come. Further, the section's educational value is high. During museum-sponsored events such as the BioBlitzes in Pittsburgh parks, for instance, the public joined the staff in collecting as many species of organisms as possible at a given locale in a twenty-four-hour period, and insects easily constituted the greatest percentage of living organisms at any given site.

Today Rawlins, as head of a large and active section that constantly interfaces with national environmental needs and policies, is outspoken about the future of entomological research and museum science in general. Articulate curators like Rawlins, with active research programs, are inevitably drawn into discussions of the purposes of research museums and their governance. He sees life sciences at the museum as moving away from research focused primarily on arcane adjustments to the classification of evolutionary groups (systematics) to a more integrated and practical focus on applied research: "The new uses are not just about phylogeny or systematics or evolution, but about specimen-based documentation for diversity, about anchoring and rendering those little records of the past.... I'm totally convinced the future of museum science will be about applied use of basic research."[48] In Rawlins's view, museums should actively manage their amazing collections for the public good. Future users of entomology collections will include biodiversity scientists, ecologists, environmentalists, organizations like the Western Pennsylvania Conservancy, and government agencies trying to address contemporary problems, as well as mainstay users from systematic entomology.

Despite the Carnegie's gigantic collection, with its acknowledged importance for research, only in recent years have insects had a large public display at the museum, raising the question of whether exhibits should reflect the scientific work that goes on in the collections. Clearly, the collection is a potentially popular one: in the 1990s, an exhibit called Backyard Monsters proved popular, and an Insect Zoo on the museum's third floor drew crowds of children and adults, allowing visitors to see curators and entomologists preparing specimens and to talk to them about their local backyard monsters. A popular feature was a working beehive, four times the size of the observation hives in other museums.[49] This popular exhibit, however, closed to make way for a changing exhibits gallery and the new hall necessary for Dinosaurs in Their Time. Marketing priorities favored the long-extinct dinosaurs, not the wonder of "living bugs." But in the future, interest in biodiversity could lead to more exhibits that unite insects, plants, and other life forms in the modern environment. Global warming, climate change, pollution, the fragmentation of living species, and the genetic disruption of species have all gained public attention: an insect collection that dwarfs all others at the museum could lead the way to richer exhibits about the contemporary natural world.

Birds

When Carnegie Museum of Natural History began collecting birds, they were still identified in the field by looking along the barrels of a shotgun. There was a saying among ornithologists: "What's hit is history, what's missed is mystery." Field photography had not yet arrived, and "sight records" without a capture or kill were received with skepticism. Museums received new species "taken" (that is, shot) by ornithologists, and the specimens were studied by anatomists who examined skeletons, skins, and even whole birds preserved in glass jars of alcohol. What we now call "bird watching" did not exist, and there were no handy pocket-sized field guides.[50] The scientific books available were large, expensive monographs, authored by "gentlemen ornithologists," featuring hand-colored lithographs of bird types found in a given region of the world or birds of a particular family. At this point, when ornithology was still in its "inventory" stage—discovering and recording species—W. E. Clyde Todd became the first curator of birds at the Carnegie Museum, in April 1899.

As a boy, Todd, born in 1874, collected eggs (a popular hobby and not yet illegal). He published his first paper at age thirteen, noting that the nesting place of the Magnolia warbler he had discovered on his grandfather's

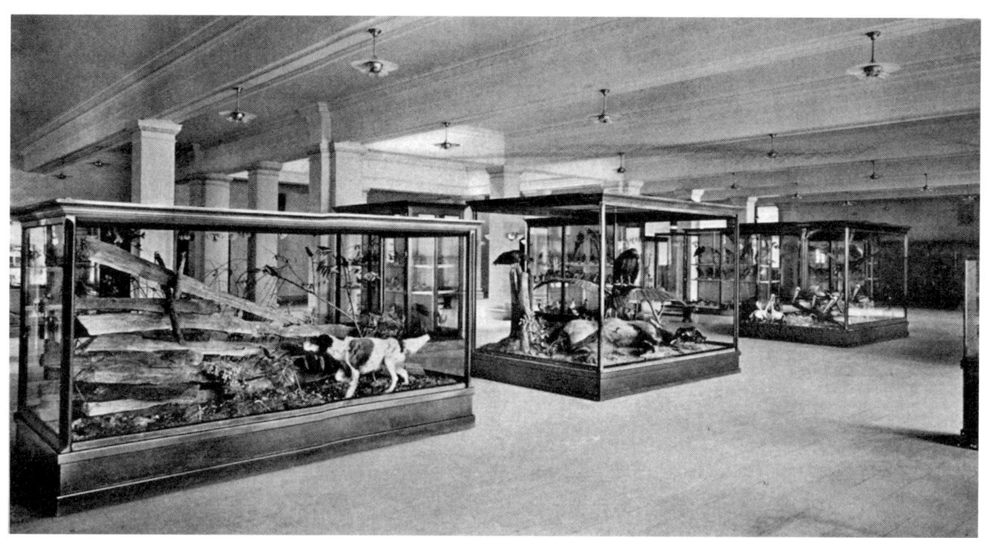

The first Hall of Birds, as pictured at the 1907 Institute, showcased the "inventory" of bird species at the museum.

farm near Sarver, Pennsylvania, was the northernmost nesting site of the species. Later a prodigious scientific writer, producing dozens and dozens of papers, Todd served as curator from 1899 until 1945 and then as curator emeritus until 1969. His best-known book is *Birds of Western Pennsylvania* (1940), one of the finest regional works on North American birds ever written, with illustrations by famous artist George Miksch Sutton.

Todd organized more than twenty-five trips to northern Canada for the museum, later expanding the museum's reach into South and Central America, as well as tropical Africa, where new species yet remained to be discovered. Todd was still personally interested in collecting eggs, and the museum's holdings of eggs were notable, but most of the specimens were study skins—the complete skin of the bird filled out with cotton in an approximate natural form, lying on its back, its crossed legs bearing a label on which were recorded the place and date of the bird's capture, its sex, and the collector's name. Sometimes additional data were included, such as the perishable colors of eyes, bills, and feet or the stage of the breeding cycle as judged by the size of the internal sex organs. To exhibit a bird, a study skin could be "relaxed" by a taxidermist, who would add glass eyes and insert wires so the bird could be mounted in a natural position. Even among precision-minded curators, Todd was notable for his accuracy, admitting to his catalog no incomplete clutches of eggs or specimens accompanied by inadequate data. When he retired at age seventy-one he had amassed a collection of well over one hundred thousand study skins, one of the half-dozen most important in the United States. The egg collection, with approximately nine thousand sets, was also nationally remarkable. After his death, it was felt that his great legacy to Carnegie Museum was his habit of scrupulous accuracy and painstaking care in research. His grandfather's farm near Sarver, where he had first hunted birds as a boy, became the first bird reserve of the Audubon Society of Western Pennsylvania: the Todd Nature Sanctuary.

When Todd retired, his position was filled by another tireless collector, Arthur S. Twomey, whose well-prepared specimens from Canada, the Bahamas, Honduras, and several African countries form a significant part of the museum's bird skin collection. In 1948, Twomey's recognized skill with the public led to his being appointed director of the newly centralized Division of Education of Carnegie Institute, a time-consuming administrative position that forced the section's daily curatorial work back upon the supposedly retired Clyde Todd and led, in 1953, to an assistant curator of birds being added to the staff, Kenneth C. Parkes. By the 1950s, the inventory of world species was approaching completion (although new species are still being discovered), and ornithology had entered the modern era of studying variations *within* bird species, focusing on avian anatomy and evolutionary relationships. Parkes was active in both these phases, working at the museum for forty-three years before retiring in 1996 and then continuing his work as a volunteer. He authored some 485 scientific publications, and his collecting expeditions to the Philippines, Argentina, and Mexico helped make the museum's Section of Birds the sixth-largest collection in the United States, its greatest strength in birds from tropical Central and South America.

By the 1960s, the public's relationship to birds was also shifting: "bird watching" had become popular. The museum responded with public programming, in 1963 hiring as an associate curator Mary H. Clench, who for the next seventeen years was a liaison between the museum and the region's bird watchers, advising home owners on attracting birds and supervising the bird-banding program at the Powdermill Nature Reserve. Her successor, Scott Wood, in 1981, let the relationship with Powdermill languish, focusing instead on reorganizing the main collection, the library, and the offices, obtaining a grant to computerize the collection's eggs, skeletons, skins, and fluids. During his eleven years at the museum, Wood upgraded the collection and facilities, but he did not pursue scientific research. His successor, Brad Livezey, moved back in the direction of research, much of it funded by the National Science Foundation. He and his colleague Richard

L. Zusi at the National Museum of Natural History studied bird evolution at the paleo-archaeological level, comparing the evolutionary anatomies of modern and fossil birds to clarify evolutionary lines of descent in bird families and species. In the 1980s such research at the frontiers of avian evolution began to make the news when scientists discovered fossil evidence of the first "feathered dinosaur" in China and demonstrated that birds were the evolutionary descendants of dinosaurs. Livezey and Zusi's research was the kind of fundamental work that would shape ornithology for decades.

Today the Section of Birds is ranked roughly as the ninth largest in the United States, the collection including approximately 195,000 specimens, encompassing 555 type specimens and examples of approximately 180 extinct birds, many collected decades and even a century ago. The importance of these older specimens, some long neglected, was revealed suddenly after World War II, when ornithological science took a revealing turn and acknowledged the devastating environmental effect of chemical pesticides. Pittsburgher Rachel Carson revealed the ruinous effects of agricultural pesticides on the environment in her award-winning book *Silent Spring* in 1962. In birds at the top of the food chain, such as fish-eating birds and birds of prey, pesticide residues interfered with reproduction, particularly with the calcium necessary for eggshells. Observers began to record female pelicans, falcons, and ospreys that laid eggs with shells so thin they would crush under the weight of the incubating parent. To track these effects, scientists needed collections of prepesticide eggs, and suddenly the Carnegie's seldom-used oology collection became a scientific treasure, for Todd had collected meticulously in the pesticide-free world before World War II. This was a classic illustration of the value of scientific museum collections—a value that can never be comprehended when they are begun.

Mammals

Mammals are characterized by the presence of hair during some time in their lives, warm blood, and the production of milk. Thus, while the Carnegie's collection of recent mammals includes living mammals that everyone knows, it also includes recently extinct species such as the Tasmanian wolf. Recent mammals are defined by the geological time period since the last ice age, about ten thousand years ago, to the present. Mammals that became extinct before this time, such as the mammoth, are in the vertebrate paleontology collection, which has material from the earlier Pleistocene period.

The first specimen in the Mammals collection (known under earlier titles such as Zoology, Taxidermy, Osteology, and Comparative Anatomy) was a kangaroo acquired in 1896. By 1910, the museum held about five hundred specimens, many from Ethiopia (then called Abyssinia and British

East Africa), donated by big-game hunter Childs Frick, the son of industrialist Henry Clay Frick. Childs Frick became the honorary curator of the section in 1926, and a volunteer research associate named Edward House was in charge of daily activities.[51] In 1938, before leaving for nine months of fieldwork in the Arctic, Kenneth Duott became the section's curator, a position he held for thirty-four years, until his retirement in 1972, aided notably by Caroline Heppenstall and John E. Guilday. After Doutt retired in 1972, Duane A. Schlitter was hired as an associate curator, and Hugh H. Genoways was hired as curator in 1976. Under their direction, the entire section—offices, collections, library, and preparation laboratory—left the Oakland building in 1979, moving two miles away to a new museum annex in East Liberty, a facility that was then considered one of the best anywhere for storage and research of mammal specimens.

Throughout the twentieth century, the section's holdings continued to grow and diversify. The North American research collection grew for sixty years, until by the 1990s it was one of the most comprehensive collections of Eastern North American mammals in the United States. In 1993, a new hall was dedicated, funded by the Hunt and Rockwell foundations, showcasing the mammals donated by Childs Frick in modern dioramas that focus on the major biomes of the African continent—an example of the environmental impulse behind modern dioramas. Yet another big-game hunter, Richard K. Mellon, also collected specimens for habitat groups to exhibit in Carnegie Museum of Natural History, notably the moose, while African missionary A. I. Good's collection, assembled over forty years with the help of his parishioners and later obtained by the Carnegie, featured West African specimens from the period before many of the forests in the area were destroyed. It is a nuance of history that the Boone and Crockett Club, founded by Theodore Roosevelt in 1887 and originally reflecting the interests of an exclusive group of big-game trophy hunters, was and still is a powerful force for wildlife conservation in the United States. The club's name honors Daniel Boone and Davy Crockett, who were seen as ethical hunters and honest men who loved the outdoors and manly pursuits. In addition to authoring the famous "fair chase" statement of hunting ethics, the club began working in Roosevelt's time for the elimination of industrial hunting, the creation of wildlife reserves, and conservation-minded regulation of hunting. It sponsored regular trophy competitions, usually held at the American Museum of Natural History in New York, but occasionally in other places such as Carnegie Museum in Pittsburgh. The big-game hunters associated with Pittsburgh, such as Childs Frick and R. K. Mellon, were part of a national network of Boone and Crockett associates who became members by invitation only. The Boone and Crockett Club had its own meeting room in the expanded Institute of 1907.

Another important piece of the collection stemmed from the Survey of Pennsylvania Mammals, conducted under Duott's direction from 1948 to 1951, netting approximately 18,000 specimens. The collection would eventually grow to include over 120,000 specimens from all parts of the world, becoming the eighth-largest collection of recent mammals in the Western Hemisphere. Today, with forty type specimens, the collection is the best in the world for mammals of Pennsylvania and adjacent areas and one of the top collections of Eastern North American mammals. Internationally, it is strong in specimens of the Eastern Arctic, Africa, South America, and Central America.

When Schlitter and Genoways arrived at the museum, the collection included a backlog of 20,000 uncataloged specimens, including material that dated back to the Great Depression and World War II. Collection manager Suzanne McLaren arrived in 1977, supported by a National Science Foundation grant, and for the next nine years grant funding was directed toward cataloging and data capture, cleaning and preparing specimens from decades-old collections, and organizing more than 50,000 specimens in the new annex.

A mammal specimen is commonly represented by a skin and a skull, although some specimens have their entire bodies preserved in formaldehyde and stored in jars of alcohol. Smaller mammals have their skins removed and are stuffed with cotton, and larger mammals have their skins tanned. Skulls are "prepared" or cleaned by flesh-eating dermestid beetles and then cleaned with an ammonia solution. "It's twenty-four-hour work," McLaren noted, "seven days-a-week, and you don't have to pay them anything."[52] All specimens are stored and labeled like books in a library and filed progressively, from the most primitive groups such as the egg-laying monotremes, opossums, and insectivores (shrews and moles) to the most advanced groups such as the carnivores and hoofed mammals. Within each group, specimens are arranged by place of geographic origin. The Mammals section also has a laboratory for biochemical and microscopic analysis and materials for many species such as frozen hearts, kidneys, livers, spleens, sperm, and muscle, as well as chromosome slides.

John Wible became the curator of the section in 1998, focused particularly on research into the evolution of the major groups of mammals. Such research unites two museum disciplines: mammalogy (recent mammals) and vertebrate paleontology (fossil mammals). This research shift toward the end of the twentieth century, with the help of newly discovered fossils, revealed important relationships among ancient and living mammals. The advent of DNA analysis in the 1970s opened up a whole different avenue of data for addressing mammal evolution, allowing scientists to reach unprecedented conclusions about higher-order evolutionary relationships among different species, including humans and primates. Thus, in mammals research, the changing nature of museum science is itself on display, allowing scientists to address questions fundamental to our understanding of our place in the global community. The modern exhibit halls of African Wildlife and North American Wildlife dropped the word "mammals" in order to emphasize biodiversity.

ANTHROPOLOGY

In the beginning, Anthropology was a catch-all: local history, archaeology, Wild West artifacts, textiles, coins and stamps, random gifts from wealthy Pittsburghers—the whole Victorian passion for collectibles coming to rest in one ill-defined area. The section itself has undergone numerous incarnations and was listed in the director's 1898 annual report (before anthropology had matured as a science) as encompassing Ethnology, Ancient and Medieval Art, Modern Arts and Manufactures, and Historical Collections, and in 1907 as including Ethnology and Archaeology, Numismatics, Ceramics, Textiles, Graphic Arts, Transportation, and Historical Collections. The collections grew in stages: an early period of archaeological work under curator Carl Vilhelm Hartman, which ended by 1908; a long period without a chief curator in which material accumulated in archaeology and ethnology and a few other categories; and then a third phase for renewed scientific fieldwork in the 1950s. By the 1980s, another phase of international research had developed, and the section finally began to develop the modern exhibition halls that its collections deserved. Today the collections in the section are worldwide in scope, with over 100,000 ethnological and historical specimens and 1.5 million archaeological artifacts.[53]

Carl Vilhelm Hartman was hired as the first curator of ethnology and archaeology in 1903. Originally a botanist and then an expert field archaeologist, Hartman continued his exacting field excavations in Costa Rica, eventually leaving behind one of the largest assemblages of Costa Rican artifacts ever made outside of that country. With his departure in 1908, the first phase of the section's archaeological work ended.

Museum director William Holland then oversaw the collection himself, with the help of his assistant Douglas Stewart and collection manager (or "custodian") Charles Hughes. Some forty years elapsed without a chief curator, a period during which the science of modern anthropology came into its own, often connected to universities. By World War I, a generation of Pittsburgh's wealthy Victorian collectors had begun to die off, and the section began to accumulate objects and even entire collections from families that no longer wanted them. Henry John Heinz, for a time the section's honorary curator, died in 1919, and some of the objects he had loaned to the museum were returned to his family; others (including teapots, ivories, Samurai armor, rare watches, and a collection of shoes from around the world) stayed at the museum. Between World War I and World War II, the "historical collections" developed in many ways. One aging industrialist, John A. Beck, in financial trouble and fearing his creditors would attach his collection, which featured some seventeen thousand items, offered it to the museum. The Indian baskets many people collected in the late nineteenth and early twentieth centuries were donated as individuals grew older and moved from spacious homes into smaller apartments. Andrew Carnegie's smoking jacket arrived, accompanied by a story from a Mr. McArdle, whose grandfather had once worked for Carnegie as a handyman. Asked by Carnegie what payment he wanted for a job he had just done, McArdle said he would like a jacket like the one Carnegie was wearing. Carnegie promptly took it off and gave it to him. A large collection of mainly Paleolithic materials came to the museum from a Russian nobleman, a colonel in the army and an engineer who had been doing mining work in Egypt when the Russian Revolution broke out, and he could not return home.

Beyond the fascinating human stories of collectors are the odd and notable objects themselves. The smallest artifacts in the anthropology collection are two fleas from Mexico, male and female, dressed in sombrero, serape, and dress, that were probably part of the tourist trade. The extensive doll collection's most celebrated member is "Miss Kochi," a Japanese doll made in response to a diplomatic effort organized in 1927 by the missionary and teacher Sidney Lewis Gulick, who encouraged U.S. children to buy dolls, dress them in Western-style costumes, and send them to Japan. Tensions between the countries were increasing, and this was a gesture of friendship. The result was a diplomatic coup, 12,739 dolls from forty-eight states welcomed by Japan with a ceremony including parades and celebrations. Fifty-eight "dolls of gratitude" were crafted by Japanese artists in response. During World War II, the Japanese government ordered the American dolls destroyed, yet hundreds were secretly saved. In the United States, about two dozen Japanese dolls survived the war, including the Carnegie's Miss Kochi.

Early exhibits were often haphazard by modern standards. Shrunken heads hung on a pegboard behind glass. "Transportation Hall" featured models of a Greyhound Bus, an airplane, and a ship; the actual Conestoga wagon used locally for Lincoln's presidential campaign in 1864; a Japanese sedan chair donated by Henry Heinz; and an eighteenth-century Portuguese coach. Once the museum began to deaccession historical artifacts to concentrate on natural history, many items went to other museums, where they were displayed to greater advantage.

A new focus on fieldwork came when the section's second curator, James Swauger, was appointed in 1949. In spite of his cheerful, informal manner, Swauger was a meticulous researcher and organizer who stayed at the museum for forty-four years. The museum also benefited when isolationism ceased for the United States with the end of World War II. As universities responded to a new public interest in social and cultural history by offering programs in archaeology and physical and biological anthropology, the importance of historic collections such as the one at Carnegie Museum became clearer. When museum director Graham Netting retired in 1974, the new director, Craig C. Black, established different priorities for the Section of Man, appointing Swauger senior curator and eventually hiring James B. Richardson III, then in the Anthropology Department of the University of Pittsburgh, as the section's chief curator. Richardson remained half-time at the university, and the museum benefited from the curatorial-academic interaction with graduate students and research associates. Eventually, it changed its name from the Section of Man, which had sexist overtones, to the more academic-sounding Section of Anthropology.

Richardson remained in charge of the department from 1978 until 1999, when he was succeeded by his colleague David Watters, another field archaeologist. Local archaeology at the museum, by this point, had an enviable record, having identified more than six thousand Native American sites in twenty-two Pennsylvania counties and having published important archaeological findings. International research continued throughout the 1990s. Richardson worked on Peruvian sites that showed how the ancient coastal region had been exposed to different ocean currents than are seen today, suggesting that ocean currents had changed over the past ten thousand years. Watters continued the tradition Hartman had begun in Central America at the turn of the century, focusing on early colonization of Caribbean islands and Costa Rica and the ecology of early inhabitants. Another curator, Sandra Olsen, worked on the early "horse culture" of the Asian plains in Kazakhstan and Mongolia, where people depended upon the domestication and uses of the horse.

For the public, anthropology at the museum came to mean the major halls that opened at the end of the twentieth century. After Carnegie Museum of Art vacated several large third-floor galleries in 1974, years of planning went into creating permanent anthropology halls to present the large existing collections. Polar World, Wyckoff Hall of Arctic Life (1983), Walton Hall of Ancient Egypt (1990), and Alcoa Foundation Hall of

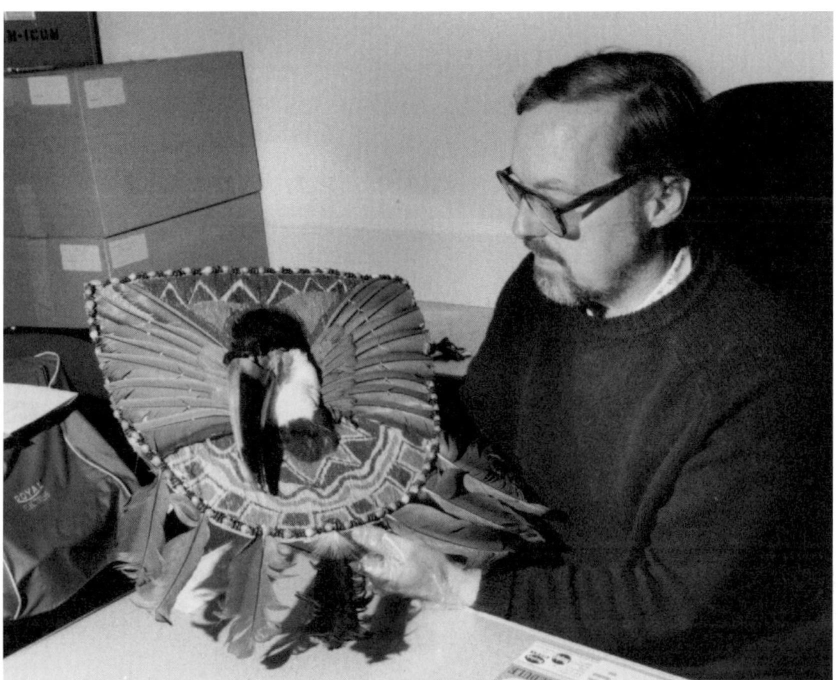

James B. Richardson III, chief curator for the museum's Section of Man from 1978 to 1999, holds a shaman's dance apron with a toucan upon it, from the Shuar (formerly the Jivaro) tribe of Ecuador.

American Indians (1998) all brought materials out of storage and showcased them in dramatic displays. In Walton Hall of Ancient Egypt is Carnegie's gift of a mummy, the first object accessioned by the museum, and also the 3,800-year-old funerary boat purchased by Carnegie after he saw an ancient Egyptian boat at Chicago's Columbian Exhibition in 1893. The Egyptian collection was amassed through the activities of the Pittsburgh chapter of the Egypt Exploration Society, which tried to give each funding chapter some integral tomb group that was being excavated, instead of dividing everything into pieces distributed among a dozen participants. The 1985 exhibit was made possible by one of the largest grants the National Endowment for the Humanities had ever made, for assessing and conserving ancient Egyptian materials. If space permitted, anthropology could easily display more of its holdings in western Pennsylvania prehistory and in South American or Costa Rican cultures. Even after sending much of its historical materials to other museums, the section's collections are the most varied of any at the museum.

In the 1800s, taxidermy was considered the best way to present information about life forms, and major cities in both Europe and America in the 1800s began to develop educational displays of animals. When Andrew Carnegie and taxidermy came together, the resulting chain of events played out for years, influencing the development of the museum itself.[54]

Taxidermy—the art of placing or mounting animal skins on frames in lifelike poses—comes from the Greek for arranging (*taxis*) and skin (*derma*). Frederic W. Webster was a leader in this art by 1880s and in 1897 became the first taxidermist at the Department of the Museum. Earlier in his career, at Ward's Scientific Establishment, which sold "prepared" specimens to interested buyers, Webster had worked with William T. Hornaday, who eventually became the director of the New York Zoo, and together the two formed the Society for American Taxidermy. In his memoirs, Hornaday wrote his employer, Henry Ward, of meeting Carnegie in Singapore—Hornaday on a trip to collect specimens, Carnegie on a world tour—and stimulating his interest in zoological matters:

I have just received an order for a tiger skin prepared as a rug, for the floor, with the head nicely stuffed, to be *first class,* and no grumbling about the price. It is wanted by Mr. Andrew Carnegie, 57 Broadway, N.Y. an American Millionaire, who owns the biggest iron works in Pittsburgh.... He is a very decent fellow although he is rich. He is also liberal, and not long since gave $5,000 to the Western University at Pittsburgh and $5,000 to his native Scotland town.... He was lost in genuine wonder and admiration at what I told him & showed him ... of Ward's Establishment, and often remarked "What a wonderful man that Prof. Ward must be!" Of course I improved all such opportunities with him. You may depend that the next time he passes through Rochester he will stop & see you & the Estab. and when he does come don't you forget who *Carnegie* is.[55]

Carnegie also remembered Hornaday and recounted their meeting in his lively travel book *Round the World* (1884):

We had the pleasure of meeting, at Major Studer's, Mr. Hornaday—a young gentleman who travels for Professor Ward of Rochester, New York, whose museum is known the world over. Mr. Hornaday's department is to keep the Professor's collections complete, and if there be a rare bird, beast, or reptile on the globe, he is bound to capture specimens. He had just returned from spending four months in Borneo, where only a supply of orang-outangs could be obtained. He returned with forty-two of the brutes, mostly shot by himself. He came one day upon two very young ones, and these he had brought here alive. They are suggestively human in their ways, and two better behaved, more affectionate babies are rarely to be met with. Let no anti-Darwinian study orang-outangs if he wishes to retain his present notions. The museum, Mr. Hornaday is advised, is now short of dugongs, and he is off for Australia next steamer to lay in a supply. The recital of his adventures are extremely interesting, and I predict that some day a book from him will have a great run.

In the absence of other commercial intelligence, I may quote the market in his line. Tigers are still reported "lively," orang-outangs "looking up," pythons show but little animation at this season of the year, proboscis monkeys, on the other hand, continue scarce; there is quite a run on lions, and kangaroos are jumped at with alacrity; elephants heavy, birds of paradise drooping; crocodiles are snapped up as offered while dugongs bring large prices. What is pig metal to this?[56]

Thus, taxidermy, not dinosaurs, first drew Carnegie to natural history—and to the idea of a natural history museum. In 1883, Carnegie gave Hornaday $500 to help support the fledgling Society of American Taxidermists; Hornaday remarked that this donation was "Andrew Carnegie's very first gift to museology."[57] Once Carnegie had created his new Department of the Museum, he quickly authorized $5,000 to be used to obtain specimens from Ward's Scientific Establishment, and one year after Carnegie Institute opened, in 1897, the board of trustees hired Webster as its first taxidermist and preparator. To assist him, the museum hired preparator Gustav Link, who helped mount many early exhibits, including a group of California condors and turkey vultures that still survives. The importance of taxidermy in Pittsburgh was underscored by Webster's then-generous salary of $1,800 per year. Holland himself, a well-known scientist and administrator, received $4,000 dollars per year, while the curator of birds and mammals, W. E. Clyde Todd, was paid $780.[58]

Holland wanted to amaze Pittsburgh and the world with dramatic displays. When the Department of the Museum opened in Carnegie Library, he bought and installed the skeletons of a giant Irish elk and a mastodon, extinct animals from ten thousand years ago, to entice visitors. The elk, with its massive antlers, was interpreted as a species that had developed a cumbersome feature that led to its own evolutionary extinction. For the 1907 building, he pursued the mounted *Diplodocus carnegii,* as well as new taxidermy mounts of mammals and birds and life-size models of American Indians. He even obtained a rare white rhinoceros specimen, a species near extinction, and Holland boasted in his 1901 annual report that only four other examples existed in the world, in Capetown, London, France, and Russia. In 1912, Theodore Roosevelt, on a tour of the museum conducted by Holland, threw his arms into the air when he saw the white rhinoceros and exclaimed, "Holland, where did you get that specimen? I am astonished at seeing it."[59]

In *Arab Courier Attacked by Lions*, two Barbary lions (a species now extinct) in the Sahara Desert of North Africa attack an Arab riding on a camel. After the Paris exhibition this popular exhibit was bought by the American Museum of Natural History in New York as part of a large German collection and was next sent to the Philadelphia Centennial Exposition in 1876. There again it was popular, and when it was returned to New York it continued to draw public interest. But after a time New York museum administrators considered it more melodrama than science, and it was old and becoming shabby, so they were ready to destroy it. Webster rescued it, paying twenty-five dollars for it in 1899, and gave it new life at Carnegie Museum in Pittsburgh. It was restored and improved by taxidermist Gustav Link, who replaced the camel driver's damaged right hand, which held the knife he used to fight the lions, with a plaster cast of his own hand. Even as a sensational version of reality, it is now considered a landmark in the art of taxidermy.

The master taxidermist Remi Santens, also from Ward's Natural History Establishment, was hired in 1906. Unlike Webster and Link, who used wooden frames, excelsior packing techniques, and early hide-tanning procedures, Santens prepared hides differently and used advanced techniques involving wires and wire cloth to obtain more lifelike poses. Replaced as chief taxidermist, Webster resigned, and Santens was joined by his younger brother, Joseph. Together they were known as innovators and were in charge when large contributions of specimens from Africa came from Childs Frick and from Theodore Roosevelt's African safaris. The Santens' mounting of two giraffes in the tallest museum case ever assembled was an admired feat in the museum world.

Related to taxidermy in the early years of the museum were the much-admired models of American Indians by Theodore A. Mills. From 1898 until his death in 1916, Mills was the museum's sculptor and model maker for ethnographic exhibits. He had worked for the U.S. National Museum, assigned by the Bureau of Ethnology to make casts of the vanishing Indian groups on the continent, and his expertise eventually led to his being asked to create the Indian displays at the new Carnegie Museum. He was then fifty-nine and came on a temporary assignment, but he so impressed director Holland that he was put on staff permanently and remained there until he died. He also made exquisite models of extinct animals for the Section of Paleontology.[60]

The year 1916 saw a change in the exhibits staff when Gustav Link died. Link was expert in preparing and interpreting birds and reptiles and collected specimens in the field that he brought back to prepare himself. At one point he captured the largest boa constrictor ever seen, on the Isle of

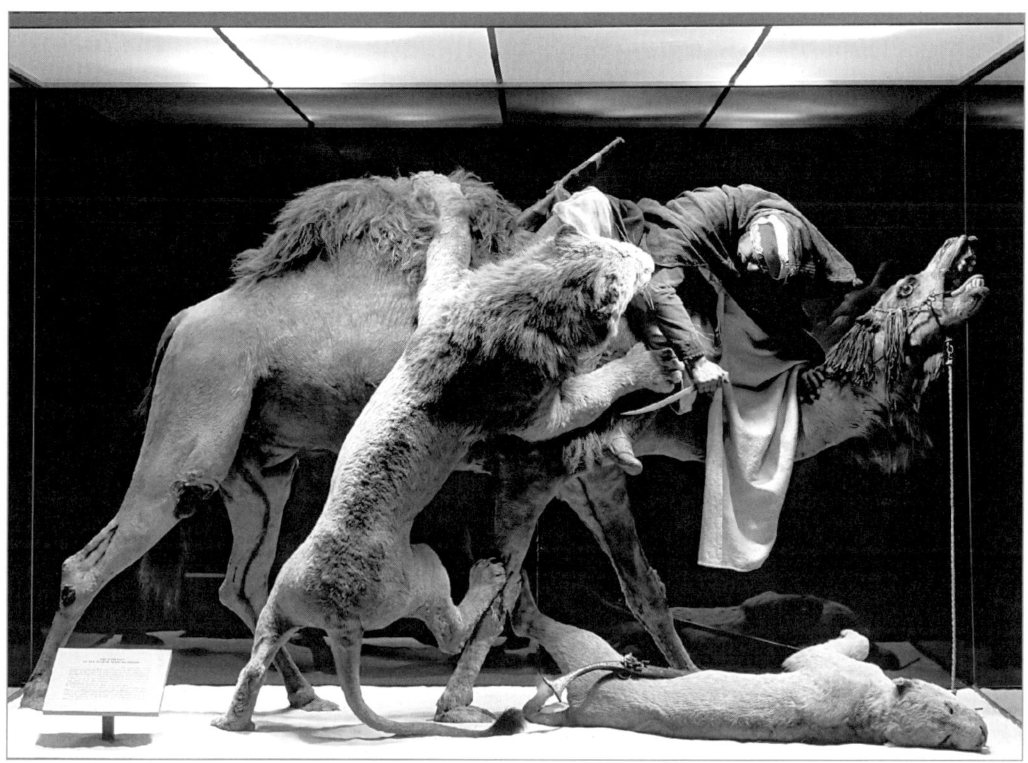

Arab Courier Attacked by Lions was a sensational exhibit at the Paris Exposition in 1867, and became a famous exhibit in the museum's Hall of Mammals.

Pines, off the coast of Cuba, in a manner described by Holland: "He slipped a bag over the head of the brute, and with the help of an assistant thrust the body of the monster into the sack, tied it up, and brought it back to the Museum, where he made a careful study of its form and value." Holland went on to say, "Mr. Link was intrepid, fearless, and indefatigable in the field, in the laboratory industrious and painstaking. In his manner modest and unassuming."[61]

Link died unexpectedly from a bite from a rattlesnake that he had collected at Ohiopyle, sixty miles southeast of Pittsburgh, a snake he fed and kept in the laboratory. He was bitten while handling the snake for University of Pittsburgh students on a behind-the-scenes tour. Bitten by snakes occasionally, he usually kept the necessary antidote in his vest pocket, but this time he did not have it. One boy on the tour pointed out the bite, but Link casually dismissed it and completed his lecture. But soon afterward the venom took its effect, and every attempt was made to save his life. A train was dispatched from New York with the antidote, but the doctor who rushed it to the scene arrived too late to save him.

By the 1920s—after the deaths of sculptor Theodore Mills and Gustav Link and the turmoil brought by World War I—the Exhibits Department was poised for change. By now, the golden age of museum dioramas had arrived, and habitat backgrounds for the specimens became increasingly important. When artist Ottmar von Fuehrer was hired in 1922, the museum entered a new phase of educational displays, with professionally painted dioramas and boxes of specimens prepared for the educational loan collection. The son of a former museum director in Vienna, von Fuehrer was the primary museum artist for nearly four decades and, with the assistance of his wife, Hannah, created many excellent backgrounds that visitors still see today.

Another notable museum hire was taxidermist Harold Clement, who joined the staff in 1927 and worked with curator Graham Netting to develop exhibits of amphibians and reptiles, including the alligator group in 1932. Herpetology exhibits had been largely ignored for years, and many of the specimens were displayed in rows of jars of alcohol, a series of dull and faded examples. World War II halted major exhibit development, but dioramas continued to be the focus of exhibits until 1948, when director Otto E. Jennings retired and Institute president William Frew died. With the advent of a new director, Wallace Richards, taxidermy took a back seat, and the museum moved toward more diversified displays. After Richards's 1952 retirement, Graham Netting, the new director, returned the museum to its traditional agenda of exhibits, the priorities shifting toward local conservation and natural history, with exhibits such as Deadline for Wildlife and a new Marine Hall. In 1964, the museum hired a preparator from Germany, Otto Epping, to revive the art of taxidermy at the museum. The last exhibit to open under Netting was Winter Bird Feeding, in 1976, featuring twenty-five species of mounted birds. Otto Epping retired soon after, in 1979, and his last job (on special contract) was to mount the beloved silverback gorilla "George" from the Pittsburgh Zoo, after it died unexpectedly in the prime of life from an abscessed tooth.

A basic principle of museum exhibits is that there is no substitute for the actual object, but exceptions have been made for educational exhibits, such as one designed for schoolchildren in Transportation Hall, featuring small models of animal pack trains, wagons, buses, and ships. It's also important to remember that in a research museum, only a tiny fraction of the collections can be displayed: as millions of specimens and artifacts accumulate, the public never comprehends the breadth and value of the collections. Similarly, there is often a disparity between the scientific importance of collections and the space devoted to public display. Entomology has always been poorly presented, considering the size and importance of the museum's holdings. Anthropology historically cycled different artifacts in and out of displays, and popular displays such as rare dolls were eventually removed once conservationists came to understand how years of light and heat from the building's skylights had damaged the materials.

Exhibits also respond to administration priorities and popular trends. Director Craig Black wanted to emphasize science and in 1976 opened an Information and Orientation (I & O) Center, which introduced visitors to the spectrum of museum research in twelve wall cases that featured photos of the staff, explanations of their work, sample artifacts and publications, and two-minute sound presentations via telephones. Later directors had different priorities, and as the I & O Center took constant maintenance and began to look dated, it was transformed first into an exhibits gallery (reflecting a national trend toward changing exhibits) and then again to include a large Natural History Store (reflecting the need for museums to produce revenue). By the 1990s, digital technology could more simply achieve the interactive mission the I & O Center had pursued twenty years earlier, including videos in exhibit areas that featured curators speaking about their work. Under director Jay Apt a new digital Earth Theater opened, talking robots were programmed to give tours, and a bank of computers was introduced to let visitors explore recent news about the global environment.

Marketing drove many exhibit decisions beginning in the mid-1990s, and after 2003, the museum had developed a strategy to rely on its trump card, dinosaurs, hoping to promote the museum as "a first-day destination" for tourists. State funds and private support were obtained, and dinosaurs emerged as an economic marketing tool for the entire city. In 2003 the city launched DinoMite Days as a marketing campaign to make dinosaurs a Pittsburgh icon and auctioned off one hundred fiberglass replica dinosaurs, creatively decorated by regional artists, to be placed in parks, plazas, and public streets. Buyers bid for the replicas in a grand auction held in the Pittsburgh Convention Center. Similar campaigns had raised large sums in many other cities, including Chicago (cows), Washington, D.C. (donkeys and elephants), and Toronto (moose), and Pittsburgh successfully raised the profile of its famous fossil dinosaur collection and was able to raise money necessary to build the new hall, Dinosaurs in Their Time. This exhibit meant the reprogramming of the entire visitor experience. People were drawn through two permanent halls to see the new dinosaur hall and then found easy access via an open staircase to the rest of the halls, including the large new hall for changing exhibits, the R. P. Simmons Family Gallery, on the third floor.

What of the classic dioramas in the modern age of museums? What of the taxidermy that first drew Andrew Carnegie to natural history? Classic dioramas and mounted specimens raise problems for administrators, who must decide whether to maintain them as works of art or to discard them in favor of new technologically oriented displays that appeal to contemporary visitors, especially children. The classic diorama is an interpretive abstraction, theatrical in nature, designed to present an ideal situation and pack that interpretive moment with scholarly details. Lovers of the classic diorama bemoaned the "imperialism of the juvenile" that rose in the mid-1980s, leading to the decline of dioramas as museum centerpieces. Thomas Hart Benton, in the *Chronicle of Higher Education,* argued that American museums had sacrificed dioramas and other classic exhibits to the programmed fun of technology, which "destroys the notion that children can enjoy quiet reflection, [and] also replaces the sense of decorum that was once a leading lesson of museums for children, with the rules of the schoolyard and chattering about technical gadgets."[62]

Related to this is the modern display mentality that emphasizes blockbuster exhibitions and hugely expensive displays, such as the Chicago Field Museum's $8 million T-rex "Sue," the most expensive fossil in the world (its conspicuous cost perhaps being its real attraction). At the American Museum of Natural History in New York, the curators mounted their enormous Barosaurus rearing up, its head fifty feet in the air, defending its young from an advancing Allosaurus. Set amid the marble columns of Roosevelt Memorial Hall, this display is awe-inspiring. It is also probably bad science. Digital and interactive technologies, on the other hand, take museum-goers into a world of detailed information and imagery that static displays can never duplicate, bypassing the old principle that museums should be home to actual specimens. Does it matter that visitors can find the same information on the Internet, in libraries, films, zoos, or theme parks?

Museum exhibits are presented with the authority of scientific research, and the public accepts them as valid, seldom sensing the social philosophy or propaganda that may be implicit in them. Powerful museum displays create impressions that can last a lifetime, and when exhibits disappear, some museum-goers experience a feeling of profound loss. In 2006, for example, Carnegie Museum sent its old, now empty cases from the Hall of Indians to Construction Junction, a resale warehouse full of doors, building remnants, and junk. One observer noticed and lamented the loss:

Sharp pangs of memory shot through me as I saw the background scenery, faded but proudly clinging to its image of a desert vista. The floors were covered with sand, rocks, and cacti and in one case, corn. Every adolescent in Pittsburgh lingered at that case. It had housed several Hopi women who were bent over

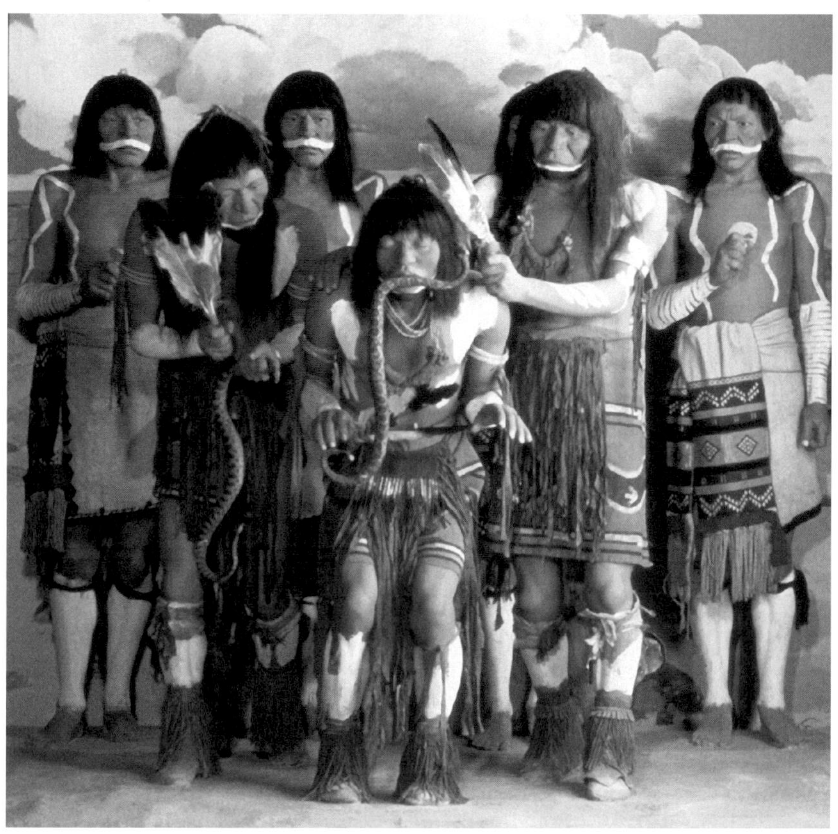

When creating a new Hall of Native Americans in the 1990s, anthropologists demolished the melodramatic and once-admired Indian snake dance group created by sculptor Theodore Mills. It was considered politically incorrect and a throwback to the old Wild West mentality of savage Indians.

those kernels, affording us all a view of their terra cotta breasts. The Hopi snake dancer, the ferocious warrior who brandished a scalp in one hand and a bloody knife in the other, the Sioux Squaw with her papoose. The fierce, the brave, the romantic, the figures struck terror as well as wonder and respect into my heart.

Countless dreams, I'm sure, were inspired by the Hall of Indians, along with sadness for a way of life that is no more. Several years ago the Hall of Indians was dismantled and in its place a new, politically correct Hall of Indians was built. The Native Americans in it are just like the rest of us. Boring and ordinary. They wear jeans and eyeglasses, construct bridges, run casinos and walk among us unnoticed and assimilated. The PC message is that we are all the same, which frankly, I would think is a given. That's not what is special about the Indians. Give me the glamour any day.[63]

Today the message in the new Hall of Native Americans is benign, attentive to a peaceful worldview. Museums everywhere have removed old sensational, violent imagery of the Buffalo Bill era to promote social harmony in a pluralist society. Exhibits change because of new science but also because of the prevailing social philosophy.

Education

Many people have been inspired by Carnegie Natural History Museum and have acknowledged the impact its collections had on their sense of themselves and the world around them. Writer Annie Dillard, a teenager visiting the museum in the 1960s, felt the power of natural history: "Week after week, year after year, after art class I walked the vast museum, and lost myself in the arts, or the sciences. Scientists, it seemed to me as I read the labels on display cases (bivalves, univalves; ungulates, lagomorphs), were collectors and sorters, as I had been. They noticed things that engaged the curious mind: the way the world develops and divides, colony and polyp, population and tissue, ridge and crystal."[64] Writer John Edgar Wideman expanded his identity as a Black American: "Under the roof of the Natural History Museum my sense of the past, of time was elaborate, extended; the past gained an immediacy and relevance that was frighteningly alien, daunting, but also included me.... My imagination was stirred and I was on my way to becoming a citizen of a world larger than Homewood."[65]

Education was central to the museum's mission from its earliest days. In his first annual report, in 1898, museum director William Holland discussed the essay contest that had been established in 1896, with students submitting compositions about the museum and its work and with prizes awarded to the best young authors. The "Andrew Carnegie Naturalist's Club" held weekly meetings for youngsters at the museum, giving them practical instruction in natural history. High school students and teachers could take special guided tours, and by 1900 the educational loan collection was operating, loaning teachers real specimens to use in their classrooms. Over time this collection would send specimens to every school and legitimate borrowing institution in western Pennsylvania. In 1921 Holland responded to the need for more educational programs by starting a program to teach teachers. Nevertheless, for decades the business of public education was largely controlled by the curatorial staff, without the stature of a separate department.

Then, in 1936, botanist Otto E. Jennings was made the museum's director of public education, overseeing an internal children's museum, a nature study contest, and lectures and classes. An institutional shift came in 1948 when the natural history and the art education programs were united under the Division of Education, supervised by ornithologist Arthur Twomey and overseeing the children's museum; the educational loan collection; adult education; radio, television, and audiovisual materials; and a traveling museum. When Twomey retired in 1974, his assistant James Kosinski became the department head, but the opening of the Scaife Gallery drew the art educators back into their own separate program. A succession of natural history educators followed: Alfred Bjelland, Susan Haggerson, Judith Bobenage, Diane Grzybec. By this point, the supervisor was known as the chair of education, overseeing a busy program that included volunteers; educational loans; interns; docents; classes for children, adults, and teachers; and special projects such as conferences, photographic competitions, birthday parties, and trips to archaeological sites important to museum research. The 1990s yielded bio-forays in which the public helped identify all the species in a narrowly defined geographic area. The late 1990s also brought the Earth Theater, with its state-of-the-art digital programs and wraparound screen, and interactive computers that allowed the public to explore current events in the natural world. By 2006, video-conferencing allowed museum scientists to be seen on monitors in school classrooms. Educationally, this allowed exciting classroom moments, close-up cameras exploring structures as familiar as a robin's nest or as unusual as a tiger beetle's compound eye. The Fisher Scientific Biotechnology Lab gave middle-school students a hands-on biotechnology lab experience, emphasizing the fundamentals of genetics, molecular biology, and microbiology.

But on a daily basis, with areas such as Bonehunter's Quarry, where children can search for fossils in the sand, or the lower-level Discovery Room, where they can touch animal skins and other specimens, the Section of Education remains a stable component of the museum's commitment to public education and a resource that parents, many of them home-schooling their children, rely upon to help children comprehend the natural world.

The Natural History Library

"Museums are all about evidence," says museum librarian Bernadette Callery, "but evidence needs to be communicated, and in science the evidence is not real until it is published. That's why research museums have natural science libraries."[66] One of the first things researchers do when returning from the field is to consult the scientific literature to verify the nature of their findings and to see whether they have discovered anything previously unknown. Natural history libraries make that literature available and accessible to researchers, giving value to past and present work and helping define the future.

To a science librarian, Callery notes, "the pleasure of working in a natural history library is not only in the marvelous materials and the interesting people who work in the field, but in the satisfaction of working in a very long tradition of knowledge. Museums are all about that—the recorded knowledge and the support of new information."[67] The modern tradition of scientific publications began in the seventeenth century, with publications by clubs of scientifically inclined gentlemen, such as the Royal Society of London, founded in 1665. Such early reports and journals were published informally and often. Although spare by contemporary standards, these publications provided both evidence of the society's proceedings and discussions and were a bond that held members together in an ephemeral world of experiments, discussions, and presentations. By the mid-eighteenth century, the Linnaean system of binomial nomenclature had given scientists an important way to standardize their approach to the natural world. From this point on, researchers were expected to be conversant with the findings of scientists from around the world, their discoveries taking place in a community.

When Carnegie Museum of Natural History opened, William Holland assumed that it would have a library. "It is utterly impossible," Holland declared, "for those who are engaged in the work of the museum to carry on their work successfully without having convenient and easy access to such books as are required."[68] Carnegie scientists began in 1896 by using books supplied by the new Carnegie Library of Pittsburgh, and before the 1907 expansion, the collection was kept in Holland's home. After 1907, the museum's library had a central location in the new Institute, a space it occupied for nearly a century. The institution had also begun publishing its own findings in 1901, with *Annals of the Carnegie Museum of Natural History* and the *Bulletin of the Carnegie Museum of Natural History,* as well as occasional special publications. Its fast-growing prestige brought literature exchanges with established institutions and started to trigger donations, such as an early bequest from John Hamilton of 219 bound volumes. The nucleus of the collection had been formed by the time Holland acquired the celebrated folios of John James Audubon, a complete set that is the library's most famous treasure. Other rare sets of books also entered the collection, including a first edition of the writings of Aldrovani, the famous Italian naturalist who had founded the museum in Bologna and published a thirteen-volume set about natural history specimens in the 1600s. Holland's personal library arrived in 1933, after his death—some 2,474 bound volumes, 469 unbound volumes, and over 6,000 reprints. Under director Andrey Avinoff, the library obtained one hundred hand-painted plates of lepidoptera by the famous artist John Abbot, and after his death came the gift of Avinoff's own two hundred watercolor plates of the *Wild Flowers of*

Western Pennsylvania and the Upper Ohio Basin, published posthumously in 1953. Today the library has about 132,000 volumes, particularly strong in multivolume sets of European journals from the nineteenth century. Beyond scientific materials, it also maintains institutional records, such as administrative and curatorial correspondence and annual reports, and is thus the starting point for any research into the history of the museum itself.

The library has benefited from strong leadership over the past century. Maud Gittings was appointed as its first custodian and stenographer, a position she held for thirty-nine years. When she retired in 1945, the first trained librarian, Anne Walgren, took over from 1945 to 1948, reestablishing the exchange program interrupted by the war. She was succeeded briefly by an expert on fishes, Arthur Henn (1949–51), then by Anna R. Tauber, who served as the librarian for thirty-two years. After her retirement in 1983, the library was headed by Gerald McKernan, Elizabeth Kwater, Elizabeth Swann, and finally Bernadette Callery, in 1995. McKernan initiated the project of machine-readable cataloging of the library's holdings, but a final comprehensive catalog was not fully achieved until twenty years later, under Callery, in 2005. At this point, for the first time, the entire collection, with all of its various departmental subsections, was included in one searchable list, with nearly the entire catalog available online. Many of the specialized books and periodicals are actually kept in the scientific sections, where researchers depend upon the literature to confirm and validate their work.

The 2005 exhibit Dinosaurs in Their Time triggered the reorganization of much museum space, and the library moved to the south wing of the original Carnegie Library building, where the Natural History Museum itself had once been installed. This required moving some nine thousand books, while two departmental collections—Birds, and Amphibians and Reptiles—moved into the central library. The library is still on the first floor and has the latest in temperature and humidity controls. There is proper storage for its valuable folios and rare materials in a Rare Book Room. Today, while the library has one-fourth less space than before, its rare materials are properly stored, and good design and efficient use of shelf space have made the collections more accessible than ever. The collections, Callery says, "are a lot happier."[69]

POWDERMILL NATURE RESERVE

The use of a natural area as a museum laboratory to study natural processes was outlined in 1948 by Graham Netting, then the museum's assistant director. Once he became director, he persuaded General and Mrs. Richard K. Mellon and Mr. and Mrs. Alan M. Scaife, in 1956, to donate eleven tracts of land totaling 1,160 acres, about sixty miles southeast of Pittsburgh, and the "Powdermill Nature Reserve, a Research Station of Carnegie Museum," was born, its mission to study natural populations of animals and plants—their life histories, behaviors, and ecological relationships.

Over the next several years, additional acreage was added to the reserve, and by 2008 it encompassed over 2,200 acres of woodlands, streams, open fields, ponds, and thickets. For over half a century, Powdermill has been a refuge for the region's plants and animals, some of which were becoming rare as their habitats were destroyed. Powdermill Run, the mountain stream that runs through the mixed deciduous forest (a second succession forest, as the land was heavily logged in the early twentieth century), is one of the few unpolluted western Pennsylvania mountain streams suited to ongoing studies of aquatic life. Powdermill's staff is dedicated to its mission, assiduously documenting changes in animal life and recording annual weather conditions. The United States has about 180 such field stations, but most of them are university affiliated and thus wedded to changing student and faculty curriculum needs. As a result, few can match Powdermill's consistent and pristine record of dedicated research.

Powdermill was part of the region's involvement in land conservation, which Graham Netting advanced through his close ties to government agencies, philanthropists, and foundations. The land conservation ethic that first emerged in the early 1930s centered on the Pittsburgh Parks Conservancy, which after twenty years embraced a larger mission and became the Western Pennsylvania Conservancy, in 1951. By this point the region's landscape displayed the environmental scars of exploitive industry: abandoned deep mines, strip mines, spoil piles, acid mine drainage, and vast stretches of clear-cut forestland. Financial and civic entrepreneurs in Pittsburgh supported the Western Pennsylvania Conservancy's mission, and they took seriously the advice of its leader, Arthur B. Van Buskirk: "Dream Big Dreams. Small dreams have no power to fire men's souls."[70]

Netting was a precise and efficient administrator, conservative in his business practices, but he fully endorsed the conservancy's quasi-religious fervor, expressed in its director Charles F. Lewis's 1957 report:

The history of a long past lies in the gorge of Slippery Rock; in the moraines of the Muddy Creek Valley; in the churning, plunging waters of the Youghiogheny at Ohiopyle; or again at the marshes of Pymatuning, in the wondrous quiet of the Powdermill Reservation, or under the noble cathedral pines of Cook Forest. To spend even a little time in deep contemplation of these varied and majestic works of nature is to realize they are, indeed, the work of God. Their perpetuation as shrines for renewed self-dedication, and as wellsprings of faith revived, is the compelling objective of this conservancy. In this undertaking, all of us are properly united in aspiration and effort.[71]

While Powdermill was not a conservancy project, it emerged from the same cauldron of idealism. Conservancy leaders were often on the board of the Carnegie Institute, while museum naturalists regularly made environmental assessments of properties to be preserved for the public. Institute presidents have held varied attitudes toward Powdermill. James Bovard, a lawyer for Mellon bank interests, kept it within the orbit of early hunting and conservation groups. James Mellon Walton kept that role intact through the 1980s, while his successor, Robert Wilburn, saw it as an increasingly interesting conservation project. Ellsworth Brown did not make it a high priority, but David Hillenbrand began to expand its administration and programs. Financially, Powdermill did not contribute to the museum's future, despite its ties to the old Pittsburgh ruling class, and in a sense it was a financial burden. In the late 1990s, director Jay Apt considered selling it, but a few trustees, notably Ingrid and Bill Rea and Tom Nimick, championed it as an important asset, part of life in the Ligonier Valley, arguing for its educational and scientific value. Apt's successor, Bill DeWalt, saw it as a force for interactive research with universities and other institutions, the role it continues to play today.

Powdermill's administrative position within Carnegie has always been complicated. Since it is owned by Carnegie Institute, its staff members are museum employees. However, it long lacked an independent board to define its mission and carry it out. Further, without an endowment, it had to raise its own funds annually. Powdermill staff members have often lived frugally on the reserve's grounds, and volunteers (including members of the museum board) have long been instrumental to its survival. For a long time, too, its facilities were spartan at best. The land R. K. Mellon donated to the Institute included a collection of old shacks and farmsteads, most without water or toilet facilities. When Powdermill's first bird bander, Robert Leberman, began living at the site, in 1961, he got his water from a hose and had to bathe in Powdermill Run. Eventually, however, all the buildings added small bathrooms and kitchens.

For years, Powdermill was administratively linked to the museum's Birds section, supported by curator Ken Parkes and his assistants Mary Clench and Scott Wood, who had oversight responsibilities. Most biological field stations band birds only in the summer or seasonally, but Powdermill operated all year long. Powdermill has captured and banded birds the same way for decades, following the method established by Leberman and the

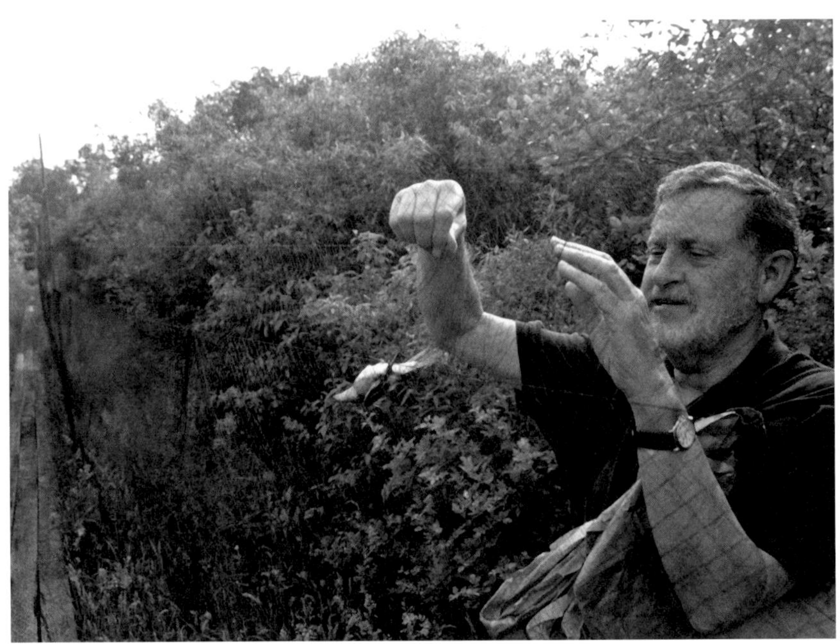

Bob Leberman removes a bird from a mist-net. He began bird-banding at Powdermill Nature Reserve—owned by Carnegie Institute—as a young volunteer. For decades, he compiled field records with scientific precision, beginning Powdermill's reputation as a national resource for ornithological research.

reserve's second chief bird bander, Robert Mulvihill. The work is still done quietly by a few core individuals, the data collected reputed to be the cleanest in existence. Nearly invisible mist nets of thin black nylon line the flight paths of birds around Powdermill's ponds and woodland paths, routinely emptied of birds by a bander who walks the line, skillfully extracting each entangled bird and placing it in a paper bag, which is closed with a clothespin and then tucked under the bander's belt. When he or she returns to the small bird-banding station, the bander extracts the bird and quickly performs a few delicate maneuvers: blowing on the bird's skull to see if its sutures have formed, indicating whether the bird is a juvenile or mature; blowing on its breast during breeding season, to see whether it has a swollen blood-rich patch, signifying that it is female with a brood of eggs to tend to. After quickly determining the bird's sex, weight, and wing length, the bander slips a numbered band on its leg before releasing it through a small window next to the table. The entire operation is smooth and gentle, taking less than a minute to complete.

When Joseph Merritt became the reserve's resident director in 1979, he encouraged a new interest in small animal research, which he pursued at Powdermill for twenty-five years. His first scientific interest was in the subnivean (under-the-snow) life of small mammals such as voles, moles, and mice—animals whose high metabolic rate drove their quest for survival in tunnels under the snow. He built up profiles of different species and their ability to survive winter climates without hibernation—a process that, if extrapolated, applied physiologically to other mammals, including humans. In 1987 Merritt published his *Guide to the Mammals of Pennsylvania.*

Merritt also established Powdermill as a retreat and center for scientific symposia and developed its reputation as a scientific enterprise worthy of national and international attention. The reserve was an able host to interns and visiting scientists from other academic institutions. Today scientists from around the world come to Powdermill, living in small cabins on the grounds, sharing meals at rustic Raven's Roost, and presenting symposia at the Nimick Nature Center. Powdermill has hosted conferences on small African mammals, shrews, the ecology of small mammals, tree squirrels, and the "evolution of human-equine relations."

When Merritt left in 2004, Powdermill was at a turning point, its scientific bona fides established but in need of more dedicated fund-raising if it were to survive and grow. Its new director, David Smith, was a retired business manager, a member of the Ligonier community with experience in developing strategic plans for nonprofit institutions. He developed the reserve's capital campaign, reorganized its programs, and expanded its facilities, from refurbishing cottages to expanding the educational center. The museum director and board asked Smith to take Powdermill into a new era of higher-profile marketing and fund-raising. Scientifically, Smith decided, the organization had to play to its strengths, and "bird research was the long-ball hitter."[72] Powdermill's "Mount Everest of Data" was irresistible to millions of bird enthusiasts around the world: impeccable information collected over more than forty years, quality photographs, a user-friendly style of field research. In 2004, the bird-banding program was renamed the Powdermill Avian Research Center (PARC). A $7.5 million capital campaign developed, and in 2005 a $3 million grant from the Richard King Mellon Foundation was earmarked for "green" expansion of the Education Center. Also in 2005, a Heinz Endowments grant of $2 million was made in honor of the late board members William H. Rea and Ingrid Rea, who had spent decades championing Powdermill.

Today at Powdermill—which receives some twelve thousand visitors annually, including three thousand students and summer campers—volunteer interns use GPS receivers to create a detailed, layered, digital map of Powdermill, capturing data on vegetation types, canopy density, species, streams, and wetlands boundaries; coordinating this data with exact points of latitude and longitude; and transferring it all to a digital Powdermill map. The resulting gigantic database can track everything that lives on the reserve: birds, mammals, amphibians, insects, and fish. A herpetology field researcher at Powdermill might inject a computer chip with a barcode under a snake's scales, then use a barcode reader to measure the animal's growth if recaptured. C. J. Ralph, a research wildlife biologist with the U.S. Department of Agriculture's Forest Service, notes that Powdermill " has the best past and present data . . . at a single station of anybody in North America."[73]

PAYING FOR SCIENCE

Museum science seems remote to everyday life, and through the years Carnegie Museum of Natural History has struggled financially to support scientific work in most of its sections. The National Science Foundation has sometimes supported research and collection development, and there have been generous grants for specific projects, but much of the cost of the curatorial staff and collection development must be borne by the endowment, which has both restricted (designed for specific projects) and unrestricted (discretionary) funds used by the central corporation and museum administration. In the 1990s, the Natural History Museum began to complain that the Institute endowment it depended upon was being used as a discretionary fund for new priorities, such as an enlarged marketing department for Carnegie Museums of Pittsburgh, and to develop Carnegie Science Center and the Andy Warhol Museum. A downturn in the stock market and a decline in the endowment's value after 2000 increased the problem. Natural History spread its budgetary shortfalls across all scientific departments, appealed for emergency "preservation" funds, and tried to avoid shrinking its small scientific staff.

Similar financial pressures were being felt by museums across the country. Even the Smithsonian Institution, with its billion-dollar budget, began to streamline and consolidate scientific research activities in 2001.[74] The New York Public Library sold its iconic painting *Kindred Spirits,* by Asher Durand, and in Philadelphia Thomas Jefferson Medical University's pending sale of Thomas Eakins's painting *The Gross Clinic* raised such indignation that two other Philadelphia museums united to match the sale price and keep the painting in the city. The Milwaukee Public Museum did not sell its patrimony, but it used its endowment to cover operating expenses, and a painful lawsuit resulted.[75] The National Science Foundation was increasingly besieged by research proposals from many organizations, and some midsize institutions began selling off valuable parts of their collections—decisions that led to controversy and protest among museum lovers. The museum consultant Tom L. Freudenheim, formerly of the Smithsonian Institution, the Baltimore Museum of Art, and the National Endowment for the Arts, argued that it was a mistake for Rust Belt communities like Pittsburgh to raise money by divesting themselves of cultural capital because no new wealth sources were immediately apparent. Freudenheim charged that there actually was wealth in such communities, but it was not coming to the aid of the typical museum: "Some of those millionaires are even trustees. . . . In the old days, writing big checks to support acquisitions and other museum programs was considered every board member's first responsibility."[76]

Carnegie Museum of Natural History has many treasures it could sell, but the option of deaccessioning assets is complex. Modern policies on deaccessioning, set by the American Association of Museums, protect the rights of the original donor, and close attention must be paid to the reason why something originally came to the museum. Another rule dictates that if a work is sold, the funds raised may be used only to acquire greater works of the same type. The deaccessioning dilemma is full of such legal intricacies; tangled value judgments must be regularly made by directors and trustees, in the face of strong public sentiment. When Carnegie Museum of Natural History sold much of its coin and stamp collection in the 1970s, it received such negative publicity that it has proceeded very cautiously ever since.

8

CARNEGIE SCIENCE CENTER AND BUHL PLANETARIUM

"Popular Science"

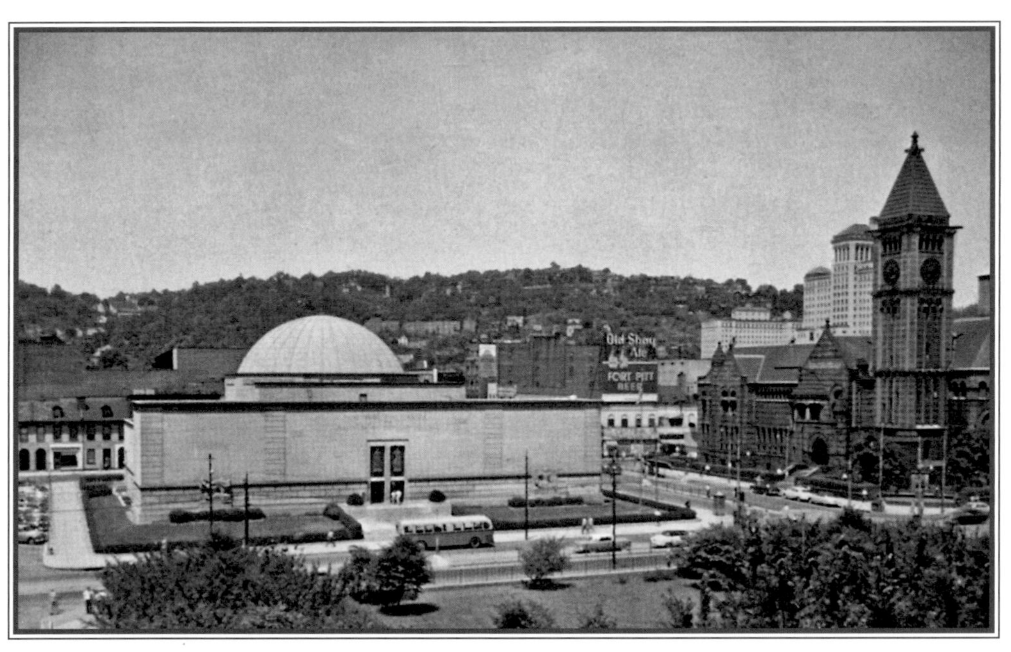

Buhl Planetarium and Science Center was located next to Carnegie's Allegheny Library on Federal Street, a convenient stop for trolleys and buses on Pittsburgh's North Side.

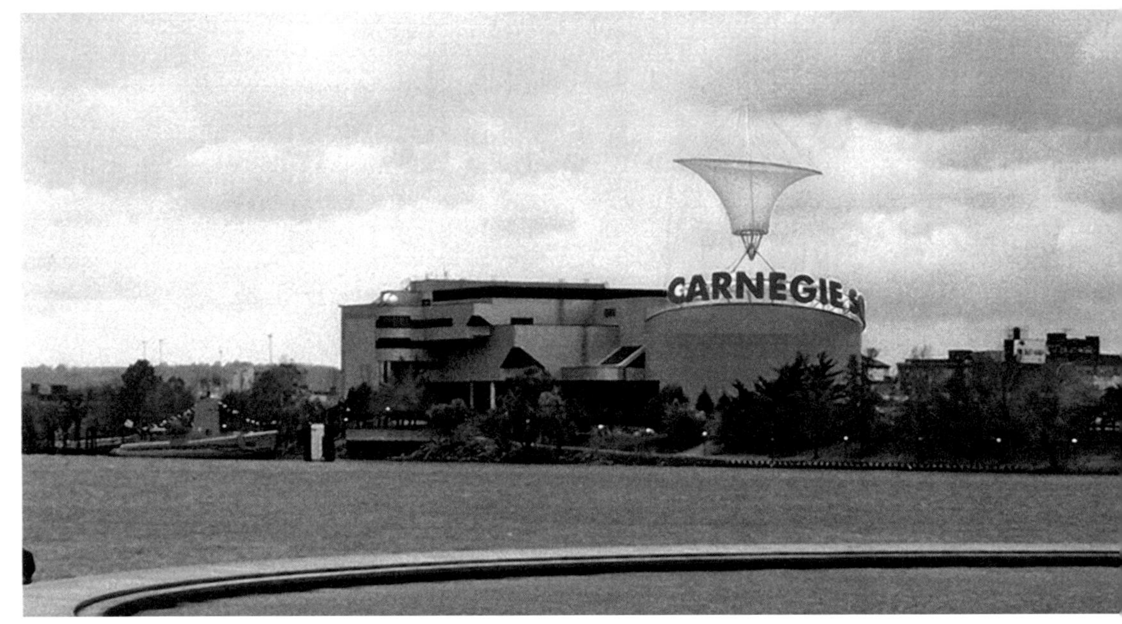

Carnegie Science Center is seen here from the fountain at Point State Park in downtown Pittsburgh.

WHEN PITTSBURGH OPENED Buhl Planetarium in 1939—the fifth planetarium in the United States—it joined the big leagues in popular astronomy, part of a trend that had started in the 1920s in Europe with the famous Zeiss system for projecting the stars and then gradually moved to the United States. Pittsburgh's planetarium was the result of a landmark grant for science education in the United States, the largest gift the Buhl Foundation had ever made. Since that time, planetariums have flourished, until by 2006 there were some five thousand science centers or comparable institutions worldwide. In Pittsburgh, the Buhl Foundation continued to support Buhl Planetarium, in 1991 transferring its endowment to Carnegie Science Center, which is widely admired for the planetarium shows it creates and distributes internationally and which has been honored nationally for its excellence in science education. While many individuals and organizations support the Science Center, the impetus for all its success can be traced directly back to Henry Buhl Jr.

Henry Buhl Jr. (1848–1927) was the co-owner of the famous Boggs and Buhl dry goods store on Federal Street, on Pittsburgh's North Side. Interestingly, he was not particularly interested in science. A sedulous planner, Buhl was not given to self-promotion and in that regard was the opposite of Andrew Carnegie. For example, when the editors of the *Cyclopedia of American Biography* asked Buhl about his own life in 1922, he modestly replied:

You say you want to include in this Cyclopedia an account of my life and activities. As to this, I am simply a merchant and have not been active at all in public matters. Therefore, I do not think that this would interest anyone specially.

Thanking you very kindly, I am Respectfully yours,

H. Buhl, Jr.

Like Carnegie, however, Buhl was altruistic and had a strong social conscience. Notably without heirs in his final years, he carefully planned the distribution of his fortune, writing and rewriting his will and eventually creating the Buhl Foundation.[1] This was the first multipurpose foundation in Pittsburgh.

Buhl's will established the foundation, with $11 million dollars, "as a memorial to my wife who, by Christian faith, lived a good and useful life and whose counsel and devotion have been my great help and comfort." Buhl gave the foundation freedom to make gifts as its board members saw

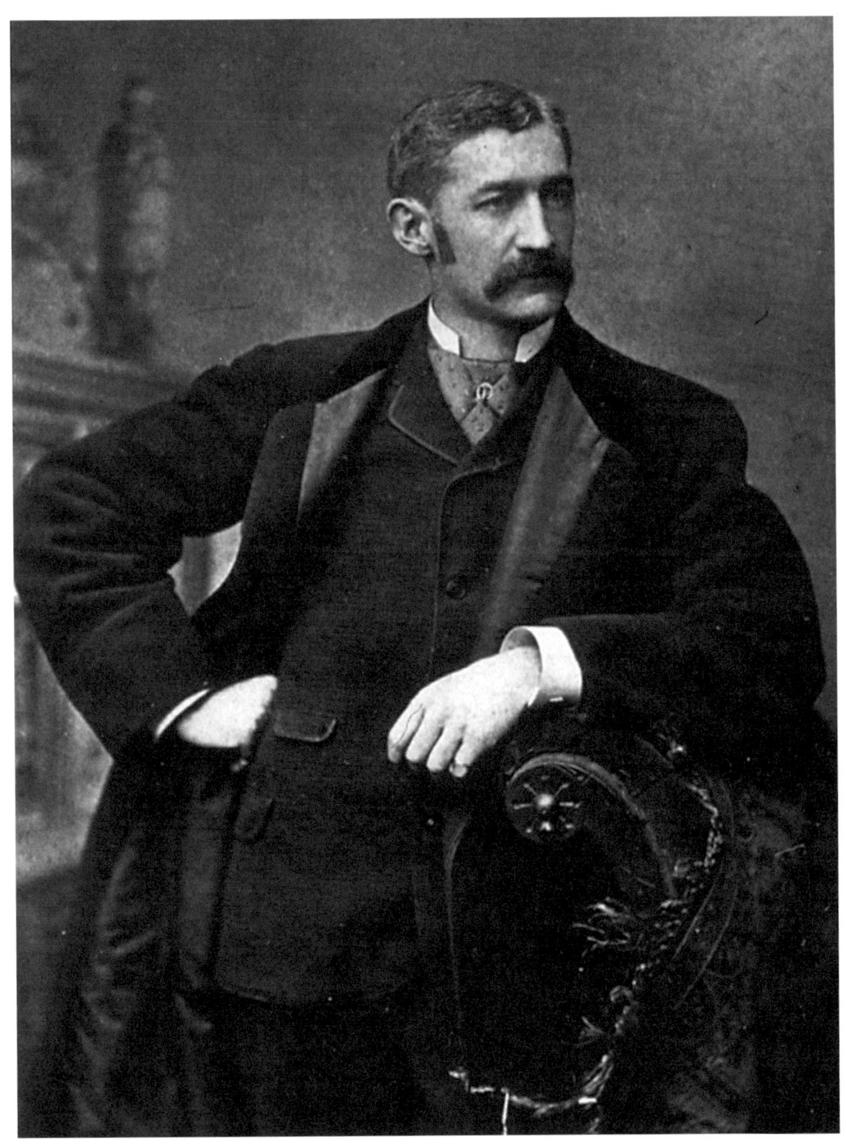

Henry Buhl Jr., co-owner of the Boggs and Buhl Department Store, created the $11 million Buhl Foundation before his death in 1927, in memory of his late wife. This broad, multipurpose foundation funded Buhl Planetarium and Science Center in 1939, and supported Carnegie Science Center in 1991.

fit, suggesting that they should first consider "the aid, needs, and well-being of the citizens of Pittsburgh, and the County of Allegheny."[2] Among the foundation's early grants were gifts to Carnegie Library of Pittsburgh to encourage continuing adult education and, later, to study and promote the new technologies that had begun to change the library profession. The 1930s, however, would bring the foundation the opportunity for which Henry Buhl's name would long be remembered.

THE PLANETARIUM AND OBSERVATORY

During the years of the Great Depression, the Buhl Foundation's members decided that the most useful gift they could make to Pittsburgh and to Buhl's beloved North Side was a planetarium and observatory. Built at a cost of $1.1 million, Buhl Planetarium and Observatory was dedicated and conveyed to the City of Pittsburgh on October 24, 1939. In 1939, the Buhl was "the latest word, both mechanically and architecturally," a temple to science, intended to lift the workers of Pittsburgh into the heavens, beyond the confines of business and industry and above the skyline of downtown Pittsburgh, which was visually etched into the perimeter of the "Theater of the Stars." The Buhl had been designed by the Pittsburgh firm of Ingram, Pratt and Boyd in the stripped-down Classical style popular in the 1930s, and the building, with its windowless walls, had an austere dignity. Its mission was to bring scientific literacy to a new generation of working-class Pittsburghers, residents of a city whose lifeblood was manufacturing and scientific entrepreneurship.[3]

Inside Buhl Planetarium, the greatest attraction was the Theater of the Stars, with its Zeiss II planetarium projector, built in Jena, Germany, whose 106 lenses could produce nine thousand star pictures. The Zeiss at the Buhl was the first projector to be installed on an elevator: it rose up dramatically into the center of the theater like a giant ant from another planet, projecting the stars on the great dome above. For children the effect was thrilling, seared into their imaginations forever. On the dome, the projector created the look of the heavens thousands of years in the past and gave viewers a glimpse of the heavens far in the future. Ironically, one of the German-built Zeiss projector's first sky shows was "Bombers by Starlight," explaining the techniques of celestial navigation by which Germany had bombed Great Britain and by which America would soon bomb Germany. Pittsburgh, the center of American steel production and war materials, was alarmed by the outbreak of war.

As other planetariums in North America and Europe opened over the next half century with more advanced technologies, the Buhl eventually became the oldest planetarium in the world still operating the classic Zeiss projector. The second most important technological feature of the Buhl was the "People's Observatory," with its ten-inch Siderostat telescope, dedicated in 1941 and first used by the public to view the planet Saturn. Designed for public access, the observatory had been built to professional standards.

Yet another fascinating exhibit was the elegant two-story Foucault pendulum, displaying the points of the compass and demonstrating why, although the Earth spins, one does not actually feel its rotation. This display was a classic in science centers worldwide, but the Buhl's pendulum was particularly elegant, a 150-pound bob swinging on a thirty-five-foot wire over a beautiful pit of Florentine marble and brass, gradually knocking down a circle of 108 silver pins as the rotating earth brought them into contact with the bob. For fifty-five years, from 1939 to 1994, when the Buhl building closed, Pittsburgh children and adults leaned over the rail, amazed at the pendulum's graceful demonstration of natural law.[4]

From the beginning, the Buhl was conceived as Pittsburgh's response to the educational needs of the city's scientific culture—which was why the phrase "Institute of Popular Science" was eventually added to its title. In this vein, the Buhl was arguably the first planetarium to have a pilot program for "interactive exhibits." These early exhibits still exist, in storage: dioramas that moved while an audiotrack played. Similarly, the Buhl's educational programs always had a hands-on quality. If you wanted to build a telescope, for example, the Buhl had an instructor who could teach you how to grind lenses the way the astronomer John Brashear did. The Buhl also offered popular classes and summer camps, including adult classes in the 1950s and 1960s that reflected the growing national fascination with astronomy and space. Generations of Pittsburgh's children took classes in science at the Buhl, its tradition of science education laying the foundation for later science education at Carnegie Science Center, which transferred key Buhl educators and successful programs to the new building in 1991.

During this conversion of the Buhl into Carnegie Science Center, a 1989 Buhl "alumni" publication detailed the careers of hundreds of children who had been students at Buhl and later became leaders and teachers in various scientific fields. Among these former students were three astronauts: Jay Apt, James B. Irwin, and Mike Fincke. James D. Duffer, a professional engineer at the Rhode Island Department of Transportation, singled out the impact of the Buhl Science Fair: "Science Fair participation sets the stage for the competitive environment that ideas, theories and the like undergo later on in life. Thus, in a sense, this was the first taste of the real world as an aspiring engineer, and the first effort at marketing one's thoughts."[5]

But the Buhl gradually fell behind technologically. By the 1980s, the

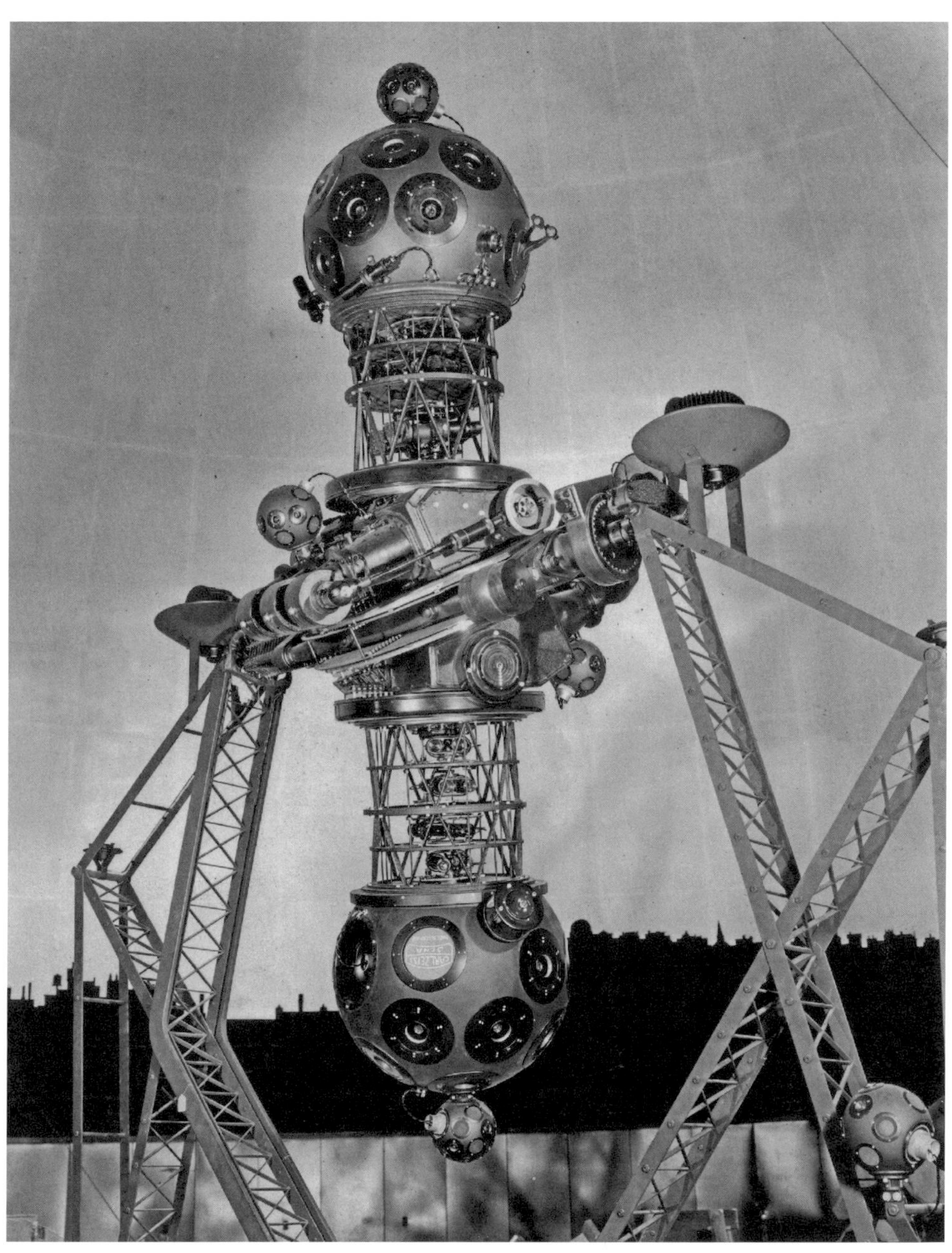

The 1939 Zeiss projector rose up on an elevator in the planetarium and thrilled Pittsburgh audiences with sky shows for decades. The Pittsburgh skyline was silhouetted on the perimeter of the dome.

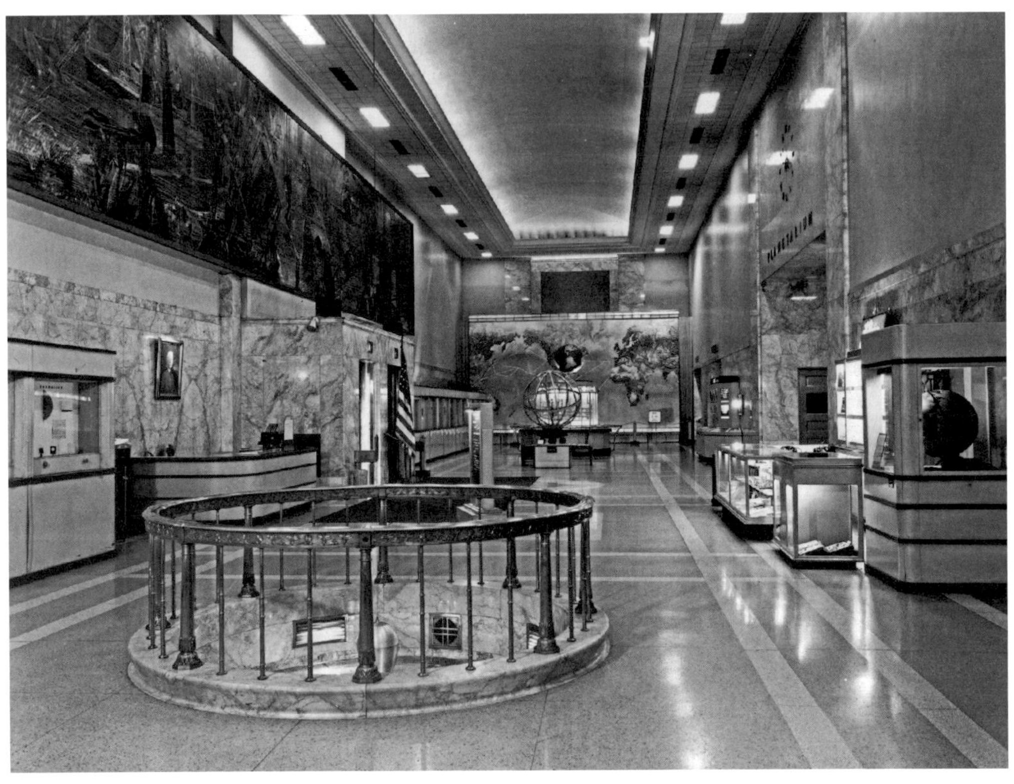

The marble-clad main lobby of the Buhl, with its elegant Foucault pendulum in the foreground, reflected the art-deco style of the building.

facility had not changed significantly in forty years, even while science itself was being transformed. Computers and databases were now common, and in the 1990s the Internet fundamentally altered the nature of scientific research. Pittsburgh educators and civic leaders recognized that the Buhl needed to be upgraded. In the short term, the mix of exhibits in the old Buhl was modernized, and various expansion concepts were proposed, including taking over the entire plaza in front of the Buhl and placing a large Omnimax theater in it, as well as placing many facilities underground. Eventually, it was decided that even with such structural changes, parking would be inadequate, and a new site had to be considered. After much administrative and political wrangling, for the first time a merger with Carnegie Institute was proposed. Robert C. Wilburn, appointed the president of Carnegie Institute in 1984, and Joshua Whetzel Jr., the director of the struggling Buhl, convinced their respective boards that a merger was best for the future of science education in Pittsburgh. Finally, in 1991, the Buhl building closed, after transferring most of its operations to the new Carnegie Science Center. The Children's Museum of Pittsburgh eventually expanded and took control of the original Buhl building in 2004, uniting it with another nearby landmark, the Old Post Office.

CARNEGIE SCIENCE CENTER

The opening of Carnegie Science Center on October 5, 1991, was a major achievement for Pittsburgh and for the larger national cause of urban science centers. At a cost of $40 million, the new center was the result of years of preparation. Not only was the new science center in a visually central part of the city, on the Ohio River facing Pittsburgh Point; it was designed with an understanding of what made other science centers effective in urban environments. Its architect, Tasso Katselas, saw the building as focused on three components: the Omnimax theater, the planetarium-auditorium space, and the exhibit space. These three were linked by a circulation pattern of ramps and staircases that gave the visitor a feeling of space; the center was not merely a functional container, but "a complex and pervasive mode of communication."[6]

The new director, Al DeSena, had been at the Buhl since 1979 and brought continuity to Carnegie Science Center programs. No opportunity for science education was neglected. The giant Omnimax theater had an entrance that allowed visitors to see the unwinding spools of film; another 300-seat Science Stage was also built, equipped for presentations; the planetarium, the most technologically advanced ever constructed, included 156 seats and a computer-driven projector (the Digistar); the observatory had a "university grade" telescope; a video wall showed live images, while the aquarium and the Miniature Railroad and Village exhibit were both expansions of traditional Buhl programs. On the second floor was a large changing exhibits gallery, and soon a Kitchen Theater was added to the third floor, focused on the science of cooking. The first floor featured a sales shop; the fourth-floor Overlook gave the visitor a view of Pittsburgh Point. "Planetarium people from all over the world are waiting to see this place," said Martin Ratcliffe, head of the new Henry Buhl Jr. Planetarium and Observatory.[7] Carnegie Science Center was soon promoting unique "destination" attractions (i.e., experiences that could not easily be found anywhere else), such as UPMC SportsWorks, the World War II submarine *Requin,* and the Rangos Omnimax Theater.

The Rangos Omnimax Theater was the first such destination experience at Carnegie Science Center—a four-story-high cinematic treat that, it was hoped, audiences would travel far to see. "Naming rights" were now a common funding mechanism for science centers, and the Rangos was a gift from the John G. Rangos Sr. Family Charitable Foundation, active in philanthropies to benefit education and health sciences. Originally, the Rangos Omnimax was used exclusively for nature films that allowed viewers, for example, to fly over the Grand Canyon or walk on the moon. But the large-format films are expensive to produce and lease and are more limited in variety and quantity than commercial films. In order to maintain public interest and audience market share, Omnimax theaters across the nation, including the Rangos, eventually began to screen commercial films in the big-screen format. When the giant cinema began to lose some of its cachet, as other big-screen theaters opened in commercial venues, Carnegie Science Center supplemented its film program with classes about the science behind the subject matter.

The Henry Buhl Jr. Planetarium was the next destination attraction. The elegant old Zeiss projector was now an antique, and the Zeiss company, although still in business, no longer supported its pre–World War II model by the 1980s, so spare parts for the old Carnegie's Zeiss projector were specially manufactured. More significantly, however, the Ziess system projected the old Earth-bound view of the universe—some ten thousand stars, with one ball of the Zeiss projecting the southern hemisphere, the other the northern hemisphere. While the operator could change the viewer's location by changing the latitude of view, and could make accurate adjustments to account for the Earth's slight wobble every twenty-six thousand years, the view remained bound to our planet, and the stars themselves appeared uniform in size in the original sixty-five-foot dome, not varied or pinpoint-like.

As Carnegie Science Center was being planned, the Digistar (digital star projector) system was already established in the planetarium business—a black and white video projector with a fish-eye lens that allowed the display of a three-dimensional image on the dome. There were still the same number of stars, but now the viewer seemed to fly through space, seeing them three-dimensionally. The Digistar could also project other three-dimensional models, such as the structure of DNA or a fly-through of the city of Pittsburgh. When the new technology was upgraded to Digistar 2 in 1994–95, the planetarium produced a show called "Journey into the Living Cell," in collaboration with the Studio for Creative Inquiry at Carnegie Mellon University and the Center for Light Microscopy at the Mellon Institute. Interactive buttons were added to the auditorium's armrests to allow the audience to control the unfolding storyline of each show, and the graphics became increasingly sophisticated. Within a few years of its opening, the new Henry Buhl Jr. Planetarium was a recognized pace-

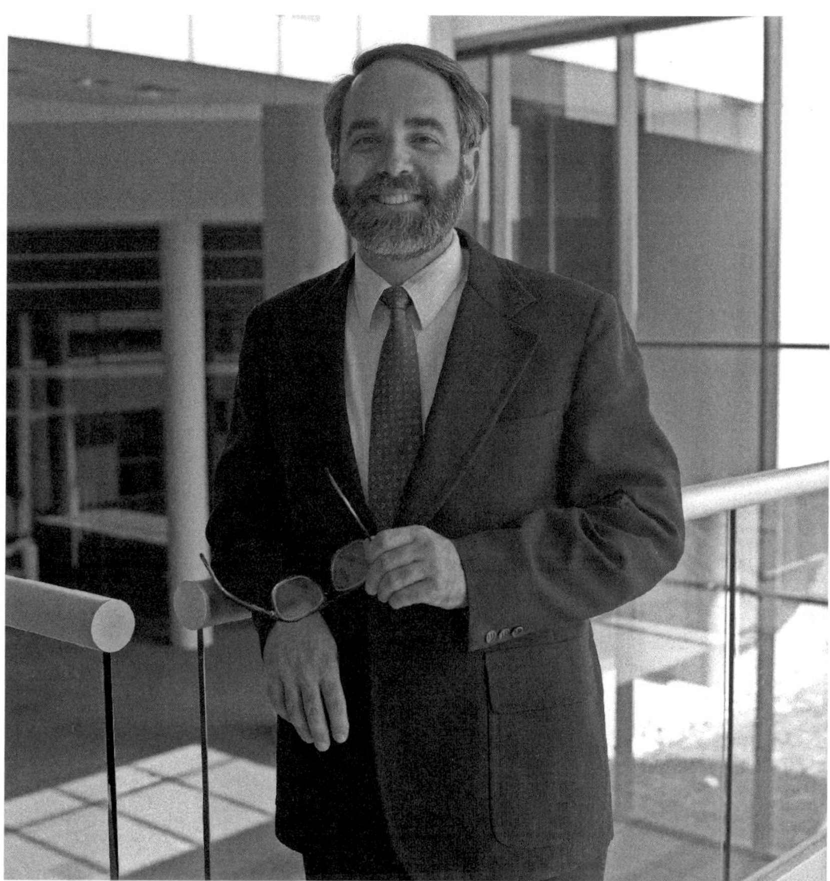

Director Al DeSena at the opening of Carnegie Science Center in 1991. DeSena had been at the Buhl Science Center for a dozen years and helped give continuity to programming at Carnegie Science Center.

setter in the field. Internationally, the packaging of original Buhl shows, with their high production values and striking content, led to a global leasing and rental program. By 2005, four hundred copies of Buhl shows were circulating in nineteen different countries, the narratives translated into fifteen languages.

The planetarium, whose distinguished directors have included Paul Olds, Martin Ratcliffe, and John Radzilowicz, remains a magnet for those who want the latest astronomical information. "When something is happening in the sky, people come here," says James Hughes, who produces many of the Buhl's original programs.[8] Audiences also come for the live star identification show, to find out what they will see that night in the sky. Space flights also drive attendance, since audiences enjoy the drama of seeing technology triumph over time and space. But real-time transmission of space flights carries risks: in 1986, at the former Buhl, the audience witnessed the *Challenger* disaster when the space shuttle exploded after takeoff. The Buhl had rented a satellite feed to watch the mission the previous weekend and was directly linked to NASA that Monday morning. The schoolchildren assembled in the planetarium to see the liftoff also saw the explosion—a horrific experience. Still, overall, space launches and transmissions are inspiring. In 2003, for example, a satellite feed let the local audience hear Pittsburgh astronaut Mike Fincke live, during his mission in space. Laser light shows in the planetarium are also popular, filling the entire screen with graphics and on average drawing about twenty thousand people a year.

The Miniature Railroad and Village, a legacy exhibit from the old Buhl, continued to expand and remained popular.[9] Paradoxically, western Pennsylvania's loss of heavy industry and the passing of traditional small-town life has enhanced the popularity of this exhibit, which provides an increasingly close look at that lost world, in a nostalgic display that attracts adults and children alike. The exhibit, which began as a hobby for wounded World War I veteran Charles Bowdish (1896–1988) of Brookville, Pennsylvania, plays to Pittsburgh's pride in its past importance as a city and provides welcome historic ballast for the groundbreaking science presented elsewhere at the science center.

Bowdish, an entrepreneur with a passion for showmanship inherited from his father, who operated a small theatrical troop and built the world's second Ferris wheel in Brookville in 1894, decided to keep himself busy after returning from the European front by making models of Brookville buildings, as part of a toy railroad display for the Christmas holidays. Soon people were asking if they could bring friends to see his display, and the exhibit brought hundreds to his door, first from Pennsylvania and then from all over the country. Gradually and meticulously, he expanded his themes, "A White Christmas" or "Indian Summer," and created increasingly elaborate miniatures and scenery, using inexpensive homegrown modeling techniques, such as beeswax for stonework, dried peas for pumpkins, and painted rice for corn.

Then, in 1952, much of his material was washed away by a local creek that flooded his home. His family had to be rescued from the flooded house by a rowboat, and the exhibit had to be moved, not only because of the flood but also because the insurance company refused to cover the thousands of visitors who were walking through his house. Bowdish submitted a proposal to Brookville's civic leaders, suggesting that they underwrite the costs of a new building to house a larger exhibit, but he did not get enough local support and began to search elsewhere, placing an ad about the "Famous

Charles Bowdish Display" in the *Pittsburgh Press Family Magazine.* Buhl Planetarium, seeking to expand its modest Lionel Christmas display in February 1954, offered Bowdish a deal: he was paid twelve dollars per day (plus living expenses) to stay in Pittsburgh and help construct the display, selling to Buhl some thirty to forty houses, barns, and other buildings, as well as three hundred trees. In Pittsburgh the exhibit's first thirty-two-day display drew 23,885 adults and schoolchildren. The next year even more visitors waited patiently in line.

Four years after Bowdish's death, in the fall of 1992, the much enhanced Miniature Railroad and Village made its debut with great fanfare at the new Carnegie Science Center. The exhibit was 60 percent larger, covering 2,300 square feet, and had 1,500 feet of track, enhanced by over 100 individual animations and over 250,000 trees. The emphasis was now on the historic and educational value of each new model, and replicas soon included steel mills, coalmines, coke ovens, and barges laden with iron ore from the Great Lakes. A loyal group of volunteers, including retirees from railroads and industry, helps maintain and present the exhibit to each new generation.

Carnegie Science Center strategically began to focus most of its attention on new science in the areas where modern Pittsburgh was increasingly strong—robotics at Carnegie Mellon University, the civic passion for sports, and the region's signature river environment. One new attraction was the World War II submarine U.S.S. *Requin.* Named after a sand shark, the *Requin* had been launched from the naval shipyard at Portsmouth, New Hampshire, on January 1, 1945, arriving in Pearl Harbor, ready to begin its first patrol, just when World War II ended. After the war it was modified and served twenty-five years during the Cold War on "picket duty," cruising the seas around the world. In 1955, when the *Nautilus* inaugurated the nuclear age of submarines, old diesel-engine submarines were gradually discontinued, and in 1968, the *Requin* was decommissioned.[10] Jim Winokur, a trustee who had served in the Silent Service during the war, was asked by Carnegie president Robert Wilburn to oversee moving the submarine from Tampa, Florida, to Pittsburgh. When the U.S.S. *Requin* was docked in the Ohio River in front of Carnegie Science Center, it was conceived as an exhibit that would attract thousands, demonstrating such scientific concepts as ballast, density, buoyancy, water pressure, and differences in living conditions above and below the water. In Pittsburgh, the fifty-year-old submarine was instantly popular, not only for its scientific interest but also because of the city's strong patriotic memories, evoking a time when Pittsburgh's steel and war materials had helped define the war effort.

Yet another of Carnegie Science Center's destination attractions opened on October 4, 2001: UPMC SportsWorks, at 35,000 square feet, was billed as

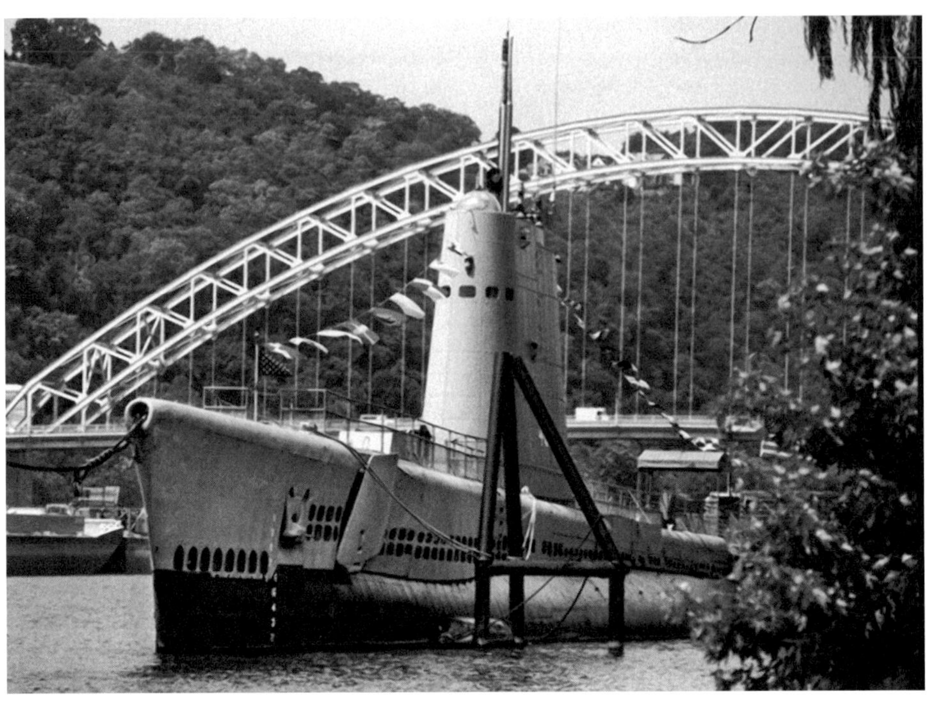

Moored in front of Carnegie Science Center, the U.S.S. Requin *is a popular exhibit about World War II technology.*

the world's largest science-of-sports exhibition, offering over forty exhibits and sixty interactive experiences designed to challenge the mind and body. Located in an older, separate building from the science center, it was five times larger than any other exhibit. Developed in partnership with the University of Pittsburgh Medical Center (UPMC), which supplied major funding and expertise from physicians and athletic trainers, the exhibit was a way to promote public health through a creative approach to sports competition. At the SportsWorks, visitors could pitch a fastball, race an Olympic sprinter, climb a rock wall, or experience hang gliding—all in an unthreatening, engaging way. And while pitching a baseball in a professional batting cage presented a physical challenge, it also taught visitors about the aerodynamics of an in-flight baseball. Next to all the exhibits were medical tips about injury prevention and rehabilitation for different sports or activities. Seddon Bennington, the center's director, called it "a positive, engaging experience for people who would not normally visit a science/education facility."[11] Indeed, the exhibit, designed to encourage family attendance, drew young adults who normally shied away from the science

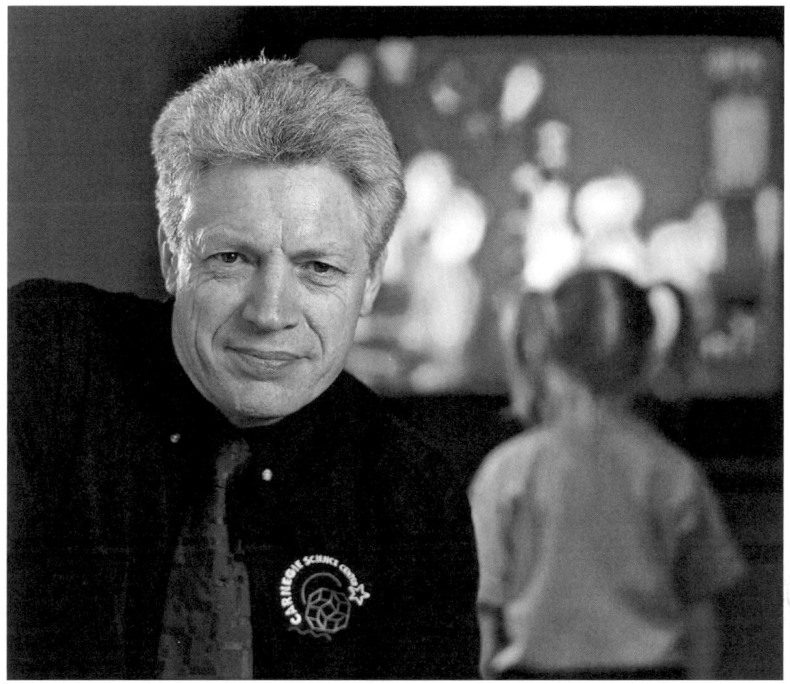

*Seddon Bennington from New Zealand was a charismatic director at
Carnegie Science Center. He promoted the outreach programs that earned
Carnegie Science Center a national award for excellence.*

center. In 2008 the older building housing SportsWorks was demolished
to make way for the new light-rail transit system serving the North Side.
A new building specifically designed for the program was erected closer to
the Science Center, and the popular activities, rebranded by a new sponsor
as Highmark SportsWorks, continued as before.

NEW DIRECTIONS

Soon after Seddon Bennington became director of Carnegie Science Center
in 1994, he began to feel that despite its offerings, the center had not fully developed its relationships with its local North Side neighborhood—or Pittsburgh with its suburbs and the larger region. As he walked to work through
the largely African American community of Manchester, he concluded
that the institution had a lot of reaching out to do to become integrated
into the fabric of the community. While the old Buhl was remembered
with great affection, Carnegie Science Center, in its new, slightly remote
location on the developing riverfront, seemed distant from people's lives.

"This was something I felt we needed to take on," Bennington said. "It has a lot to do with sincerity.... We needed to think about how we can partner with the community itself, and be a good neighbor, and build economic growth that way."[12]

In 1994, a large number of Pittsburghers were still grasping at the technological future, and Carnegie Science Center defined its role as focused on preparing the public for new industries, new careers, and the future of the region. While suburban Pittsburgh was largely middle-class, the science center, on the urban North Side, seemed inaccessible to the neighborhood. "We needed to connect in a meaningful and affordable way," Bennington said. "We couldn't just wave free tickets around. We had to meet with the grassroots organizations in the community."[13] Bennington also felt that beyond Allegheny County, a broader audience might be found in lower-income and depressed rural communities. The Bennington era thus became one of expansion into local communities through outreach programs. Carnegie Science Center developed ambitious programs to take its classes on the road, bringing educational programs not only to challenged Pittsburgh neighborhoods, such as the Hill District, but across western Pennsylvania, in partnership with Subaru, which provided cars allowing teachers to take their materials to distant towns. It was this effort that led to a national award to Carnegie Science Center for its community outreach programs.

Bennington's sense of mission also inspired his staff, mostly consisting of people whose passion, he said, was to "share science." Personally interested in the arts, Bennington further extended his vision to expanding the science center with a new, iconic building: "I wanted a building that opened people's eyes to the strength of the topography around us ... the rivers and so on. I wanted a building that was equal to that. I wanted people to be able to feel that strength ... to have a new insight for what Pittsburghers take for granted."[14] A 1996 study focused on expanding the science center by developing the Miller Building (which would temporarily house SportsWorks), but as an old factory-style structure, the Miller Building was less than ideal, and the board agreed that the best plan was instead to dramatically transform the existing science center.

In spite of all the excitement generated around this idea, the great disappointment of Bennington's tenure was the failure of his expansion plan with the famous architect Jean Nouvel, who had been selected after an international competition. Nouvel could give Pittsburgh the type of signature building that museums around the world were trying to construct as tourist magnets. The concept he produced was striking: a showplace fronting on the Ohio River that could be admired from downtown, including a Science Park on the surrounding grounds. But the projected build-

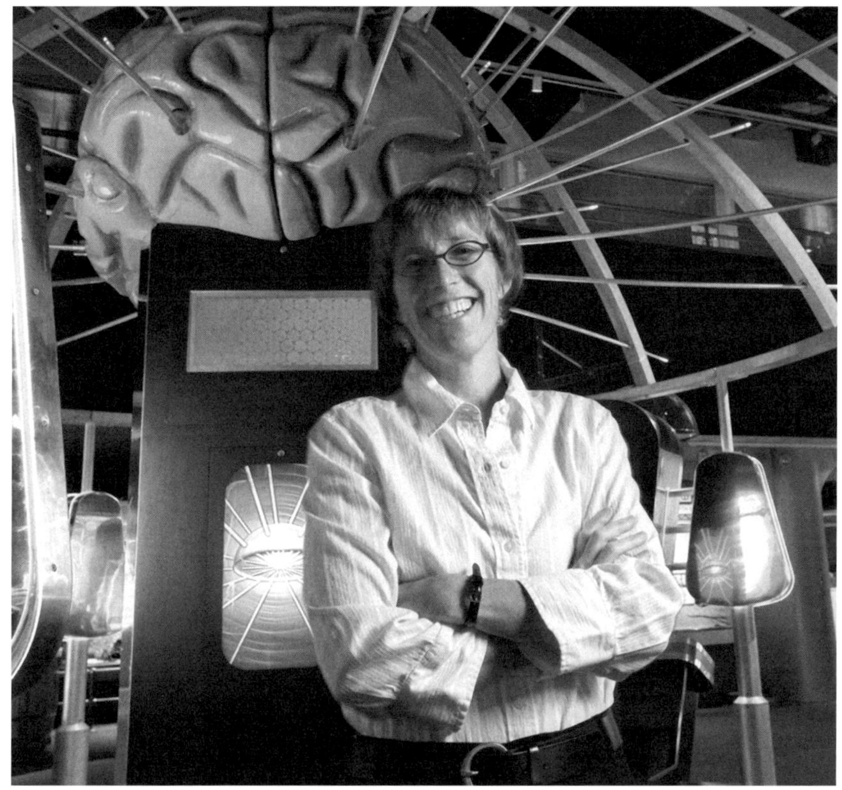

Director Johanna (Jo) Haas fought real estate and public transportation battles on the developing north shore, as the Science Center found itself bookended on the east by Heinz Field and on the west by Rivers Casino.

ing was soon $20 million over budget just on paper, and other economic factors soon came into play. Carnegie Museums of Pittsburgh was under increasing financial pressure, having been drawing down its endowment, and in 2002 the American stock market plunged, further reducing available resources. Financially, this signature building proved beyond reach, and the contract with Nouvel ended in a lawsuit for the recovery of some of the funds paid in advance.

Other changes soon followed. Bennington resigned in November 2002, Johanna (Jo) Haas taking over as the new director in October 2003. Haas, the first woman director of any of the Carnegie museums, continued to pursue Bennington's focus on outreach programs. She wanted "to change people's minds about science and to establish inquisitive, thoughtful, curious, competent people of all ages.... Science matters. Every day science, math, and technology drive both simple and complex things in the world

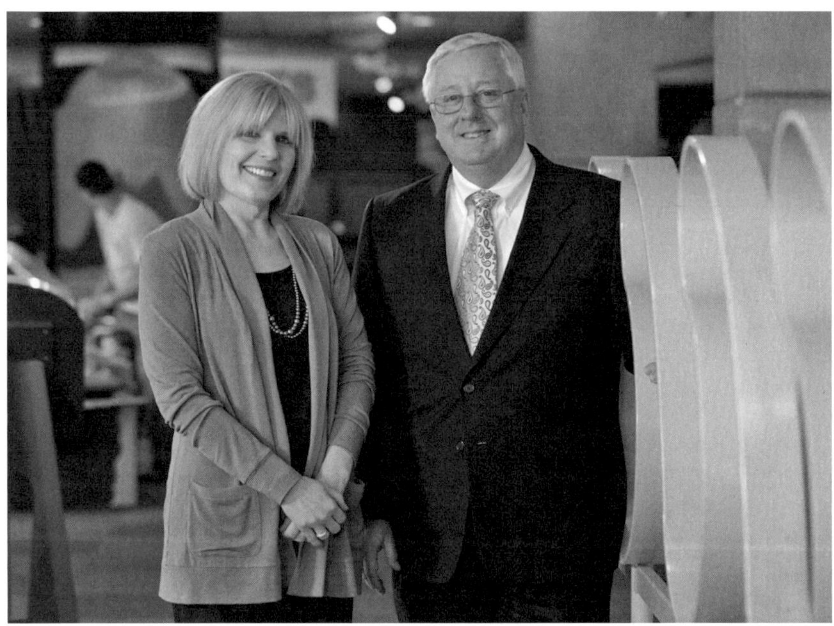

The joint appointment of Anne M. Metzger and Ron Baillie in 2009 marked the first time that Carnegie Museums of Pittsburgh had a permanent, dual codirectorship.

around us. The Science Center can play a significant role in demystifying and revealing the science in our everyday lives."[15] She was in place when Carnegie Science Center received the 2003 National Award for Museum Excellence, achieved by Seddon Bennington, bestowed by the Institute for Museum and Library Services at the White House. The award recognized Carnegie Science Center's exceptional record of service to the community, making it a symbol of successful museum outreach programs and an example of national standards. Haas resigned in 2008, and two of the center's executives, educator Ron Baillie and marketing expert Anne M. Metzger, were named permanent codirectors of the center in 2009—the first time any of the Carnegie museums had permanent codirectors and a sign of president David Hillenbrand's and the Board of Trustees' willingness to break with executive tradition and strike out in a new direction.

Science centers have caused controversy within the museum profession. In the 1970s and 1980s, a national debate began among museum professionals about the identity and mission of science centers and the new phenomenon of children's museums. In traditional collection- and discipline-based museums, curators preserve and interpret objects for the public. Thus,

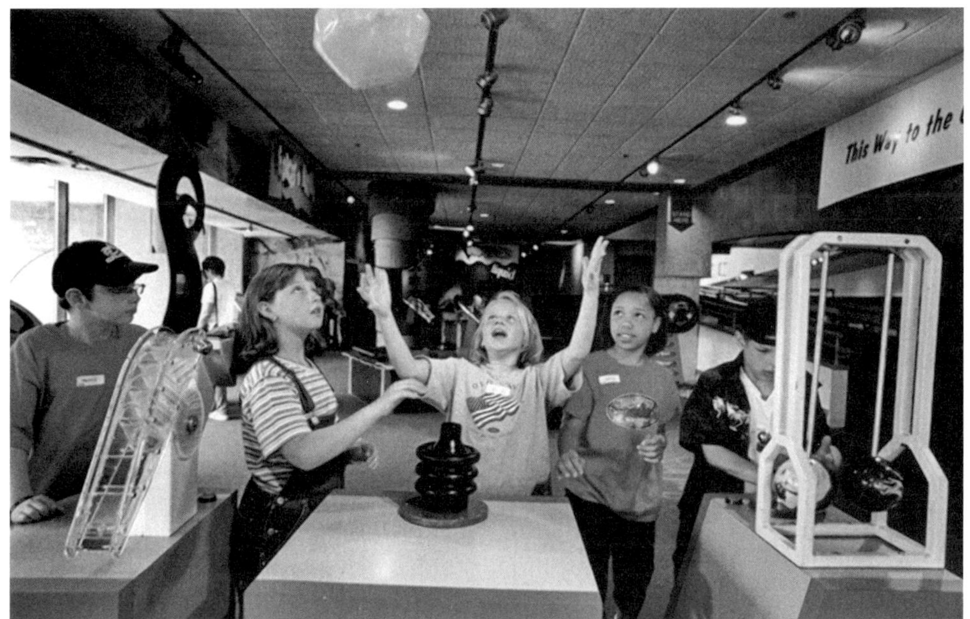

In the hands-on SciQuest exhibit, children discover for themselves scientific processes such as magnetic forces, lasers, aerodynamics, and embryology.

at Carnegie Museum of Art and Carnegie Museum of Natural History, education is driven from the top down, by expert curators who interpret collections within their scholarly and scientific disciplines. But the educational world of science centers and children's museums is structured differently, focused on the bottom-up behavior of children and adults; on people reacting to natural phenomena and real objects; on the way they touch, maneuver, or walk inside designed spaces. More broadly, the museum field was also struggling with the question of whether to recognize parallel educational experiences available at theme parks such as Walt Disney World, or through the National Park System, or at urban entertainment centers. In the science center field, the Association of Science Technology Centers (ASTC), formed in 1973, attended to an ever-growing membership, but the traditional American Association of Museums (AAM) debated whether it could grant equal status to institutions that had no collections and no curators.

To social historian and critic Roy Lubove, such new facilities were "fated to become a kind of first-level technological amusement park that presented science as 'fun.'" Fun meant, first and foremost, as many interactive exhibits as possible, discouraging solitary contemplation. Lubove argued that making science accessible to all was the same as "dumbing [it] down," reducing it "to the level of games and distractions for young children and their adult equivalents."[16]

Pittsburgh's new science center, however, proved very popular—and united popular science with a vision of post-industrial Pittsburgh. Its mission was to promote the movement of the region's young people from a past of heavy industry toward the high-tech economy of the future, and in that sense Andrew Carnegie's goal to bring science to the masses was now successfully recast in modern terms.

9

THE ANDY WARHOL
MUSEUM

"He Harvested Ideas from Everything"

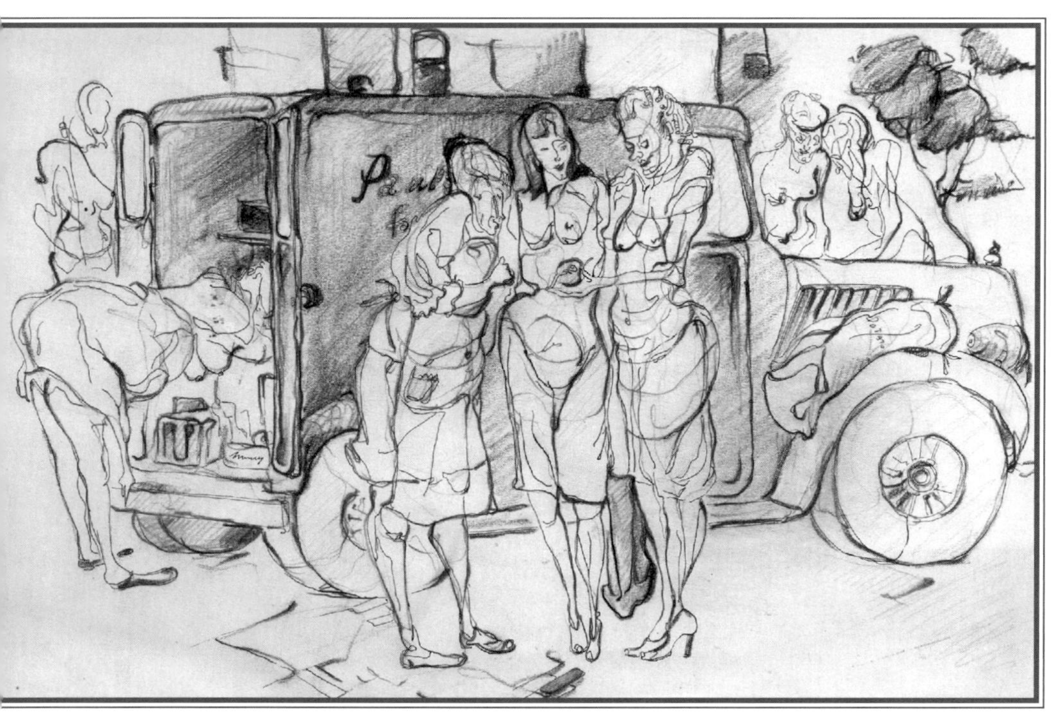

Andy Warhol, Women and Produce Truck, 1946. To save his college career, Andy
was required to do sketches in the summer of 1946, like this one of his brother Paul's grocery
truck in the Strip District. He succeeded in selling his sketches for twenty-five cents,
received a college award of twenty dollars, and was allowed to complete his degree
at Carnegie Institute of Technology.

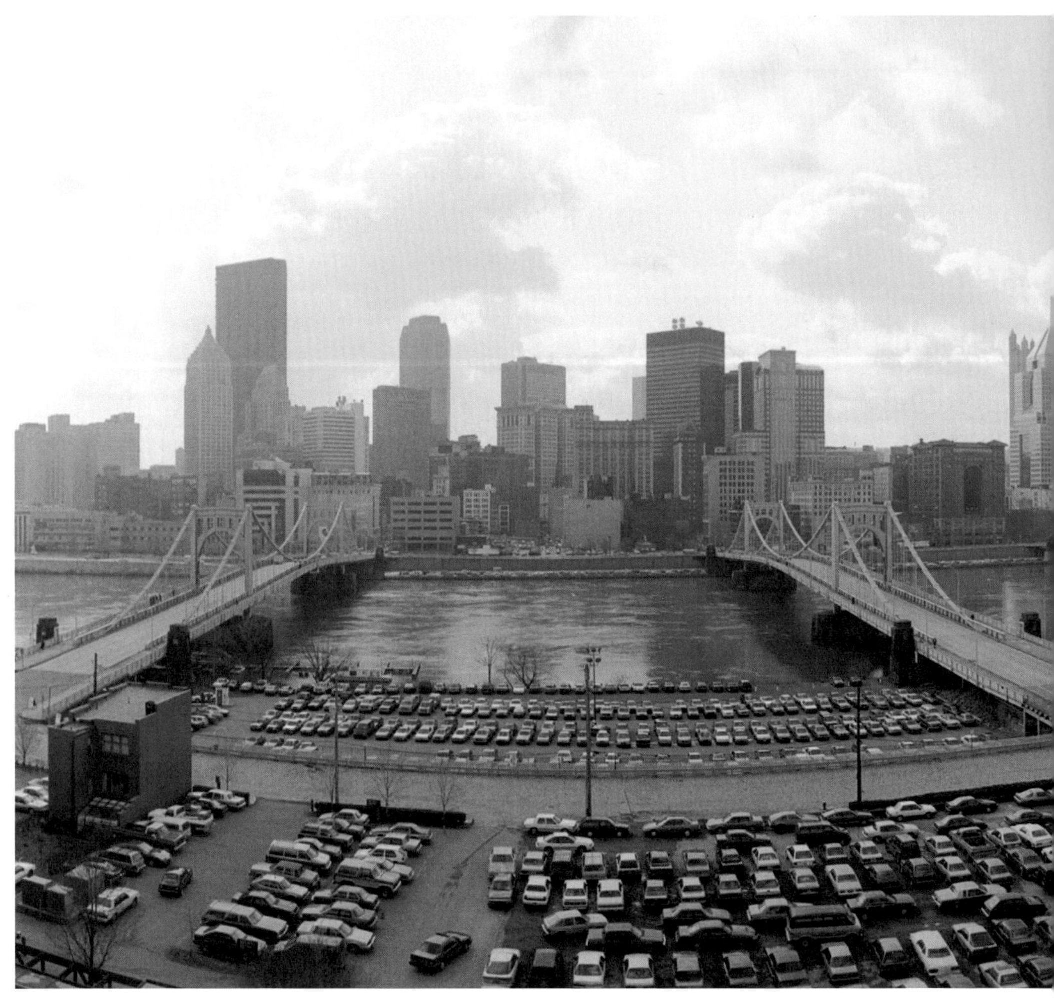

*The Volkwein Music building on the North Side in 1992 shortly before it became
The Andy Warhol Museum. This 1911 building resembled industrial warehouses
converted to art galleries in New York and was close to Pittsburgh's Downtown Cultural
District across the Seventh Street Bridge, which was renamed the Andy Warhol Bridge*

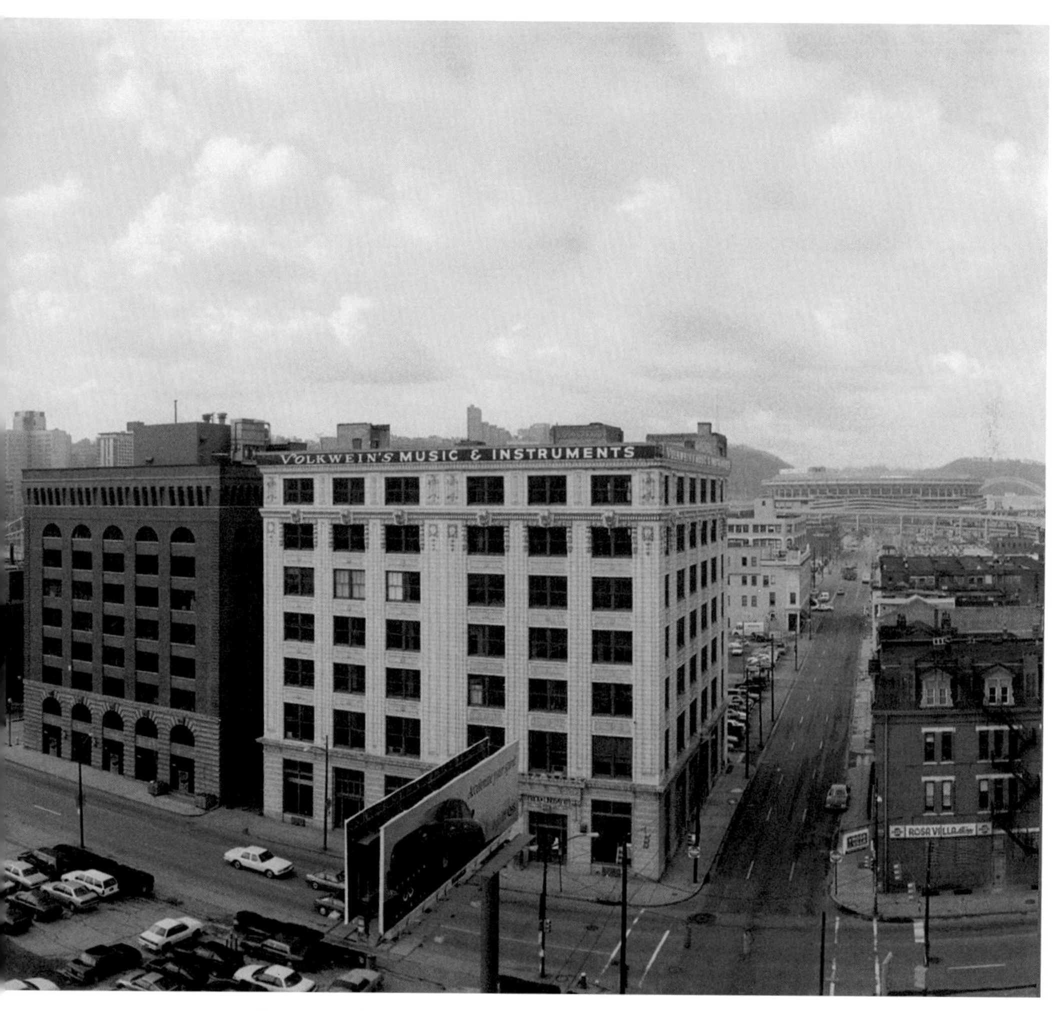

*in 2005 on the museum's tenth anniversary. The area was soon transformed when
Alcoa built its headquarters on the riverfront and a linear park developed along the
Allegheny River. On Sandusky Street, to the right, Three Rivers Stadium can be seen; it
was replaced in 2001 by PNC Park for the Pittsburgh Pirates, which is even closer to the
museum on Sixth Street.*

He harvested ideas from everything that was going on around him and thrived on a cacophony of experiences which he edited and then subjected to his own order.

Tom Armstrong, second director of the Andy Warhol Museum

AT FIRST GLANCE, Andrew Carnegie and Andrew Warhola seem to have little in common. Born nearly a century apart, they were children of different ages, Carnegie (1835–1919) the symbolic entrepreneur of the American industrial age, Warhol (1928–87) the most celebrated Pop artist in the New York scene of the 1960s–80s.[1] On closer examination, however, the two had much in common. Both were from poor immigrant families and spent two decades growing up in Pittsburgh. Their youthful years were dominated by their mothers, and their families' European religious traditions shaped their lives in subtle ways. Both exhibited their singular skills as children, Carnegie as the optimistic young master of his coworkers and Warhol as the watchful observer, living imaginatively in the world of popular entertainment. Both left Pittsburgh to seek success in New York, there applying the work ethic they had learned in their mill-town home. Carnegie, the industrialist who made and sold the replicated rails, girders, and steel plate from his mills, in time was drawn into the world of culture and art. Warhol, from the start interested in making art, called his studio "The Factory," replicating prints and images and finally declaring business to be the highest form of art. He would love to be replaced by a machine, he said: "I like boring things. I like things to be exactly the same over and over again."[2]

Significantly, both Carnegie Museum of Art and the Carnegie Institute of Technology shaped Andy Warhola's career as an artist. Joseph Fitzpatrick taught Warhola for four years, from fourth through eighth grade, first in art classes at the Institute and then at Schenley High School. Warhola was also enrolled in the commercial art program in the School of Fine Arts at Carnegie Tech, there pressured to achieve in a demanding curriculum that stressed performance and technique rather than a liberal arts philosophy.[3] A critical moment came when he was dismissed from school for marginal grades and undistinguished work at the end of his freshman year, in spring 1946. In their review of Warhola's performance, two faculty members argued that he deserved a second chance and suggested that he enroll in summer school, prove his worth, and be readmitted. He took this advice

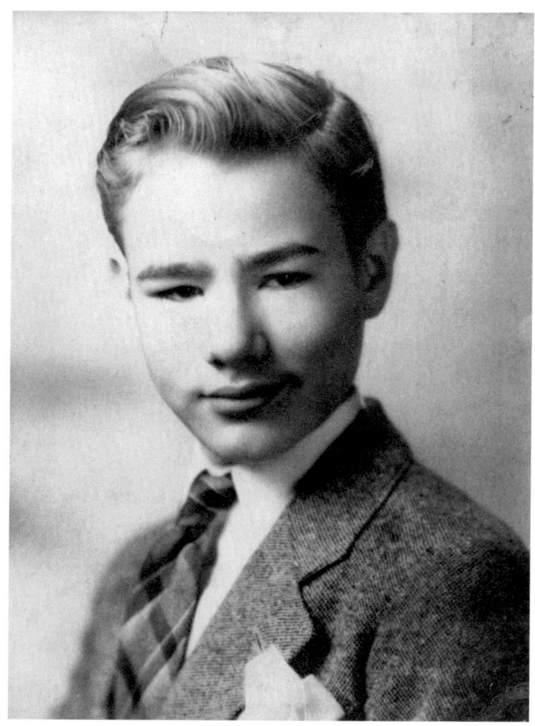

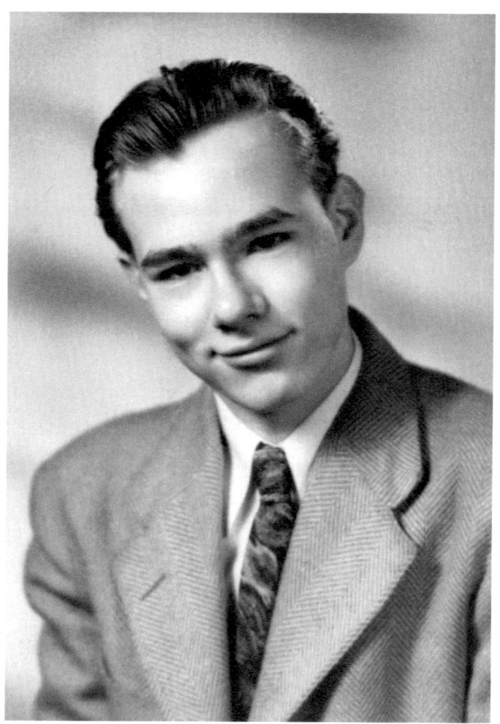

Andy Warhola, one month before his fourteenth birthday in 1942. He was taking art classes at Carnegie Institute at that time.

Andy's Schenley High School graduation picture, taken when he was about sixteen. He would soon attend Carnegie Tech, where he majored in commercial art.

and excelled at his summer art class, taking drawing trips to Oakland and to the Strip District, where his brother ran a fruit and vegetable truck. He produced an excellent collection of sketches, won the forty-dollar Leisser Prize for freshman artwork, and had his first one-man show in the school's fine arts gallery.

At Carnegie Tech, Warhola saw drawings and posters by Toulouse-Lautrec, as well as a major exhibit of magazine art, and learned about the similarities between commercial and fine art. He saw Ben Shawn's drawings and developed his own broken-line technique. At the end of his sophomore year, he chose to focus on pictorial design, a path that led him to commercial art.

His creativity was evident. He worked in the display department of Joseph Horne's department store in downtown Pittsburgh, where he impressed his manager with his creative window displays. He won a twenty-dollar prize on the 1948 "Carnegie Day," celebrating Carnegie's birthday, for his colorful rainbow painting of the glass at Phipps Conservatory, based on the perception that the glass was made up of reused plate-glass photographic negatives. In his senior year, he was the art editor of *Cano,* the school's monthly publication of creative writing, a foretaste of his later work in magazine design.

By the time he left Carnegie Tech and Pittsburgh, Andy Warhola was primed to succeed as a commercial artist in New York's marketplace, dropping the "a" from his last name to become "Andy Warhol." Like Carnegie in his early years, he was a workaholic, and he produced an astonishing amount of art, working at night and on holidays, when most people relaxed. Also like Carnegie, religion was a deep and constant, though largely hidden, current in his life. While Carnegie's Presbyterian Scottish roots never made him a practicing churchgoer, he nevertheless adhered to the Scotch-Presbyterian tradition of doing good works, often in secret, and rewarded with "Hero medals" those who made personal sacrifices to help others. Warhol kept his Byzantine rite Catholicism largely out of sight while living in New York, but he went to mass weekly and in the 1980s volunteered to help the homeless by distributing food. His religious feelings had been inculcated largely by his mother, Julia, who adhered to Old World religious traditions and took her three sons to Saint John Chrysostom Stanislaus Church in the "little Russia" section of South Oakland several times a week. It was here that young Andy first saw on the church iconostasis screen the stylized figures of saints and martyrs that would later influence his portraits of icons of popular culture (Marilyn Monroe, Jackie Kennedy), which have a similar religious intensity.

Too clever by far to publicize in New York his déclassé roots in Pittsburgh, Warhol privately stayed in touch with his brothers in Pittsburgh for thirty-eight years, while publicly declaring himself a rootless working-class everyman artist: "I prefer to remain a mystery, I never like to give my background and anyway, I make it all up different every time I'm asked."[4] Ironically, Warhol's life during the Depression had been so circumscribed that he never ventured beyond a few miles from his house: he was much more a native Pittsburgher than Andrew Carnegie. Since he disowned Pittsburgh in public during his life, Pittsburgh did not honor him as a native son—a problem with which future directors of the Andy Warhol Museum would have to contend. In New York, he worked in many media, coming to symbolize the edgy, provocative style of the 1960s and 1970s. The center of a group of admirers and hangers-on who experimented with sex, drugs, and art world celebrity, Warhol himself was a brilliant documentary observer of the excesses of this social era, a passive voyager rather than a full participant.

Decades after his death, it is necessary to recall what a polarizing fig-

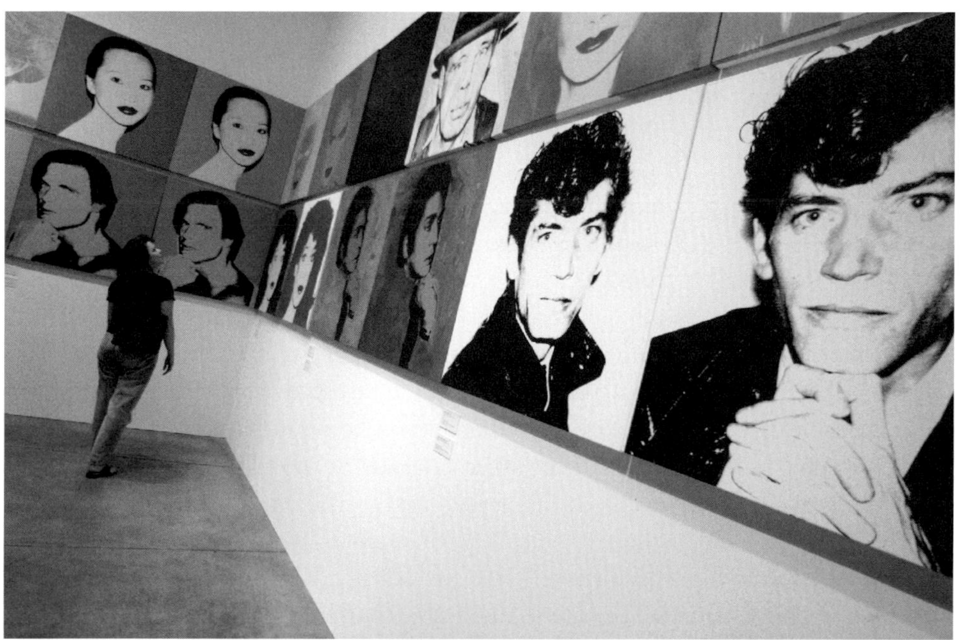

A museum visitor looks up at Warhol's celebrity portraits in the Entrance Gallery.

ure he was in the art world. Some artists and critics disdained Pop Art and thought Warhol a fraud and an opportunist; others considered his cool omnipresence and playful indifference in the midst of the turbulent New York scene the height of sophistication. Nat Finkelstein, in his cynical memoir of the Factory years, writes, "Andy Warhol's greatest work of art was Andy Warhol." "Andy's strategy," Finkelstein notes, "was organized like an air-raid through radar-protected territory. He would drop these showers of silver foil out of the plane to deflect the radar. Behind this screen of smoke and mirrors, there was Andy at work. That was the real function of the entourage. It was a way to get attention away from Andy, while he hid behind them, doing his number. The entourage was there to distract the attention, to titillate and amuse the public, while Andy was doing his very serious work."[5] Admirers like the philosophic critic Arthur C. Danto said that Warhol had "an artistic corpus which consisted of comic-strip heads, soup cans, Brillo cartons, and like images from what cultural critics were disposed to take as typifying the mindless, tasteless, thoughtless inanities of American popular culture, too sunk in banality to rise even to the level of Kitsch."[6] But Danto argues that Warhol thus creatively approached the very boundaries of art, making movies, for example, in which nothing moved, or urinating on a canvas to produce "oxidation paintings." In 1967, Warhol famously said, "If you want to know all about Andy Warhol, just look at the surface."[7] Danto adds, "But there is more to it than that. He turned the world we share into art, and turned himself into part of that world, and because we ourselves are the images we hold in common with everyone else he became part of us. So he might have said, if you want to know who Andy Warhol is, look within. Or for that matter, look without. You, I, the world, we are all of a piece."[8]

A personal turning point came for Warhol in 1967, when he was shot by a demented woman named Valerie Solanis. Warhol was declared clinically dead but miraculously survived. Afterward, he avoided hospitals, declaring fatalistically that if he ever entered one again he would not emerge alive. This proved prophetic: in 1987, after a decade of medical problems, his admission to New York Hospital for seemingly routine gallbladder surgery turned fatal, and he died unexpectedly of complications. The rich and famous flocked to his funeral in New York. His burial beside his parents in a suburban Pittsburgh cemetery saw a much smaller group in attendance, including his old art teacher, Joseph Fitzpatrick.

CREATING THE
ANDY WARHOL MUSEUM

After Warhol's death, books about him flourished, from biographies and art criticism to tell-all memoirs by Factory survivors and superstars. In spite of all the controversy surrounding his life and work, twenty years after his death he was acknowledged as a great artist who had died midcareer and been enshrined as an American original whose common subjects had universal appeal. The prices of his art soared, a familiar pattern in the art market. This increasing worldwide fame was probably due in no small part to the Andy Warhol Museum, whose traveling international shows reached large audiences, cultivating new admirers and new, wealthy collectors. The Andy Warhol Museum thus, arguably, brought order to the chaos of Warhol's artistic legacy. But how did this Pittsburgh museum—in simultaneously the most logical and the most unlikely of locations—come to pass? A single-artist museum is difficult to create under any circumstances, in the United States or anywhere, and the unique set of circumstances that led to the Andy Warhol Museum was particularly unlikely. Warhol's untimely death, however, had triggered an unlikely combination of forces, the resulting museum "the product of a triple entente of divergent interests that had to learn how to cooperate with each other," according to the historian Avis Berman.[8] These converging forces were the legacy of the artist's multimillion-dollar estate, in the control of the Dia Foundation and the newly formed Andy Warhol Foundation; the nascent notion of a permanent gallery for Warhol's art in New York; and the Carnegie Institute's suddenly aggressive pursuit, under Robert Wilburn, of a large collection of Warhol's work.

In New York, the Dia Foundation (from the Greek word for "through") had been Warhol's greatest patron. One of its founders, the art dealer Heiner Friedrich, had long been fascinated by Warhol's art and had discussed with Warhol the idea of opening a small museum dedicated to his work, even mentioning Pittsburgh. This drew a typically elliptical response from Warhol: "'Why Pittsburgh ... why not New York?' ... He was not really so interested to have a museum in Pittsburgh, I think, because of his memories, and because New York was the place where all his fame unfolded, but he was very precisely allowing everything to happen."[9] Dia honored its connection to Warhol even after its own financial fortunes began failing in 1984, when it stopped purchasing art and making grants to artists, mounting three Warhol-designed exhibitions of his work in SoHo. In 1985, Dia was overhauled, Friedrich resigned, and the smaller organization focused mainly on lending and exhibiting works of art.

Still, when Warhol died, Dia owned nearly two hundred of his works. One of the foundation's first efforts, under its executive director Charles Wright, was to find a proper home for the Warhol oeuvre. Wright first approached the large New York museums that already had Warhol works in their collections—the Metropolitan, the Museum of Modern Art, the Whitney Museum, the Brooklyn Museum—but none wanted a large, permanent display. Rebuffed, Dia began to look elsewhere.[10] At the same time, another foundation had developed quickly after Warhol's death: the Andy Warhol Foundation for the Visual Arts, its general purpose, stipulated in Warhol's will, to promote the visual arts. Directing this foundation were Warhol's brother John Warhola; the chief administrator of the Warhol Studio, Vincent Fremont; and the executor of Warhol's estate, his friend and business manager Fred Hughes, who became the chief executive officer of the Warhol Foundation.

Meanwhile, back in Pittsburgh, James A. Fisher, the chair of the Development Committee of Carnegie Institute, began actively to pursue a possible collaboration between Carnegie Institute in Pittsburgh and the New York foundations. A friendship developed between Hughes and Fisher, and soon Hughes, along with Charles Wright of the Dia Foundation, began to consider a collaboration that would allow much of Warhol's art to be housed in one location. John R. Lane, former director of Carnegie Museum of Art, advised the Dia Foundation to contact Carnegie's Robert Wilburn,

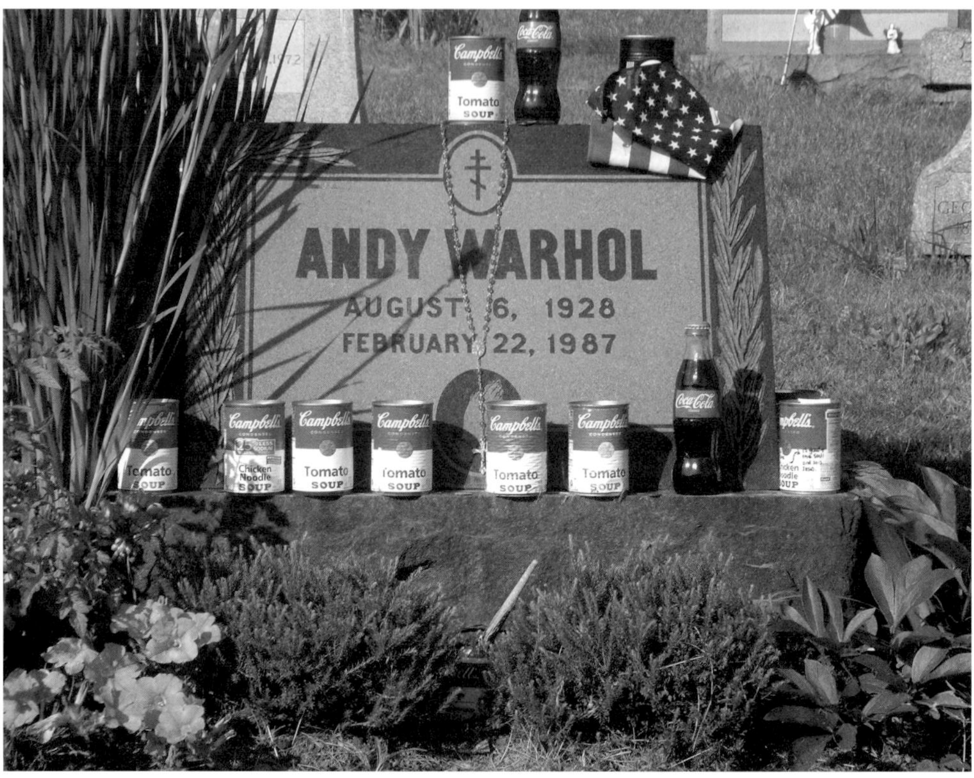

Andy Warhol's grave in St. John the Baptist Byzantine Catholic Cemetery in Bethel Park, a Pittsburgh suburb. Visitors constantly leave gifts at the site, and Carnegie Museum of Art educator Madelyn Roehrig began to date and photograph them. This photo is "Figments: Conversations with Andy, 062509."

who was immediately interested. "The first time I heard about it, I felt it was something we had to get for Pittsburgh," said Wilburn. "We had very few paintings by Andy Warhol in our collection, and we saw that as being a great gap, particularly since he was from Pittsburgh.... It was very important to get the paintings to Pittsburgh. We had to make it happen."[11] Convinced that the collection had to come to Pittsburgh, if not specifically to Carnegie, Wilburn assembled a meeting with Hughes and a large group of city officials, Carnegie Institute decision makers, and representatives from the Heinz and Hillman foundations. It soon became apparent that Carnegie Institute was the key to providing organizational stability for housing the new collection, and Carnegie Museum of Art's long commitment to contemporary art was a perfect philosophical fit. Importantly, the Andy Warhol Foundation's Fred Hughes was willing to match the Dia's contributions and go even further, filling out the artist's ouevre with materials including photographs, paintings, prints, drawings, films, videotapes, and archival records. The museum would reflect both Andy Warhol and his era.

The Dia Foundation's Charles Wright felt strongly that the Warhol collection belonged in a building with the same industrial feel that Warhol himself had designed for his exhibits, and the discussion soon shifted to real estate opportunities. Pittsburgh was full of old warehouses, and the Carnegie favored adapting an older building rather than erecting a new one. The chief financial officer of Carnegie Institute, Andrew Hungerman, spent a great deal of time reviewing possible locations: the old Buhl Science Center on the North Side (too ornate), the empty Duquesne Brewery (a money pit), and a former jail and furniture store on the South Side. Hungerman went to New York to see the Dia's Soho gallery, and with this model in mind, he focused more clearly on replicating its ambience in a Pittsburgh building. Finally, on August 24, 1988, he took a key group of decision makers to a building he knew was a good match—the 1911 Volkwein Music and Instruments Company building at 117 Sandusky Street, just across the Seventh Street Bridge, on Pittsburgh's North Side.

In the joint venture agreement of September 29, 1989, the Andy Warhol Museum was legally established as an entity in which each of the three participating organizations had legal rights and responsibilities. The Dia decided that the art would come to the museum as gifts, not loans, and the result would be a comprehensive collection detailing Warhol's life as an artist. The Dia promised to donate 79 works, the Warhol Foundation 650, while even more materials were promised as they were itemized and archives assembled. The Carnegie would buy the Volkwein building and have it renovated by the architect Richard Gluckman, who had been associated with Dia projects since 1977. The Carnegie also guaranteed professional treatment of the works and provided the financial system for running the institution. At this point, Senator John Heinz III, a charismatic and wealthy Republican from Pennsylvania, lent his energies to the project, not only because it was potential economic boon for Pittsburgh but also because it righted a historic situation in which so much art collected by Pittsburghers had left the city.

Meanwhile, the Andy Warhol Foundation, formed out of necessity after Warhol's unexpected death, began to undergo significant change. None of its directors was experienced in running a nonprofit organization, and Hughes, who had multiple sclerosis, had begun to deteriorate physically. Hughes thus enlisted the help of the consultant Archibald Gillies, who had experience in nonprofit management. Gillies eventually became the president of the foundation, but he and Hughes began to disagree over its promised future gifts, Gillies unconvinced that so much art should be given to the new Pittsburgh museum.

Back in Pittsburgh, too, difficulties surfaced. A year and a half elapsed before the sale of the building became final, with a price tag of $20 million ($15 million for the purchase and $5 million for an endowment). The collection to be housed, meanwhile, had grown to eight hundred works of art, plus archival materials. In the meantime, Richard Gluckman's designs for the recently acquired Volkwein building had produced the understated industrial appearance that Hughes admired, the art to be the museum's prominent feature, not the building itself. But unlike a new industrial-style building built to museum specifications, the rehabilitated Volkwein building needed the full set of museum requirements: storage areas, offices, a theater, a bookstore, a coffee shop, sophisticated security, climate control systems, skylights, an elevator, staircases—all improvements that raised the initial costs projection of $25 per square foot to $110.

In the meantime, Carnegie Museum of Art had hired a new curator of contemporary art, Mark Francis, on October 1, 1989. He would succeed John Caldwell as the curator of the next Carnegie International, in 1991, and he would also act as the first director of the Warhol Museum. The squabbling between the Carnegie and the Warhol Foundation over which paintings were to be contributed continued into the 1990s under Francis's watch, even as he assembled the 1994 Carnegie International art exhibition. Simultaneously, Carnegie Museum of Art director Phillip Johnston faced the reality of a deepening recession: no patrons came forward to give millions to realize the Warhol project, and Wilburn continued to struggle to get public money. At a crucial moment, Senator John Heinz pledged $5 million to support the project from his two family foundations, but he died tragically and unexpectedly in a plane crash on April 4, 1991, and Wilburn was forced to resume his campaign to raise public money from the same legislators he had tried to convince before. Eventually coming up with a plan for an appropriation from the state operating budget for three successive years, rather than a capital gift, Wilburn finally succeeded and thus avoided cancellation of the project. When Senator Heinz's widow, Teresa Heinz, honored his intentions by pledging $7 million to the project, the Warhol Foundation finally decided to give half the number of paintings proposed, along with some other works. This still left $15 million to be raised from other sources, before construction could begin. The unrelenting Wilburn eventually obtained $6 million from the state of Pennsylvania, to the amazement of other art museum directors around the country, bringing the total to $13 million. The remaining $2 million was secured from local foundations and business, including the Hillman Foundation and Alcoa. The project had by this point become so large, and

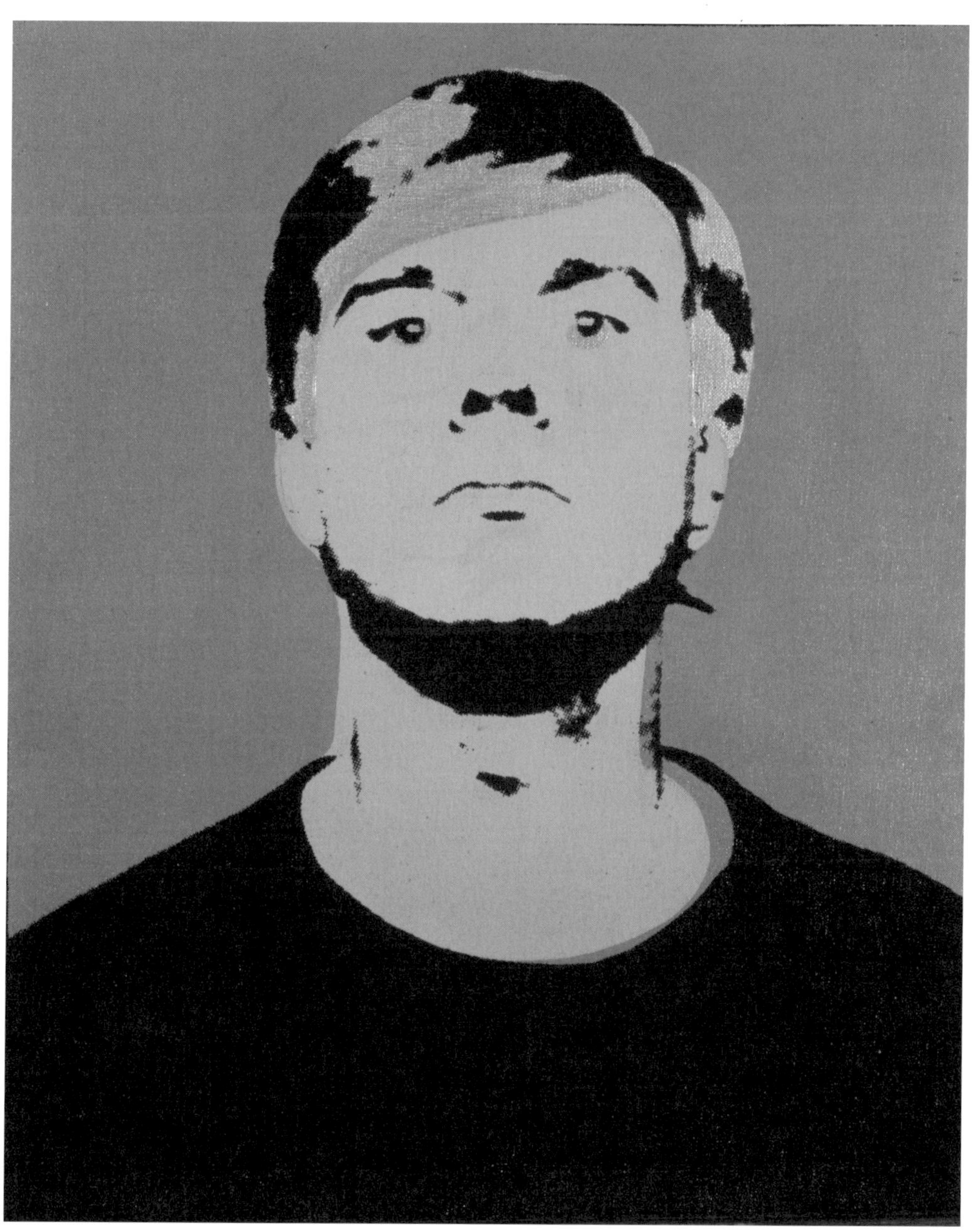

This Warhol self-portrait was used on banners to brand the Seventh Street Bridge when it was renamed the Andy Warhol Bridge in 2005.

required such staffing and support, that the endowment needed to operate the museum had to be increased to $35 million, an additional $20 million beyond what had been raised.

Any potential conflict between New York and Pittsburgh was resolved by the Warhol Foundation's Archibald Gillies, who said the Andy Warhol Foundation should be in the business of giving grants to young artists, while the museum should be in the business of promoting Warhol's art and legacy. The foundation and the museum also agreed that while the art would come to Pittsburgh for exhibition and care, the licensing rights to reproduce anything Warhol had made (except film and video) would remain with the foundation. Thus, the foundation also became the watchdog for policing the world for Andy Warhol imitations—a challenge it was better equipped take on than was the museum. This licensing decision produced an interesting symbiosis in which the Andy Warhol Museum effectively raised the international profile of Warhol to even higher levels with successful traveling exhibitions, while the Andy Warhol Foundation maintained the rights to reproduce works of art under his name. This is not the usual way art museums control and use the reproduction rights to art in their collections, usually collecting the fees generated by licensing others' use of images. But Andy Warhol's commercial value was different from that of most other modern artists, and his broad involvement in pop culture invited a range of reuse that was extremely lucrative.

RUNNING THE
ANDY WARHOL MUSEUM

Thus, British art curator Mark Francis became the first director of the Andy Warhol Museum, which held some 900 paintings and 1,500 drawings, prints of all Warhol's films, almost all of his published prints on paper and in books, and many hundreds of photographs and Polaroid images. The museum, which opened to local and national acclaim on May 14, 1994, displayed this cornucopia by using vitrines on the different gallery floors to show Warhol's progress over different decades, along with a wall displaying *Interview* magazine covers, a space for screening his films, and a study center where archivists helped researchers and meticulously opened the mysterious sealed boxes (the "Time Capsules") in which Warhol had methodically deposited his ephemera throughout the years.

Initially, the museum showcased the permanent displays and had a modest changing exhibition schedule, but it soon became obvious that a more dynamic changing exhibition schedule and a more determined outreach program were necessary if the museum was to stay popular over the

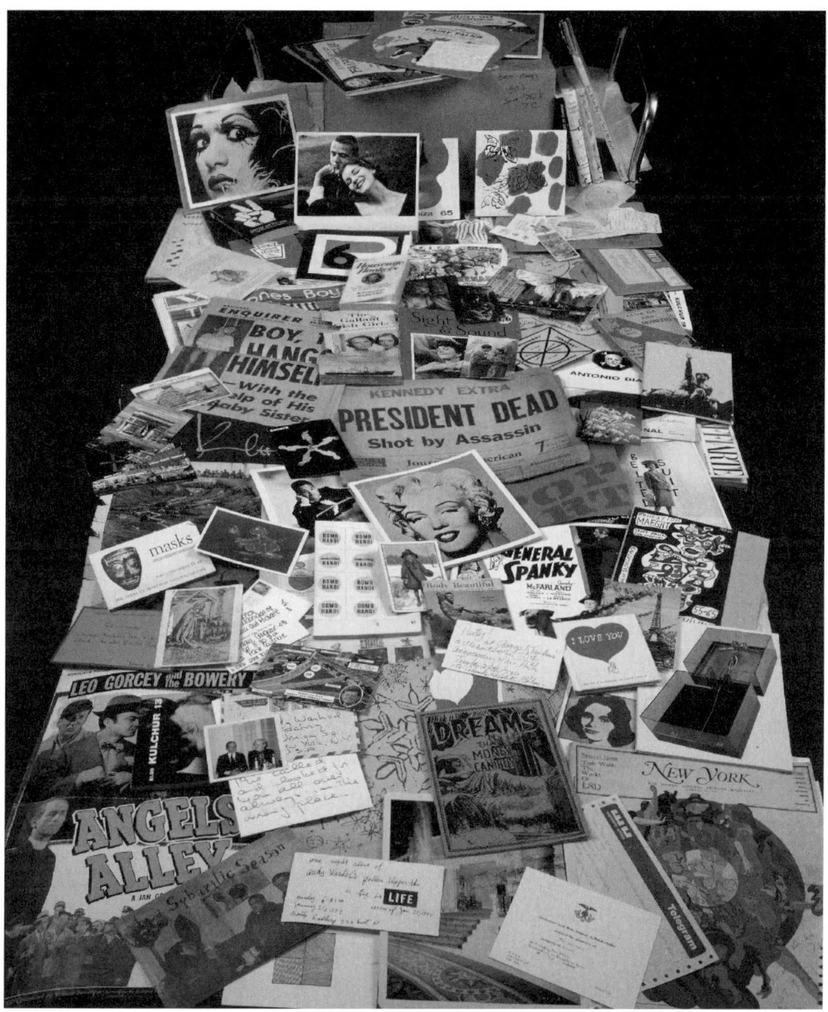

A typical Warhol Time Capsule and its contents.

long run. It needed creative educational programs, more engagement with the city's cultural life, and exhibits that would challenge the public with their emphasis on Warhol's own provocative, counterculture spirit. It also had to be a fully independent stand-alone museum, with a separate board, its own aspirations, and an international agenda. Otherwise, it would become nothing more than a mausoleum to a twentieth-century artist. All of this implied a level of fund-raising and international support beyond that for which Mark Francis had been hired.

The April 1993 appointment of Thomas Armstrong III seemed the ideal solution to the museum's challenges: Armstrong had directed the

Whitney Museum of American Art from 1974 to 1990 and was known for his diplomatic flair and his fund-raising abilities. Too, Armstrong had known Warhol and been an early advocate of his art. Now, asked about moving to Pittsburgh, he said:

Well, when I was being interviewed for the job, I was fascinated that one of the people who had given the museum a great deal of money—and who was a leading member of the community—was a very conservative person. I said, "Do you know anything about Andy Warhol?" thinking that if he'd found out certain details of Andy's life, he would be somewhat taken aback. And he said, "I know about Andy Warhol, but the museum is good for Pittsburgh." I think that's a wonderful civic spirit. In New York there are so many museums that they're taken for granted. In Pittsburgh individual institutions are important, and they're really perceived to have an impact on the city.[12]

The financial challenge the museum faced was immediate, and Armstrong quickly made a fund-raising trip to Europe with a Warhol trustee to see whether he could interest wealthy European patrons in supporting the new museum. This expedition, however, failed, and Armstrong was also clearly reluctant to work closely with Museum of Art director Phillip Johnston and his board, preferring instead to cultivate a few wealthy patrons on his own. After his first efforts for large gifts failed, Armstrong, after less than two years, decided to return to New York. Clearly, major patronage support for the Warhol would have to come from Pittsburgh. Clearly, too, the Warhol would have to market itself aggressively beyond Pittsburgh if it were to survive.

The national search for the third director of the Andy Warhol Museum led to the appointment of Thomas Sokolowski in May 1996. A lively, articulate art historian, Sokolowski, over the next decade in Pittsburgh, led the museum toward its goal of being both a unique international institution and an asset to the city. He saw Warhol as part of a great tradition and as a native son Pittsburghers could admire: "What Warhol did in his time, in his context, was not so different, formally, from the way Leonardo created memorable portraits in the Renaissance using tempera and oil glazes. People have gotten the misconception that because Warhol was an excellent self-publicist he was not really a serious artist. He was a serious artist and very aware of—increasingly aware of—the artist's role in the art world, especially when he made references to an image, like that of Marilyn Monroe. He knew what Leonardo had done, and wanted other people to be savvy enough about art to see his own references to it."[13] Sokolowski saw Warhol's Factory and his entourage as rooted firmly the tradition of great artists' workshops, where many assistants were central to a successful enterprise. Sokolowski

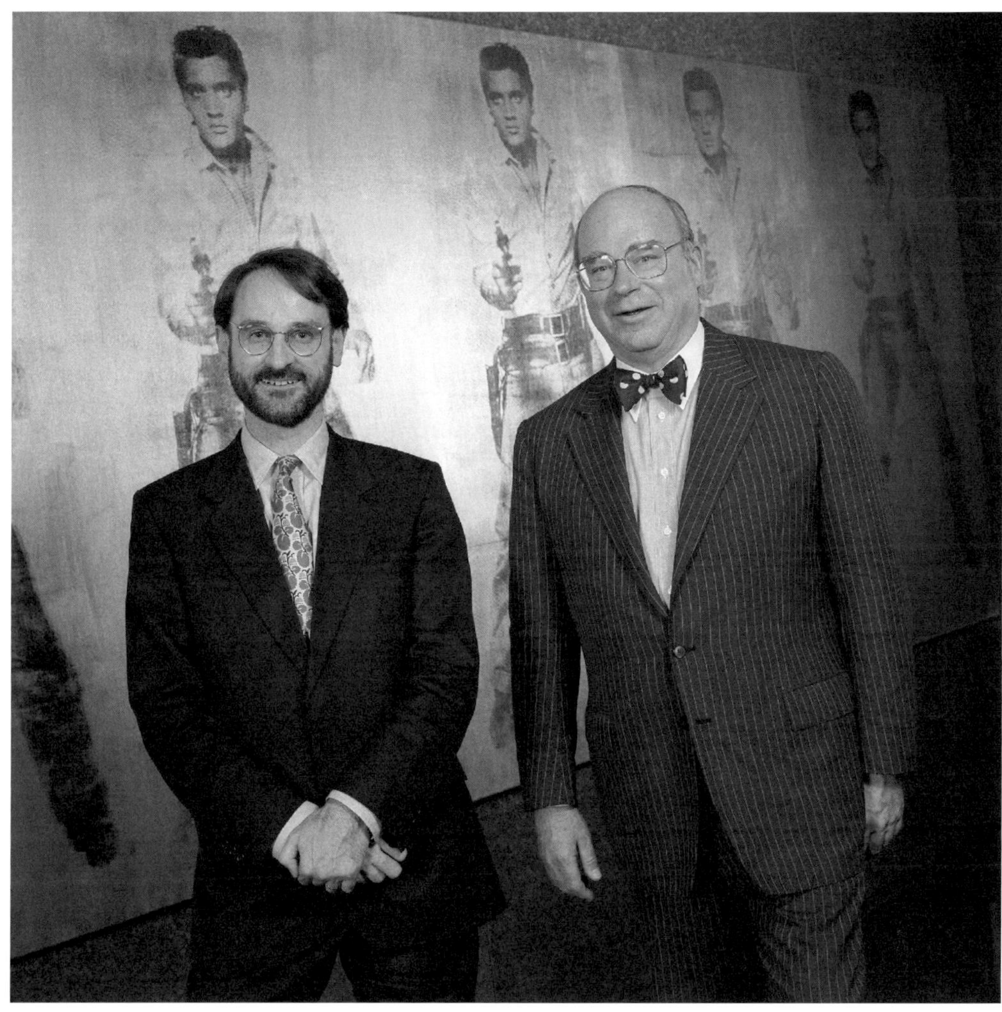

First director Mark Francis and second director Thomas Armstrong III, when the museum opened in 1993.

also downplayed the gap between the artist's origins and his public indifference to Pittsburgh, which many Pittsburghers resented.

While Mark Francis had been both director and chief curator, an assistant curator, Margery King, was hired in 1994. One of the museum's first tasks was to mount an international exhibition to be held in Brazil, through the U.S. Information Agency. Tailoring such traveling exhibitions for other countries soon became one of Sokolowski's most successful strategies, and the Warhol brand of art gained new admirers worldwide. In Pittsburgh, the display of the permanent collection changed several times a year to give

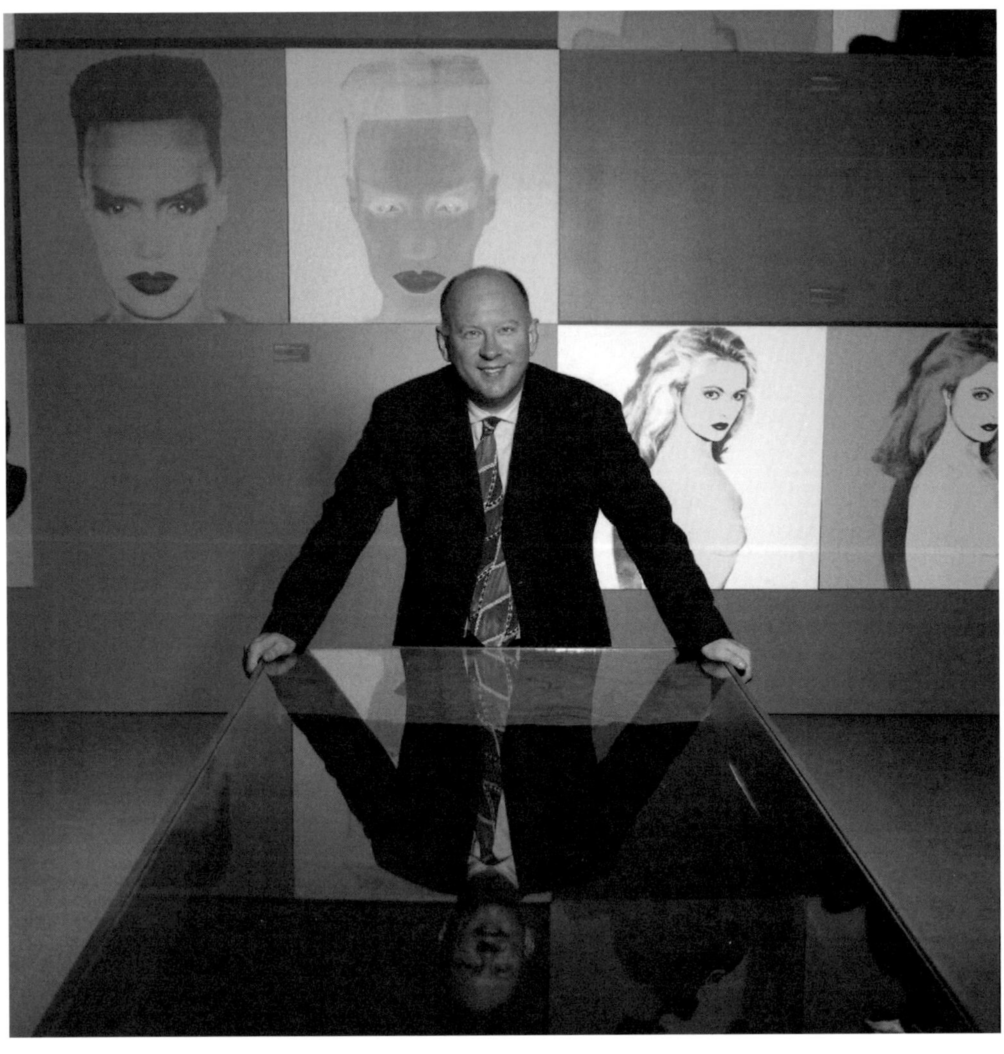

Tom Sokolowski brought new energy to the museum and gave it an expansive and counterculture mission that made it unique.

the public constantly fresh experiences and to rotate works on paper back into storage before they were affected by exposure to light. Public relations became a high priority for Sokolowski, and he quickly tapped into a youth-minded counterculture Pittsburgh audience, an audience whose members were typically left out of the educational programs at Carnegie Science Center, Carnegie Museum of Art, and Carnegie Museum of Natural History. Sokolowski held that "if you are going to ask people to make a donation, whether it's $50 or $50,000, there has to be something that they think is worthwhile. Any institution, whether it's the Carnegie or a hospital, or a

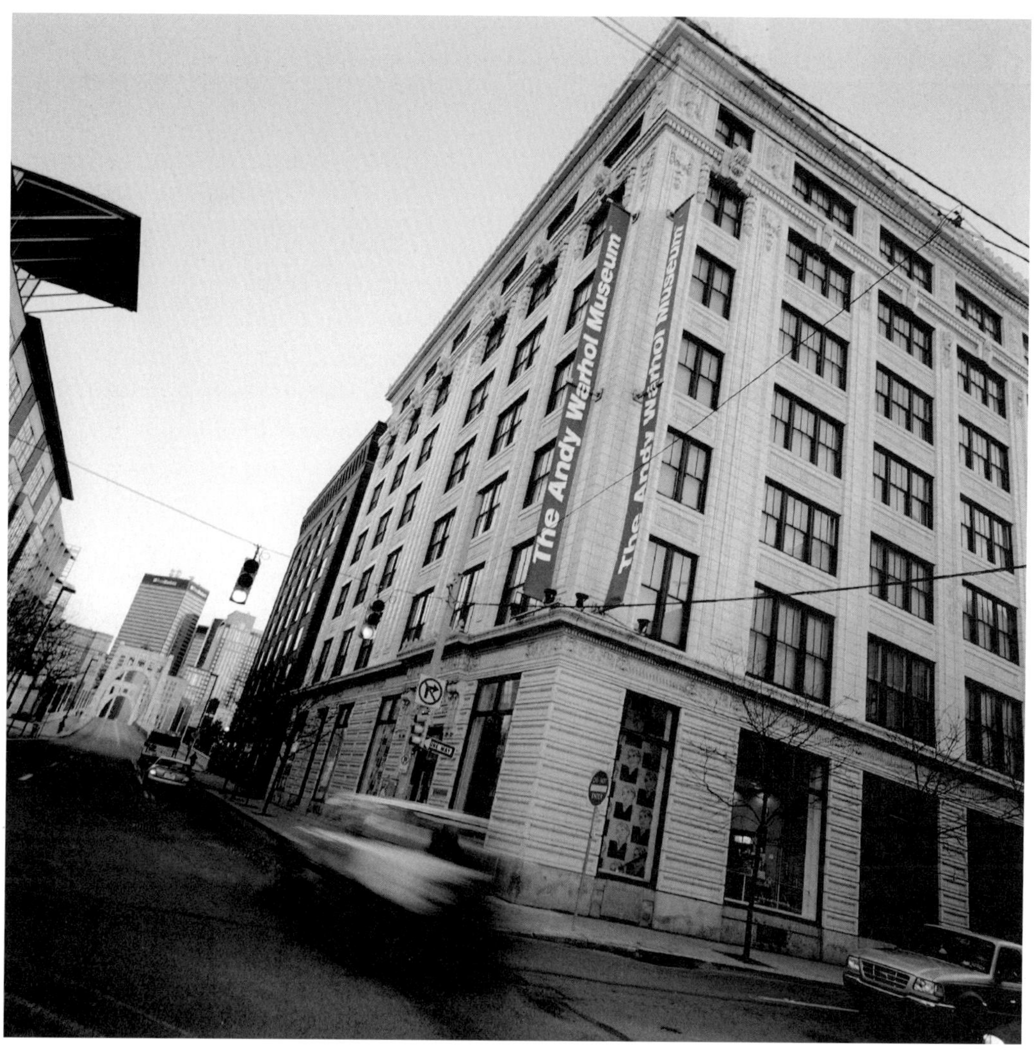

The exterior of the Andy Warhol Museum is seen here from street level.

university, or a methadone clinic, has to be seen to be serving some part of the populace to deserve support."[14]

As time passed, the success of Sokolowski's strategies became ever clearer. Audience surveys revealed that the Warhol drew its first-time visitors—some 80 percent of the total, according to Sokolowski—from an international pool, as well as from western Pennsylvania. The Andy Warhol Museum had become a first-day destination for tourists to Pittsburgh.

The museum's ambition was made clear in 1996 with the exhibit Andy Warhol 1856–1986, Mirror of Time, a show that opened in Tokyo. An even greater success a few years later was Andy Warhol: A Retrospective, which traveled to thirteen cities in twelve Eastern European countries, including Russia, Hungary, and states formerly within the Soviet eastern bloc, such as Slovakia and Lithuania, as well as Greece. The U.S. Bureau of Educational and Cultural Affairs promoted the show as a display of American cultural influence, capitalizing on the gradual breaking up of the Soviet political empire that had begun a decade earlier. The show had great appeal to Eastern Europeans because of Warhol's family roots in the Carpathian Mountains. One artist viewing the exhibition observed: "In Soviet times, we were told that Western art was useless, meaningless.... This exhibit has given me a whole new perspective, not just on Warhol but on Western art."[15]

Like the Museum of Art in its early years, the Andy Warhol Museum has also had a limited staff. Associate curator Margery King left in 2003 during the downsizing of staff throughout Carnegie Museums of Pittsburgh, and Tom Sokolowski filled in as curator, as well as serving as director. Conservator John W. Smith managed the Archives Study Center, a central service of the museum. Smith also served as the museum's interim director between Tom Armstrong's departure and the arrival of Tom Sokolowski in 1996. In Smith's dozen years in Pittsburgh, the Warhol archives emerged as a national resource. He was followed by his assistant conservator Matt Wribican, who had long done the critical work of making the facility available to researchers. The conservation of the artwork was demanding, and conservators traveled with the art to oversee installation and maintenance. Security at the Andy Warhol Museum was also state-of-the-art, considering the value of the works housed there. One guard recalled an odd incident at the Security Office when movement was electronically detected in the hallways and stairwell that led to the higher floors. The guard who was dispatched to the site discovered that one of the *Silver Clouds* (metalized polyester film filled with helium) had escaped from the room where air currents kept it floating in the air and was now traveling down the stairwell.[16]

Geralyn Huxley moved from the Film Section of Carnegie Museum of Art to become the Warhol's assistant curator of Film and Video, the collection including 237 films and almost 4,000 videotapes. Jessica Gogan, in charge of "Education and Interpretation," developed a great array of partnerships and programs in concert with Pittsburgh groups, as well as national organizations: community programs; school programs; weekend Factory programs allowing visitors to experiment with Warhol's techniques; teacher lesson plans; online resources; a list of Carpatho-Rusyn events; and connections to gay, lesbian, bisexual, and transgender groups. The exhibition's educational component also engaged its audience with controversial topics, such as "Andy Warhol's Electric Chairs: Reflecting on Capital Punishment in America."

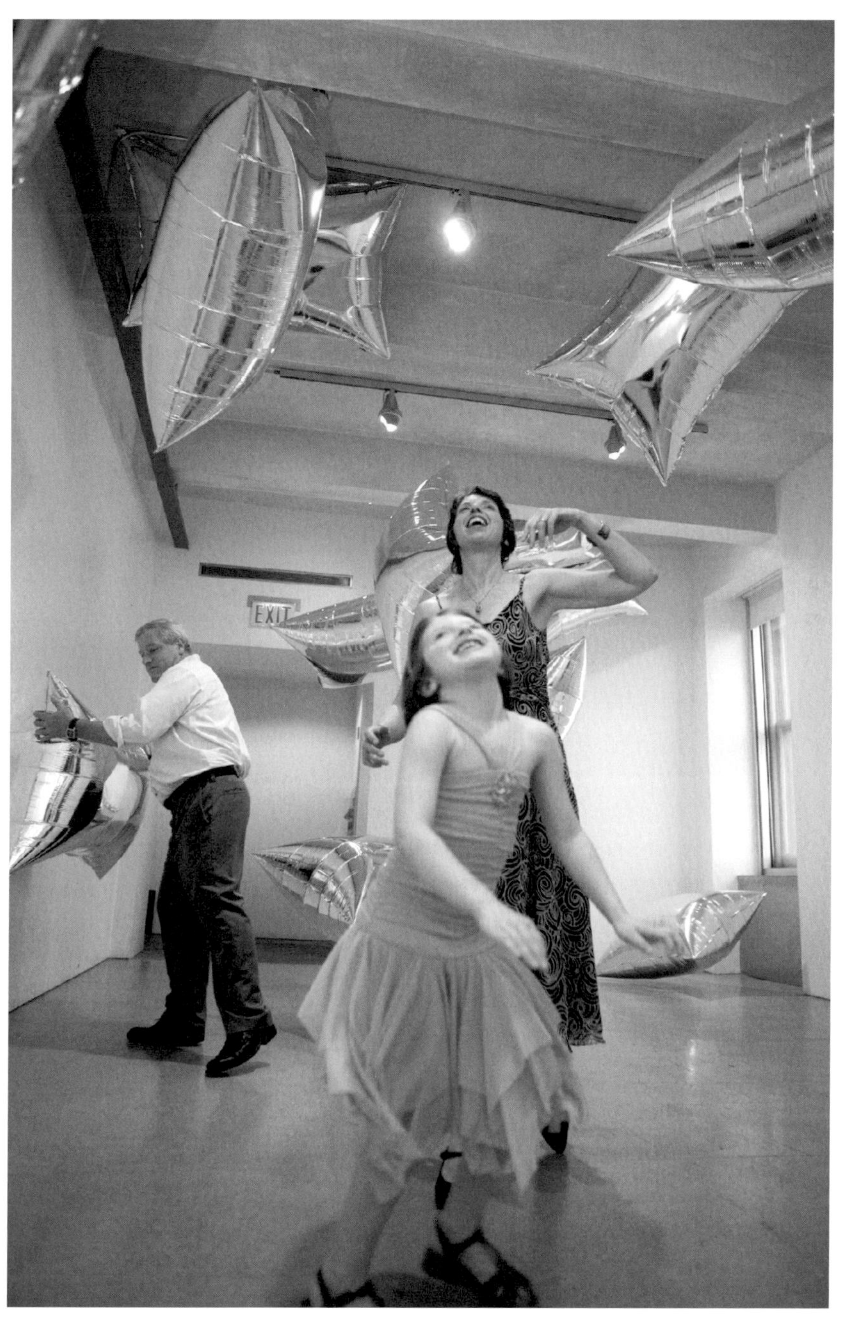

Visitors interact with the Silver Clouds *installation.*

When the search for a new president of Carnegie Institute was launched in 2005, the candidates overwhelmingly felt that the Andy Warhol Museum had the most potential of any of the four Carnegie museums of Pittsburgh. It was truly one of a kind, whereas other cities also had (often much larger) art and natural history museums and science centers. Warhol board member Jim Wilkinson pointed out, "To see a great collection of Andy Warhol's art there is only one place in the world—on Pittsburgh's North side. The Warhol draws more international visitors than all the other museums combined."[17] Thus, the Warhol avoided becoming merely a mausoleum for a dead artist, evolving instead into dynamic center for the arts. It has followed Warhol's example in being multidisciplinary, involved in film, television, commercial art, and socially provocative. As the museum's deputy director maintained, "It is the only adequate and responsible way to present what he stood for."[18]

Sokolowski stepped down at the end of 2010, saying that after fourteen years, it was time. Eric C. Shiner, a native of the western Pennsylvania area, became the Milton Fine Curator of Art and served as acting director while the museum began a national search for the next director to carry the museum into the future.

1 0

IN SUMMARY

Andrew Carnegie's palace of culture has impacted generations of people in Pittsburgh and the United States, and internationally. After such a rich, complex story has been told, a brief summary is in order to bring out its key points. First, Andrew Carnegie's steadfast interest in building a library system and a cultural center for the working class in the smoky, blighted industrial city where he had made his fortune lasted for decades, from the 1880s until his death in 1919. Pittsburgh's Carnegie Institute and Library was his first great experiment in large-scale philanthropy and certainly gave him lessons that he would use in later benefactions, which ultimately led to the creation of the Carnegie Corporation in 1911, at that time the world's largest philanthropic organization.

Second, Carnegie Library of Pittsburgh became a model for urban and small-town library systems that was copied throughout the United States and in other countries of the English-speaking world. Through the work of Pittsburgh's library directors, several of them leaders in the American Library Association, this experiment in free public libraries spread throughout the world. Back at home, Carnegie Library remains a powerful force for public education, and Pittsburgh itself is acknowledged as one of the more literate cities in the nation. Pittsburgh's library early established an urban children's library and instituted the first program to train children's librarians. It "Americanized" immigrant families by teaching them English and helping with citizenship tests. During two world wars, it supplied the home front with practical literature about industry and science and was a leader in developing useful libraries for soldiers and sailors overseas. During the Great Depression and other hard economic times, it was a refuge of culture and civilized behavior for people whose daily lives were filled with hardship. Its creative approach to service formed the basis for the Library for the Blind and Physically Handicapped and for lending libraries in department stores, schools, homes, and bookmobiles that served neighborhoods and suburbs.

Successive library administrations were paradoxically blessed and

287

cursed by being housed in the splendid 1895 building, and a century passed before the public and politicians outgrew the myth that Carnegie had personally endowed it in perpetuity. Generations of civic leaders mistakenly believed that tax support and other financial aid were not needed. In 1993, with the implementation of the Allegheny County Regional Asset tax, the library instantly became the largest recipient of county tax support and finally achieved a kind of financial stability that tied it to the fluctuating revenues of Allegheny County. This public support is appropriate and long overdue: a 2006 economic impact study of the library's importance revealed that 70 percent of city residents between the ages of thirteen and thirty-six held Carnegie Library of Pittsburgh cards, as did one-fifth of the residents of Allegheny County. Carnegie Library was by far the most heavily used cultural asset in the region, bringing obvious economic benefits.

Notable too is the fact that the Institute as a whole has nurtured and administered a broad swath of cultural services, including at the start the now world-famous Carnegie Mellon University, whose governing board was a subdivision of the board of Carnegie Institute until 1959. With such an amalgam of interests—music, natural history, art, education—the Institute in Oakland was the unchallenged center of all things cultural in Pittsburgh and western Pennsylvania, and along with the library it stimulated Oakland's growth into an outstanding university town and the third-busiest population center in the state of Pennsylvania.

It is also important to acknowledge the impact of the conservative strain of the Scotch-Irish Presbyterians who founded the Institute and have long supported its growth. While this conservatism might have prevented the Museum of Art from buying controversial works, it also helped the Natural History Museum work with the Western Pennsylvania Conservancy to establish a strong basis in land conservation. Further, the expectation of doing good work quietly for the masses, without personal self-congratulation or praise, has characterized generations of Institute board members and benefactors. Pittsburgh's great families—the Mellons, the Heinzes, the Hillmans—generously led the way in this respect, and many other patrons followed. Thanks to their support, the Museum of Art built the large Sarah Scaife Gallery in 1974, while the Natural History Museum developed a two-thousand-acre research station. The Institute helped support the privately funded state-of-the-art Carnegie Science Center (1991), which brought science education into the modern era and emphasized Pittsburgh's research and economic strengths. The Andy Warhol Museum (1994), initially sponsored by Carnegie Museum of Art, developed an independent life as a museum. It celebrates the counterculture and exhibits Warhol's art globally and has become a first-day destination for tourists in Pittsburgh.

Carnegie Museum of Art, with the Carnegie International, established a strong presence in the international art world, despite the disruptions of two world wars and the Great Depression and the frustrations of various directors. And true to Carnegie's vision for literacy in the visual arts, it has maintained an educational program that has trained hundreds of thousands of schoolchildren, including Philip Pearlstein and Andy Warhol.

Carnegie Museum of Natural History also extended its reach over time, diversifying into many areas of scientific research even as it became the "Home of the Dinosaurs." It made world news early in the twentieth century by duplicating in plaster the sensational large dinosaur fossil *Diplodocus carnegii* for the British Museum, and it also sent replicas to other museums in international capitals. Carnegie relished seeing his upstart Pittsburgh museum occupy the international stage. Eventually, from being a Victorian catch-all for the antiquarian interests of Pittsburgh industrialists, it evolved into a natural science research institution that explores frontiers from birds and mammals to insects, botany, and geology, highly regarded for the scientific work of many of its energetic curators. Regionally, it has long been a force for the conservation movement and has taken the lead in important local projects like developing the site of old Fort Pitt into modern Point State Park. As its mission continues to change, it consistently demonstrates enlightened museum stewardship in sharing and deaccessioning many of its local history artifacts, so that other institutions, such as the Senator John Heinz History Center, can highlight them to greater public advantage.

This, then, is an American success story of some power, showing how a grim industrial center in mid-America became, through the generosity of a great patron, a cultural center of national importance, in the course of a century transforming the city itself into a great place to live. Other philanthropists followed Andrew Carnegie's lead, as he hoped they would, and scores of dedicated managers steered the institutions Carnegie founded through the tumultuous twentieth century and into the twenty-first.

This was always a symbolic story, a story about a mission and a struggle for success in America, just as Carnegie's own life had been.

APPENDIX

Interview Subjects

Unless publication details are noted, these may be found in the William Oliver Special Collections Department, Carnegie Library of Pittsburgh. If no taped copy of an interview is available, the note "transcript only" appears. The note "etc." indicates that subsequent interviews were conducted following the initial interview.

Abbreviations

AWM	Andy Warhol Museum
CI	Carnegie Institute
CLP	Carnegie Library of Pittsburgh
CM	*Carnegie Magazine*
CMA	Carnegie Museum of Art
CMH	Carnegie Music Hall
CMNH	Carnegie Museum of Natural History
CSC	Carnegie Science Center

Andy Warhol Museum symposium, AWM, February 28, 1999

Jay Apt, CMNH, director, April 15, 1997

Charles C. Arensburg, Pittsburgh History and Landmarks Foundation, *CM*, November 1976

Jane Arkus (Leon Arkus's widow), CMA, December 5, 2003

Leon Arkus, CMA, director, October 1974, etc.

Richard Armstrong, CMA, director, May 28, 1996, etc.

Ron Baillie, CSC, educator, March 22, 2006

Gene Baro, CMA, International curator, June 11, 1982

Linda Batis, CMA, curator of works on paper, November 9, 2004

John Bauer, CMNH, retired staff member, model for artist Andrey Avinoff, November 22, 2004

Christopher Beard, CMNH, curator of vertebrate paleontology, March 4, 1997, etc.

Jim Bender, CI, personnel, financial services, May 31, 2005, etc.

Seddon Bennington, CSC, director, August 30, 1994, etc.

Sidney Bergman, CMNH, honorary curator of ancient glass, October 23, 26, 1975

David Berman, CMNH, curator of paleontology, January 2005

Alfred Bjelland, CMNH, assistant director, *CM,* September 1976

Craig Black, CMNH, director, June 2, 1975

Marsha Bol, CMNH, anthropologist, Native American exhibit, July 16, 1997

Doreen Boyce, CSC, head of Buhl Foundation, July 13, 2004

Ed Breuggman, CI, financial services director, *CM,* October 1978

Ellsworth Brown, CI, president, May 14, 2004, etc.

Selma Burke, CMA, sculptor, January 27, 1975, etc.

Bernadette Callery, CMNH, librarian, November 12, 2005

Carnegie Institute security guards, *CM,* April 1974

Carnegie International curators, CMA, 1982–2004 (symposium held by Friends of the
    Carnegie International, November 2003)

Carnegie Veterans, interview with retired employees, November 5, 2005

Larry Carra, Carnegie Mellon, theater director, *CM,* October 1975

Robert Croneberger, CLP, director, January 28, 1987, etc.

Sylvester Damianos, CMA, architect of gallery reconstruction, October 29, 1976

Mary Dawson, CMNH, curator of paleontology, January 1976

Al DeSena, CSC, director, May 11, 2005

Bill DeWalt, CMNH, director, June 30, 2002, etc.

Mary Dewalt, CMA, docent, February 2, 2005

Sally Dixon, CMA, curator of film and video, October 1973

Jim Dugas, CMA, exhibits staff, artist, October 28, 2004

Maryellen Dwyer, art and natural history docent, *CM,* December 1974

Herb Elish, CLP, director, March 3, 2004

Dolores Ellenberg, CI, director of development, October 12, 2006

Joseph Falgione, CLP, regional library administrator, July 20, 2006

Attilo Favorini, University of Pittsburgh, theater director, *CM,* February 1976

Robert Feller, CMA, expert on painting restoration, *CM,* March 1974

James Fisher, CI, trustee, *CM,* October 1975; October 8, 2002

Joseph Fitzpatrick, CMA, art educator, June 25, 1986

Mark Francis, AWM, director, March 19, 1990

Charles Froom, CMA, gallery redesigner, 1985

Hugh Genoways, CMNH, curator of mammals, January 1997

Alice Guilday, CMNH, wife of former curator, secretary to the president, January 21,
    2004

Johanna Haas, CSC, director, June 29, 2004

Robert Haller, Pittsburgh Filmmakers, *CM,* November 1977

Deborah Harding, CMNH, anthropology collection manager, February 23, 2005

Theodore Hazlett, CI, director of A. W. Mellon Educational and Charitable Trust,
    June 20, 1977

Samuel Hazo, International Poetry Forum, *CM,* January 1974

Betty Hill, CMNH, collection manager, vertebrate paleontology, November 21, 2002

David Hillenbrand, CI, president, November 2, 2005

James Hillman, Jungian psychiatrist, panel discussion on "The Soul of Pittsburgh,"
    CM, January 1987

Nicholas Hloppoff, CMA, furniture restorer, April 28, 1975

Henry Hofstott, CI, trustee, December 12, 2005

Laura Hoptman, CMA, International curator, October 11, 2002

Walter Read Hovey, CMA, honorary curator, head of Pitt Fine Arts Department, *CM,* May 1975

James Hughes, CSC, planetarium producer, March 22, 2006

Charlie Humphery, AWM, board member, April 12, 2005

Cy Hungerford, Pittsburgh cartoonist, *CM,* May 1976

Geralyn Huxley, AWM, curator of film, November 15, 2006

Sheila Jackson, CLP, main library services, June 9, 2006

Arthur Jaffe, CI, director of development, September 1, 2004

Phillip Johnston, CMA, curator of decorative arts, director, December 13, 1989

William Judson, curator of film, *CM,* October 1976; May 14, 2007

Paul Kaminski, CI, financial and general services, January 16, 2007, etc.

James King, CMNH, director, January 4, 1989, etc.

Paul Koch, CMH, organist, *CM,* March 1975

Peter Krass, author of biography *Carnegie* (2002), October 10, 2002

Anthony Landreau, CMA, curator of art education, *CM,* March 1976

John (Jack) Lane, CMA, director, August 21, 1984

Robert Leberman, CMNH, bird bander, May 12, 2005 (transcript only)

Louise Lippincott, CMA, curator, December 4, 2006

Brad Livezey, CMNH, curator of birds, May 5, 2005

Kathy Logan, CLP, music and art librarian, October 11, 2006

Emmy Magel, art and natural history docent, *CM,* December 1974

Gladys Maharam, CLP, deputy director, June 19, 2006

George McComb, CI, financial administrator, November 3, 2004 (transcript only)

Sue McLaren, CMNH, collection manager, mammals, April 14, 2005

Medieval historians, *CM,* February 1974

Joseph Merritt, CMNH, director, Powdermill Nature Reserve, mammalogist, *CM,* Summer 1984

Barbara K. Mistick, CLP, director, May 1, 2006

Ruth Crawford Mitchell, founder, Pitt Nationality Rooms, *CMS,* Summer 1975

Cliff Morrow, CMNH, head of exhibit design, *CM,* April 1975

Robert Motherwell, artist, Man and Ideas speaker, February 1976

Robert Mulvihill, CMNH, ornithologist, June 6, 2005

Tracy Myers, CMA, curator of Heinz Architectural Center, July 26, 2007

William Neil, CI, financial and general services, November 3, 2003

Graham Netting, CMNH, director, March 4, 1987

Sarah Nichols, CMA, curator of decorative arts, October 11, 2005, etc.

Jean Nouvel, CSC, architect, March 14, 2002

D. J. Oshry, CI, fund-raising administrator, December 23, 2003

David Owsley, CMA, curator of decorative arts, *CM,* June 1974

Timothy Pearce, CMNH, curator of mollusks, May 15, 2007

Barbara Phillips, CMA, assistant director, August 22, 1984

Mary Kay Poppenberg, CI, director of marketing, December 8, 2004

John Rawlins, CMNH, curator of invertebrate zoology (insects), November 1994, etc.

Ingrid and Bill Rea, CI, trustees, Powdermill supporters, May 11, 2002

Jim Richardson III, CMNH, curator of anthropology, November 17, 1979, etc.

Judith Selwyn, CI, conservationist, September 20, 1989

Jim Senior, CMNH, exhibit design, December 18, 2002, etc. (transcript only)

Ben Shaktman, Pittsburgh Public Theater, director, *CM*, October 1975

David Smith, CMNH, director of Powdermill, June 6, 2005

Tom Sokolowski, AWM, director, August 1996

William Stein, CI, director of marketing, October 16, 2006

Tey Stitler, CMA, director of marketing, January 24, 2008

John Sutton, CMNH, data collections manager, *CM*, September 1977

Jim Swauger, CMNH, anthropologist, assistant director, June 30, 1986, etc.

Eileen Twigger, CMH, manager, October 2, 2007 (transcript only)

Arthur Twomey, CMNH, director of education, *CM*, December 1974

Fred Utech, CMNH, botanist, *CM*, June 1977

Ann Wardrup, CI, trustee, Museum of Art committee, March 30, 2004

John Warhola, AWM, older brother of Andy Warhol, February 29, 2007, etc.

Paul Warhola, AWM, older brother of Andy Warhol, February 26, 1997

Dave Watters, CMNH, curator of anthropology, January 11, 2005

Don Wentworth, CLP, reference librarian, May 20, 2005

Robert M. West, CMNH, director, July 11, 2005

Joshua Whetzel, CSC, first director, December 11, 2002

John Wible, CMNH, curator of mammals, with Sue Wible, CMNH, collection manager, April 14, 2005

Robert Wilburn, CI, president, January 24, 1985, etc.

Donald Wilkins, CMH, pipe organ musician, October 6, 2007 (transcript only)

Suzanne Wilkinson, CMA, docent, February 2, 2005

Marc Wilson, CMNH, curator of mineralogy, May 30, 1996

James Winokur, CI, trustee, November 27, 2002

Matt Wribican, AWM, archivist, November 15, 2006

NOTES

Abbreviations

CI	Carnegie Institute
CLP	Carnegie Library of Pittsburgh
CM	*Carnegie Magazine*
CMNH	Carnegie Museum of Natural History

Researching Annual Reports

The Carnegie Institute and Carnegie Library of Pittsburgh annual reports are held in two collections at Carnegie Library of Pittsburgh: Special Collections and the Pennsylvania Department. Carnegie Museum of Natural History annual reports (part of Carnegie Institute reports but sometimes printed separately) are also held in the Carnegie Museum of Natural History Library. The Carnegie Museum of Natural History Library is the easiest to use for research on the natural history museum.

Using Carnegie Magazine for Research

Beginning in April 1927, *Carnegie Magazine* was published monthly (or later ten times a year, by combining several issues into one Summer issue) through 1981. In 1982 it became a larger-size publication with color, published bimonthly, with six issues (e.g., January–February, March–April, etc.). In 2005 it became quarterly, with Spring, Summer, Fall, and Winter issues. Changes in the magazine over eighty-three years reflected the economics of publishing and different management policies toward using the magazine as a marketing tool. The magazine is also identifiable by volume and issue number and in the early years used the academic style of numbering pages consecutively throughout a bound volume.

The magazine went online in 1996 with feature articles, and back issues from that date to the present may be found on the Carnegie Museums of Pittsburgh site, as "Carnegie Online." See http://www.carnegiemuseums.org/cmag/.

For many years printed indexes in the back of each bound volume were the only tool for the researcher. But as editor, with the help of volunteers, in 1981 I produced a comprehensive index for volumes from 1927 to 1981, in a limited quantity. A few copies of this index are still available in the libraries of the art and natural history museums and at Carnegie Library of Pittsburgh. After 1982 indexes continued to be published at the end of each bound volume (which by then included two years of publication), but these indexes were finally discontinued a few years after the magazine went online and began using a digital index.

Preface

1. Andrew Carnegie, telegram to William Nimick Frew, 1894.

2. Whitehead, *Museum of Fine Arts Boston*, ix.

1. The Carnegie Years

The *Autobiography of Andrew Carnegie* (1920), the essential source to which all Carnegie's biographers refer, is probably the best thing Carnegie wrote, although it is occasionally unreliable, as later scholars have found out. He stopped writing it at age seventy-nine in 1914 and died before completing it. Louise Carnegie commissioned its publication the year after his death. She also commissioned Burton Hendrick to write the authorized biography, *The Life of Andrew Carnegie*, in 1932. Hendrick had access to primary materials that many other biographers did not, but his *Life* is also a sanitized version of a controversial person. Hendrick cowrote a biography of Louise Carnegie in 1950, an overlooked work that is rich in personal details about her life with her husband.

The scholarly *Andrew Carnegie* by Joseph Frazier Wall (1970) was the reigning biography on the subject for some thirty years. David Nasaw's *Andrew Carnegie* (2006) is likely to displace it as a more easily digested story, and Nasaw used many of Hendrick's original materials and other primary sources, which led him to new insights. Another well-written recent biography is Peter Krass's *Carnegie* (2002), which begins with a critical view of the subject but warms as the life unfolds. Easily overlooked but important to understanding Carnegie's writings is George Swetnam's literary biography *Andrew Carnegie*, in Twayne's U.S. author series, which is full of examples of Carnegie's prose. *Meet You in Hell* (2005), by Lee Standiford, is a good treatment of the relationship between Andrew Carnegie and Henry Clay Frick.

The dedications of Carnegie Institute and Library are well documented in two publications: "Dedication Souvenir of Carnegie Library of Pittsburgh PA, Programme and Catalogue" (Nov. 1895; a 95-page pamphlet that includes prepared remarks by the architects, president, directors, and other dignitaries), Pennsylvania Department, Carnegie Library of Pittsburgh, available online at http://www.carnegielibrary.org/research/ pittsburgh/Carnegie/mrac1.html; and *Memorial of Celebration of the Carnegie Institute at Pittsburgh, PA* (Apr. 1907; a well-illustrated 465-page case-bound volume printed by the Board of Trustees that includes Carnegie's speech at the occasion, as well as elaborate remarks from many national and international dignitaries).

Carnegie's gifts to Pittsburgh and all his other philanthropies are well documented in *A Manual of the Public Benefactions of Andrew Carnegie*, compiled and published by the Carnegie Endowment for International Peace in 1919, and *Forty Years of Carnegie Giving*, a summary authored in 1941 by Robert M. Lester, secretary of Carnegie Corporation of New York. A brief summary of Carnegie's many benefactions was published in pamphlet form by Carnegie Corporation of New York in 1987, entitled "The Carnegie Trusts and Institutions."

1. Andrew Carnegie to Henry Codman Carter, Jan. 1897, in Hendrick, *Life*, 2: 252.

2. *Memorial of Celebration*, 58.

3. Quoted in Swetnam, *Andrew Carnegie*, 33–34, 67–69.

4. Krass, *Carnegie*, 19. Nasaw, however, contends that William was not deprived of work by the new steam-power looms in Dunfermline, as Andrew said. The first power looms in Dunfermline did not weave the fine linen products that William specialized in. Rather, William was unable to sell his linens in Glasgow for export trade because of a U.S. economic embargo in the 1840s on imported British textiles (*Andrew Carnegie*, 21).

5. Nasaw, *Andrew Carnegie*, 160.

6. Quoted in Swetnam, *Andrew Carnegie*, 35. Carnegie opens the book rousingly with a first chapter called "The Republic."

7. Quoted in Van Slyke, *Free to All,* 20–21.

8. Nasaw, *Andrew Carnegie,* 646–67. Nasaw quotes from Samuel Clemens's memoirs, unpublished during his and Carnegie's lifetimes: *Mark Twain in Eruption,* 36–52.

9. Andrew Carnegie to John Ross, 1906, in Wall, *Carnegie,* 881. Here also is the observation about millionaires who laugh being rare.

10. *Manual of the Public Benefactions,* 201. This work, compiled by the Carnegie Endowment for International Peace, is the best source of the official language Carnegie used to found institutions and distribute his wealth.

11. Wall, *Andrew Carnegie,* 882–83.

12. Pritchett, "Andrew Carnegie," 2ff., 19.

13. Lester, *Forty Years of Carnegie Giving,* 6–13.

14. William Frew, quoted in Carnegie Institute, "Presentation of the Carnegie Library," n.p.

15. The online version of Andrew Carnegie's 1895 dedication speech may be found at http://www.carnegielibrary.org/research/pittsburgh/Carnegie/mrac1.html.

16. Tarbell, *Story of Carnegie Tech,* 23. The quotation is from Carnegie's dedication speech, but the details of the gift can also be pursued in chapter 2 of Tarbell's history, "The Founding and the First Day" (21–35).

17. Lester, *Forty Years of Carnegie Giving,* 6, 11.

2. Building a Palace of Culture

The basic sources for the building history are the two architectural historians of the Pittsburgh History and Landmarks Foundation, James D. Van Trump and Walter Kidney, plus the scholarly art historian Margaret Henderson Floyd, the author of *Architecture after Richardson.* Van Trump, in *An American Palace of Culture,* is unexcelled as a richly styled observer of the emotions a building creates in the viewer, while Kidney, in *Pittsburgh's Landmark Architecture,* is more objective. Floyd, a thorough student of Henry Hobson Richardson and his partners who designed Carnegie Institute and Library, is full of information about the sources of architectural details in the building, as well as in other buildings the firm designed in Pittsburgh, such as the first branch libraries.

My title, *Palace of Culture: Andrew Carnegie's Institute and Library in Pittsburgh,* is drawn from the title of Van Trump's 1970 book, which has been out of print for some time. Jamie Van Trump was a friend of mine, and as the editor of *Carnegie Magazine* I had the opportunity to publish his essays. The Pittsburgh History and Landmarks Foundation graciously permitted me to use a variant of his title as my own.

An excellent overview of the Institute and the Oakland developments following it is the art historian Franklin Toker's *Pittsburgh: A New Portrait.* Toker's 2009 edition of his 1986 Pittsburgh history is now the standard.

1. *Memorial of Celebration,* 55.

2. Bauman and Muller, *Before Renaissance,* 24.

3. See Aurand, *Spectator and the Topical City,* 218; Bauman and Muller, *Before Renaissance;* "A Growing City," *Pittsburgh Post,* May 9, 1890.

4. The best account of the park's development is Barbara Judd's "Edward M. Bigelow: Creator of Pittsburgh's Arcadian Parks."

5. Alberts, *Pitt,* 57. See also Bauman and Muller, *Before Renaissance,* 45.

6. Tarbell, *Story of Carnegie Tech,* 25.

7. Carnegie to William Frew, Oct. 1894, in "Andrew Carnegie/Library of Congress," vol. 28, quoted in Wall, *Carnegie,* 817, 1100.

8. Evert and Gay, *Discovering Pittsburgh's Sculpture,* 189.

9. Carnegie to William Frew, telegram, Nov. 4, 1895, in "Andrew Carnegie/Library of Congress," vol. 34, quoted in Wall, *Carnegie*, 817, 1100.

10. Floyd, *Architecture after Richardson*, 236.

11. Floyd, *Architecture after Richardson*, 218.

12. Floyd, *Architecture after Richardson*, 218.

13. Cynthia Field, interview with the author, 1991. This interview took place during Field's 1991 visit to Pittsburgh to review Carnegie Institute's request for national designation as a historic building. See also R. J. Gangewere, "What the Muses Hold," *CM*, Jan.–Feb. 1992, 13.

14. Van Trump, *American Palace of Culture*, 25.

15. Van Trump, *American Palace of Culture*, 23.

16. Van Trump, *American Palace of Culture*, 30.

17. Van Trump, *American Palace of Culture*, 32.

18. Van Trump, *American Palace of Culture*, 20.

19. Chabon, *Mysteries of Pittsburgh*, 50.

20. Kidney, *Henry Hornbostel*, 88.

21. *Bellefield Boiler Plant.* This hardbound report with photographs, no author noted, is the major source of the boiler plant's history.

22. Van Trump, *American Palace of Culture*, 21.

3. The High Command—A Century of Governance

Organizational history for museums is a pastiche of materials, from annual reports to memoirs, scholarly catalogs, and appreciative accounts of collectors. After 1927, *Carnegie Magazine* provided an ongoing record of the life of Carnegie Institute and Library, a forgivably self-serving log of the comings and goings of presidents, directors, and curators. Over time, the magazine has come to be published less frequently and to be used more as a promotional tool than as a complete record of the Institute's ongoing life.

Parallel to the decline of the magazine was the demise of the published annual report as an unbiased look at the institution's corporate life. As museums became more financially competitive over the twentieth century, their annual reports morphed toward marketing goals, favoring long, grateful lists of donors and benefactors, with little space devoted to staff changes, administrative strategy, or financial details. Carnegie Institute's annual reports eventually ceased being a useful public resource in the 1990s.

Taped interviews with many Carnegie Institute notables are available in the William Oliver Special Collections Department, CLP. See the list of interview subjects in the appendix.

1. Morley, *Recollections*, 2: 111.

2. "Letter to Mayor Wm. J. Diehl," Nov. 15, 1900, Minutes of Carnegie Institute, Book I, Board of Trustees, CI, Special Collections and Pennsylvania Department, CLP. See also the Library, CMNH, and the President's Office, CI.

3. From an address given at Union College, Schenectedy, Founder's Day, 1896, Special Collections and Pennsylvania Department, CLP.

4. R. L. Duffus, "Is Pittsburgh Civilized?" Oct. 1930, 537–45, quoted in Lubove, *Pittsburgh*, 59.

5. Duffus, "Is Pittsburgh Civilized?" quoted in Lubove, *Pittsburgh*, 59.

6. Aline Saarinen in *The Proud Possessors*, quoted in Katz and Katz, *Museums U.S.A.*, 67.

7. Walker, *Self-Portrait with Donors*, 106.

8. "Mr. Frew's Address," in "Dedication Souvenir."

9. Jordan, *Encyclopedia of Pennsylvania Biography*, 9: 191ff; CI, Annual Report, 1915.

10. Jordan, *Encyclopedia of Pennsylvania Biography*, 9: 191ff.

11. The 1898 "Founder's Day Report" includes this remark and the poetic aside on civilization (6–7). See Pennsylvania Department, CLP.

12. Founder's Day Report, 1898.

13. Lester, *Forty Years of Carnegie Giving*, 10.

14. *CM*, Apr. 1928, 4.

15. *CM*, Apr. 1928, 4.

16. See Church's regular column "Through the Editor's Window," in which he commonly railed against Hitler and the Nazi occupation (*CM*, 1941–43).

17. *CM*, Oct. 1943, 131.

18. *CM*, Oct. 1947, 67–68.

19. *CM*, Oct. 1947, 67–68.

20. *CM*, Oct. 1947, 67–68.

21. *CM*, Feb. 1948, 195.

22. *CM*, Mar. 1948, 227.

23. *CM*, Jan. 1969, 5–8.

24. *CM*, Jan. 1968, 7.

25. CI, Annual Report, 1980, 8.

26. William Neil, interview with the author, Nov. 3, 2003.

27. R. J. Gangewere, "We Are the Carnegie," *CM*, Sept.–Oct. 1986, 5.

28. Ellsworth Brown, interview with the author, May 14, 2004.

29. Neil, interview, Nov. 3, 2003.

30. Bill Zlatos, "Salaries Soar as Museum Funds Sink," *Pittsburgh Tribune Review*, Nov. 3, 2002.

31. Doreen Boyce, interview with the author, July 13, 2004.

32. Patty Tascarella, "Carnegie Museums Closes Marketing Department; Layoffs Expected," *Pittsburgh Business Times*, Dec. 5, 2002.

33. Charlie Humphrey, interview with the author, Apr. 12, 2005.

34. Brown, interview, May 14, 2004.

35. "Globetrotting Executive Lands Dream Job at Carnegie Museums," *Journal of Philanthropy*, Oct. 12, 2005.

36. David Hillenbrand, address to all staff, Nov. 2, 2005.

37. Brown, interview with the author, Jan. 9, 2006.

38. Mencken, "The Libido for the Ugly," in *Prejudices: Sixth Series*, 187.

39. *CM*, Dec. 1975, 15.

40. Sam Roberts, "An American Portrait," *Pittsburgh Post-Gazette*, Dec. 15, 2006. Roberts cites Robert D. Putnam, the author of *Bowling Alone: The Collapse and Revival of American Community*.

41. R. J. Gangewere, "Andy Warhol: A Retrospective," *CM*, July–Aug. 2000, 21.

4. Carnegie Music Hall

Roland Leich's "The Music Hall at Carnegie Institute," published in *CM* in Sept. 1981, is the only public summary of the hall's use through the years, oriented toward the famous musicians who have performed there. The Music Department of Carnegie Library, however, has rich records of the hall's use and historical records of the politics of management when it was the home of the Pittsburgh Symphony Orchestra.

For the early history of the Pittsburgh orchestra, see Wolfe, "Short History of the Pittsburgh Orchestra." Wolfe's account, a master's thesis in library science, is held in the collection of the Music Department, CLP.

1. Walter Damrosch, *Memoirs,* quoted in Nasaw, *Andrew Carnegie,* 357.

2. Roland Leich, "Music Hall at Carnegie Institute," *CM,* Sept. 1981, 15. Leich was a professor of music at Carnegie Mellon University and the program annotator for the Pittsburgh Chamber Music Society.

3. See Nasaw, *Andrew Carnegie,* 356.

4. Toker, *Pittsburgh,* 98; Floyd, *Architecture after Richardson,* 205.

5. Leich, "Music Hall at Carnegie Institute," 18.

6. Andrew Carnegie, dedication speech at Carnegie Library, 1895. The "Dedication Souvenir" for the event contained all the details of the ceremony, with remarks by dignitaries, but Carnegie's speech was not published until later.

7. "Dedication Souvenir."

8. *Pittsburgh Leader,* Jan. 27, 1897.

9. McCullough, "Play On," 2. The late C. Hax McCullough Jr. was a writer and a supporter of the Pittsburgh Symphony who wrote several books about Pittsburgh's musical scene. His history of the Pittsburgh Symphony Orchestra from 1896 to 1910 was almost complete when he died in 2007. Information on the symphony was generously provided by his wife, Jean McCullough.

   For Carnegie's remarks, see "Founder's Day 1898, at the Carnegie Institute, Pittsburgh, PA.," 16–17.

10. *Pittsburgh Dispatch,* Jan. 24, 1897.

11. McCullough, "Play On," 16.

12. "Victory for Herbert," *Pittsburgh Times,* Nov. 4, 1898, quoted in Wolfe, "Short History," 178.

13. *Pittsburgh Post,* Nov. 18, 1899.

14. Wolfe, "Short History," 227.

15. Wolfe, "Short History," 133.

16. Wolfe, "Short History," 134.

17. C. E. Russell, *Cosmopolitan,* 1909, clippings file, CLP. (The clippings files of the CLP sometimes do not contain page numbers or exact dates.)

18. Russell, *Cosmopolitan,* 1909.

19. McCullough, "Play On," 13.

20. Roy Ambrose, in CI, Annual Reports, 1927, 1928.

21. Wall, *Andrew Carnegie,* 430.

22. Thomas Baker, "Hail and Farewell," *CM,* Feb. 5, 1932, 279–81.

23. "The New Organist," *CM,* Sept. 6, 1932, 101.

24. R. J. Gangewere, "Interview with Leon Anthony Arkus," *CM,* Oct.–Nov. 1974, 312–15.

25. Eileen Twigger, interview with the author, Oct. 2, 2007.

26. Twigger, interview, Oct. 2, 2007.

27. Twigger, interview, Oct. 2, 2007.

5. Carnegie Library of Pittsburgh

Carnegie's library philanthropy has triggered a number of histories, including George S. Bobinski's *Carnegie Libraries: Their History and Impact on American Public Library Development* (1969), Theodore Jones's *Carnegie Libraries across America: A Public Legacy* (1997), and Abigail Van Slyke's *Free to All: Carnegie Libraries and American Culture* (1995). Margaret Henderson Floyd's *Architecture after Richardson* also describes the central library and the branches. See the appendix for interviews with many significant library figures.

1. Bobinski, *Carnegie Libraries,* 12, quoting "Mister Carnegie's Investments," *Library Journal* 27 (June 1902).

2. Evert and Gay, *Discovering Pittsburgh's Sculpture,* 5.

3. Carnegie, *Autobiography,* 45.

4. This charge was first leveled in print by Washington Gladden, the minister of the First Congregational Church of Columbus, Ohio. See Van Slyke, *Free to All,* 19, quoting an article published in the *Outlook* in 1895.

5. Bobinski, *Carnegie Libraries,* 63.

6. Van Slyke, *Free to All,* 4.

7. Van Slyke, *Free to All,* 36.

8. Quoted in drama critic Christopher Rawson's "Book Set Mostly Does Justice to Wilson's Cycle," *Pittsburgh Post-Gazette,* Oct. 31, 2007.

9. Library director Barbara Mistick triggered the local economic analysis: "Report on the Economic Impact of Carnegie Library," by the Center for Economic Development (CED) at Carnegie Mellon University, published in 2006. The national analysis was Jack Miller's "America's Most Literate Cities 2004," University of Wisconsin, Whitewater, and is included in the Carnegie Mellon Report.

10. Robert Croneberger, interview with Bob Hoover, *Pittsburgh Post-Gazette,* Dec. 5, 1993.

11. Gladys Maharam, interview with the author, June 19, 2006.

12. Barbara Mistick, interview with the author, May 1, 2006.

13. CLP, Annual Reports, 1903–7, 15–16.

14. William T. Harris, quoted in CLP, Annual Report, 1904, 25–26.

15. Alberts, *Pitt,* 287.

16. Christopher Monkhouse, "The ABC's of an Architectural Library in Pittsburgh: Anderson, Bernd and Carnegie," *CM,* Mar.–Apr. 1996.

17. Carnegie, dedication speech, 1895, in "Dedication Souvenir," 10.

18. See CLP, Annual Reports, 1903–7, 15–16.

19. See Ralph Munn's unpublished history of Carnegie Library (1969), 20, available at http://www.carnegielibrary.org/research/Pittsburgh/Carnegie/mrac2f.html. See CD (P.333).

20. Munn, unpublished history (1969), 37.

21. John N. Berry III, obituary editorial, *Library Journal,* Apr. 1, 1998.

22. Eleanor Jo (Joey) Rodger, quoted in R. J. Gangewere, "Editorial: Remembering Robert C. Croneberger, 1937–1998," *CM,* May–June 1998.

23. Bob Hoover, "Close-Up," *Pittsburgh Post-Gazette,* Dec. 5, 1993.

24. Herb Elish, interview with the author, Mar. 3, 2004.

25. Quoted by Bob Hoover, *Pittsburgh Post-Gazette,* Sept. 29, 2004.

26. Quoted by Bob Hoover, *Pittsburgh Post-Gazette,* Sept. 29, 2004.

27. Mistick, interview, May 1, 2006.

28. Mistick, interview, May 1, 2006.

29. The calculation of $40,000 in 1895 being equivalent to $1,021,000 in 2009 was made by a Carnegie Library reference librarian.

30. Van Slyke, *Free to All*, 102.

31. Quoted in Stephanie Franklin, "Libraries of the Twenty-First Century," *Pittsburgh Tribune Review*, Dec. 17, 2002.

32. The study was released on Apr. 27, 2006, and its conclusions were summarized by Carnegie Library of Pittsburgh in a news release on that date.

6. Carnegie Museum of Art

General collection catalogs were published by several of the museum's directors (Leon Arkus [1973], John R. Lane [1985], and Philip Johnston [1995]), each reflecting the perceived highlights of the permanent collection at that time. In addition, catalogs of the Carnegie Internationals were published regularly, eventually becoming ambitious treatises.

Historical discussions of specific collections can also be found in catalogs assembled by a number of scholarly curators. Especially noteworthy are Henry Adams's *American Drawings and Watercolors in the Museum of Art, Carnegie Institute* (1985), Diane Strazdes's *American Paintings and Sculpture to 1945 in the Carnegie Museum of Art* (1992), and Vicky Clark's *International Encounters: The Carnegie International and Contemporary Art, 1896–1996*. Kenneth Neal presents a thorough study of the museum's early years in *A Wise Extravagance: The Founding of the Carnegie International Exhibitions, 1895–1901* (1996). Jason T. Busch's *Decorative Arts and Design Collection Highlights* was published in 2009. Also see the interviews listed in the appendix.

1. Carnegie, dedication speech, 1895, in "Dedication Souvenir."

2. Neal, *Wise Extravagance*, 50.

3. Neal, *Wise Extravagance*, 188.

4. Andrew Carnegie to William H. Frew, Oct. 24, 1894.

5. Andrew Carnegie to William H. Frew, Feb. 2, 1896, in Wall, *Carnegie*, 833.

6. Carnegie, dedication speech, 1907, 60, Pennsylvania Department, CLP.

7. Adams, *American Drawings and Watercolors*, 6.

8. Strazdes, *American Paintings and Sculpture*, 456–57.

9. Adams, *American Drawings and Watercolors*, 7. Adams quotes from "Essays on Our Leading Citizens: John Wesley Beatty, " *Harpoon*, May 1913, and "A Talk with John Beatty about the Carnegie Art Gallery," *Library*, Sept. 8, 1900, among other sources.

10. Quoted in Strazdes, *American Paintings and Sculpture*, xviin.24.

11. For a useful summary of major works the museum acquired from Internationals, see Donald Miller, *Pittsburgh Post-Gazette*, Oct. 8, 2004.

12. Neal, *Wise Extravagance*, 54–55.

13. See the 1914 Founder's Day speech, quoted in Neal, *Wise Extravagance*, 122.

14. Christian Brinton, 1913, quoted in Neal, *Wise Extravagance*, 14.

15. Anna Seaton-Schmidt, "Pittsburgh's Show of Sane Art," *Boston Evening Transcript*, Apr. 2, 1913, quoted in Neal, *Wise Extravagance*, 61n.18.

16. Neal, *Wise Extravagance*, 121.

17. Neal, *Wise Extravagance*, 140.

18. Mary Cassatt to John Wesley Beatty, Oct. 6, 1909, CI, Museum of Art records, 1896–1940, Archives of American Art.

19. Platt, "Gambling, Fencing, and Camouflage.

20. Strazdes, *American Painting and Sculpture,* xviii.

21. Strazdes, *American Painting and Sculpture,* xix. Strazdes in general provides a good description of the operation of the museum during Saint-Gauden's era.

22. Donald Miller, "Carnegie International: Historical Perspective," *Pittsburgh Post-Gazette,* Oct. 31, 1999.

23. Quoted in Christine O'Toole, "Golden Years," CM, Spring 2007, 27–29.

24. Gordon Bailey Washburn, "Popular Questions and Unpopular Answers on Modern Art," *CM,* Nov. 1962, 302.

25. Altshuler, "Modern World Is Our Business.'"

26. Strazdes, *American Painting and Sculpture,* xxiv.

27. James Winokur, interview with the author, Nov. 27, 2002. See also "The New Director of Fine Arts," *CM,* Dec. 1962, 337; Strazdes, *American Painting and Sculpture,* xxiv.

28. Jane Arkus, interview with the author, Dec. 5, 2003; Jane Arkus, email to the author, July 11, 2007.

29. Edward Larrabee Barnes, "Architectural Notes," *CM,* Oct.–Nov. 1974, 324–26.

30. Gangewere, "Interview with Leon Anthony Arkus." See also CI, Annual Report, 1974, 71.

31. Gangewere, "Interview with Leon Anthony Arkus."

32. Jane Arkus, email to Tey Stitler, communications director, CMA, Feb. 11, 2008.

33. Quoted by Jack Lane, in "Carnegie International Curators Symposium," Nov. 2003 (taped symposium, archived at CMA; transcript in author's personal collection).

34. CI, Annual Report, 1985, 33.

35. Quoted by Lane, in "Carnegie International Curators Symposium," Nov. 2003.

36. John Russell, "Art View: The Best and the Biggest in Pittsburgh," *New York Times,* Nov. 17, 1985.

37. Quoted by Lane, in "Carnegie International Curators Symposium," Nov. 2003.

38. *CM,* Nov.–Dec. 1996, 6.

39. 1999 International, catalog, 99.

40. Richard Armstrong, quoted in 2004 International, catalog, 9, 8, 17.

41. Mary Thomas, "Forty Artists to Explore 'Life on Mars' in International," *Pittsburgh Post-Gazette,* Feb. 22, 2008.

42. CI, Annual Report, 1917.

43. Margaret Lee, "Many Happy Returns," *CM,* Jan. 1945, 227.

44. *CM,* Feb. 1932, 275.

45. Lee, *CM,* Jan. 1945, 227.

46. *CM,* 1950, 344.

47. Donald Miller, "Thinking of Fitz.," *CM,* Mar.–Apr. 1987, 21.

48. In 1953, Fitzpatrick wrote an article about teaching beginners, especially adults: "The Joy of Learning," *CM,* Oct. 1953, 281. See also Mar. 1950, 266ff; Mar. 1951, 78ff. An overview of Fitzpatrick's years in Pittsburgh can be found in an interview by R. J. Gangewere, "Joe Fitzpatrick: Look, to See, to Remember, to Enjoy," *CM,* Mar.–Apr. 1987, 20ff. See also, in the same issue, Miller, "Thinking of Fitz."

49. Dillard, *American Childhood,* 212.

50. Decorative Arts presented its history in wall panels in 2003 in the exhibit Very Familiar: Celebrating Fifty Years of Collecting Decorative Arts. Historical information here comes from this text. The first catalog of the collection was published in 2009: Busch; Decorative Arts and Design Collection Highlights.

51. Sarah Nichols, interview with the author, July 9, 2007.

52. David T. Owsley, interview with the author, *CM*, June 1974, 226. Not all of the taped interview was included in the published article.

53. Nichols, interview, July 9, 2007.

54. See Haller, *Crossroads*.

55. See references to Sally F. Dixon and the film program in *CM*, 1970, index.

56. Bill O'Driscoll, "Pittsburgh's Close-Up," *Pittsburgh City Paper*, Apr. 6, 2006.

57. Marilynn Uricchio, quoted in Haller, *Crossroads*, 64.

58. Bill Judson, interview with the author, May 14, 2007.

59. Pat Lowry, "In Cutback, Carnegie Drops Film, Video Unit," *Pittsburgh Post-Gazette*, Jan. 8, 2003.

60. Caroline Abels, "Carnegie Cuts Stun Art Experts, Filmmakers," *Pittsburgh Post-Gazette*, Jan. 9, 2003.

61. Abels, "Carnegie Cuts Stun Art Experts."

62. Louise Lippincott, telephone interview with the author, July 20, 2007.

63. Virginia Lewis, "One Hundred and Eleven Prints: The Gift of Kenneth Seaver to Carnegie Institute," *CM*, Feb. 1949, 230–33.

64. Linda Batis, interview with the author, Nov. 9, 2004.

65. R. J. Gangewere, "James Bliss Austin, a Rare Collector," *CM*, Mar.–Apr. 1989, 8.

66. Phillip Johnston, "Welcome to the Heinz Architectural Center," *CM*, Nov.–Dec. 1993, 14.

67. Tracy Myers, interview with the author, July 26, 2007.

7. *Carnegie Museum of Natural History*

Two popular books about dinosaurs are Tom Rea's *Bone Wars: The Excavation and Celebrity of Andrew Carnegie's Dinosaur* (2001) and Leonard Krishtalka's *Dinosaur Plots and Other Intrigues in Natural History* (1989). Another resource is Helen McGinnis's *Carnegie's Dinosaurs* (1982). Most of the curators publish in scientific journals, but they sometimes publish separate volumes of interest to a larger audience. Examples are Joseph E. Merritt's *Guide to the Mammals of Pennsylvania*; Don W. Dragoo's study of the Native Americans of western Pennsylvania, *Mounds for the Dead: An Analysis of the Adena Culture*; and Christopher K. Beard's *The Hunt for the Dawn Monkey*.

Also of note is the work of two collection managers who have worked unofficially as historians. Betty Hill, the collection manager of Vertebrate Paleontology, developed a master list of all staff employed by the institution since its founding, and Stephen Rogers, the collection manager of Birds, and of Amphibians and Reptiles, has studied the fascinating role of taxidermy in museum exhibits. In addition, the history of each of the museum's sections may be found at http://www.carnegiemnh.org. The appendix lists interviews with many individuals who were essential to the history of the museum.

1. Edward O. Wilson, "That's Life," *New York Times*, Sept. 6, 2007.

2. John Rawlins, email to the author, Dec. 3, 2007.

3. John Wible, with the collection manager Sue Wible, interview with the author, Apr. 14, 2005.

4. Alberts, *Pitt*, 50. In all his communications with Carnegie, it is clear that Holland knew how to flatter the founder.

5. McGinnis, *Carnegie's Dinosaurs*, 17.

6. Carnegie Institute, *Exhibition of Andrey Avinoff*.

7. Shoumatoff, *Russian Blood*, 152.

8. Shoumatoff, *Russian Blood*, 152.

9. Quoted in Shoumatoff, *Russian Blood*, 196.

10. John Walker, quoted in Shoumatoff, *Russian Blood*, 196.

11. John Bauer, interview with the author, Nov. 22, 2004.

12. When Jennings died in 1964, a number of obituaries detailed his achievements. See esp. the booklet Graham Netting wrote, "In Memoriam: Otto Emery Jennings, 1877–64," published by the museum; and Leroy K. Henry's piece in the journal of the Pennsylvania Academy of Science, vol. 38 (1964): 18–20.

13. Mary Dawson, interview with the author, Nov. 27, 2006.

14. CI, Annual Report, 1959, 54.

15. Robert West, interview with the author, July 12, 2005. Despite his short stay at the Institute, West offered a shrewd and wide-ranging critique of the Pittsburgh museum and the museum profession.

16. Quoted in *CM*, July–Aug. 1996, 6–7.

17. Caroline Abels, "Museum Chief Brings Experience to New Job," *Pittsburgh Post-Gazette*, Feb. 15, 2001.

18. Samuel Taylor, telephone interview with the author, Jan. 29, 2009. Taylor also wrote a position paper in 2008 that outlined his views: "Putting Science First at Carnegie Museum of Natural History."

19. Much of the information in this account comes from the "History of the Section of Invertebrate Paleontology," PAIS publication no. 6, 2007. See also the paleontologist Mary Dawson's description in *CM*, Sept.–Oct. 1988, 12–18.

20. John L. Carter, "Spineless Wonders in the Bayet Collection," *CM*, Feb. 1973, 71.

21. Graham Netting, "Interminable Reaches of Time," *CM*, Dec. 1965, 336.

22. Marc Wilson, interview with the author, Aug. 14, 2007. A taped interview with Wilson (May 30, 1996) is on file in the William Oliver Special Collections Department, CLP. Samuel Eliot Morrison's monumental two-volume study *The Discovery of America* quickly reinforces the notion that greed for gold and silver drove the early navigators to explore and colonize the Western hemisphere.

23. Richard Souza, "Minerals of the Carnegie Museum of Natural History," supplement to *Mineralogical Record* 21, no. 5 (1990): 9–10. Souza is the main historian of the section's early years, and the details provided here are from his account.

24. This acquisition and the beginnings of a permanent collection are noted in Carnegie Museum, Annual Report, 1898, available in the Special Collections and Pennsylvania Department, CLP, and Library, CMNH.

25. Quoted in Kathryn M. Duda, "A Gem of a Mineral Collection," *CM*, Nov.–Dec. 1996, 14–17.

26. John E. Guilday, an associate curator of Vertebrate Paleontology, and Elizabeth Hill, a curatorial assistant, together examined the section's history in *CM*, Oct. 1979, 18–27. Much of the following account comes from their description.

27. Quoted in McGinnis, *Carnegie's Dinosaurs*, 15.

28. John E. Guilday, "Caves, Bones and Ice Age Owls," *CM*, May–June 1982, 20.

29. See McGinnis, *Carnegie's Dinosaurs*, 71–73.

30. Melissa Hendricks, "Tales from the Crust," *Johns Hopkins Magazine*, Apr. 2001.

31. John Altdorfer, "A Rare Bird," *CM*, Winter 2006, 22.

32. Timothy Pearce, interview with the author, May 15, 2007, and Pearce's later editorial notes, May 15, 2007.

33. J. José Parodiz, "Invertebrates," *CM,* Sept. 1980, 12.

34. James Waldo Fawcett, "Investigator of River Life Who Has Searched Local Streams Is an Interesting Figure," *Pittsburgh Gazette Times,* July 26, 1914, Ortmann's vertical file, Pennsylvania Department, CLP.

35. A. E. Ortmann, "Correlation of Shape and Station Freshwater Mussels (Naiades)," *Proceedings of the American Philosophical Society* 19 (1920): 269–312.

36. Biography of George Hubbard Clapp, typed manuscript, 1939, vertical file, Pennsylvania Department, CLP.

37. Frederick Utech, "Botany," *CM,* Summer 1979, 6–13. Much of the history of the section comes from Utech's article.

38. Sue A. Thompson, "BioBlitz," *CM,* May–June 1998.

39. Jennifer Bails, "DNA Plays a Role in Park's Revival," *Pittsburgh Tribune-Review,* Mar. 2, 2006.

40. Bails, "DNA Plays a Role."

41. Dorothy Pearth, "Trees for Tranquility," *CM,* June 1973, 231. Pearth was assistant and then associate curator from 1954 until her retirement in 1978, when she became curator emeritus.

42. Rachel Rivera, "Rafting Iguanas Survive 200-Mile Journey in Caribbean Sea," *Science World,* Jan. 11, 1999. See also the University of Connecticut publication *Advance,* Oct. 19, 1998.

43. Rivera, "Rafting Iguanas."

44. Rivera, "Rafting Iguanas." See also *Advance,* University of Connecticut publication, Oct. 19, 1998.

45. Neil Richmond, "Amphibians and Reptiles: Their Differences," *CM,* May 1971, 199.

46. Jack McCoy, "Amphibians and Reptiles," *CM,* Mar. 1981, 25–33.

47. An overview of the section's history may be found at http://www.carnegiemnh.org. Much of the history presented here is from Ginter Ekis, "Entomology," *CM,* Jan.–Feb. 1984, 22–29.

48. John Rawlins, interview with the author, June 15, 2007.

49. Kathryn Duda, "Backyard Monsters," *CM,* July–Aug. 1998.

50. Kenneth Parkes, "The Section of Birds," *CM,* Summer 1981, 8. Parkes provides the best review of the section's history.

51. The history of the section until 1980 is in Hugh Genoways and Duane A. Schlitter, "The Section of Mammals of Carnegie Museum of Natural History," *CM,* Summer 1980, 30–36. The Carnegie Institute's annual reports also contain information about its development, the collection manager Suzanne McLaren the most exacting historian.

52. Suzanne McLaren, interview with the author, Apr. 14, 2005.

53. Much of the material in this section is from interviews I conducted with the curators Jim Richardson III (Feb. 22, 2005) and Dave Watters (Jan. 11, 2005) and with the collection manager Deborah Harding (Feb. 23, 2005). Also see the account of the section's history, *CM,* Nov. 1980.

54. Stephen Rogers, "Stuffed Animals." Rogers is the collection manager for Birds and for Amphibians and Reptiles, and his rich account forms the basis for much of this section. Like former collection manager Betty Hill in Paleontology, Rogers is an internal historian of the museum's past. Betty Hill's comprehensive list of museum staff is used heavily throughout this section.

55. William Hornaday to Henry Ward, 1878, quoted in James Andrew Dolph, "Bringing Wildlife to Millions: William Temple Hornaday, the Early Years: 1854-1896," Ph.D.

diss., University of Massachusetts, 1975 (Ann Arbor: UMI) and in Stephen Rogers, "Stuffed Animals."

56. Carnegie, *Round the World,* 141.

57. Quoted in Stephen Rogers, "Stuffed Animals," n.16. See also Hornaday, *Two Years in the Jungle.*

58. Stephen Rogers, "Stuffed Animals."

59. William Holland, "The White Rhinocerus: How This Great and Rare Beast Made Its First United Stated Appearance in Pittsburgh," *CM,* Jan. 1933, 239–41. See also Stephen Rogers, "Stuffed Animals," n.25.

60. James Swauger, "Where Are the Indians?" *CM,* June 1947, 13; *Annals of Carnegie Museum* 11, Nov. 1917, 9–11.

61. Carnegie Museum, Annual Report, 1916, 5–7, available in the Special Collections and Pennsylvania Department, CLP, and Library, CMNH.

62. Benton, "Decline of the Natural-History Museum." Benton was the pseudonym of an associate professor of English at a Midwestern liberal arts college who wrote about academic culture for the *Chronicle.*

63. "Don't Ask Oscar," unsigned column, *Seen,* Mar. 2006, 31.

64. Dillard, *American Childhood,* 211.

65. John Edgar Wideman, "Ten Great Science Museums: Carnegie Museum of Natural History," Nov. 1993, http://discovermagazine.com/1993/nov/tengreatsciencem300.

66. Bernadette Callery, interview with the author, Nov. 12, 2005. Another key source for this section is Anna Tauber, "The Library of Carnegie Museum of Natural History," *CM,* Oct. 1981, 25–29.

67. Callery, interview, Nov. 30, 2005.

68. CI, Annual Report, 1898.

69. Callery, interview, Nov. 30, 2005.

70. Arthur van Buskirk, quoted in Netting, *Fifty Years of the Western Pennsylvania Conservancy,* 79. One of Netting's projects as director emeritus of the museum was to summarize the work of the conservancy in this publication.

71. Quoted in Netting, *Fifty Years of the Western Pennsylvania Conservancy,* 116.

72. David Smith, interview with the author, June 6, 2005. Also see various articles about Smith and Powdermill in *CM,* 2005–9.

73. Quoted in Christine H. O'Toole, "Powdermill Takes Wing," *CM,* Fall 2006, 16–20.

74. "Nota Bene," *Academe,* 2001; Elizabeth Olsen, "Embattled Smithsonian Official Resigns, *New York Times,* Mar. 27, 2007.

75. Dave Umhoffer and Avril D. Lank, "Former Museum Official Charged," *Milwaukee Sentinel-Journal,* Oct. 11, 2006.

76. Tom. L. Freudenheim, "Buffalo's Defeated Art Lovers May Still Spark a Revolution," *Wall Street Journal,* Mar. 20, 2007.

8. Carnegie Science Center and Buhl Planetarium

The best general introduction to the Carnegie Science Center is the special issue of *Carnegie Magazine* devoted to its opening (Sept.–Oct. 1991), with articles about Henry Buhl, the evolution of the science center, comments by the architect, and detailed floor plans. Glenn A. Walsh, the historian of Buhl Science Center, has detailed most of its history online: http://buhlplanetarium.tripod.com/Buhlbriefhistory.html. See the appendix for interviews with individuals who have worked at the science center.

1. See "Merchant, Philanthropist, Pittsburgher, 1848–1927," a summary published by the Buhl Foundation. The story of Henry Buhl's life may also be found in R. J. Gangewere, "Henry Buhl, Jr., and 'the Everlasting Getting On with It,'" *CM,* Dec. 1989, 4.

2. "Merchant, Philanthropist, Pittsburgher."

3. See Walsh's Web site: http://www.planetarium.cc. See also Kidney, *Pittsburgh's Landmark Architecture,* 177.

4. In the mid-1990s, the pendulum was displayed at Carnegie Science Center, but the original marble pit remained at Buhl Planetarium. Then in 2004, when the Children's Museum of Pittsburgh opened in the refurbished Buhl facility, the pendulum was returned to the original building. See Lillian Thomas, "Foucault Pendulum Helps Us Get the Drift of the Earth's Spin," *Pittsburgh Post-Gazette,* Feb. 21, 2005.

5. James D. Duffer received a B.S. from the University of Pittsburgh and an M.S. in naval architecture and marine engineering from MIT. Glenn A. Walsh, the historian of Buhl Science Center, details most of Buhl's history online at http://www.planetarium.cc. Included is a digital version of the 1989 publication "Lives Touched . . . Worlds Changed, Fifty Years of Alumni Achievements," detailing the educational experiences of Buhl schoolchildren.

6. *CM,* Sept.–Oct. 1991, 38.

7. *CM,* Sept.–Oct. 1991, 91.

8. James Hughes, interview with the author, Mar. 22, 2006.

9. Patricia Rogers, "History of the Carnegie Science Center's Miniature Railroad and Village." Rogers, the program manager, wrote this guide for volunteers and visitors, held in the Miniature Railroad and Village office, CSC.

10. See Abby Mendelson, "The Science Center Submarine," *CM,* July–Aug. 1990, 28ff.

11. Seddon Bennington, interview with the author, Nov. 27, 2002.

12. Bennington, interview, Nov. 27, 2002.

13. Bennington, interview, Nov. 27, 2002.

14. Bennington, interview, Nov. 27, 2002.

15. Jane Ellen Robinet, "Jo Hass, Energized," *CM,* Sept.–Oct. 2004.

16. Lubove, *Twentieth Century Pittsburgh,* 188–90.

9. The Andy Warhol Museum

The shelves are laden with books about Warhol, ranging from scholarly and popular biographies to personal memoirs and catalogs of his art. Warhol, with the help of friends and editors, also produced books himself, including the ghostwritten *The Philosophy of Andy Warhol (From A to B and Back Again)* (1975). Two years after the artist's death, the Museum of Modern Art in New York published a comprehensive scholarly catalog entitled *Andy Warhol: A Retrospective* (1989).

When the Andy Warhol Museum opened, it published *The Andy Warhol Museum* (1994), including an overview of the museum's development by director Tom Armstrong. Under director Tom Sokolowski, the museum also published an illustrated catalog of its holdings, with comments by the museum staff, as well as Warhol's thoughts: *Andy Warhol 365 Takes: The Andy Warhol Museum Collection* (2004). Also see the pertinent interviews listed in the appendix.

1. Much of the information that follows is adapted from R. J. Gangewere, "Two Andy's from Pittsburgh," *CM,* May–June, 1994, 20ff.

2. Warhol said this repeatedly in various forms, and it became something of a motto. See *Andy Warhol: A Retrospective,* 457; *Andy Warhol and Pat Hackett,* 80.

    Warhol at one point declared, "Business art is the step that comes after art.

I started as a commercial artist, and I want to finish as a business artist. After I did the thing called 'art' or whatever it's called, I went into business art. I want to be an Art Businessman or Business Artist" (*Philosophy of Andy Warhol*, 186).

3. Andy's classmate Bernard B. Perlman gives a full explanation of Warhol's schooling in "The Education of Andy Warhol," in *Andy Warhol Museum*, 147–65.

4. Quoted in Bockris, *Life and Death of Andy Warhol*, 221.

5. Finkelstein, *Andy Warhol*, 8 (unpaginated).

6. Arthur C. Danto, "The Philosopher as Andy Warhol," in *Andy Warhol Museum*, 74, 89.

7. Quoted in Danto, "Philosopher as Andy Warhol," 90.

8. *Andy Warhol Museum*, 90.

9. Heiner Friedrich, interview with Avis Berman, Apr. 22, 1993, cited in *Andy Warhol Museum*. Berman wrote a piece entitled "The Right Place: The Founding of the Andy Warhol Museum" (*Andy Warhol Museum*, 16–36), which is the primary source of information about this subject. The interview with Friedrich was also deposited in the collection of the Andy Warhol Museum.

10. Avis Berman, in *Andy Warhol Museum*, 19.

11. Robert C. Wilburn, interview with Avis Berman, Apr. 8–9, 1993, in *Andy Warhol Museum*.

12. Thomas Armstrong III, interview with Lisa Liebman, *Interview*, May 1994.

13. Tom Sokolowski, interview with the author, CM, Aug. 1996.

14. Sokolowski, interview with the author.

15. Gangewere, "Andy Warhol."

16. Jim Barnhart, interview with the author, Feb. 10, 2007.

17. Jim Wilkinson, interview with the author, Aug. 29, 2007.

18. Colleen Criste, telephone interview with the author, Oct. 8, 2006.

BIBLIOGRAPHY

Adams, Henry. *American Drawings and Watercolors in the Museum of Art, Carnegie Institute.* Pittsburgh: Carnegie Institute, 1985. Dist. University of Pittsburgh Press.

Alberts, Robert C. *Pitt: The Story of the University of Pittsburgh 1787–1987.* Pittsburgh: University of Pittsburgh Press, 1986.

Altshuler, Bruce. "'The Modern World Is Our Business': The Carnegie International in the Gordon Bailey Washburn Years, 1950–1962." In Clark, *International Encounters,* 107–9.

Andy Warhol: 365 Takes: The Andy Warhol Museum Collection. Pittsburgh: The Andy Warhol Museum, 2004.

Aurand, Martin. *The Spectator and the Topical City.* Pittsburgh: University of Pittsburgh Press, 2006.

Bauman, John, and Edward Muller. *Before Renaissance: Planning in Pittsburgh, 1889–1943.* Pittsburgh: University of Pittsburgh Press, 2006.

Beard, Christopher K. *The Hunt for the Dawn Monkey.* Berkeley: University of California Press, 2004.

The Bellefield Boiler Plant, Pittsburgh, Pennsylvania: A Review of the Origin and Expansion of the Boiler Plant. December 1967.

Benton, Thomas H. "The Decline of the Natural-History Museum—An Academic in America." *Chronicle of Higher Education,* October 9, 2006.

Bobinski, George S. *Carnegie Libraries: Their History and Impact on American Library Development.* Chicago: American Library Association, 1968.

Bockris, Victor. *The Life and Death of Andy Warhol.* New York: Bantam Books, 1989.

Brignano, Mary. "Giving—the Good Life: A Panorama of the Carnegie and the People Who Created It." Unpublished manuscript. Pittsburgh: Carnegie Institute, ca. 1985.

Busch, Jason T. *Decorative Arts and Design Collection Highlights, Carnegie Museum of Art.* Pittsburgh: Carnegie Museum of Art, 2009.

Carnegie, Andrew. *The Autobiography of Andrew Carnegie.* Boston: Northeastern University Press, 1986.

————. *The "Gospel of Wealth": Essays and Other Writings.* Sel. and intro. David Nasaw. New York: Penguin Books, 2006.

————. *Round the World.* New York: Charles Scribner's Sons, 1884.

Carnegie Corporation of New York. "The Carnegie Trusts and Institutions." Pamphlet. Ed. Sara L. Engelhardt. Privately printed.

Carnegie Endowment for International Peace, comp. *A Manual of the Public Benefactions of Andrew Carnegie.* Ed. S. N. D. North. New York: Charles Scribner's Sons, 1919.

Carnegie Institute. *The Andy Warhol Museum.* New York: Distributed Art Publishers, 1994.

————. *The Carnegie Museum of Art, Collection Highlights.* Collection catalog. Intro. Phillip Johnston. Pittsburgh: Carnegie Institute, 1995

————. *Catalogue of the Painting Collection: Museum of Art.* Collection catalog. Intro. Leon A. Arkus. Pittsburgh: Carnegie Institute, 1973.

———. *An Exhibition of Andrey Avinoff: The Man of Science, Religion, Mysticism, Nature, Society and Fantasy.* Collection catalog. Text by Virginia E. Lewis. Intro. Walter Read Hovey. Pittsburgh: Carnegie Institute, 1953.

———. "Presentation of the Carnegie Library to the People of Pittsburgh with a Description of the Dedicatory Exercises, November 5, 1895." Printed by order of the Corporation of the City of Pittsburgh.

———. *Museum of Art, Carnegie Institute Collection Handbook.* Collection catalog. Intro. John R. Lane. Pittsburgh: Carnegie Institute, 1985.

Chabon, Michael. *The Mysteries of Pittsburgh.* New York: William Morrow and Company, 1988.

Clark, Vicki, ed. *International Encounters: The Carnegie International and Contemporary Art, 1896–1996.* Pittsburgh: Carnegie Institute, 1996.

Dillard, Annie. *An American Childhood.* New York: Harper and Row, 1988.

Dragoo, Don W. *Mounds for the Dead: An Analysis of the Adena Culture.* Annals of Carnegie Museum, vol. 37. Pittsburgh: Carnegie Museum, 1963.

Evert, Marilyn, and Vernon Gay. *Discovering Pittsburgh's Sculpture.* Pittsburgh: University of Pittsburgh Press, 1983.

Finkelstein, Nat. *Andy Warhol: The Factory Years, 1964–1967.* New York: St. Martin's Press, 1989.

Floyd, Margaret Henderson. *Architecture after Richardson: Regionalism before Modernism—Longfellow, Alden and Harlow in Boston and Pittsburgh.* Chicago and London: University of Chicago Press, in association with the Pittsburgh History and Landmarks Foundation, 1994.

Haller, Robert. *Crossroads: Avant-garde Film in Pittsburgh in the 1970s.* New York: Anthology Film Archives, 2005.

Hendrick, Burton. *The Life of Andrew Carnegie.* 2 vols. New York: Doubleday, 1932.

Hendrick, Burton, and Daniel Henderson. *Louise Whitfield Carnegie: The Life of Mrs. Andrew Carnegie.* New York: Hastings House, 1950.

Hornaday, William T. *Two Years in the Jungle: The Experiences of a Hunter and Naturalist in India, Ceylon, the Malay Peninsula and Borneo.* New York: Charles Scribner's Sons, 1885.

Hovey, Walter Read. Introduction. In *An Exhibition of Andrey Avinoff: The Man of Science, Religion, Mysticism, Nature, Society and Fantasy.* Pittsburgh: Carnegie Institute, 1953.

Jones, Theodore. *Carnegie Libraries across America: A Public Legacy.* New York: John Wiley and Sons, 1997.

Jordan, John W. *Encyclopedia of Pennsylvania Biography.* 10 vols. New York: Lewis Historical Publishing Company, 1918.

Judd, Barbara. "Edward M. Bigelow: Creator of Pittsburgh's Arcadian Parks." *Western Pennsylvania Historical Magazine* 58 (January 1975).

Katz, Herbert, and Marjorie Katz. *Museums U.S.A: A History and a Guide.* New York: Doubleday and Company, 1965.

Kidney, Walter. *Henry Hornbostel: An Architect's Master Touch.* Pittsburgh: Pittsburgh History and Landmarks Foundation, 2002.

———. *Pittsburgh's Landmark Architecture: Historic Buildings of Pittsburgh and Allegheny County.* Pittsburgh: Pittsburgh History and Landmarks Foundation, 1985.

Kinard, Agnes. *Celebrating the First 100 Years of the Carnegie in Pittsburgh, 1895–1995.* Published by the author, 1995.

Koskoff, David E. *The Mellons: The Chronicle of America's Richest Family.* New York: Thomas Y. Crowell Co., 1978.

Krass, Peter. *Carnegie.* Hoboken, NJ: John Wiley and Sons, 2002.

Krishtalka, Leonard. *Dinosaur Plots and Other Intrigues in Natural History.* New York: William Morrow, 1989.

Lester, Robert M. *Forty Years of Carnegie Giving, 1901–1941.* New York: Charles Scribner's Sons, 1941.

Lubove, Roy, ed. *Pittsburgh.* New York: Franklin Watts, 1976.

———. *Twentieth Century Pittsburgh: Government, Business and Environmental Change.* New York: John Wiley and Sons, 1969.

————. *Twentieth Century Pittsburgh: The Post-Steel Era*. Pittsburgh: University of Pittsburgh Press, 1996.

McCabe, Colin, ed. *Who Is Andy Warhol?* London and Pittsburgh: British Film Institute and Andy Warhol Museum, 1997.

McCullough, C. Hax, Jr. "Play On: A History of the Pittsburgh Orchestra, 1896–1910." Unpublished manuscript, 2007.

McGinnis, Helen. *Carnegie's Dinosaurs*. Pittsburgh: Carnegie Institute, 1982.

Memorial of Celebration of the Carnegie Institute at Pittsburgh, PA. Pittsburgh: Board of Trustees, 1907.

Mencken, H. L. *Prejudices, Sixth Series*. New York: Knopf, 1927. Reprint, New York: Octagon Books, 1927.

Merritt, Joseph E. *Guide to the Mammals of Western Pennsylvania*. Pittsburgh: University of Pittsburgh Press, 1987.

Morley, John, Viscount. *Recollections*. 2 vols. New York: MacMillan Company, 1917.

Morrison, Samuel Eliot. *The European Discovery of America*. 2 vols. Oxford: Oxford University Press, 1971–74.

Museum of Modern Art. *Andy Warhol: A Retrospective*. Ed. Kynaston McShane. New York: Museum of Modern Art, 1989.

Nasaw, David. *Andrew Carnegie*. New York: Penguin Press, 2006.

Neal, Kenneth. *A Wise Extravagance: The Founding of the Carnegie International Exhibitions, 1895–1901*. Pittsburgh: University of Pittsburgh Press, 1996.

Netting, Graham. *Fifty Years of the Western Pennsylvania Conservancy*. Pittsburgh: Western Pennsylvania Conservancy, 1982.

Paolucci, Antonio, ed. *Great Museums of Europe: The Dream of the Universal Museum*. New York: Millan Skira, 2002.

Park, Michung. "Adolph Martin Foerster: His Life and Music." Ph.D. diss., Peabody Conservatory of Music, Peabody Institute of Johns Hopkins University, 1996.

Physick, John. *The Victoria and Albert Museum: The History of Its Building*. Oxford: Phaidon-Christie's, 1982.

Platt, Susan. "Gambling, Fencing, and Camouflage: Homer Saint-Gaudens and the Carnegie International, 1922–1950." In Clark, *International Encounters*, 67–91.

"Presentation of the Carnegie Library to the People of Pittsburgh with a Description of the Dedicatory Exercises, November 5th, 1895." Printed by order of the Corporation of the City of Pittsburgh.

Pritchett, Henry S. "Andrew Carnegie: Anniversary Address Delivered before the Carnegie Institute of Technology on November 24, 1915." Cleveland. Privately printed, 1915.

Putnam, Robert D. *Bowling Alone: The Collapse and Revival of American Community*. New York: Simon and Schuster, 2000.

Rea, Tom. *Bone Wars: The Excavation and Celebrity of Andrew Carnegie's Dinosaur*. Pittsburgh: University of Pittsburgh Press, 2001.

Rogers, Stephen. "Stuffed Animals: The Art of Taxidermy—A History of Taxidermy at the Carnegie Museum." Unpublished manuscript, 2006.

Sanger, Martha Frick Symington. *Henry Clay Frick: An Intimate Portrait*. New York: Abbeville Press, 1998.

Schaefer, Ludwig F. *Evolution of a National Research University, 1965–1990: The Stever Administration and the Cyert Years at Carnegie Mellon*. Pittsburgh: Carnegie Mellon University Press, 1992.

Shoumatoff, Alex. *Russian Blood: A Family Chronicle*. New York: Coward, McCann and Geoghegan, 1982.

Standiford, Les. *Meet You in Hell: Andrew Carnegie, Henry Clay Frick, and the Bitter Partnership That Transformed America*. New York: Three Rivers Press, 2006.

Strazdes, Diane. *American Paintings and Sculpture to 1945 in the Carnegie Museum of Art*. Pittsburgh: Carnegie Institute, 1992.

Swetnam, George. *Andrew Carnegie*. Boston: G. K. Hall and Co., 1980.

Tarbell, Dean Arthur Wilson. *The Story of Carnegie Tech, 1900–1935*. Pittsburgh: Carnegie Institute of Technology, 1937.

Thomas, Clarke M. *A Patrician of Ideas: A Biography of A. W. Schmidt.* Pittsburgh: Pittsburgh History and Landmarks Foundation, 2006.

Toker, Franklin. *Pittsburgh: A New Portrait.* Pittsburgh: University of Pittsburgh Press, 2009.

Twain, Mark [pseud., Samuel Clemens]. *Mark Twain in Eruption.* Ed. Bernard DeVoto. New York: Grosset and Dunlap, 1940.

Twitchell, James B. *Branded Nation: The Marketing of Megachurch, College, Inc., and Museumworld.* New York: Simon and Schuster, 2004.

Van Slyke, Abigail A. *Free to All: Carnegie Libraries and American Culture 1890–1920.* Chicago and London: University of Chicago Press, 1995.

Van Trump, James D. *An American Palace of Culture: The Carnegie Institute and Carnegie Library of Pittsburgh.* Pittsburgh: Carnegie Institute and Pittsburgh History and Landmarks Foundation, 1970.

Violet, Ultra [pseud., Isabelle Dufresne]. *Famous for Fifteen Minutes.* New York: Harcourt Brace Jovanovich, 1988.

Walker, John, *Self-Portrait with Donors: Confessions of an Art Collector.* Boston: Little, Brown and Company, 1974.

Wall, Joseph. *Andrew Carnegie.* 1970. Reprint, Pittsburgh: University of Pittsburgh Press, 1989.

———. *The Andrew Carnegie Reader.* Pittsburgh: University of Pittsburgh Press, 1992.

Warhol, Andy. *The Philosophy of Andy Warhol (From A to B and Back Again).* New York: Harcourt Brace Jovanovich, 1975.

Warhol, Andy, and Pat Hackett. *POPism: The Warhol 60s.* New York: Harcourt Brace Jovanovich, 1980.

Whitehead, Walter Muir. *Museum of Fine Arts Boston: A Centennial History.* Cambridge: The Belknap Press of Harvard University Press, 1970.

Wolfe, Richard James. "Short History of the Pittsburgh Orchestra, 1896–1910." Master's thesis, Carnegie Library School, Carnegie Institute of Technology, 1954.

Wilson, Ellen. *The Carnegie.* Pittsburgh: Carnegie Institute, 1992.

ILLUSTRATION CREDITS

Abbreviations

AWM	The Andy Warhol Museum
CM	*Carnegie Magazine*
CMA	Carnegie Museum of Art
CMNH	Carnegie Museum of Natural History
CSC	Carnegie Science Center
ARS/NY	Artists Rights Society, New York

End Papers

Robert Qualters, *Untitled* (A boy in Carnegie Hall of Architecture) 1985, watercolor on paper, gift of the artist to Robert J. Gangewere.

1. The Carnegie Years

Unless otherwise noted, many images in this book, including all historic photos and cartoons of Andrew Carnegie and those of his Institute and Library, the early exhibits, and many early administrators are published through the generosity of the Pennsylvania Department, Carnegie Library of Pittsburgh.

2. Building a Palace of Culture

41: View of cast of the Abbey Church of St.-Gilles-du-Gard, CMA/Tom Little.

Floorplans

67, 68, 70, 72, 74, 76: Historic floorplans and images published with the assistance of Mike Kanaroi.

46, 60, 61, 62: Modern floorplans courtesy of Susan Geyer. All images courtesy of Carnegie Library of Pittsburgh.

3. The High Command

65: Carnegie portrait, CMA
74, 78, 80, 83, 86: *CM*
86: Terry Clark

4. Carnegie Music Hall

97: Stephen Foster portrait, CMA

Color Signature

Photograph of the Carnegie Institute and Library by Hector Corante. Courtesy University of Pittsburgh Press.

John Kane, American, 1860–1934, *The Cathedral of Learning,* 1930. Oil on canvas. CMA, John O'Connor, Jr. Fund. 72.9.

Pascal Adolphe Jean Dagnan-Bouveret. *Christ and the Disciples at Emmaus,* 1896–1897. Oil on canvas. CMA, Gift of Henry Clay Frick. 98.5.

John White Alexander. *Apotheosis of Pittsburgh,* detail from the mural program *The Crowning of Labor,* 1905–7. Oil on canvas. CMA, purchase, 07.08.

Winslow Homer, *The Wreck,* 1896. Oil on canvas. CMA, purchase, 96.1.

Life Magazine cartoon: Carnegie Library of Pittsburgh.

Photograph of Lynn Zelevansky by Bob Donalson, *Pittsburgh Post-Gazette.* Includes Alberto Giacometti, *Walking Man I,* 1960, Bronze. CMA, Pittsburgh: Patrons Art Fund, 61.48. © 2011 Succession Giacometti/Artists Rights Society (ARS), New York/ADAGP, Paris. Also includes in background Mark Rothko, *Yellow, Blue on Orange,* 1955. Oil on canvas. CMA, Fellows Fund, Women's Committee Acquisition Fund, and Patron's Art Fund. 74.55. © 1998 Kate Rothko Prizel & Christopher Rothko/Artists Rights Society (ARS) New York.

Georges Rouault, *The Old King,* 1916–1936. Oil on canvas. CMA, Patrons Art Fund, 40.1. © 2011 Artists Right Society (ARS), New York.

Entry to Warhol Museum, Andy Warhol, *Self-Portrait,* 1986. AWM/Richard Stoner. © 2011 The Andy Warhol Foundation for the Visual Arts, Inc./Artists Rights Society (ARS), New York.

Andy Warhol, *Andrew Carnegie,* 1981. Acrylic and silkscreen on canvas. CMA, Richard M. Scaife American Painting Fund, 81.107. © 2011 The Andy Warhol Foundation for the Visual Arts, Inc./Artists Rights Society (ARS), New York.

Andy Warhol, *Andrew Carnegie,* 1981. Acrylic and silkscreen on canvas. CMA, Gift of the Andy Warhol Foundation for the Visual Arts, 88.20. © 2011 The Andy Warhol Foundation for the Visual Arts, Inc./Artists Rights Society (ARS), New York.

Photograph of Andrew Carnegie, 1896: Carnegie Library of Pittsburgh

Photograph of Carnegie Science Center: CSC.

Photograph of Dinosaurs in Their Time exhibit: CM, Josh Franzos.

paternalism, Carnegie's, 10–12, 108, 132
Patron's Art Fund, 140–41, 149
Pauer, Emil, *99,* 101–2
Pearce, Timothy, 203, 206
Pearlstein, Philip, 289
Pennsylvania: libraries in, 17, 120–21;
    supporting Andy Warhol Museum,
    276
Pennsylvania Railroad, Carnegie
    working for, 6–7
personality, Carnegie's, 12–13, 18
Peterson, Olof A., 196, 198
philanthropy, 67, 87, 90, 103; Carnegie's
    attention to, 13, 19–20, 287; Carnegie's
    beliefs about, 3–4, 20, 26–27; Car-
    negie's legacy from gifts, 16–17, 108;
    Carnegie's weariness of trying to give
    away wealth, 14, 16; Louise Carnegie's
    role in, 21–22, 24, *66;* public parks
    as good gift for, 26–27; through
    Carnegie Corporation of New York,
    16; total gifts to Carnegie Institute
    and Library, 24, 287. *See also* Gospel of
    Wealth
Phipps Conservatory, 26, *31, 32*
Pittsburgh, 3; artistic tastes of, 134,
    145; attractions in, 89–90, 165, 249;
    Carnegie Institute's importance to,
    87, 287; Carnegie offering library to,
    17–18; Carnegie's move away from,
    24; Carnegie's pride in achievements
    of, 101, 174; changing economics of,
    78–79; collection of photographs
    of, 169; desire for Warhol's art to be
    in, 274–75; image of, 80–81, 87, 231;
    library funding from, 114, 118, 123, 126;
    minerals in development of, 189–91;
    as organ capital of the world, 104–5;
    renaissance of, 143, 181; ruling class of,
    64–67; strengths of, 243, 247, 257, 287;
    Warhol's roots in, 270, 281
Pittsburgh Library Board, 18
Pittsburgh Orchestra Association,
    hosting traveling orchestras, 102
Pittsburgh Symphony Orchestra, *99;*
    conductors of, 98, 100–101; financial
    problems of, 97–98; history of, 98–
    103; playing at Music Hall, 93, 96–97
Powdermill Avian Research Center
    (PARC), 241
Powdermill Nature Reserve, 77, 237–42,

288; Apt proposing sale of, 184; bird-
    banding program at, 218, 239–41;
    educational programs at, 189, 241;
    facilities at, 184, 239, 241; research at,
    209, 241
President's Office, 42, 65
Price, Vincent, 145
Pritchett, Henry S., 16–17, 63, *66*
public outreach, 218; by Andy Warhol
    Museum, 278–79, 284; Carnegie
    Science Center's focus on, 259–62;
    by Institute, 74–77, 80; by libraries,
    112–13, 115–18, 122–23, 127, 287

Radcliffe, Martin, 253
Radzilowicz, John, 255
Ralph, C. J., 242
Rangos Omnimax Theater, at Carnegie
    Science Center, 253–54
Ratcliffe, Martin, 255
Rawlins, John, 176, 206, 214–15
Raymond, Percy E., 187
Rea, Ingrid and William, 213, 239, 241
Reed, W. H., 194
religion: Andy Warhol's, 270; in
    Pittsburgh ruling class, 65–66
Requin submarine, at Carnegie Science
    Center, 253, 257, *258*
research, 216, 252, 284; displays
    explaining staff's, 198–202, 231;
    importance of museum collections in,
    186, 205, 215; library of natural history
    museum in, 235–37; at natural history
    museum, 186, 198–202, 205, 207–8,
    214–15, 218–19, 224, 289; NSF grants
    for natural history museum's, 214,
    242; at Powdermill Nature Reserve,
    238, 240–42
Rhind, John Massey, 32, 33–37, *34–36*
Richard King Mellon Foundation, 77, 79,
    188, 241
Richards, Wallace B., 181, 230
Richardson, Henry Hobson, 28, 111
Richardson, James B., III, 224, *225*
Richmond, Neil D., 212, 213
Rockwell Foundation, funding Hall of
    Mammals, 220
Roehrig, Madelyn, *274*
Rogers, Stephen, 213
Roosevelt, Theodore, 227–28
Root, Elihu, 16

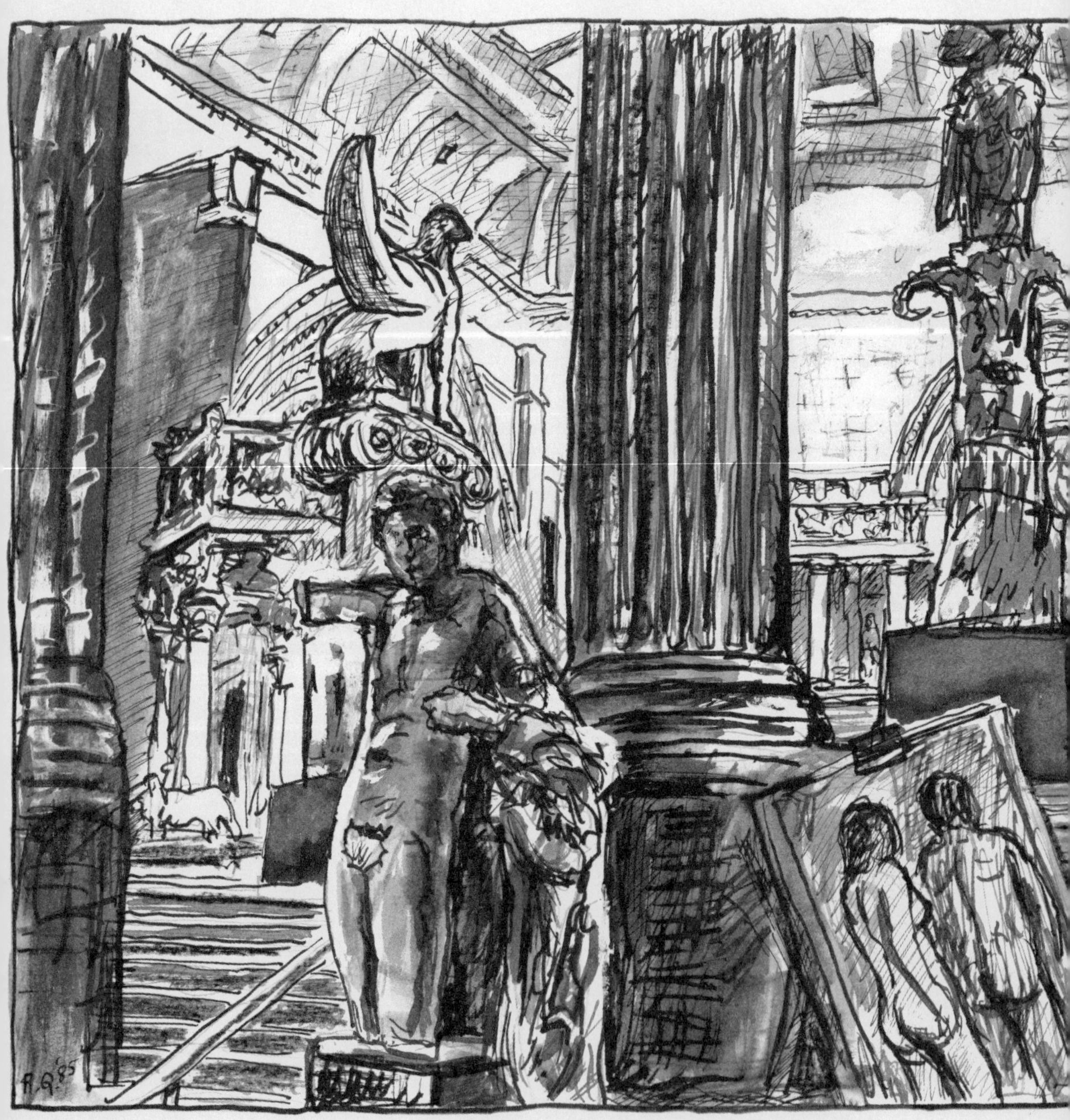